T OR SEED BUTTER

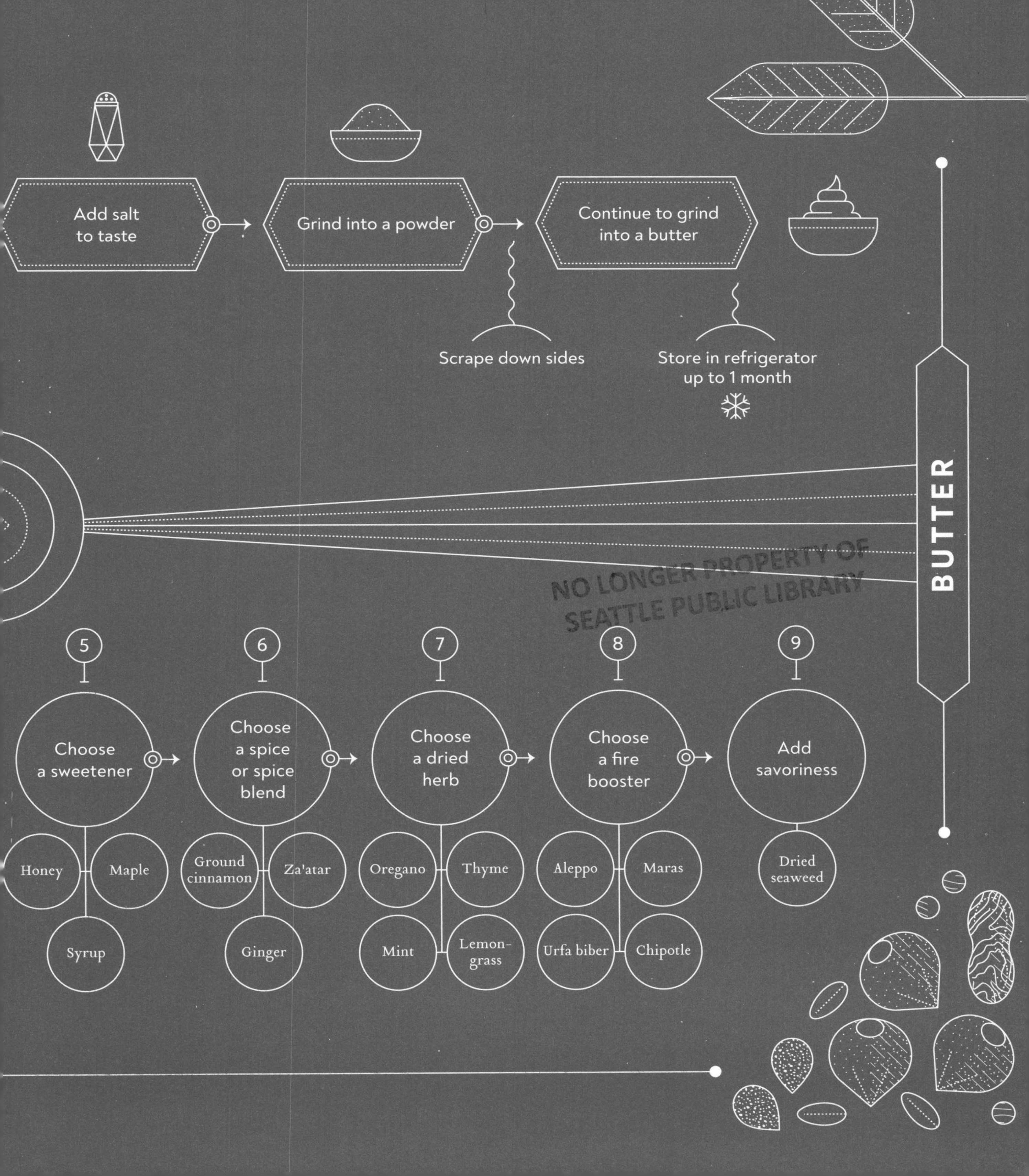

Add salt to taste → Grind into a powder → Continue to grind into a butter

Scrape down sides

Store in refrigerator up to 1 month

BUTTER

5 Choose a sweetener
- Honey
- Maple
- Syrup

6 Choose a spice or spice blend
- Ground cinnamon
- Za'atar
- Ginger

7 Choose a dried herb
- Oregano
- Thyme
- Mint
- Lemon-grass

8 Choose a fire booster
- Aleppo
- Maras
- Urfa biber
- Chipotle

9 Add savoriness
- Dried seaweed

IN THIS GROUNDBREAKING new cookbook, Nik Sharma gives us an entirely new way to become a better cook: through the science of flavor and sensation. Nik is a molecular biologist, a beloved food blogger, a columnist for the *San Francisco Chronicle* and *Serious Eats*, and the author of the buzz-generating cookbook *Season*. Here is science plus beauty, an exploration of flavor through more than 100 delicious, meal-centering recipes—rich curries, layered salads, creamy casseroles—plus more than 150 of Nik's uniquely evocative photographs.

Nik is famous for the deeply flavorful and unique recipes he develops, drawing on his Indian heritage, his time in the American South, and his deep love of cooking. Nik is a home cook, and these are recipes for people trying to put good food on their tables.

Every time you cook, you're trying to hit 7 notes: brightness, bitterness, saltiness, sweetness, savoriness, fieriness, and richness. These are the flavors that make our food sing. When you eat, you rely on a variety of senses and feelings—taste, sight, aroma, sound, mouthfeel, and emotion—to perceive these sensations. Through recipes, introductions,

and more than 40 illustrations, we learn the simplest ways to play up any and all of these sensations to cook the most flavorful food.

Nik also demonstrates how approachable spices, fresh herbs, and commonplace pantry items can transform simple dishes. This accessible primer on food chemistry includes a dozen of Nik's own food experiments, such as how to get the crispiest caramelized onions.

At last, here is a science-based cookbook that marries ease with beauty, highlighted through vibrant illustrations and Nik's gorgeous photography.

"If you're interested in flavor—and every cook is, that's what we constantly think about—this book is for you. A fascinating look at how flavor works and how memory and emotion, where we come from and where we end up, influence how we cook and what we eat. I haven't learned so much from a single book in a very long time. I'm now cooking my way through it."

—**DIANA HENRY**
food writer and author of the James Beard Award–winning *A Bird in the Hand*

"Nik Sharma has created an irresistible book that makes you want to immediately jump into the kitchen. There is not a single recipe that I would not want to cook; I am dying to make them all! This book helps you understand the deep complexities that surround our food and how much it can mean to us."

—**PATI JINICH**
chef, cookbook author, and host of *Pati's Mexican Table* on PBS

"Fascinating, enlightening, and beautiful, Nik's book is a masterpiece. The recipes are simply gorgeous."

—**NIGEL SLATER**
author of *Greenfeast*

"Nik Sharma answers the hows and whys of taste from a scientific perspective as well as one from a well-seasoned cook. The multicultural flavors are sure to entice anyone's taste buds to spring into action (I have my eye on the Chocolate Miso Bread Pudding and the Coffee-Spiced Steak). Anyone wanting to take a deep dive into how to make food taste better will revel in Nik's thoroughly researched—and gorgeously photographed—treatise on the topic."

—**DAVID LEBOVITZ**
author of *My Paris Kitchen* and *Drinking French*

"In *The Flavor Equation*, Nik marries the art and science of cuisine. His recipes speak to the technicalities of success, with weights provided for unwieldy vegetables and herbs, and ample explanation of the hows and whys of key ingredients; but more importantly, Nik's recipes speak to the experience of success—how a dough should feel beneath your hands, the way asparagus will turn more vibrant with heat, or how the telltale sizzle of corn on the grill signals it's time to turn the cob. This isn't a book about controlling every variable, nor is it one that suggests our hearts alone can guide the way. Rather, it offers a holistic approach to cooking at home, one that celebrates both chemistry and emotion, in both the creation and enjoyment of our meals."

—**STELLA PARKS**
pastry chef and author of *BraveTart: Iconic American Desserts*

"Nik Sharma explains flavor—and our perception of it—by combining the science and chemistry of food and cooking with the working of our senses, memories, and emotions. Along the way, we get loads of tasty tips, lists, and geekily creative "maps" on everything, including the art of food styling, the behavior of starches for thickening, food pigments, and how ingredients are paired differently in cuisines around the globe. *The Flavor Equation* is not only a newer and bigger (and more fun) way to think about flavor, it's also a treasure trove of useful information and ideas, juicy tidbits, and exciting dishes—just open the book to any page—bound to make us better, more present, more interesting, and more joyous cooks and eaters."

—**ALICE MEDRICH**
cookbook author and dessert chef

$$
\begin{array}{r}
\text{Emotion} \\
\text{Sight} \\
\text{Sound} \\
\text{Mouthfeel} \\
\text{Aroma} \\
+ \quad\quad \text{Taste} \\
\hline
\text{Flavor}
\end{array}
$$

THE FLAVOR EQUATION

THE SCIENCE OF GREAT COOKING EXPLAINED
+ MORE THAN 100 ESSENTIAL RECIPES

Nik Sharma

Foreword by Christopher Kimball

Illustrations by Matteo Riva

CHRONICLE BOOKS
SAN FRANCISCO

For Floyd Cardoz,
who made Goan cuisine shine bright.

For Michael,
who makes me laugh.

Library of Congress Cataloging-in-Publication Data

Names: Sharma, Nik, author. | Riva, Matteo, illustrator.
Title: The flavor equation : the science of great cooking explained in
  more than 100 essential recipes / Nik Sharma ; illustrations by
  Matteo Riva.
Description: San Francisco : Chronicle Books, 2020. | Includes
  bibliographical references and index.
Identifiers: LCCN 2020023603 | ISBN 9781452182698 (hardcover) |
  ISBN 9781452182858 (ebook)
Subjects: LCSH: Cooking. | Cooking—Technique. | LCGFT: Cookbooks
Classification: LCC TX714 .S497 2020 | DDC 641.5—dc23
LC record available at https://lccn.loc.gov/2020023603

Manufactured in China.

MIX
Paper from
responsible sources
FSC™ C104723

Prop styling by Nik Sharma.
Food styling by Nik Sharma.
Design by Lizzie Vaughan.
Typesetting by Howie Serverson.

The photographer wishes to thank the Biological
Imaging Facility, University of California, Berkeley.

10 9 8 7 6 5 4

Ajinomoto is a registered trademark of Ajinomoto Co., Inc.; Alinea
is a registered trademark of The Alinea Group LLC; Cadbury is a
registered trademark of Cadbury UK Limited Corporation; Gjelina
is a registered trademark of Fresco's Gym LLC; King Arthur Flour is
a registered trademark of The King Arthur Flour Company, Inc.;
Lao Gan Ma is a registered trademark of Guiyang Nanming
Laoganma Special Flavour Foodstuffs Co., Ltd.; Lee Kum Kee is
a registered trademark of Lee Kum Kee Company; Lyle's Golden
Syrup is a registered trademark of T&L Sugars Limited Company;
Maggi is a registered trademark of Societe des Produits Nestle;
Maldon is a registered trademark of Maldon Crystal Salt Company;
Marmite is a registered trademark of Conopco, Inc.; Namu Gaji is a
registered trademark of David Lee; Nestlé is a registered trademark
of Societe des Produits Nestle; PBS is a registered trademark of
Public Broadcasting Service Corporation; San Francisco Chronicle is a
registered trademark of Hearst Communications, Inc.; Serious Eats is
a registered trademark of Serious Eats LLC; Vegemite is a registered
trademark of Bega Cheese Limited.

Chronicle books and gifts are available at special quantity
discounts to corporations, professional associations, literacy
programs, and other organizations. For details and discount
information, please contact our premiums department at
corporatesales@chroniclebooks.com or at 1-800-759-0190.

Chronicle Books LLC
680 Second Street
San Francisco, California 94107
www.chroniclebooks.com

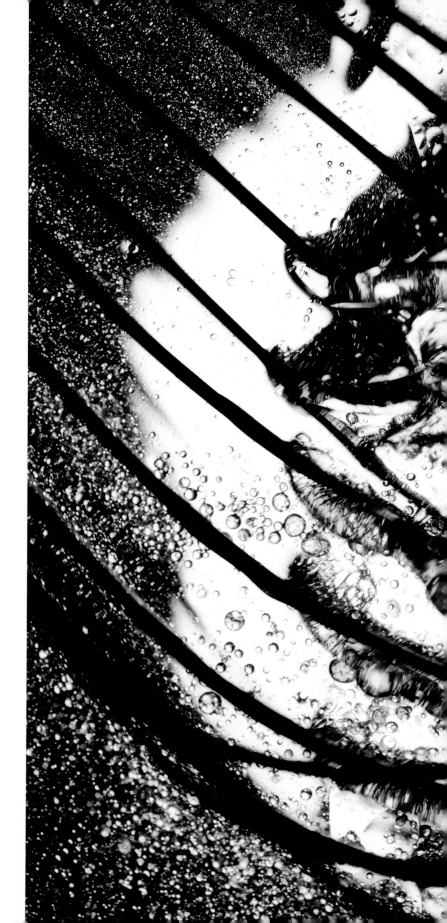

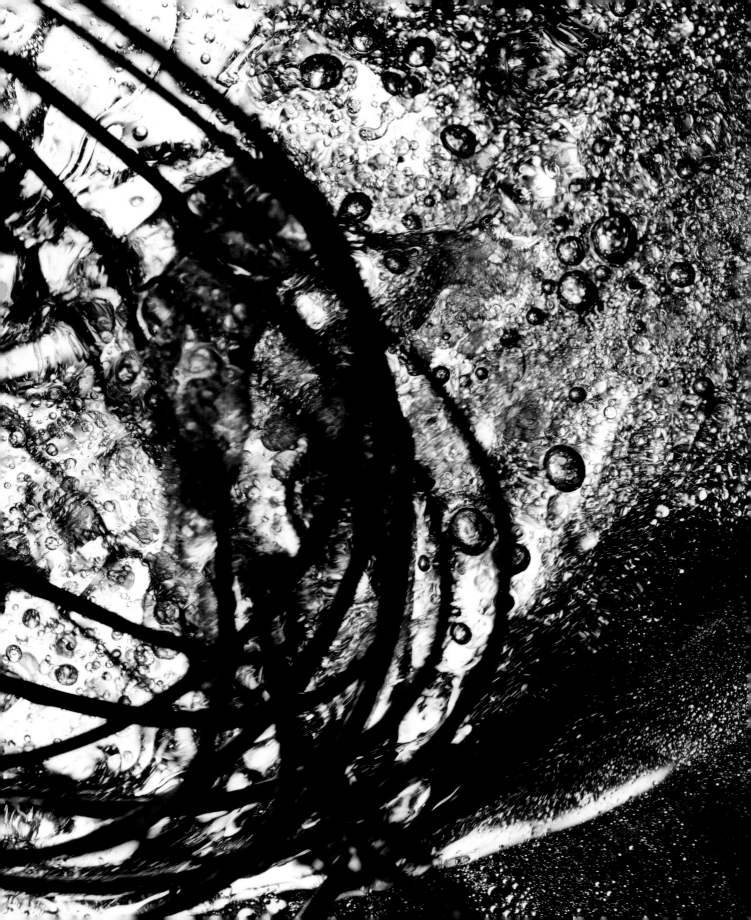

Foreword

I have spent more than 40 years trying to understand food science. I started with Harold McGee's classic *On Food and Cooking*, which, to this day, I find both brilliant and impenetrable. Next, I used Shirley Corriher's *CookWise* and *BakeWise*, both of which bridged the gap nicely between science and cooking. I worked with Bob Wolke (*What Einstein Told His Cook*), a man with a sense of humor and good storytelling skills. Finally, I have worked for many years with Guy Crosby, Milk Street's in-house food scientist, who answers our day-to-day questions, such as "Why can't you make mayonnaise during a thunderstorm (or can you)?" and "Why did a duck braised in red wine explode in the oven?"

Crosby admitted that he restricted his answers to my questions based on his perception of my ability to understand. Over the years his description of gluten became more and more complex, starting with gluten content, moving on to glutenin and gliadin, then discussing prolamins. This reminds me of my sixth-grade science teacher who, when I asked if molecules actually looked like his colorful wooden balls and dowels, told me they did not. "Why?" I asked. He replied, "Because that's all you can handle." The message was clear: There is something deeply unfamiliar behind the curtain, something way beyond the ken of the average home cook.

Enter Nik Sharma. I first interviewed Nik years ago on *Milk Street Radio* and was won over by his combination of authenticity and enthusiasm for his adopted home—he grew up in Bombay and moved to America—stirred by his love of marrying Indian and American culinary traditions. His father hailed from northern India and his mother from Goa, places with cuisines that are about as similar as Lowcountry seafood is to Vermont

pot roast, so he was well prepared for the future. His food has always reflected the underpinning of flavor from his childhood, a lesson that he puts to good use no matter what and where he is cooking.

The Flavor Equation is written by someone who understands flavor first. This is not a book for geeks who want to dive deep into amino acids, gels, and osmosis. This is a book about how to turn out food that optimizes flavor. For Sharma, flavor is visceral and complex. It is emotion, sight, sound, mouthfeel, aroma, and taste. Flavor is also brightness, bitterness, saltiness, sweetness, and savoriness. The cooking of India, which incorporates dozens of regional and local cuisines, perfectly represents this complexity.

In northern European cuisines, dishes tend to be played in a major key. In plenty of other spots around the globe, home cooks are playing music that is chromatic and even atonal at times, finding the notes between the notes to make you sit up and ask, "What did I just taste?" It is subtlety and daring all in one forkful.

Nik Sharma and others are teaching us that good food is not about technique per se: years standing in front of the stove, advanced knife skills, and mastering pastry technique. It's about crafting flavor through an understanding of what flavor actually is. This style of cooking doesn't have to be precarious or even highly skilled, but it does have to thoughtful. Sharma shows us how to make tomato soup, lamb chops, chicken salad, fruit crisps, and spareribs in new ways by thinking about the push and pull of texture and flavor. This offers a transformational way forward for anyone who wants to grow from good cook to great cook, all without classic French training.

—Christopher Kimball
founder, Milk Street

Introduction

What makes a recipe cooked in a home kitchen or the meal served at a restaurant taste spectacular and delicious? What makes it inviting and special? Why do we like some foods more than others? The answers to these questions lie in our perceptions of flavor.

Flavor symbolizes different things to different people. It might represent the aroma and taste of a dish prepared with love by a parent or grandparent, or an opportunity for food culture to be passed on to a younger generation. For some, it might jog the memory of a meal that provided comfort when the world was harsh or represent a path to an immigrant who longs to connect with the country of their birth as well as their adopted home.

Flavor is much more than a distinctive smell or taste; it involves our emotions, and sometimes memories, intertwined with our sense of the sounds, colors, shapes, and textures of our food. These components together make what I refer to as the Flavor Equation:

$$\frac{\text{Emotion} + \text{Sight} + \text{Sound} + \text{Mouthfeel} + \text{Aroma} + \text{Taste}}{\text{Flavor}}$$

A fresh, crisp apple smells and tastes wonderful by itself: a bit sweet and a bit tart, accompanied by a fruity scent. Slice the fruit, dip it into a bit of almond butter, and bite into it; it will take on a whole new flavor profile. Dip another slice of the apple into caramel sauce, and it again delivers a whole new eating experience. This is flavor: a combination of aromas and tastes that makes eating such a marvelous and exciting experience.

But while the classic definition of flavor includes aroma and taste, our senses of sight, smell, sound, and mouthfeel (texture), intertwined with our emotions and memory, all help shape this extraordinary experience.

I couldn't afford to attend culinary school, and most of what I've learned to cook comes by way of watching the cooks in my life: my maternal grandmother, my mom, and the wonderful pastry chefs I worked with at Sugar, Butter, Flour bakery. I read scores of cookbooks and newspapers. As an eager young cook, my mind was filled with questions, and every time an opportunity arose, I'd ask my teachers. I wanted to know why things worked and why they didn't. I wanted to know why people responded to food in different ways.

As a cook and a food writer, I use food as a way to connect my past with my present and future—to weave a thread between my life in India, my life in America, and the people and places I've seen and met along the way. Certain aromas and tastes seem to become more special over time than others. What I didn't fully appreciate and understand at the time was how many different factors shaped both the way in which flavor was created and how these factors influenced my perception of a meal.

I found recipes to be an excellent tool from which to learn. More than just a skeleton of instructions, a recipe reflects a point of view and a glimpse into the past. Within the instructions is hidden the logic behind why certain ingredients are combined. The recipes that stick with me are those that explain the nuts and bolts of the players and their actions. These snippets of information help me understand why things work; they provide clues and ideas to fix failures, and they help me construct my own recipes.

What we define as "delicious" is a combination of elements that come together as one holistic experience. Knowing how and why our ingredients behave and the effect these have on flavor is what made me a better cook—and this knowledge will make you a better cook too. In this book, we will tackle each of these elements—emotion, memory, sight, sound, mouthfeel (texture), aroma, and taste—individually to understand the role they play in everyday cooking. *The Flavor Equation* will help you become more confident in the kitchen because you will eventually learn how flavor works and use that to your advantage.

If you're trying to use starch to thicken a sauce that already contains a large amount of acid, you need to know why the sauce isn't thickening. For years, I've tried to make paneer (a type of Indian cottage cheese) resemble the store-bought stuff that I can buy here in American grocery stores and that I ate in India; it turned out that it mattered what type of milk I used, due to protein structure and denaturation. When making a savory broth, knowing how the chief umami molecules bring out flavor helped me create a delicious, rich broth with a powerful punch without adding meat. These are some examples of what you will learn in this book.

At its core, much of what we do in the kitchen and at the table is experimentation, not only with aroma and taste senses, but also what we see and hear and the emotions they trigger in us. Some of my behaviors are tied to memory; others might be explained by evolution and genetics. I avoid cooking or writing recipes for the Indian squash *doodhi*, bitter melons (*karela*), or turnips, nor will I eat excessively ripe bananas, not only because I strongly dislike the texture, smell, and taste of these foods, but also because my parents forced me to eat the first two vegetables as a kid—which scarred me for life. As an adult, I exercise my free will by staying away from these foods.

Our relationship with our food is complex and influenced by our genes and our environment. Some of us prefer sweet foods to bitter tastes more strongly than others; what's written in our genetic makeup explains some of this. Where we grew up, our cultures, and the people we interact with also influence our food behaviors and preferences. For example, I love the scent of malt vinegar, limes, and the spicy flavor of Goan chouriço, as these are ingredients familiar to me since childhood and part of the cuisine I grew up eating. Increased access to new cultures in different parts of the world through technology and travel creates an opportunity for us to learn and experience the new—which eventually becomes more and more familiar. Country-specific and even region-specific ingredients and foods are now not only the subjects of cookbooks but also popular in our local markets. Take the example of the fermented tea kombucha, which originated in Manchuria; it now sits on the shelves of every major grocery store in America and shows up on restaurant and cocktail menus in a myriad of exciting colors, flavors, and applications.

Let's rewind a little, so I can tell you a bit about my journey with cooking and my obsession with flavor. My romance with cooking and flavor started where many cooks begin: at home, in my parents' kitchen. The first twenty-some years of my life were spent in Bombay, India (to me it will always be Bombay, the city I was born and raised in, though it's now called Mumbai). I started to cook out of necessity and curiosity. Because both my parents worked, and neither was particularly fond of cooking, they focused on feeding us with what they could quickly put together. I grew bored eating the same food again and again; this led me to delve into my mother's collection of cookbooks and recipe cuttings from magazines and newspapers.

My maternal grandmother, Lucy Carvalho, was an excellent cook, and any excuse to visit her was also an excuse for me to eat more of her food. I'd taste and try to figure out what she did to make her food so delicious. By the time I was old enough to be left alone at home, I got bold and began tinkering in the kitchen. Through my mom and grandmother, I learned to pay attention to the fragrance of dry spices as they toasted, and how to listen to the song of a *paratha* (a buttery, flaky flatbread) as it sizzled on the hot pan, singing "Flip me!" Learning to pay attention to these sensory cues made me a better cook.

My love for biology and chemistry began in early childhood, but the first chemistry lab I took in high school gave me concrete evidence of how food and science were interconnected. As part of an experiment to understand pH, acids, and bases (alkalis/soaps), my professor dipped a piece of turmeric-coated filter paper into a soap solution. It quickly went from a bright orange-yellow to a deep red. She then took the same strip and dipped it into a tube of vinegar, and it instantly switched back to yellow. At the end of class, I snuck a few strips of turmeric paper to see if this would work at home. It did.

As time progressed, I got adventurous and a bit sneakier, and I brought more experiments home. My parents indulged my interest: One Christmas, my mom gave me a little chemistry set. It was splendid; in the box were six glass test tubes, a rack, and a few chemicals including baking soda and iron filings. Within a few weeks, I had cracked the tubes by heating them directly over our gas stove, and my desire to have more fun was stoked. My dad took me to Princess Street in the south side of Bombay, where laboratory-grade equipment was sold, and I picked out a few hard glass borosilicate test tubes and beakers. Every weekend, I'd pull out a wooden board to set up my "lab." My earliest experiments involved attempts to isolate the pigments in mangoes and spinach leaves by crushing them down and sneakily adding whiskey. I once left a hot beaker on my bed, accidentally burning a hole in my bedsheets. You can bet I got reprimanded.

Back in Bombay, I signed up for courses in biochemistry and microbiology. We learned how to extract pectin from orange and apple peels, use chilled alcohol to wash the starch we collected from corn kernels and potatoes, stain the yeast and bacteria present in *dosa* and *idli* batters, and ferment fruit juices. Food made its way into some of my other classes too: In immunology, we learned about antibodies, and all I could focus on was the role papayas played in elucidating the structure of the antibody. Raw papayas contain an enzyme called a protease that cuts the antibody protein into chunks that help scientists determine its structure. In India, raw papaya was an ingredient we sometimes incorporated into our meat marinades, and now I knew why: It tenderizes meat by breaking down proteins. These lessons gave me a lens through which to look at the food I was cooking at home and gain a deeper appreciation for why things worked the way they did in the kitchen.

The similarities between the standard recipe format in cookbooks and the way we jotted down our experiments in class were striking. Even the buffers and growth media that I learned to make had recipes! Ingredients were listed in the order in which they first appear in the instructions, and when a group of different ingredients were added in a single step, the ingredients were listed from the largest to the smallest quantity, in the exact same manner by which a cook would write a recipe down. Experiments needed to be repeated to make sure our results could be replicated, and sometimes we'd try to answer a question using a few different methods to make sure our results were indeed correct. Later, when I started my blog, *A Brown Table*, I felt that my life in science had somewhat equipped me for food writing and recipe development, because I viewed everything I did in the kitchen as a way to improvise and learn; to revisit ideas and make them better.

When I came to America to attend grad school, I explored a new world. The people I met and the restaurants I dined at represented a kaleidoscope of cultures from all over the world. I tried to eat out often to taste and experience new flavors and textures. I started to notice similarities and differences in the food I ate in the United States and the food I knew from India. Some things seemed to be favorites no matter where you went: Meat and potatoes were comfort foods; vanilla in European desserts performed the role that cardamom did in many Indian desserts. But there were striking differences too. Many of the European-style dishes I tasted and learned to cook in America relied on using ingredients that complemented and enhanced the flavors of the key components of the dish, quite unlike the approach I'd seen in kitchens back in India, which emphasized the use of contrasting ingredients. Mexican and Cajun food caught my attention for their use of bold, contrasting flavors that reminded me of Indian cuisine.

Not long ago, I read a study that piqued my interest and validated some of my observations about the differences I noticed in the way I flavored my food compared to the way my friends and family members did. Scientists who had sifted through thousands of recipes available from databases in North America and Korea were able to compare how people from distinctively different parts of the world use flavor when they cook. (To be clear, the definition of what really encompasses North American and East Asian cooking is a bit oversimplified in this discussion and there are limitations to this dataset; it's important to acknowledge the distinct regional differences in cuisines before we take a quick dive into some of the images from this study.)

By determining the most prevalent ingredients from several online recipe databases and comparing the types and amounts of different flavor substances present in them, scientists were able to get a deeper understanding of how flavors are used in different parts of the world. In North America, butter is more popular (41%), while in East Asia, soy sauce predominates (47%). The scientists then attempted to determine if a region's cuisine can be identified by the use of specific signature ingredients that were most frequently mentioned in recipe databases. Ingredients that share common flavor substances are linked together by lines, the thickness of each line representing the number of shared substances. The size of the circles gives an indication of how popular these ingredients are in recipes; the larger the circle, the more frequent its appearance. North American cooking uses milk, butter, vanilla, eggs, cane molasses, and wheat—many of which share multiple flavor compounds (for example, butter and vanilla share at least twenty flavor molecules). In contrast, East Asian recipes use soy sauce, scallions, sesame oil, rice, soybeans, and ginger,

CULTURAL AND REGIONAL DIFFERENCES IN FLAVOR PAIRING

Cultural and regional diversity affects the way we combine ingredients and pair the flavors we cook with.

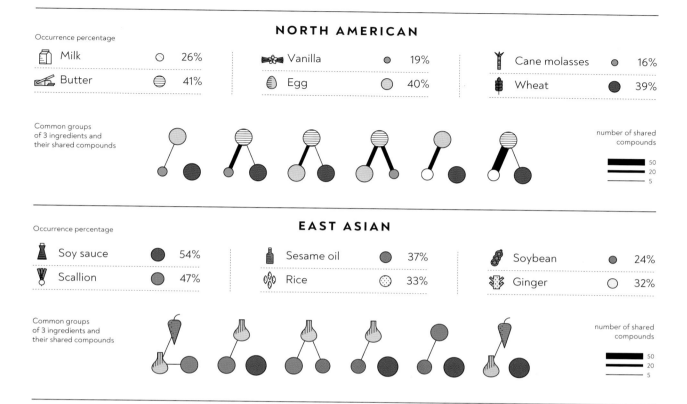

NORTH AMERICAN

Occurrence percentage

Milk ○ 26%	Vanilla ● 19%	Cane molasses ● 16%
Butter ⊖ 41%	Egg ● 40%	Wheat ● 39%

Common groups of 3 ingredients and their shared compounds

number of shared compounds
— 50
— 20
— 5

EAST ASIAN

Occurrence percentage

Soy sauce ● 54%	Sesame oil ● 37%	Soybean ● 24%
Scallion ● 47%	Rice ● 33%	Ginger ○ 32%

Common groups of 3 ingredients and their shared compounds

number of shared compounds
— 50
— 20
— 5

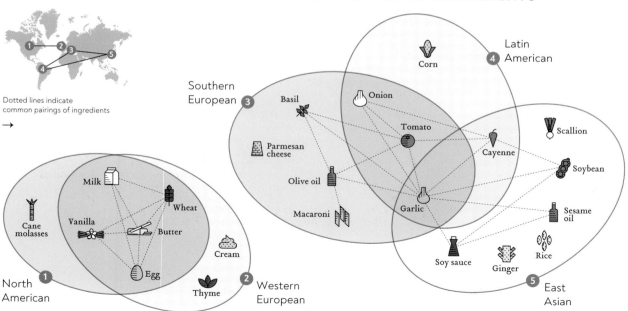

REGIONAL CO-OCCURRENCE OF COMMON INGREDIENTS

Dotted lines indicate common pairings of ingredients

→

Latin American ④
Corn

Southern European ③
Basil
Onion
Tomato
Parmesan cheese
Cayenne
Scallion
Soybean
Olive oil
Garlic
Sesame oil
Macaroni
Rice
Soy sauce
Ginger
East Asian ⑤

Cane molasses
Milk
Vanilla
Butter
Wheat
Cream
Egg
Thyme
North American ①
Western European ②

Adapted from Ahn, Y., Ahnert, S., Bagrow, J. et al. "Flavor network and the principles of food pairing." *Scientific Reports* 1, 196 (2011).

which share fewer flavor molecules and yet are often paired (for example, sesame oil and scallions share close to five different flavor molecules). The charts on page 13 illustrate these results, which demonstrate distinct patterns in our approach to cooking and flavoring our food.

Researchers then used a bit of math to define and select six of the most prevalent and authentic ingredients along with ingredient pairs in five regional cuisines—North American, Western European, Southern European, Latin American, and East Asian. They observed a close relationship between North American and Western European cuisines, whereas Southern European cuisine had more in common with Latin American cuisine than it did with Western European cuisine, which can be explained by history and colonialism. I find all these results fascinating because they question the principles by which we view and pair different flavors in our cooking.

All these figures illustrate that our relationship with flavor in our food, our cooking choices and behavior, are strongly influenced by the culture where we grew up. As more data from websites and cookbooks is gathered and studied, I would not be surprised if we see a more detailed and distinct view of regional cuisine differences with respect to flavor preferences and relationships. In addition, as people immigrate and bring new flavors with them, these flavors eventually start to mingle into the adopted countries' cuisines and become assimilated into their new surroundings, much as chillies made their way from Mexico to the rest of the world via colonialism and are now integral parts of many cuisines, including those of India, China, and Korea. Some of these boundaries across flavor molecules might also disappear over time. If you quickly skim through the ingredients in some of my recipes, you'll notice my most frequent players include limes, onions, cilantro, chillies, brown sugar or jaggery, tomatoes, and olive or grapeseed oil. Most of these ingredients are unlike each other in their flavor profiles, but they still work.

Flavor is much more than a set of rules or guidelines. Living in the United States required me to adapt what I knew from before to what I was experiencing in my present. My earliest experience with Chinese food came from India (it's called Indo-Chinese food and originated in Kolkata, where some of the Chinese Hakka community immigrated many years ago), but in the United States, the menu is remarkably different. Spices that are common to Indian cuisine became a part of the Chinese immigrant community's repertoire, creating a singular combination of flavors that works beautifully. In my own way, I started to change the way I cook and flavored my food. Sometimes I'd add

fried paneer to a kale salad or use tamarind instead of balsamic vinegar in my caprese; these substitutions revealed combinations that were familiar yet different and special in their own ways.

As I learned to play with flavors and appreciate their nuances and effects on cooking, I wanted to write and share my perspective on how food and flavor evolve through experiences as time passes. And that is what I set out to do with my blog, *A Brown Table*, and my food writing for many outlets, especially my column in the *San Francisco Chronicle*. I quit my work in research and worked as a pastry cook at a small California patisserie called Sugar, Butter, Flour. There I got to learn how flavors were integrated into pastries and about the aspects of food styling and presentation. The chefs taught me to recognize the importance of how fat, flour, and sugar come together in various ratios to produce varying textures in different desserts.

I started to pay more attention to ingredients and foods, to how a strawberry straight off the vine tastes juicier than one from a store. I observed how different ingredients behaved with each other in a recipe; how dried red chilli flakes would turn hot oil bright red and hot but never produced a comparable effect when mixed with cold water. When I added aromatic spices, like green cardamom, to cake batters, I noticed how the intensity of the aroma varied depending on the stage at which it was added; if it was added directly to the butter initially, it gave me a more long-lasting effect than if I added it toward the end. I'd question the chefs I worked with as well as the home cooks who invited me to their homes to eat. When I got an opportunity to travel, I'd ask farmers and food producers why some types of cabbage were better suited than others to braise or roast, or why honey can taste very different depending on the type of bees and the flowers they had fed on.

When my husband and I moved to Oakland, I quit my job at the pastry shop and took on a new role. I worked as a food photographer for a startup company that cooked and delivered meals to people within the city. It was a tremendous learning experience; before, I'd relied on information I gleaned directly from customers or readers of my blog, but now the startup's data engineers were analyzing what types of dishes clicked the most with people via data collected by the app. I saw firsthand how color, shapes, and descriptions had a huge influence on which dishes people identified with the most. After a year and a half or so, I left the startup and moved into freelance food writing, creating my own recipes and taking photos. I also wrote a cookbook, *Season*.

Flavor is made up of many parts.

One part is driven by our emotions and memories, while the other part we decipher using our senses: sight, sound, mouthfeel (texture), aroma, and taste. Think of the last time you cooked something; let's say it was a caprese. You pick out tomatoes based on their vibrant colors and shapes and their wonderful aroma. You slice through the tomato and feel the flesh give away under the sharp edge of the knife. Now in goes the large ball of creamy, smooth mozzarella, a sprinkle of crunchy salt and cracked fresh black pepper, a splash of sweet-sour balsamic vinegar and borderline-pungent olive oil. You might crush and throw in few basil leaves. There's so much going on at every stage of this prep. Your senses are in overdrive, guiding you along the way as you cook, and then come into play once again when you take a bite. You taste salty, sweet, sour, savory, along with the fresh aroma of herbs and luxurious nature of fat. These elements, all together, are what make most of us love a caprese.

Aroma and taste are the two most talked-about components of flavor. Even a simple dish can wow dinner guests if it smells and tastes good. Brown gravy, for instance: It's probably not the most eye-catching color, but there's a nine-out-of-ten chance that it tastes fantastic because of all the different aroma and taste molecules bundled into it. Stir in a bit of lime juice and sprinkle on some fresh herbs, and its deliciousness soars to new heights.

When I yearn for some specific food, the first thing that comes to my mind is the aroma. Thinking about the sweet scent of coconut mixed with rosewater in a Goan coconut cake (called *baath*) makes my heart burst with unbridled joy. As I learned to cook, I noticed how onions would transform from an eye-burning pungency to mellow sweetness when heated. This would then help soften the punch of heat in a chilli-loaded pork vindaloo when added along with a little bit of sugar. My grandmother kept a large amber bottle of vinegar next to her salt jar right by her stove. She'd add vinegar, taste, and then add salt. I didn't pay much attention to this at the time; much later, in my own kitchen, I realized that she was first adding a sour ingredient, followed by salt. Her actions were wise and scientific, as sour ingredients tend to minimize the need for salt, because acids help increase our perception of saltiness. She was using this property to add less salt to her food.

While the taste of fat is controversial among scientists, there is no denying that we look to it as a flavoring agent in our food, and I felt strongly that it deserved its own spot in this book. Fieriness is the strangest phenomenon; we learned to love ingredients such as chillies and pepper that irritate our nerves. It gets its own chapter as well. Many of us find these ingredients exciting and go out of our way to add them to our food.

In this book, you will learn how we use our sight, sound, texture, smell, and taste to combine with our emotions and memories in everyday life as we cook. I've laid out the workings behind these concepts and included several practical "Case Studies" as well as recipes to give you an appreciation of what really unfolds as you cook in the kitchen, but also to show you how all the science comes together.

The science behind the actions and reactions in these recipes will help guide you, so you will know what's happening and why, and consequently make you a better, more confident, creative, and flexible cook. For every recipe, I call out or build on important concepts using the Flavor Approach. With this information at your disposal, you will have the principles that will help you build flavor into your own food.

I've also included a short primer for those of you who want to dig a bit more into the science behind how our food molecules work, want a primer on the biochemistry of cooking ingredients, or want to explore the biology of our bodies and their relationship with flavor.

The Flavor Equation is a synthesis of the various components and the knowledge I've accumulated over time that helped me understand how to cook with flavor in the kitchen. We can all make our food delicious and memorable. Let's travel on this journey of flavor together.

THE
FLAVOR
EQUATION

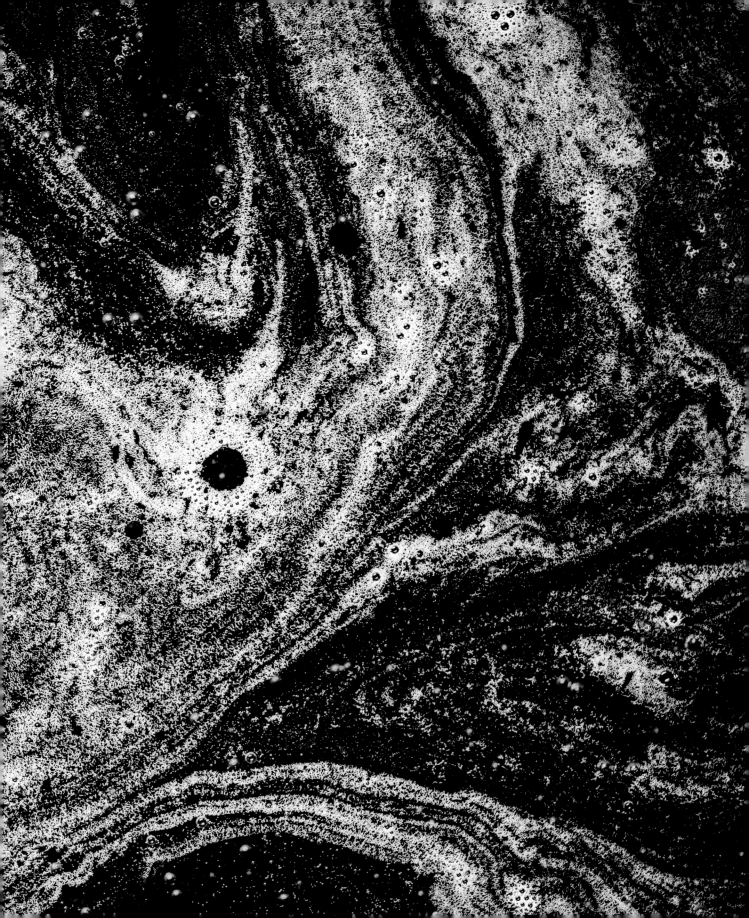

Emotion

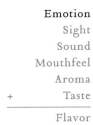

Emotion
Sight
Sound
Mouthfeel
Aroma
+   Taste
─────────────
Flavor

While I wrote this book, several unrelated events occurred; now when I go back and sift through the pages or think about a particular recipe, certain memories immediately come to mind.

The first time I wrote and tested the date syrup recipe (page 324), my neighbor's home in Oakland was in the process of being burgled in broad daylight, and I called 911 to inform the cops (who arrived in a timely manner and prevented the theft). By the time this book comes out, I will have moved to Los Angeles; during our move, I froze several large batches of the Black Pepper Chicken (page 260) for my husband to take with him when he first drove down there. These memories are now intricately tied to these dishes in my mind; making date syrup now reminds me of that burglary, and Black Pepper Chicken is the one dish I quickly associate with our move to Los Angeles.

The flavors in our food and our emotions are interconnected and have the power to influence each other. At times, a spoonful of tart and sweet custardy lemon curd can immediately create a notion of immeasurable happiness in my mind. When I'm down with a cold, a bowl of hot chicken broth can provide much-needed comfort. When I'm tense, my appetite disappears.

We often write and talk about love being one of the most important ingredients during cooking. My fondest memories are of times spent watching my grandmother cook over her large gas range in her kitchen, learning to butter slices of bread with my grandfather that would accompany the thin shaved slices of salted beef tongue. What you eat and the flavors you experience transform, over time, into a repository of flavors that can evoke a variety of emotional responses, from sheer joy to absolute disgust. Our brain pays careful attention and files away memories of these reactions. This learning process between

flavors and emotion is constant. Of course, there are certain ingredients whose flavors I still run away from; the aroma of turnips, for some unfathomable reason, makes me queasy.

By the time I was a teenager, I had worked out a game plan to get myself out of trouble: make hot tea for my parents when they came home from work. It usually worked very well; the sweet hot tea infused with ginger and cardamom would soften their reactions to whatever I had done wrong that day, and my sentencing would be less severe. If I were really lucky, I'd be free. How things taste can affect our judgment; in one study, people who drank a sweet beverage viewed certain moral actions favorably, while those who drank a bitter drink rated them otherwise.

You see something delicious at a bakery and immediately start to crave a bite; that first bite of chocolate cake feels wonderful. The fragrance of warm bread straight out of the oven is irresistible. When we eat food, the flavor components present in the meal interact with the receptors (see Aroma, page 41, and Taste, page 48) that line the surfaces of our nose and mouth and set off a series of chemical and electric signals from the nerves to the brain. The brain then uses a mechanism of reward and aversion for the different flavors. The sweet taste of sugar creates a reward, while a bitter food might induce aversion.

There is some room for fluidity in our choices. Our brain has the powerful ability to overcome certain tastes. Your first bitter taste of coffee, for instance, might seem unpleasant, but after drinking coffee repeatedly, you eventually start to like it. Sometimes a food or taste that

EMOTION AND TASTE

Emotion and taste influence each other.

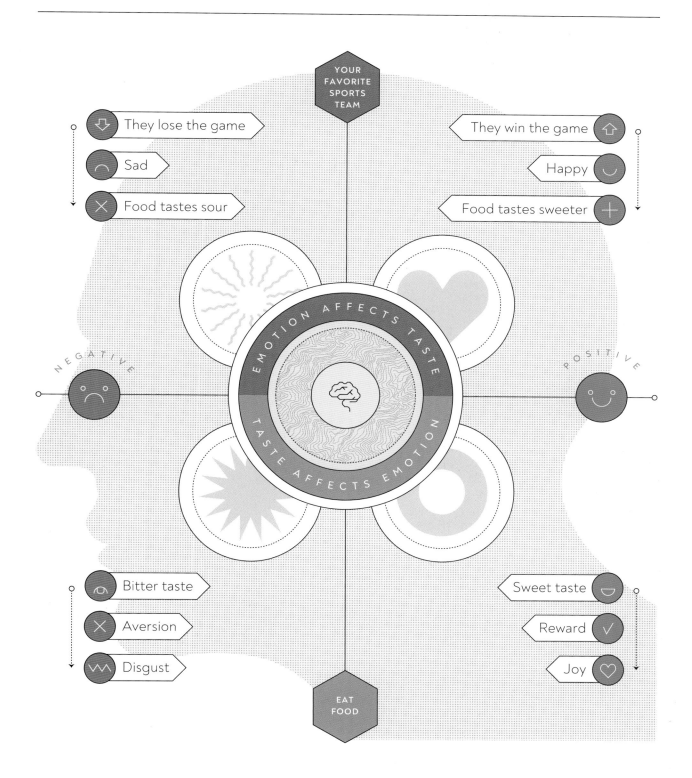

YOUR FAVORITE SPORTS TEAM

They lose the game

Sad

Food tastes sour

They win the game

Happy

Food tastes sweeter

NEGATIVE

POSITIVE

EMOTION AFFECTS TASTE

TASTE AFFECTS EMOTION

Bitter taste

Aversion

Disgust

Sweet taste

Reward

Joy

EAT FOOD

was once pleasant can become unpleasant and undesirable. Think of a meal that you once ate that made you sick; even if it had been a favorite food, after that experience you may find you can't bring yourself to eat a single bite.

This relationship between emotion and flavor is especially evident at social events. Foods served at celebrations are glorious and dazzling, with all sorts of flavors (as well as colors and textures) to evoke a sense of exceptionalism and induce positive emotions. At special events, my family and friends in India served platters of aromatic biryanis, rich fried breads, creamy stews, or delicate sweets ornately decorated with bits of shiny silver foil called *varak*. At funerals, the food was much more somber—often something simple like a bowl of mashed potatoes or boiled rice that gave a sense of soothing comfort. We might even prepare the beloved food of the deceased as a way to remind us of the good times. Around the world, we use food to communicate our innermost thoughts and emotions.

The flavors in our food can affect our emotions, and emotions can influence our perception of flavor.

As we experience and learn more about our food, our brain pays attention and makes notes for us in the form of memories. Of the different components in the flavor equation, aroma is one of the senses most strongly associated with memory. Where I live in California, the weather is usually dry and warm for the better part of the year, and I sometimes miss the heavy monsoons of India and the rain showers of summer in Washington, DC. When that happens, I immediately start imagining the scent in the air that rises when the first droplets of rain hit the soil (that "fresh rain" aroma, called *petrichor*, actually comes from a combination of plant oils, ozone, and geosmin, a compound secreted by actinomycete soil bacteria, whose spores are released when rainwater falls).

Sometimes I get nostalgic about a sweet or a meal I ate as a kid and can't find anymore; I start to imagine and remember how that aroma smelled, and its intensity builds up to the point where I find myself looking for a way to eat it or cook it at home. Our sense of smell is used by physicians as a marker to detect and diagnose diseases; the loss of the ability to smell is considered an early symptom in the development of Alzheimer's disease, a medical condition characterized by progressive memory loss. The next time you think about food or memory, try and think about what you imagined first; most likely it will be an aroma.

Restaurant chefs strive to create memorable meals and provide a rich dining experience. A home cook's intent might be slightly different—it might be to feed a family or entertain—but we all want to eat good food. We often manipulate our emotional memories during cooking; for example, the resin asafetida is used by Indian cooks to imitate the flavor of alliums such as garlic and onions in certain communities where these ingredients are not permitted. Asafetida contains a chemical called dimethyl trisulfide as well as other sulfur-containing substances present in alliums, so it can be used to re-create that aroma when garlic and onions must be left out. When my paternal grandmother became a widow, she gave up eating onions and garlic based on an archaic superstitious belief that it might induce "impure thoughts"; she switched to using asafetida in her cooking. When asafetida met the hot oil, it gave off an aroma that triggered her flavor memories of the onions and garlic.

Vegan cooks employ the Indian salt *kala namak* (see page 139). Its sulfurous smell creates an "eggy" aroma. When egg whites are heated between 158°F and 212°F [70°C and 100°C], the egg white protein ovalbumin unfolds and the sulfur-containing groups in the amino acids are exposed and oxidized, releasing a gas, hydrogen sulfide, described as sulfurous or egg-like.

When a whole egg is boiled, the iron in the yolk reacts with the sulfur in the ovalbumin and gives off a stronger egg aroma. (At low concentrations, this smell is pleasant, but at high concentrations, as produced by rotten eggs, the aroma becomes noxious.) Kala namak is rich in sulfur and iron (in addition to sodium chloride). When this salt is mixed with water, the egg-like hydrogen sulfide is released, a property that chefs take advantage of (see how kala namak intensifies the egg flavor in Salt-Cured Egg Yolks, page 312). In each instance, ingredients that share similar aromatic, sulfur-containing molecules are used to play with our memories of scents we've been exposed to over the course of our lives.

Sight

We first eat with our eyes.

This was an early lesson I picked up when I started my blog, *A Brown Table*. Before people cooked my recipes, they'd first look at the photos of the ingredients and the food. The colors and shapes of visuals are critical in helping whet our appetites and making decisions about food; they help build our perception of what we eat. The local farmers' market presents a vast spectrum of colors and shapes; the bright orange pumpkins, the bundles of fresh scallions, and the clusters of blood-red cherries stacked in the stalls entice and attract your attention at every corner. The rising popularity of images of food and cooking videos on social media platforms is perhaps one of the most powerful testaments to the impact of visuals on eating.

Yet the adage "Don't judge a book by its cover" is true, especially when it comes to brown-colored food. Not everything that tastes delicious looks good. In fact, one of the challenges I often face when styling and photographing dishes such as curries, stews, and gravies that are various shades of brown is how to make them appealing and enticing enough for people to want to cook them. That's where the power of a garnish comes in; a few sprigs of fresh cilantro, parsley, or mint soften the look with their bright verdant tones and give the dish an appealing visual contrast.

The color in food comes from molecules called dyes or pigments, and as cooks, we're constantly trying to take advantage of the colors in our ingredients. Hard-boiled eggs can be cured in a mixture of vinegar and red beet juice that stains the outer white of the egg a light pink. In India, rice grains are often stained with saffron, turmeric, or beet juice mixed in water or milk to create a colorful display in pilafs and biryanis.

In my college chemistry lab, we ground fresh spinach leaves to a thick paste with an organic solvent (a carbon-based liquid). Tiny dots of these liquids were then dried on sheets of white blotting paper and exposed to a different type of organic solvent. As the paper got wet, different colors arose and separated across the paper from that one green spot. Bands of yellow, orange, and various shades of green appeared: These spots of colors were pigments hidden within the green spinach leaves. When we repeated the experiment with cooked spinach leaves, a whole new set of colors showed up.

Many pigments present in food can alter their appearance in response to changes in the environment, like heat or acidity, and this can affect the outcome of how a dish might appear. Canned spinach has a shade of green different from the fresh leaves because of the effect of cooking heat on the pigments.

Green vegetables contain a family of pigments called chlorophylls. When vegetables like broccoli, peas, and green beans are cooked for short periods of time by methods such as blanching or stir-frying, you'll see the color change to a more vibrant green. As the vegetable heats, the gases trapped between the tissue's cell walls warm up and expand; this causes the cell walls to collapse, increasing the visibility of the green chlorophyll pigment. Heat also plays a second role; it helps to destroy a plant enzyme called chlorophyllase, an enzyme that is responsible for breaking down chlorophyll to a brown pigment.

If green vegetables are cooked too long, their color starts to change to a dull olive gray. The prolonged heating causes the cells to release acids, which push out the magnesium atom in the center of the chlorophyll molecule, causing it to turn dull green. Cooks should avoid adding acids like lemon juice or vinegar to blanching water, but a pinch of baking soda can help retain some of the bright green color; the alkaline nature of baking soda counteracts

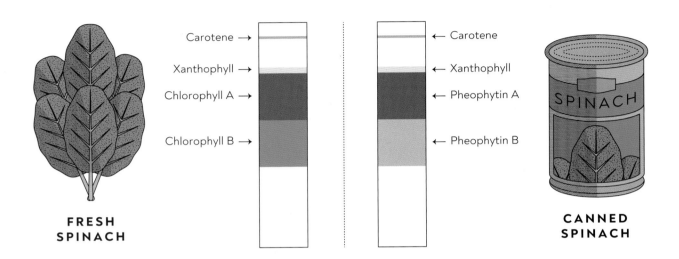

FRESH
SPINACH

Carotene →
Xanthophyll →
Chlorophyll A →
Chlorophyll B →

← Carotene
← Xanthophyll
← Pheophytin A
← Pheophytin B

CANNED
SPINACH

some of the effects of the plant acids by locking the magnesium in the pigment. Once the vegetables are cooked and ready to serve, they can be drizzled with lemon juice without altering the color. However, some vegetables that are rich in pectin may turn soft or mushy when exposed to baking soda, so the amount of baking soda and cooking time must be carefully adjusted.

Heat can change the color of some vegetables, notably those rich in anthocyanin pigments. Anthocyanins are highly water soluble; heating in water releases the pigment from the storage compartments in the vegetable called *vacuoles*, and the pigment leaches out. Heat also destroys the anthocyanin pigment; as the purple color disappears, the green chlorophyll pigments that were initially hidden become visible. Purple beans like the Royal Burgundy variety and purple asparagus both turn green after cooking; red cabbage loses it color when cooked for a long period of time. On the other hand, blueberries (which contain large amounts of different types of anthocyanins) do not lose their color during heating, as when making pie filling; the acidic conditions from lemon juice (commonly added to blueberry pie fillings) as well as the acids in blueberries themselves ensure a low pH; heating blueberry juice at a pH of 2.1 stabilizes the anthocyanins, and the high concentrations of added sugar help stabilize the anthocyanin

pigments and minimize color loss. In addition, blueberries contain varying amounts of the polysaccharide pectin, which can form complexes with some types of anthocyanins and stabilizes and protects them (Roasted Fruit with Coffee Miso Tahini, page 125, utilizes this principle).

Pigments like the blue anthocyanins in blueberries are also sensitive to pH changes. If you crush fresh or frozen blueberries in a small amount of water, you'll end up with a deep red color. Stir in a teaspoon of baking soda and it will turn blue. When blueberries are crushed, the anthocyanin pigment stored in the skin is released, contacts the acids in the pulp, and turns red. Diluting with a large quantity of water or adding a bit of baking soda neutralizes the acid and the number of free hydrogen ions [H+] and turns the anthocyanin back to blue.

When I make a batch of my chilli oil (page 283) or the Indo-Sichuan Sauce (page 318), the oil takes on a bright-red shade of crimson. Both chillies and tomatoes used in these recipes contain a fat-soluble pigment of the carotenoid family (see Lipids, page 335) that dissolves in the hot oil as they cook, giving the oil a deep red color. Carotenoids include the red lycopenes of tomatoes and chillies as well as the xanthophylls, like the zeaxanthin of corn. In green plants, carotenoids are hidden behind a veil of chlorophyll, revealed only when the chlorophyll is degraded as seen in

TABLE OF COMMON FOOD PIGMENTS

The pigments responsible for the different types of colors naturally present in our fruits, vegetables, and meats can be sorted into two groups based on whether they dissolve in water or fat.

Water-Soluble Food Pigments	Pigment Subtypes		Color	Found In				
Anthocyanins			acidic pH = red to pink neutral pH = purple alkaline pH = blue, green, yellow, to colorless (as pH keeps increasing)	Blueberries	Pomegranates	Grapes	Purple beans	
Anthoxanthins			Colorless or pale yellow	Cauliflower	Spinach	Onions	Green leafy vegetables	
Betalains	Betacyanin		Red	Beets	Amaranth	Rhubarb	Swiss chard	Prickly pear cactus
	Betaxanthin		Yellow	Red and yellow beets	Yellow Swiss chard	Yellow-orange pear cactus		
Myoglobin			Purple-red in meat, when exposed to oxygen, changes to varying shades of red depending on the type of meat: cherry red for beef; dark cherry red for lamb; grayish-pink for pork; pale pink for veal. Turns brownish-red over time due to conversion to metmyoglobin.	Meat				
Hemoglobin			Red in the presence of oxygen; greenish when oxygen is removed.	Blood	Meat that comes into contact with blood			
Polyphenols and tannins			Brown	Quince	Red wine	Sumac		

Fat-soluble food pigments

	Pigment Subtypes		Color	Found In				
Chlorophylls	Chlorophyll-a		Blue-green	Green leafy vegetables	Bell peppers	Beans	Peas	Green chillies
	Chlorophyll-b		Dull yellow-green	Chicories				
Carotenoids	Carotenes	Alpha-carotene	Yellow	Carrots	Sweet potatoes	Green leafy vegetables	Mangoes	
		Beta-carotene	Orange	Carrots	Oranges	Green leafy vegetables	Apricots	
	Xanthophylls	Lycopene	Red	Tomatoes	Watermelon			
		Lutein	Yellow	Egg yolks				
		Capsanthin	Red	Paprika	Red chillies			
		Crocetin	Yellow	Saffron				
		Bixin	Red	Annatto				
Curcumin			Orange-yellow turns red when exposed to an alkaline pH (e.g., baking soda)	Turmeric				

a ripening bell pepper that slowly morphs from green to red. Some pigments, like the orange beta-carotenes of oranges and sweet potatoes, provide the foundation for the production of vitamin A. Some of these pigments create flavor compounds: The beta-carotene in green tea leaves produces some of the key flavor compounds in tea.

Colors in food can also develop through food reactions. When fresh fruit and vegetables are sliced or bruised, the broken cells release enzymes that produce a brown color that is considered unappealing. Cooks will immerse the slices in cold water and lemon juice to prevent or reduce this. The caramelization of sugars and the Maillard reaction (more on this later) that occur when food is heated also create brown pigments that make many sweet and savory dishes appetizing and attractive.

We've learned to associate certain colors and flavors in our food over time. Orange in a fruit can make us anticipate a sweet taste; chillies in various shades of red evoke the fiery sensation of heat. For my *San Francisco Chronicle* column, I once photographed and styled a bunch of cherry tomatoes in various colors from red to yellow to orange for a recipe, and it caused a bit of confusion. Some folks emailed to ask if the yellow and orange orbs were garlic pods (which weren't included in the instructions); others assumed they might be some other ingredient I'd accidentally left out. Tomatoes come in more shapes, sizes, and colors than many people realize, and this lesson taught me how much readers might rely on a photograph not only for the outcome of a dish but also how they may associate specific colors with an ingredient.

A FEW TIPS ON WORKING WITH FOOD PIGMENTS

+ Anthocyanins change their color with a change in the pH, so adding an acid such as lemon juice or an alkali such as baking soda can alter the color from varying tones of bluish-purple to red.

+ Betacyanin, the red pigment in beets, is sold as beet powder and can be used to create pink colors in dishes. You can mix a little powder in water or milk and use it to color rice, as in some biryanis and pulaos, or in desserts (see No-Churn Falooda Ice Cream, page 200, and Peppermint Marshmallows, page 196).

+ When baking cakes or desserts with red beets, I use a trick I learned from the book *Sweet: Desserts from London's Ottolenghi.* Crush a vitamin C (ascorbic acid) tablet to a fine powder, sprinkle it over the grated beets, fold to coat well, and add the beets to the cake batter when you're ready to bake (use a 1500 mg vitamin C tablet for every 8¾ oz [250 g] of grated red beets). Vitamin C preserves the color of betalain pigments by protecting them from enzymes that cause them to turn brown. Lemon juice is a good source of vitamin C, but I usually

don't add it to cake batters unless called for, because the high amount of citric acid can affect the texture of the cake. Betalain pigments are also sensitive to alkaline pH and will turn dull and brown on exposure to ingredients such as baking soda, so keep them away (the vitamin C method and incorporating the ingredients just before baking both help reduce this effect).

+ Turmeric can be used to impart a bright orange-yellow color to savory dishes, as is done in Caldine (page 301). Turmeric is pH sensitive; if you mix a little baking soda with it, it will turn red.

+ To get the maximal bang for my buck from an expensive spice such as saffron, I grind the threads with a little salt (for savory preparations) or sugar (for sweet preparations) using a mortar and pestle to form a powder and use that to cook with. Salt and sugar act as abrasives and help break down the saffron. Reserve a few whole strands to use as a garnish (see the Polenta Kheer, page 185, and the Saffron Swirl Buns, page 193).

+ If you're worried about staining kitchen surfaces or your hands, first look up the solubility of the pigment in the table (see page 23). Pigments that are water soluble will typically not dissolve in oil; if the final outcome of the dish won't be affected by traces of oil, you can grease your kitchen surfaces and hands with a little cooking oil and then proceed with the recipe; the colors will slide off surfaces and your skin.

+ When working with ingredients such as yellow carrots, I add a few drops of lemon juice to prevent the polyphenol oxidase enzyme from turning the pigment to brown.

+ The anthocyanin pigments present in fruits and vegetables such as purple carrots and berries can be stabilized by adding a few teaspoons of whey protein (the proteins present in the liquid portion of yogurt and curdled milk).

GEOMETRIC SHAPES + COMPOSITION

I often play with shapes when I compose my photos. In image 1, a set of circular shapes in the form of serveware focuses the eye's attention to the mayonnaise in the bowl, while the knife on the side adds subtle detail as it intersects them. In image 2, different types of quadrilateral shapes create a mazelike effect and the illusion that the cake is being lifted and presented. In both images, neutral backdrops let the colorful food take center stage.

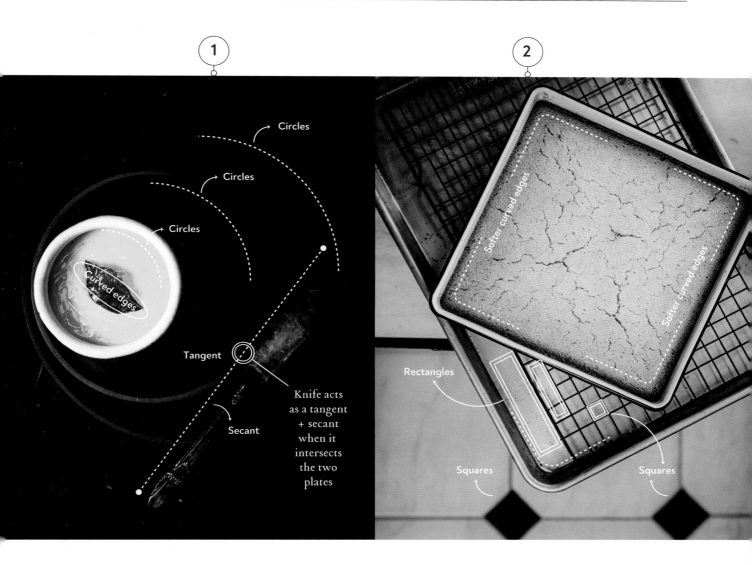

Note how the yellow, green (image 1) & the golden-brown (image 2) colors
pop out in these two photos and everything else draws your attention to the food.

When I worked as a photographer for a food delivery startup, the data engineers and analysts analyzed how customers responded to the food photos on the app as a way to determine what made a dish more appealing to their audience. The analysts studied many variables: the food styling and presentation (which was important to my work there), the seasonality and type of ingredients the chefs used, and the cost, just to name a few. By determining how long customers spent looking at a particular dish and whether or not they purchased the meal, the analysts could establish a conversion rate that they used to understand customer behavior and provide menu options based on people's preferences. The chefs created recipes for menus based on repeated customer behavior and their displayed preferences combined with customer feedback. Visuals also affected customer expectations and behavior; customers often wanted their meal to turn out the way it was styled in the photo. This behavioral data not only helped the chefs design menus that met their customers' desires, but also gave me a deeper insight into food styling and presentation to make their food more desirable.

As I learned to style food for my photographs, I began to pay close attention to the colors and shapes of ingredients and pair them with props that drew attention to the food to make it attractive. I picked up clues on color pairing by sifting through home design catalogs and noted how photographers composed images for architectural magazines by playing with shapes. If you browse through my photographs, you'll notice my love of circular shapes and how, as much as possible, I avoid plates with rectangular shapes when I style or entertain.

I've taken apart two photos that I photographed for this book to give you a sense of how I tinker around with geometric shapes and colors when I style and photograph food (see image, page 25). In the first image, I play with circles by nesting different-size round plates to create eccentric rings (circles that do not intersect with each other but share different points of origin) and use a small white pot against the black plates to draw attention to the mayonnaise, while the knife is placed at an angle to the two black plates (which simultaneously serves as a tangent and a secant, depending on the plate you look at). In the second image, I weave a pattern of rectangles and squares and skew them a little at different angles to create an illusion that the cake pan is moving toward you. In each case, my

preference is for props with neutral colors, so the color of the food draws your eye in immediately.

It turns out there's scientific support for my preferences for certain geometric shapes over others. In a study of people's responses to shapes, participants preferred curved shapes over sharp angular edges. One reason might be that sharp edges—the jagged blade of a sharp serrated knife or broken glass—signal threat and danger. In a separate study, brain imaging experiments recorded when people were shown images of emotionally neutral curved and sharp objects (such as a wristwatch with either a circular dial or a rectangular dial). Despite the fact that these images were emotionally neutral, the amygdala—the part of the brain that processes and triggers a fear response—was activated when people were shown images of otherwise neutral sharp-cornered objects; they preferred curved objects, such as a round cake pan versus a square pan.

There are some exceptions, especially for shapes that people have learned to associate with certain tastes over time. When the chocolate manufacturer Cadbury introduced a chocolate bar with circular edges instead of their classic rectangular bars, consumers were irate; they thought the new circular shaped bars tasted too sweet, though the company claimed the recipe was unchanged. Sweetness is often associated with curved shapes, and bitterness with angular shapes. In the case of chocolate, a bitter note in the flavor is prized by many consumers, and over time we've learned to associate the rectangular shape of the original chocolate bars with the quality of the chocolate and its taste. In this case, consumers felt the new curved bars tasted sweeter and less bitter.

Food engineers also use shapes to improve the perception of flavor in our food. Let's stay with chocolate. By studying the shape of the human mouth, engineers at Nestlé's research centers created different shapes of chocolate to improve the perception of flavor. Depending on its shape, a piece of chocolate can melt and dissolve more slowly or more quickly, releasing its flavor molecules at different rates—and thus affecting our perception of its aroma, sweetness, and bitterness.

The relationship between sight and flavor perception is complex, but by playing with the way in which food is presented to the eater, we have exciting new opportunities to create a stimulating and satisfying food experience.

CASE STUDY: THE TASTE OF COLORS AND SHAPES

Over time, we start to associate not only colors but also shapes with the food we eat. Inspired by the work of experimental psychologist Charles Spence at Crossmodal Research Laboratory at the University of Oxford in the United Kingdom, who studies how people perceive flavor with respect to their environment, I ran a short experiment—an informal scientific poll. I asked a bunch of people a few questions on what tastes they most commonly associated with different colors and shapes. The results were interesting. In some cases, the answers were more obvious, as a lot of our perceptions are based on observations we notice in our environment. For example, among the responses, the color green implied bitter (bitter greens), while sharper-edged forms like triangles were associated with salty (salt crystals).

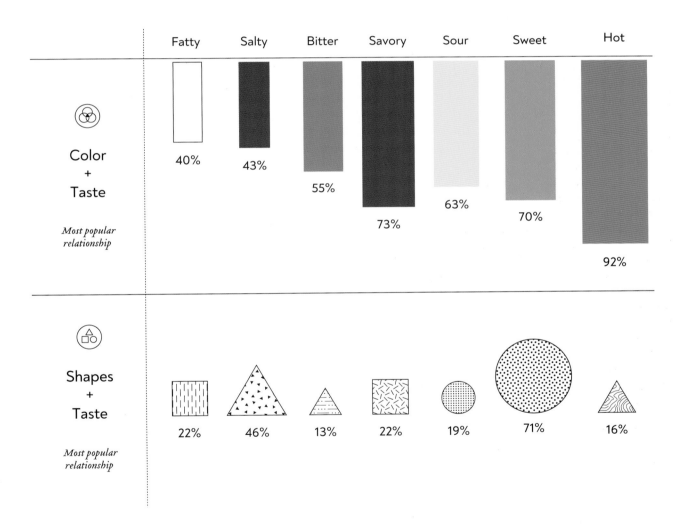

Sound

Emotion
Sight
Sound
Mouthfeel
Aroma
+   Taste
—————————
Flavor

Radio and television producers, food scientists, and product designers all devote large amounts of time and money to understand how sounds can be used to make their food products alluring to us.

At home, we rely on sound quite a bit in the kitchen; we look for certain sounds during eating and pay attention to certain sounds when we cook.

If you've watched episodes of *The Great British Bake Off*, the judges often use sound as a measure of the baker's skill; they'll tap croissants or listen to the crunch that occurs when a crispy pastry is cut through. Sounds can indicate quality. Freshness can be conveyed by the crunchy sound of a vegetable, like a stick of celery as it breaks, the crisp sound of potato chips or pappadums as they shatter, and the hollow sound that comes from tapping a perfectly ripe watermelon. Sounds can make eating food pleasant and enjoyable; think of crispy carrots coated with crunchy rice crumbs (page 178) or the sound of hot tea pouring into a teacup. Sometimes, the more intense the sound, the better: When using a new bottle of club soda to make grapefruit soda (page 120), the crackling sound of the bubbles will be louder and faster than that from a bottle kept open for a while.

Certain sounds can act as cues during cooking and give us an indication of how to proceed. When preparing the *tadka* (a flavor-boosting spice concoction of spices infused in a hot fat or oil), the crackling sound that arises when the mustard seeds sputter in the pan of hot oil indicate that the oil is hot enough to draw the flavors from the seeds; within a few seconds, that sound ceases and it's time to take the pan off the heat. The popping sound of corn kernels exploding as they expand in the presence of heat is used as a gauge to determine the cooking time

when preparing a big bowl of popcorn for movie night. Depending on how vigorous the air bubbles in my tea kettle sound, I can get a rough sense of whether the water is hot enough for my tea. Some people, especially those with visual impairment, use sound as an essential tool when they work in the kitchen. Alarms, stopwatches, and audible thermometers are helpful to monitor endpoints when cooking, and these days, more sophisticated high-tech options that employ artificial intelligence have entered our lives in the form of a new wave of "smart" kitchen appliances that can tell us when food needs to be removed from a pan or the oven.

Sounds can also affect the perception of flavor. Some restaurants might play a curated list of music to enhance the dinner experience; others take might it a step further. At the Fat Duck restaurant run by Chef Heston Blumenthal in the UK, you listen to the sounds of breaking ocean waves while eating the Sound of the Sea, a dish made with seaweed and seafood; by evoking our association of seafood and breaking surf, the pairing is meant to positively enhance the dining experience.

We pick up sound through auditory receptors, tiny hair cells (not actual hair, but they look hairy) inside the inner ear in an organ called the *cochlea*. The hair cell contains stereocilia, a bundle of hairlike processes that can pick up sound. Sound waves enter through the outer ear and travel through the ear canal toward the eardrum, and the eardrum begins to vibrate. The intensity of the vibrations depends on the intensity of the sound. The vibrations are transferred to the cochlea, a snail-shaped structure filled with a fluid that moves in response to the sound vibrations. The hair cells lining the surface of the cochlea pick up the sound vibrations and convert the sound vibrations into electrochemical signals in about ten microseconds and send this via nerves to the brain. The brain in turn processes the information to tell us the source and quality of the sound, and we react accordingly.

Sometimes the start of a meal can be marked by a short speech, a song, a chant, or the ringing of a musical instrument such as a gong or a bell. The purpose is to create the ambience in which the food will be eaten, and often the sound is a way to make the guests conscious of the story behind the meal: a remembrance of a person or people, the land in which the food originated, or a cause.

At Chef Grant Achatz's Alinea in Chicago, sound plays an important part of the dining experience first by eliminating it, then by reintroducing it. Prior to consuming a meal with a lot of crunchy textures, such as the frozen pearls of English pea soup, cards are handed out to all the guests in the room, asking them to stay silent. With the room quiet, the stage is set: The sound of the frozen soup pearls as they rhythmically fall into the bowls, followed by the sounds of guests crunching on the soup, creates a spectacular and dramatic experience of sound and flavor.

Research has been conducted to determine whether air pressure changes or cabin noise are responsible for airline passenger preferences for beverages and meals in flight. The studies simulated the air pressure and/or sounds experienced in a commercial airplane cabin at cruising altitude. A combination of factors seems to reduce both odor and taste perception. The low humidity in a pressurized cabin dries out the surface of the cells lining the nose and odor receptors, and the perceived amount of salt, sugar, and savoriness (umami, or glutamate) in foods is lowered. Sound and its intensity can also influence the perception of taste. If you're asked to taste a set of solutions with a taste molecule such as a salt, up to a certain point you'd expect

to taste increasing saltiness as the concentration of the salt increased. In one study, scientists asked whether noise, such as the engine noise that passengers experience during a flight, affect our perception of taste. To answer this, they asked people to taste solutions of different taste molecules to cover the five basic tastes—sour, salty, sweet, bitter, and savory (umami); their responses were recorded in the presence and absence of loud sounds that simulated airline cabin noise. Out of the five basic tastes, only sweet and savory were significantly affected. In particular, the perception of umami increased in the presence of loud noise, while the perception of sweetness started to decrease.

Sound can also have a negative impact on eating; loud sounds can be distracting and make it hard to concentrate. I once met a person who cringed at the sound of foods like potato chips being eaten, so much so that she needed to leave the room every time. She suffers from *misophonia*, a condition in which certain sounds trigger strong emotional or physiological responses; the continuous sound of crunching chips or chewing of food made her increasingly uncomfortable.

In discussing the influence that sounds can have on our perception of taste, we've covered the sounds that food makes as well as the role of music and ambient noise. The sound of spoken words can also influence our perception of taste. For example, in one study separate soundtracks were played, one with the word "bitter" and the other the word "sweet," while people ate honeycomb candy (page 199), a bittersweet treat prepared by caramelizing sugar. The candy eaten while hearing the word "bitter" was perceived as significantly more bitter than the one eaten while hearing the "sweet" soundtrack.

The next time you're eating or cooking, pay attention to the sounds around you and the sounds the ingredients and food make, and take note. Are these sounds amplifying a sensation, or are they acting as indicators that help you cook?

Mouthfeel

Emotion
Sight
Sound
Mouthfeel
Aroma
+   Taste
_____
Flavor

The sensation of taste begins in the mouth, where we begin ingesting our food in its initial physical form.

The tongue and teeth start to explore and investigate the food's surface and physical character; simultaneously, they try to answer many questions. How soft does a roasted carrot feel? Is a chocolate chip cookie chewy or crisp? Will the peanut brittle yield to pressure from your teeth? This physical sensation produced by food textures is called mouthfeel.

When you take in your first morsel of a food, your tongue kickstarts the process of chewing by attempting to move the food around your mouth toward your teeth. The teeth start to crush every bite into smaller pieces, chopping and pulverizing. If you're eating a bowl of the Hakka noodles (page 216), notice how your tongue first explores the silky-smooth texture of the noodles. As your teeth begin to break down the food, you start to notice the crunchiness of the stir-fried cabbage and the tenderness of the bits of chicken. These different physical sensations start to work in concert to build a pleasurable eating experience.

We are able to appreciate the texture of food in our mouth thanks to highly specialized cells called *somatosensory receptors*. Some of these, the *mechanoreceptors*, sense when food touches the mouth, the pressure the weight of a heavy liquid such as oil or a piece of food presses against our tongue, the texture of a ruffled chip or waffle, the sponginess of a slice of a bread, and the fizz of bubbles of carbon dioxide trapped inside beer or champagne. The nociceptors sense pain; thermoreceptors detect temperature and help protect us from burning or freezing, and we've evolved to use them to our advantage in enhancing the eating experience. As we will see later, the pain receptors help in the perception of heat from chillies and black pepper in our food, and this led to the development of a whole new dimension of flavor for us to add to and appreciate in our food. A bowl of hot soup tastes much nicer on a cold day; a glass of chilled lemonade on a hot summer day is refreshing. Temperature plays a very important role in our perception of taste.

Later we will see how warm and cool temperatures change the perception of different tastes; for example, sweet foods taste sweeter when warm. Somatosensory receptors participate in a phenomenon called *chemesthesis*, a broad range of sensations including pain, temperature, vibration, pressure, and touch, that occur when we consume food. The tingling sensation that you feel on your lips when you taste a fresh lemon, the fiery burning sensation of a hot bird's eye chilli, the cooling sensation produced by crushed spearmint in a salad, and the sensation of bubbles bursting in your mouth as you drink a glass of club soda are all examples of chemesthesis.

Once food or drink comes into contact with a receptor, the mechanoreceptors get to work and sense the different physical aspects of the food to determine its characteristics. The information from these receptors travels by a combination of electrochemical signals through the nerves directly to the brain, which translates this information to tell you what exactly you are experiencing. If it's pleasurable, your brain rewards you; if it's not pleasant, you might do your best to avoid eating it.

We each have our own chewing preferences, and some scientists sort us into four different mouthfeel categories (see table, facing page).

While one goal of cooking is to build the aroma and taste notes in a dish, another is achieving the right textures. Imagine a scoop of chocolate ice cream that lacks

FOOD MOUTHFEEL CATEGORIES

Some scientists classify us by our preference for different food textures.

Category	Prefer	Examples of food
CHEWERS!	Food that can be chewed for a long time	Gummy bears, Apples, String cheese, Oatmeal cookies, Brownies
CRUNCHERS!	Food that is crunchy	Crisp apples and pears, Potato chips, Chocolate with nuts, Celery sticks
SUCKERS!	Food that dissolves slowly	Hard candies, Peppermints, Lollipops
SMOOSHERS!	Food that is creamy	Ice cream, Greek yogurt, Bananas, Custards and pudding

the desired soft texture, or the disappointment of eating mushy, overcooked green beans.

Let's examine two types of common food textures—crispiness and the thickness of sauces—and how we can achieve them.

Making Food Crispy

Heat is often used to achieve crispiness in food. Toasting and deep-frying (see Gunpowder Oven "Fries," page 144) are techniques known for their ability to create crispy textures. In both cases, this is achieved by getting rid of moisture on the surface.

One way to give old bread a new lease on life is to transform it into croutons by toasting. Croutons are a great illustration of the effect of heat on the texture of food. By starting out with stale sourdough bread that's been left sitting out for a day or two, you're already beginning with a lower water content. Cut the bread into bite-size cubes and toss the pieces with a bit of salt and any spices you might like, along with a generous splash of olive oil. Spread them out on a baking sheet lined with parchment paper and toast them in the oven at 350°F [177°C] for 8 to 10 minutes, until they turn crispy and golden brown.

The same principle operates in frying: Food is cooked in oil or fat at a high temperature, above the boiling point of water (212°F [100°C]) for a specific period (see table, facing page). Heat performs two roles; it drives the water out of the food and also helps build flavors through the caramelization of sugars and the Maillard reaction, in which sugars and proteins react to produce a complex array of flavor molecules, and the food takes on a golden-brown color.

In some cases, crispiness can be achieved by melting the fat and evaporating the water out of the skin of poultry like chicken or turkey while they roast in an oven at a high temperature. You can roast a whole chicken by the dry or wet method; I'm partial to the wet method: First, because it always gives me a crispy skin with an inner soft and tender texture that never dries out, and second, you can build on flavor by basting the chicken with the concentrated juices in the pan.

To dry roast, cook a 3½ to 4 lb [1.6 to 1.8 kg] chicken at 425°F [218°C] for 45 to 55 minutes. To wet roast, use about 2 cups [480 ml] of stock or wine in the roasting pan and cook the chicken at 450°F [232°F] for 1 hour to 1 hour 10 minutes, basting the chicken with the liquids in the pan every 15 minutes. In both cases the chicken is done cooking when the internal temperature in the thickest part of the bird registers 165°F [74°C] on an instant-read thermometer and the skin turns golden brown and crispy.

For a crispier batch of chicken wings (page 95), a roast chicken (whole or cut) (pages 263 and 225), or a crusty steak, air drying the meat makes a noticeable difference in the crust that forms after cooking. Pat the meat dry with clean paper towels, season with a little fine sea salt, and then let it air dry in the refrigerator, uncovered, overnight to maximize exposure and thereby increase the rate at which the water escapes. A few things happen here: The salt moves from the skin surface into the meat by diffusion, while the water inside the tissue starts to move outward. This happens because the concentration of salt and water is different on the outer and inner surfaces, so they try to achieve a balance with the goal of reaching equilibrium. Some of the water that comes to the surface evaporates, while the salt starts to change the structure of the meat proteins it meets along its way (see the discussion of protein denaturation, page 334), making them much more palatable. The result is a chicken with a crispy skin on the outside and juicy, tender meat on the inside. This is also called *dry brining*.

In wet brining, meat, poultry, or fish is submerged in a large quantity of salted water along with herbs and spices for flavor, for anywhere from a few hours to a day or two. In this method, the meat retains more water once cooked, and proteins become more soluble (see the Basics of Brining, page 34, for how this enhances flavor).

Tossing french fries, vegetables, and chicken wings with dry ingredients like flour or cornstarch before frying helps to create a crispy texture. The starch molecules in these ingredients absorb the moisture at the surface and form a gel. When the starch hits the hot oil, it loses the water and shrinks to form a crispy crust on the surface. Frying vegetables coated with a batter or with a layer of dried crumbs produces a crust that will crunch delightfully when eaten.

Thickening a Sauce

Many custard and sauce recipes call for thickening. A thickened liquid will move less freely and will also linger much longer on the palate, consequently increasing the time you get to experience its full flavor potential. Various kinds of starches and proteins can thicken liquids.

STARCHES

On my trips back home to India, I make it a point to eat a lot of Indo-Chinese food, a cuisine that's largely been

Achieving Crispiness in Food by Frying

FOOD CHARACTERISTICS THAT AFFECT RESULTS

+ **Protein, fat, or sugar**—The amount that's inherently present in the food. Foods rich in sugars (sweet potatoes) can burn faster; some that are rich in fats that can liquefy at high temperatures can fall apart.

+ **Size**—The smaller the size, the faster food will cook. Cut everything in similar-size pieces so they cook evenly and at the same rate.

+ **Structure**—Spongy vegetables like eggplants, mushrooms, and zucchini can absorb a lot of oil when frying. Before frying, sprinkle cut pieces of these vegetables with a bit of salt and let them sit for 30 minutes. Discard any residual liquid, rinse them clean quickly under cold water, and pat them dry with kitchen towels.

+ **Color**—The darker the food, the faster it absorbs heat, so the risk of burning is high. Use a lower frying temperature if possible or a shorter cooking time.

+ **Reheating**—Fried food is best eaten as soon as it's done, hot off the stove, but if needed, you can reheat the food in an oven at 350°F [177°C].

OIL/FAT

+ Most recipes call for neutral oils when frying. Flavored oils like mustard or olive can leave an aftertaste, which may or may not work with the taste of the food being fried.

+ Know the smoke point of your oil/fat. Since we typically fry food between 325°F and 375°F [165°C and 190°C], the oil needs to remain stable and not smoke when heated at these temperatures.

+ Avoid too low a temperature. Adding too much food at once lowers the oil temperature so the crust takes longer to form and the food can feel greasy.

+ Use fresh oil. Food cooked in repeatedly used oil will soak up much more oil than that fried in fresh oil.

+ Avoid too high a temperature. If the oil is too hot, the food's exterior will burn before the interior gets a chance to cook.

+ How much oil to use will depend on the application and the thickness of the food. Tiny pieces of food like nuts need less oil; chicken wings need more.

COOKING TOOLS

+ A smaller pan or pot will need less oil.

+ Use a slotted spoon or a spider to move the food around when frying. The perforations in the spoon let the excess oil drain away.

+ Use an instant-read thermometer to note and maintain temperature.

+ Once fried, transfer the food to a dish lined with paper towels or a dry kitchen towel to absorb any excess oil, or arrange them on an elevated wire rack to drain the oil.

+ Maintain crispiness by keeping the fried food on a wire rack over a baking sheet or a cooling rack (this allows the steam to escape from the bottom and prevents the food from getting soggy).

absent from the menus of most Indian restaurants in America. Originally developed by the Chinese Hakka community that settled down in Kolkata (Calcutta), the food reflects a singular and unusual blend of spices and dairy with Chinese influences. Cornstarch is used in Chinese cooking to thicken several sauces, as well as in the Manchow Soup (page 255). A slurry of cornstarch prepared in a small quantity of water is whisked into the hot liquid. As the starch heats up, it creates a meshwork that holds the water, producing a gloriously velvety texture.

Once the soup thickens, you should avoid agitating it any further, as this would break the meshwork, releasing the trapped liquid and causing the soup to thin. The use of starch as a thickener isn't confined to Asian cooking; the French use a mixture of fat or oil with flour and cook it by heating to form a roux, which can then be used to thicken sauces and soups alike.

Starch is a carbohydrate, one built from several sugar molecules and produced by plants to store fuel for all their growing needs. Every granule of starch contains two types of chains of sugar—amylose and amylopectin—that contain many repeating molecules of the sugar glucose. When the plant needs energy, it cuts and releases the glucose units from these chains to burn.

When starch is mixed with water and heated, the granules undergo a series of changes that help thicken the liquid. The components of the starch granules dissociate and then reassociate in a new order to form a gel-like structure.

When starch is first mixed with cold water, the starch granules swell. The amylose and amylopectin molecules are held together by hydrogen bonds. When the liquid is heated, the starch granules absorb more water, and the bonds between the amylose and amylopectin molecules break; thus, they hydrate. Amylose molecules, being much smaller than amylopectin molecules, leach out of the starch granule and dissolve in the water, turning the liquid viscous. The temperature at which this occurs is called the thickening or gelatinization temperature because it varies by the source of starch at which it begins to thicken (amylose thickens at higher temperature than amylopectin, for example; see the table on thickening, page 339). (The word *gelatinization* is a bit confusing and might give the wrong impression that the protein gelatin is somehow involved, so I instead refer to this as thickening, as author Harold McGee does in his book *On Food and Cooking*.) If the liquid is cooled, the amylose and amylopectin reassociate into a new ordered structure to form a gel, a process called *retrogradation*. When the gel is left to stand, it contracts, shrinks, and releases water; this is called *syneresis* or weeping.

Depending on the situation, retrogradation of starch can be a headache or a blessing for cooks. In cooking, it occurs when starch-based foods are frozen and thawed or when water migrates in starchy foods. This lowers the quality of both food texture and nutritional value. Retrogradation is responsible for bakery goods going stale, as it can create a hard, firm crumb, reduce crispiness, and change aroma and flavor. But it can also be desirable, as in the production of starch-based noodles, croutons, breadcrumbs (see Rice Crumbs, page 310), and even fried rice. In croutons, starch retrogradation helps keep the outer layer hard and crunchy while the inner layer is soft. When fresh bread is baked, we let it cool before slicing to allow retrogradation to occur; otherwise the hot bread would be gummy in the center. When the bread is hot, water enters the starch granule and makes it soft; as it cools, the water moves out and the bread firms up.

THE BASICS OF BRINING

+ Meat is exposed to salt, either dissolved in water (wet brining) or rubbed dry over the surface (dry brining).

+ Salt changes the structure of proteins in both the skin and the meat, and some proteins solubilize.

+ Water retention increases, and pores in the muscle expand, helping flavor molecules that are small enough to pass through the tissue.

+ Depending on the thickness of the cut of meat and the amount of salt present, salt travels a short distance within the meat.

+ Depending on the concentration of salt used, the amount of salt diffusing into the meat starts out at a high rate but eventually reduces (in the case of a 10% solution of salt, it drops after 3 hours of brining).

+ Saltiness and water retention are greater in meat brined in salted water than in dry-brined meat.

EGG PROTEIN CHART

Physical and chemical changes that occur in eggs during heating.

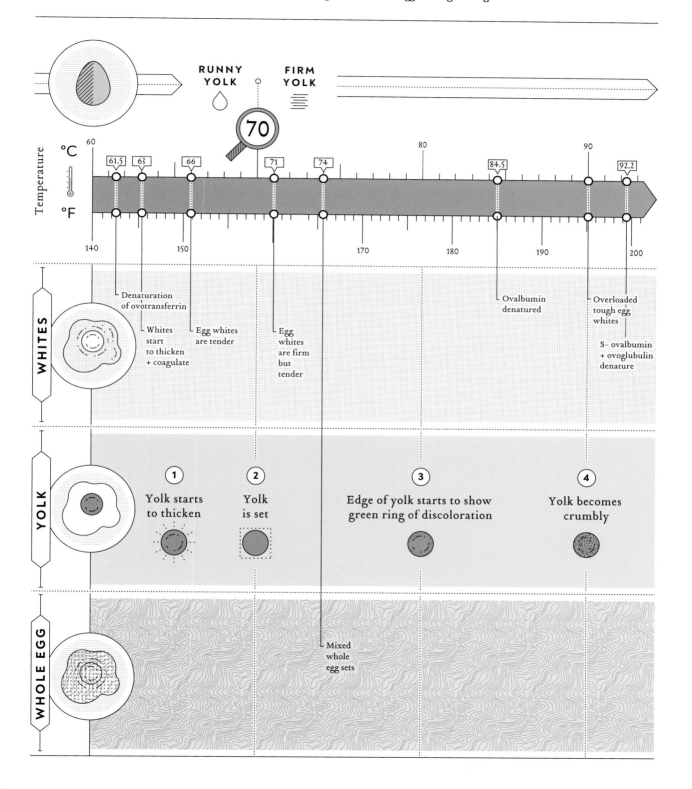

RUNNY YOLK

FIRM YOLK

70

Temperature

°C

°F

60 — 61.5 — 63 — 66 — 71 — 74 — 80 — 84.5 — 90 — 92.2

140 — 150 — 170 — 180 — 190 — 200

WHITES

Denaturation of ovotransferrin

Whites start to thicken + coagulate

Egg whites are tender

Egg whites are firm but tender

Ovalbumin denatured

Overloaded tough egg whites

S- ovalbumin + ovoglubulin denature

YOLK

1. Yolk starts to thicken
2. Yolk is set
3. Edge of yolk starts to show green ring of discoloration
4. Yolk becomes crumbly

WHOLE EGG

Mixed whole egg sets

Over time, syneresis can occur, as the bread releases water from its gel structure and turns stale and hard.

Not all starches are created equal; depending on the plant source, they can have different amounts of amylose and amylopectin, which affects their behavior in cooking (see the table, Types of Starches and Their Properties, page 340) and are categorized as either waxy or floury. Waxy starches contain little to no amylose, while floury starches have a higher amount of amylopectin.

Choose the starch that works best for your needs; knowing the amount of amylose or amylopectin gives you an indication of how the starch will behave when heated and cooled while the thickening temperature helps gauge when the liquid start to thicken. For example, tapioca starch is a better choice for thickening custard bases for ice creams, since the granules do not release water as the ice cream, sitting at room temperature, warms and starts to soften. When you want a clear, transparent sauce or pie filling, use a starch that has a higher amount of amylopectin. Depending on the recipe or use, you could also mix a grain starch like cornstarch with a root starch like tapioca. A quick trick to thicken a watery sauce, stew, or curry is to add potatoes or breadcrumbs while cooking; they absorb water and create a thicker texture.

To save a buck or two, I once purchased a rather large jar of cornstarch; not surprisingly, it lasted a questionably long time in my kitchen. Even though I stored it in an airtight jar, free from moisture, I eventually noticed that it would no longer thicken liquids as it once had; instead, I kept adding more, and the results were less than satisfying. It turns out that starch has the ability to react with oxygen over time, especially when stored in the presence of sunlight, and it will slowly lose its ability to thicken liquids. If you notice this dwindling thickening power while cooking, increase the amount of starch to get the desired level of thickness, or get a fresh supply.

Other sources for starch include chickpeas—flour made by grinding the dried beans works as a good thickener and can be used in a roux, as featured in the recipe for Roasted Cauliflower in Turmeric Kefir (page 83). Just remember, unlike other pure starches, which have no noticeable taste, chickpeas have a distinctive flavor. See the starch tables on pages 339 and 340 for more information on which starch will work best for you.

PROTEINS

Proteins can also act as thickening agents for sauces; an example is egg-based custard (see the Sweet Potato Honey Beer Pie, page 129, and Hazelnut Flan, page 126).

All proteins, including the ones in an egg, are made up of amino acids linked together to form long chains.

When heated or whisked, protein undergoes a process called *denaturation* in which the chains rearrange themselves, ultimately leading to a change in the protein molecules' shape. Once denatured, the protein molecules can clump together in a process called *coagulation*, as when an egg is fried and the thin, watery albumin becomes firm and opaque as it cooks. Protein coagulation always follows protein denaturation.

When you prepare an egg-based custard, the proteins in the egg white and yolk start to change. The chains within the proteins form new links and attach to each other, forming a large network that locks in the water and thickens the sauce. But watch carefully—as the temperature continues to rise, the proteins will continue to denature and change their shape, which can lead to coagulation and curdling at temperatures above 185°F [85°C] (see Egg Protein Chart, page 35). To prevent curdling, cook the sauce in a heavy-bottomed saucepan to ensure even transfer of heat, cook over low heat, and monitor the temperature with an instant-read thermometer. You can also use a *bain-marie*, a special type of double pot in which the lower pot contains simmering water, heating the sauce that thickens in the upper pot.

Examples of baked custard are flan and custard pie. For flan, the custard is cooked at a low temperature on the stove and then transferred to a baking dish that is set in a water bath and baked in a 350°F [177°C] oven. The temperature never rises above the boiling point of water, and the egg proteins start to denature and firm up. The trick is to remove the pan when the flan is tender yet firm to the touch on the sides and jiggles only slightly in the center. This applies to the custard filling in pies like pumpkin and sweet potato, except this custard bakes in a pastry shell, not a water bath.

FATS AND OILS

When I took French in school, as part of the immersion experience, we each had to cook something from the country. My French textbook featured a two-page-long description on making mayonnaise. The goal of this exercise wasn't really learning the proper way to cook French food; it was a lesson in composing verbs and tenses properly. So you can guess what happened. The mayonnaise didn't turn out quite right; it simply refused to thicken (my mom salvaged it). A few years later, I would learn the basics of mayonnaise well, in a surprising place: my chemistry class.

Fats hate water, and water reciprocates; there is no love lost between them (see Lipids, page 335). They are

two foes that even when shaken together aggressively in a bottle of vinaigrette will stubbornly revert to their original separate positions. They represent a colloid: a mixture of two liquids that are physically incompatible. You need to coax them to play together, just as a parent must with two siblings. The addition of a bit of mustard or an egg yolk brings them together. The "coaxer" that creates this friendship between fat and water is an *emulsifying agent* or *emulsifier*, the process by which this takes place is called *emulsification*, and the result is an *emulsion*. Egg yolks (which contain a lipid called *lecithin*), mustard (which contains a carbohydrate called *mucilage*), the pectin (a carbohydrate) present in cells of tomatoes and garlic, and milk proteins (casein) are some of the most frequently used kitchen emulsifiers. Dispersion of one liquid into another is almost always achieved by applying some kind of mechanical force, like shaking them together in a sealed jar or whisking in a bowl.

An emulsifier spreads out one *liquid* phase into another (it could be either fat or water, depending on their amounts) by surrounding and forming a protective coat around small liquid droplets, creating a homogenous mixture. The liquid that forms the coat is the *continuous* phase; there is usually more of it than the liquid that forms the droplets—the *discrete* phase. The emulsifier stabilizes this system by forming a connection between the water and oil phases, holding them together.

In the kitchen, we use two common types of simple emulsions: *water-in-oil* (less water and more oil), such as butter and the Lebanese *toum*, which combines oil and lemon juice (page 315), and *oil-in-water* (less oil and more water), such as cream. A vinaigrette made with olive oil is an example of a water-in-oil emulsion where droplets of vinegar are dispersed within a large volume of oil. In mayonnaise, oil is dispersed into water (vinegar, lemon juice) with the help of an emulsifying agent like an egg yolk, creating an oil-in-water type emulsion.

Because salad leaves get wet during washing, gently dab them dry with a clean towel or use a salad spinner to get rid of the excess water. Any water on the surface of the leaves will repel the vinaigrette and prevent the leaves from getting coated well.

OIL AND WATER EMULSIONS

A closer look at some of the emulsions we prepare in the kitchen.

Food	Water			Food Emulsion	Emulsifying Agent
Mayonnaise	Oil	+	Vinegar	Oil-in-water	Egg yolk (proteins + lecithin); some recipes use mustard powder (mucilage)
Aioli	Oil	+	Vinegar	Oil-in-water	Egg yolk (proteins + lecithin), mustard powder (mucilage), garlic (pectin)
Toum	Oil	+	Lemon juice	Water-in-oil	Garlic (pectin)
Tomato vinaigrette	Oil	+	Vinegar	Water-in-oil	Tomato (pectin), garlic (pectin)

Oil

Water

Oil-in-water → emulsion

← Water-in-oil emulsion

FACTORS AFFECTING EMULSIFICATION

+ **Mechanical Force**—Both shaking and whisking create liquid droplets, which helps disperse them. Proteins aid emulsification as protein molecules denature and change their shape.

+ **High Temperature**—If the temperature is too high, the emulsion will fall apart because the molecules gain more energy and move faster. Additionally, if there are proteins in the mixture, there's a risk of coagulation from excessive denaturation, so the sauce might become lumpy.

+ **Low Temperature**—Too cool a temperature and the molecules won't have enough energy; instead, they will stick together in their separate phases. Freezing an emulsion might not always work; when warmed up, the fat phases can separate from the water phase.

+ **Evaporation**—Leaving an emulsion exposed to air for a prolonged period of time can lead to water evaporation, changing the ratios of the fat and water. Keep the emulsion in an airtight container.

A FEW COMMON TEXTURE BOOSTERS USED IN COOKING

Cooking food involves appreciating and creating textures. Here are some of the different ingredients that add various textures to our food.

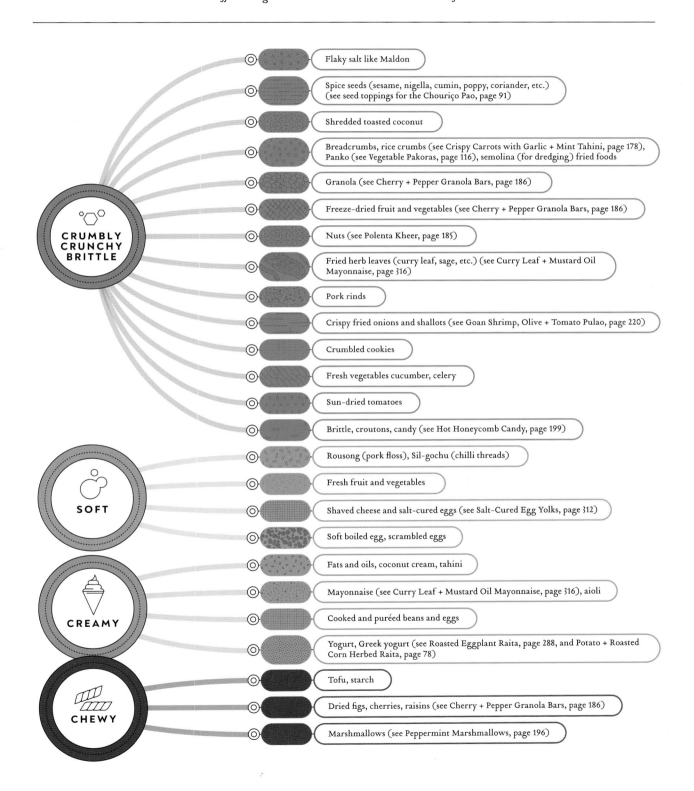

CRUMBLY CRUNCHY BRITTLE

- Flaky salt like Maldon
- Spice seeds (sesame, nigella, cumin, poppy, coriander, etc.) (see seed toppings for the Chouriço Pao, page 91)
- Shredded toasted coconut
- Breadcrumbs, rice crumbs (see Crispy Carrots with Garlic + Mint Tahini, page 178), Panko (see Vegetable Pakoras, page 116), semolina (for dredging) fried foods
- Granola (see Cherry + Pepper Granola Bars, page 186)
- Freeze-dried fruit and vegetables (see Cherry + Pepper Granola Bars, page 186)
- Nuts (see Polenta Kheer, page 185)
- Fried herb leaves (curry leaf, sage, etc.) (see Curry Leaf + Mustard Oil Mayonnaise, page 316)
- Pork rinds
- Crispy fried onions and shallots (see Goan Shrimp, Olive + Tomato Pulao, page 220)
- Crumbled cookies
- Fresh vegetables cucumber, celery
- Sun-dried tomatoes
- Brittle, croutons, candy (see Hot Honeycomb Candy, page 199)

SOFT

- Rousong (pork floss), Sil-gochu (chilli threads)
- Fresh fruit and vegetables
- Shaved cheese and salt-cured eggs (see Salt-Cured Egg Yolks, page 312)
- Soft boiled egg, scrambled eggs

CREAMY

- Fats and oils, coconut cream, tahini
- Mayonnaise (see Curry Leaf + Mustard Oil Mayonnaise, page 316), aioli
- Cooked and puréed beans and eggs
- Yogurt, Greek yogurt (see Roasted Eggplant Raita, page 288, and Potato + Roasted Corn Herbed Raita, page 78)

CHEWY

- Tofu, starch
- Dried figs, cherries, raisins (see Cherry + Pepper Granola Bars, page 186)
- Marshmallows (see Peppermint Marshmallows, page 196)

Aroma

Emotion
Sight
Sound
Mouthfeel
Aroma
+   Taste
Flavor

A few years ago, for a brief span of time, I gave up coffee. In the months that followed, I quickly learned how much I missed this drink. Every stroll past a coffee shop was a strong reminder.

The aroma of freshly roasted coffee beans escaping through the shop's windows and doors would make me pause just so I could take a deep breath and inhale that scent and imagine what that steaming cup of coffee would taste like. This is the power of aroma and our ability to sense smell, which scientists call *olfaction*. Aroma is the sense most strongly associated with our memory; when we reminisce about food or drink, it's their unique scents that we recollect, and rarely their taste (see Emotion, page 18). (Just in case you're wondering, I eventually did go back to drinking coffee.)

What Is Aroma?

Grab a piece of your favorite chocolate bar (in my case, it's usually the ones with bits of toasted hazelnuts), use your fingers to clamp your nose shut, and put the chocolate in your mouth. Slowly start to eat it and pay attention to what you taste and smell. The sweet and bitter notes will be prominent; depending on how the chocolate is prepared, you might also notice some sourness. But can you pick up the smell of the cocoa? Probably not. Now release your fingers from your nose and continue to eat the chocolate. Now you can smell the rich scent of the cocoa along with the other flavor molecules in the bar; this is aroma. This aroma or scent is a mixture of various types of tiny flavor compounds small enough to quickly vaporize into gas at room temperature and travel in the air right to your nose.

People vary in their ability to sense smells. Some folks are much more sensitive to detecting odors than others, while there are some afflicted with a medical condition called *anosmia*, losing the ability to smell.

How Aromas Work

Our ability to smell is one of the most powerful senses we're gifted with. This ability can warn us of impending danger when we smell smoke from a burning fire or the risk of sickness when we detect the putrid smell of rancid butter. It helps us build familial bonds as a baby learns its parents' scents. It can also entice and make us hungry when we smell the perfume of rosewater and cardamom mingled with coconut in a cake (see Coconut Milk Cake, page 306).

When we inhale, aroma molecules travel through air to the cells lining the back of the nose—the olfactory epithelium. Here these molecules dissolve and interact with the odor receptors, which send an electric signal to the brain. We have more than four hundred different types of odor receptors that can detect more than one trillion types of aromas at extremely low quantities (in a tiny number of parts per billion). How does this work? A single aroma molecule can bind more than one type of odor receptor, and a single type of odor receptor can bind more than several different types of aroma molecules. As a result, we can detect a variety of combinations of aroma molecules, which helps us discriminate among the various aromas of the foods we eat.

+ Aromas are volatile; they turn to gas quickly at room temperature. The warmer the air, the faster they volatilize.

+ Dried spices can be ground just before you add them to a dish. Heating helps release their aromas. Toast whole or ground spices in a dry skillet for 30 to 45 seconds on medium-high heat until you just start to smell them, then add them to the dish.

+ To infuse spices and herbs, you can break them down by hand, using either a mortar and pestle or a blender, and steep them in water, alcohol, or a fat or oil, with or without heat. You can also make your own seasoning blends by grinding them with coarse crystals of salt or sugar.

+ For most dried herbs, use half the amount you would if you were using fresh. There are some exceptions, like curry leaves and makrut lime leaves, for which you need to use *more* of the dried than the fresh.

+ In colder foods like ice creams or sorbets, you might need to use a bit more of the aromatic ingredient to get a robust scent.

Chocolate alone has more than six hundred types of aroma molecules; an apple contains three hundred different types of aroma molecules. Individually, none of these aroma compounds smell like a piece of chocolate or an apple slice, but when present in that particular combination and in certain amounts, they create a characteristic fragrance that we recognize as the food's signature aroma. If you smell a spice mix like garam masala or Chinese five-spice, it often doesn't smell like the individual spices that go into making those blends; these blends each possess their own unique aroma.

Our relationship with odor starts early in our mother's womb. Odor receptors begin to form within the first eight weeks, and as early as the second trimester, the fetus starts to pick up the scent of odor molecules in the mother's amniotic fluid. What the mother eats during pregnancy can play an important role in what a newborn baby might be interested in; for instance, newborn babies show an interest in garlic and anise odors if their mothers consumed food containing garlic or anise while pregnant. This might also explain our cultural preferences for certain types of food aromas, depending on where we grew up. In India, cinnamon was a spice typically added to savory dishes in my mother's rice pilafs or ground into garam masala, but when I came to America, I'd notice the scent of grated cinnamon in a freshly baked apple pie and find it intoxicating. A single ingredient used in two different dishes with outstanding results, savory and sweet.

Biology plays an important role in our ability to sense odors; women may be much better than men when it comes to sensing certain odors because they possess a greater number of nerve cells for the odor receptors to

talk to. Age can also influence our ability to smell. As we get older there is steady decline in the number of odor receptors, one reason why young children often find the aromas from spices more intense and overwhelming than an adult will. Our genes can play a role in our preferences for certain aromas and the smell of fresh cilantro is perhaps one of the most well-known examples of this behavior attributed to a genetic mutation. Indians and Mexicans use cilantro liberally when they cook, and I consider it one of the freshest herb scents, but some folks find this aroma repulsive and describe the taste as soapy. For some, this aversion toward the aroma isn't etched in stone but can be altered; these people can try to cook cilantro in a different way to overcome the aroma they dislike. My friend Alex dislikes cilantro, but he's a big fan of the broiled oysters from my book *Season*. That dish features a spiced cilantro topping that is cooked—in all likelihood, cooking transforms its aroma and flavor profile.

One area of research that's become increasingly popular among food scientists is the arena of phantom aromas. Once in a while you might imagine a smell that isn't actually around you. Aroma is the sense that is most strongly associated with memory (see Emotion, page 18), and this relationship can be manipulated during cooking to trick our brain to reconstruct what it perceives the food should taste like. Ham is a salt-cured meat, and we've learned to associate the aroma of ham with saltiness. In a taste experiment, the presence of "ham aroma" in food samples convinced a group of people that their food tasted saltier. You can play with this yourself. If you repeatedly use aromatic spices such as cardamom, cinnamon, rosewater, and vanilla in desserts, you start to associate those aromas

AROMAS BY CHEMICAL STRUCTURE

The aromas in our food are built by various cooking methods or naturally through biochemical reactions.

Non-enzyme-based aromas can arise during cooking when food is exposed to heat. Examples: Maillard reaction, caramelization, oxidation of lipids.

Enzyme-based aromas can arise naturally by enzymes produced by plant and animal cells. Microorganisms like bacteria can also produce some of the off-putting aromas.

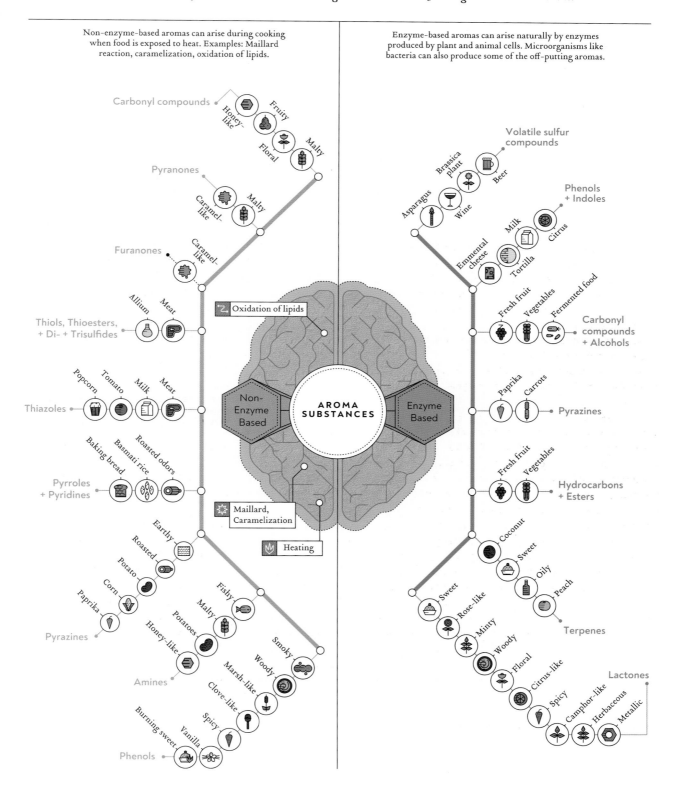

with sweetness. The next time you make a dessert such as Polenta Kheer (page 185), cut back on the amount of added sweetener and add a bit more of the "sweeter" aromatic spice. Your dinner companions will probably find that the dessert tastes very sweet.

The Family of Aroma Molecules

AROMA MOLECULES HAVE THESE THREE FEATURES:

1. They are small and light in weight (a molecular weight of less than 300 daltons). Lighter molecules travel faster through air.

2. They are volatile at room temperature, so they can travel through air to the nose.

3. They can talk with odor receptors.

Aroma molecules have a good side and bad side. The same aroma molecule that creates the signature scent of one food can be responsible for an odor considered unpleasant in a different food. Often the signature scent of an ingredient relies on the presence of one aromatic molecule; these are called *key odorants*.

PERFUME EXPERTS SORT AROMAS INTO THREE CATEGORIES:

1. Top notes (head notes)—These are the first aromas you detect and also the ones that fade away immediately.

2. Middle notes (heart notes)—These are the main aromas you detect after the top notes.

3. Bottom notes (base notes/drydown)—These are the notes you detect for a long time.

A second way to describe aroma molecules is by their chemical structure; see Aromas by Chemical Structure, page 43.

Aroma in Cooking

In Bombay, every Saturday I'd go with my dad to the market near our home. Spectacular displays of fresh fruits and vegetables in various shapes and colors would be arranged in wicker baskets or wooden crates in stalls, while patrons like my dad haggled and bargained with the sellers for the best price possible (a skill I've yet to develop). But even before the bargaining began, my dad would pick up the vegetables he wanted to purchase, carefully inspect them for any physical damage, and bring them close to his nose and smell them. Anything that smelled funky, he'd put back. This was my first important lesson in understanding the importance of aroma: It could be used as a measure of quality to decide what was good to buy or not.

Produce isn't the only place where your sense of smell is useful. You can tell the age and quality of seafood by how "fishy" it smells. As fish ages, trimethylamine oxide (TMAO) in its gut breaks down and produces a "fishy" odor.

As I learned to cook with my mother and grandmother, I noticed how aromas were carefully built into the food we prepared. If we made a stock or a dal, either spices or aromatic ingredients like onions, garlic, and ginger were cooked in fat over heat to release their aromas and draw them into the fat. Sometimes aromatic ingredients were added toward the end, just before the food would make its way to the table—like fresh lime zest scattered over a slice of pound cake, so you'd smell the citrus aromas immediately.

When you're cooking, smell your ingredients as often as possible. A bottle of balsamic vinegar from two different producers will vary in their aromas as well as flavor profiles. Because most aroma molecules are highly volatile, they start to evaporate as they're exposed to air. Temperature can also have an effect: The warmer the room, the more quickly the aroma molecules evaporate and escape. I like to rub the palms of my hands together when I'm trying to smell a spice like a vanilla bean, dried smoked chilli flakes, or even a glass of wine; the gentle dose of heat this generates helps increase the rate at which aroma molecules turn to gas, and you will pick up a stronger scent.

Buy dry, whole spices and herbs in small amounts based on your needs and store them away from sunlight, in airtight containers in a cool, dark place. Extracts made from vanilla or mint are usually made in alcohol, and they will evaporate quickly; open the bottles briefly, taking as much as you need, and immediately cap and seal them tightly. For some dishes, fresh herbs are added just before serving to take full advantage of their aroma, but in other dishes, these can also be incorporated into the dish and cooked (see Herb + Paneer Pulao, page 80). When herbs and spices are dried, not only do they lose water and shrink in volume, but their essential oils can also undergo chemical changes; in some instances, the amount of these oils decreases drastically on drying and storage. With some dried herbs, like bay leaves, dill, oregano, and mint, I usually use half of what I would have used were it fresh. However, this rule doesn't always work, especially for ingredients like dried basil, citrus peels, curry leaves, and makrut lime leaves; the dried stuff just isn't as potent as its fresh counterpart. With these, I double and sometimes even triple the amount of dried leaves in the recipes; I smell and taste first and then increase the amount I use depending on their quality.

We can also introduce aroma into our food through the popular and ancient technique of *smoking*. Smoking is used as a supplementary method, along with salting and drying, to preserve foods like fish and meat. The smoke from burning wood contains certain chemicals called *tarry substances* that get deposited on the food, giving it that characteristic smoky aroma and also preventing bacterial growth. Enclosing the food in a chamber helps concentrate volatile aromatic compounds that are released as the wood burns and impart a much stronger flavor (most home and commercial smokers and smokehouses are designed to take advantage of this principle).

There are two main ways to smoke food: cold and hot.

In *cold smoking*, the smoke is generated in a separate chamber from which it travels to the food. The food is not exposed to heat; the temperature stays below 85°F [30°C]. Some cold-smoked meats, like bacon, must be cooked before eating, while fish like salmon can be eaten raw.

Cheese, *lapsang souchong* (a type of smoked tea from China), hard-boiled eggs, and chipotle chilli peppers (smoked and dried jalapeños) can also be flavored by this method.

In India, food is sometimes smoked using the *dhungar method*, in which an onion is hollowed out in the center (a bowl will also suffice), filled with melted ghee, and then placed near the cooked dish. A piece of live charcoal is dropped into the bowl and the dish is covered for a few minutes. The hot charcoal burns the ghee, producing smoke that is absorbed by the food. You can try this for yourself when you make the Dal Makhani (page 292), and you can apply this method to other foods; it works well with roasted vegetables such as eggplant (try this with Roasted Eggplant Raita, page 288).

In *hot smoking*, the food is exposed to smoke in an enclosed chamber directly over heat so it cooks and absorbs the smoke flavors simultaneously. You can salt or brine your food prior to smoking, but consider also cooking it a little more after smoking to build new flavor molecules and enhance the texture; for example, by searing the skin of smoked chicken thighs on a hot pan. Not only does this add a delicious crust but it also builds new flavor molecules via the flavor reactions, namely caramelization and the Maillard reaction.

You don't have to smoke your food to enjoy that smoky aroma. You can impart smokiness by using presmoked ingredients—smoked salt or sugar, bacon, a few drops of liquid smoke, or smoked tea leaves such as lapsang souchong.

MAKE YOUR OWN FLAVORING EXTRACTS

Extracts are made by adding the flavoring ingredients to alcohol, which acts as a solvent to dissolve and draw out the aromatic molecules from these ingredients, and the end result is a concentrated liquid rich in aroma. A little bit of these flavoring agents goes a long way. Always store extracts in a cool, dark place away from sunlight, which can destroy some of the aromatic molecules over time. I prefer to store all my extracts in dark amber glass jars to avoid damage from all sources of light. Once infusing is complete, you can divide and store the liquid in smaller bottles or jars.

Vanilla Extract

MAKES 1 CUP [240 ML]

6 good-quality vanilla beans

1 cup [240 ml] clear unflavored vodka or rum

Cut the pod in half lengthwise, scrape out the seeds, and transfer the pods and the seeds to a small, dry glass container that can be sealed so it is airtight. Pour in the vodka and press the beans down to submerge them completely. Seal tightly and shake. Store in a cool, dark place for 6 to 8 weeks before using; shake occasionally. Discard the pods and use the liquid with the seeds as a flavoring extract in desserts.

Green Cardamom Extract

MAKES ¼ CUP [120 ML]

20 green cardamom pods, coarsely cracked

½ cup [120 ml] clear unflavored vodka

Place the cardamom husks and cracked seeds into a small, dry glass container that can be sealed so it is airtight. Pour the vodka over the cardamom, seal the lid tightly, and shake. Store in a cool, dark place for 6 to 8 weeks; shake occasionally. Strain the liquid before using.

Citrus Extract

MAKES ½ CUP [120 ML]

2 large lemons, limes, or navel oranges, or 3 oz fresh peels

½ cup [120 ml] clear unflavored vodka

If using oranges, rinse them under cold running water. Using a citrus zester, extract the zest and place it in a small, dry glass container that can be sealed so it is airtight. Pour the vodka over the peels and press down to submerge. Seal the lid tightly and shake. Store in a cool, dark place for 6 to 8 weeks; shake occasionally. Strain the liquid before using.

VARIATION: EXTRACTING BY HEAT USING SOUS VIDE The preceding methods are cold extraction; you can also use heat extraction, which reduces the time required to extract the aromatic molecules and gives you better control of the process. Prepare your extracts as for cold extraction but in heat-proof jars, such as canning jars. Set up the sous vide device in a container filled with water, place the jars in the bath, and heat to 130°F [55°C]. (The boiling point of pure alcohol is 173.1°F [78.4°C], but since vodka is an 80 proof [40%] mixture of water and alcohol, the liquid behaves a bit differently. Vodka will boil at 212°F [100°C], which is actually nearer the boiling point of water.) Let the ingredients infuse in the water bath for 4 hours. A few minutes before the infusions are done warming, prepare a separate bath containing ice water. Transfer the infused jars to the ice water bath to chill completely. Strain the chilled liquid, transfer to dark amber jars, and store.

Taste

Emotion
Sight
Sound
Mouthfeel
Aroma
+ **Taste**

Flavor

The final component of the flavor equation,
but perhaps the one we seek the most, is taste.

How Taste Works

Throughout our lives, taste, like aroma, guides us to seek out food that nourishes and to reject the food that might be detrimental to our health. Taste is intimately connected to memory. As we eat and taste food over time, our brain files away little snippets of information that help us associate food tastes with memories, either good or bad. Sweet- and savory-tasting foods signal a source of nutrients and energy for the body; bitter- and sour-tasting foods alert us to potentially harmful toxins and chemicals.

Just like the rest of our senses that use the special proteins called receptors, taste works in a similar fashion. However, we must think beyond the taste map of the tongue that many of us learned in our high school textbooks. Taste receptors for different tastes are not confined to specific regions of the tongue; rather, they are present all over the oral cavity. Taste buds containing taste receptor cells not only line the tongue surface but also coat the soft palate, the throat, and, to a lesser extent, the epiglottis and esophagus. Taste receptors are also present in the gut and lungs, where they act as sensors that can regulate our appetites and help protect us from harmful substances.

A single taste bud has 50 to 150 specialized taste receptor cells arranged in a tight bundle like an onion to form a tiny pore. Within this small pore, extending from the surface of each taste receptor cell are a bunch of microvilli, hairlike extensions that contain the taste receptors. Running through the taste cells are a network of specialized nerves that respond to the taste molecules present in food (or any

foreign substance). The tongue is an easy place to observe taste buds; on its surface, those little visible bumpy projections are the papillae that house them.

When we eat and chew food, our teeth break the food down into smaller bits that start to get dissolved in saliva. The taste molecules, or tastants, then travel through the pores of the taste buds, where they meet the taste receptors on the microvilli. When a taste molecule binds with a receptor, it immediately sends a signal through the nerve to the brain, which then tell us what kind of taste is present in the food we're eating.

Taste is subjective and personal and can be learned over time.

What you eat less of, you start to sense more of. If you cut back on the amount of salt or sugar in your food, you'll start to pay attention to the natural sweetness in unsweetened milk or appreciate the innate saltiness of a tomato or fish. Your experience depends on how much of a particular taste molecule is present and how it interacts with other tastes; for example, how sweet-and-sour tastes behave with each other in a juicy mango.

Biology plays an important role in determining our taste patterns and behavior. You might meet a supertaster who is highly sensitive to the taste of food. Supertasters have far more taste buds than most people, so they have a greater sensory ability. You can check this out for yourself. Put a drop of food-safe blue dye on your tongue: a supertaster's tongue will have very few blue colored patches because the surface is very bumpy, covered by a larger number of papillae and taste buds.

TYPES OF TASTE

Beyond providing pleasurable flavors in our food, our tastes (including Richness and Fieriness) evolved as tools to guide and protect us.

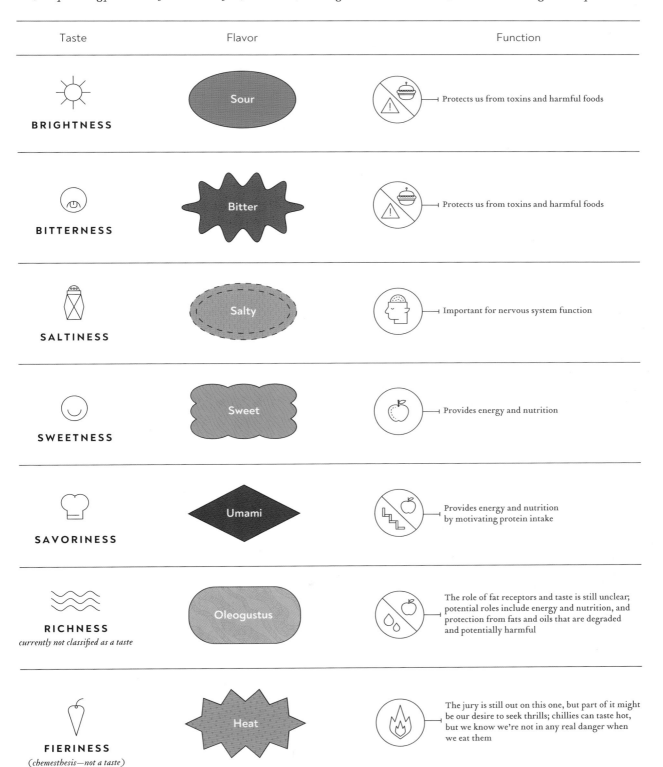

Taste	Flavor	Function
BRIGHTNESS	Sour	Protects us from toxins and harmful foods
BITTERNESS	Bitter	Protects us from toxins and harmful foods
SALTINESS	Salty	Important for nervous system function
SWEETNESS	Sweet	Provides energy and nutrition
SAVORINESS	Umami	Provides energy and nutrition by motivating protein intake
RICHNESS *currently not classified as a taste*	Oleogustus	The role of fat receptors and taste is still unclear; potential roles include energy and nutrition, and protection from fats and oils that are degraded and potentially harmful
FIERINESS *(chemesthesis—not a taste)*	Heat	The jury is still out on this one, but part of it might be our desire to seek thrills; chillies can taste hot, but we know we're not in any real danger when we eat them

Changes in the genes that produce our taste receptors can affect the way we respond to tastes. Variations in the DNA sequence of a gene that encodes one of the bitter taste receptors (the gene is called T2R38) affects our appreciation of bitter cruciferous vegetables like broccoli. People with these variations are highly sensitive to bitter tastes, tend to avoid bitter-tasting foods, and have a strong preference for sweeter foods. However, given time and attention we can learn over time to appreciate bitter-tasting foods. We learn to love chocolate, coffee, and broccoli, but what is not yet known is whether we actually start to like these foods for their bitterness or for the other tastes that are present in them.

Sometimes a medical injury or illness can destroy our ability to taste. In a deeply moving episode of Netflix's *Chef's Table*, Chef Grant Achatz, of the celebrated restaurant Alinea in Chicago, shares his journey with his diagnosis of tongue cancer and how he lost his ability to taste. After completing chemotherapy and radiation, his cancer went into remission and his ability to taste slowly recovered, one taste at a time. Interestingly, the first taste he noticed come back was sweetness, the taste that informs us if a particular food is an energy source.

Tastes and Receptors

Based on their responses, taste can fall into three categories for most animals: pleasant, unpleasant, and indifferent. However, humans can differentiate taste among five basic, distinct categories: *saltiness*, *sourness*, *sweetness*, *bitterness*, and *savoriness* (*umami*).

The fiery heat that you feel on your tongue when you eat chillies is technically not a taste but rather, as we will see, a response to pain. There are some cultural differences in how tastes are classified; in ancient Ayurvedic texts, pungency (hot) and astringency (but not umami) are considered types of taste. Pomegranate juice, though sour and sweet, can create a sensation of dryness in the mouth; this is astringency. More recently, a growing body of research supports the existence of receptors that detect a sixth taste—oleogustus, or the taste of fat, which I've given its own chapter (see Richness, page 270).

On our planet, living organisms need water to function and survive. Both humans and animals rely on thirst to regulate their appetite for water. Thirst helps us sense water and also create a sensation of taste through special channels—aptly named *aquaporins*, or water pores—in our taste receptor cells. In some instances, certain sweeteners, such as saccharin and acesulfame, have the unusual ability to induce a phenomenon called the "sweet water aftertaste." Very high amounts of artificial sweeteners like saccharin block the sweet taste receptors. When you rinse with water, it removes the sweetener, the taste receptor is no longer blocked, and there is an immediate sensation of sweetness in the mouth. You might also pick up on this phenomenon after you eat an artichoke; a naturally occurring chemical, *cynarin*, acts in the same manner as saccharin. After it's washed away by a drink of water, it leaves a sweet aftertaste in your mouth.

Some ingredients can enhance the basic tastes, leaving a sensation of continuity in the mouth, called *kokumi*. Kokumi is derived from the Japanese word *koku*, which refers to the substance or body of a food or drink. Calcium, glutathione, and some types of peptides (see also Proteins, page 333) create this taste by working through special calcium-sensing receptors in our taste buds.

Qualifications to Be a Taste

When scientists study taste, they measure the response of the brain, nerves, and taste receptors (if they've identified them) by recording the electric and biochemical responses to different tastants or foods. These experiments help scientists determine whether the response indeed qualifies as a taste.

One of the most important experimental tasks is identifying a receptor that responds specifically to the taste molecule. Sometimes, scientists find more than one type of receptor to be responsive to a taste; bitter-tasting foods can kick off more than twenty-five types of taste receptors.

The criteria for what makes a taste "official" are hotly debated, but the following are some of the key points that determine whether a taste merits inclusion in the list. At present, the official basic tastes that satisfy these criteria are sour, bitter, salty, sweet, and savory (umami). As research progresses and advances are made, it is highly likely that other tastes will be classified as basic tastes. Here are the criteria:

+ A basic taste should not be produced by any combination of other basic tastes. A sour taste should not be produced by bitter or bitter by sour.

+ There should be a receptor or receptors that responds specifically to the food molecule.

+ A basic taste should be found in foods universally.

HOW TASTE BUDS WORK

On the tongue are tiny, bumpy projections called papillae. Of the four types of papillae, only circumvallate, foliate, and fungiform are associated with taste buds. Filiform papillae are responsible for appreciating the textures in our food (mouthfeel). Each papilla contains a collection of taste buds which in turn contains the taste pore, through which the taste cells and nerves sense the different tastes in our food.

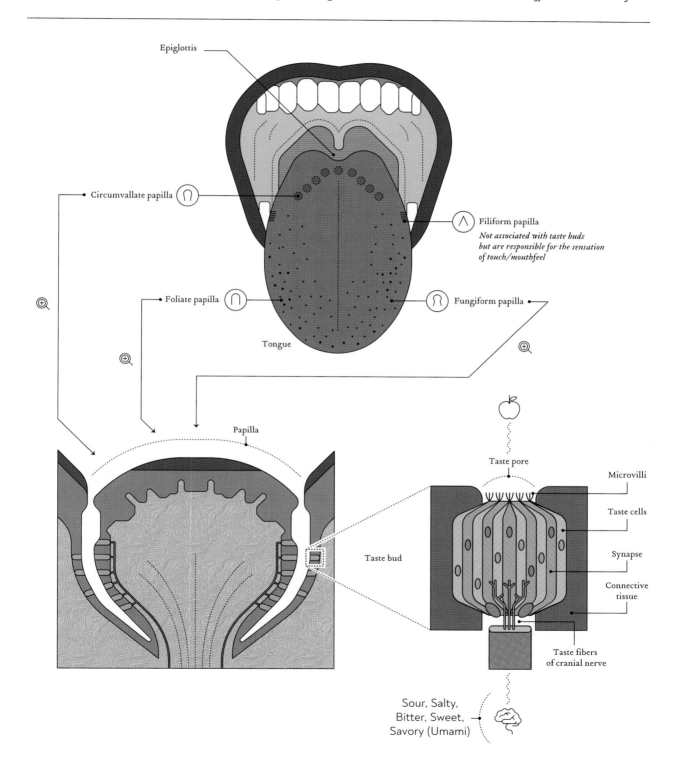

Epiglottis

Circumvallate papilla

Filiform papilla
Not associated with taste buds but are responsible for the sensation of touch/mouthfeel

Foliate papilla

Fungiform papilla

Tongue

Papilla

Taste pore

Microvilli

Taste cells

Synapse

Connective tissue

Taste bud

Taste fibers of cranial nerve

Sour, Salty, Bitter, Sweet, Savory (Umami)

II.
RECIPES +
THE ANATOMY
OF FLAVOR

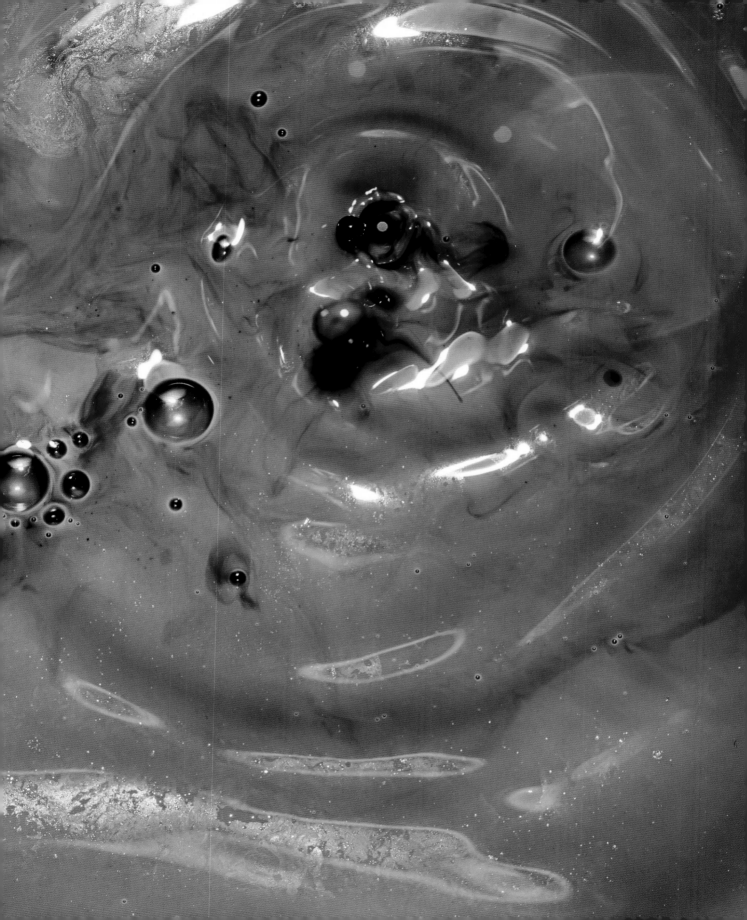

IF YOU LOOK CLOSELY AT ANY RECIPE,
you'll notice that the essential elements—
headnote, ingredient list, and method—all
work in concert to build flavor. The headnote
reveals the inspiration or thinking behind the
recipe, usually toward achieving a sensation or
reliving a nostalgic taste memory.

The list of ingredients is more than just a list of amounts
and the order in which they will be used; it also gives you
some hints as to why an acid might be added at the start
or toward the end of the recipe, or why spices are toasted,
cooled, and ground. The method expands on the ingredient list and tells you exactly what to do with them. It gives
you cooking time ranges as well as visual and sound cues.
The method is where the flavor reactions occur; new flavor
molecules are created, older ones might be modified, new
textures are created—the complex set of aroma, taste,
and pigment molecules created by the caramelization and
Maillard reactions that happen when we heat our ingredients. And while the final look and taste of a dish might
evoke memories, even rolling cookie dough during the
holidays can bring back fond memories or become the
stage for a new memory.

Prepping and cooking the ingredients demands that you
pay attention to sight, sound, aroma, and taste. I use a
qualitative approach to flavor testing a recipe, a.k.a. my
"hedonic scale." My question is "How does the dish taste?"
Pitted on a vertical line are the various outcomes—meh, ok,
very tasty—and factors that inform these outcomes—too
salty, too bitter, too creamy, too oily—are plotted along
the continuum.

The breakdown on the facing page of the steps involved
in preparing the Roasted Cauliflower in Turmeric Kefir
(page 83) is a more detailed and intricate representation of
my simple scale, and reveals how the different components
of the flavor equation come into play.

ANATOMY OF A RECIPE

A recipe is made up of many parts: the ingredients, the cooking methods used, and our senses and emotions working in concert.

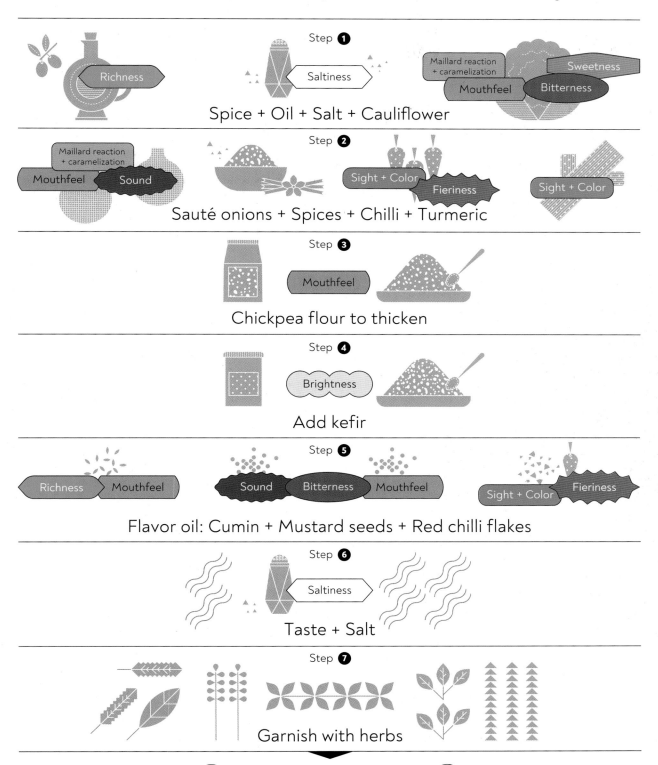

Step 1 — Richness · Saltiness · Maillard reaction + caramelization · Mouthfeel · Sweetness · Bitterness

Spice + Oil + Salt + Cauliflower

Step 2 — Maillard reaction + caramelization · Mouthfeel · Sound · Sight + Color · Fieriness · Sight + Color

Sauté onions + Spices + Chilli + Turmeric

Step 3 — Mouthfeel

Chickpea flour to thicken

Step 4 — Brightness

Add kefir

Step 5 — Richness · Mouthfeel · Sound · Bitterness · Mouthfeel · Sight + Color · Fieriness

Flavor oil: Cumin + Mustard seeds + Red chilli flakes

Step 6 — Saltiness

Taste + Salt

Step 7

Garnish with herbs

EMOTION! HAPPINESS!

FLAVOR MAP OF A STOCK

Use this as a general guide to help build flavor in your stocks.

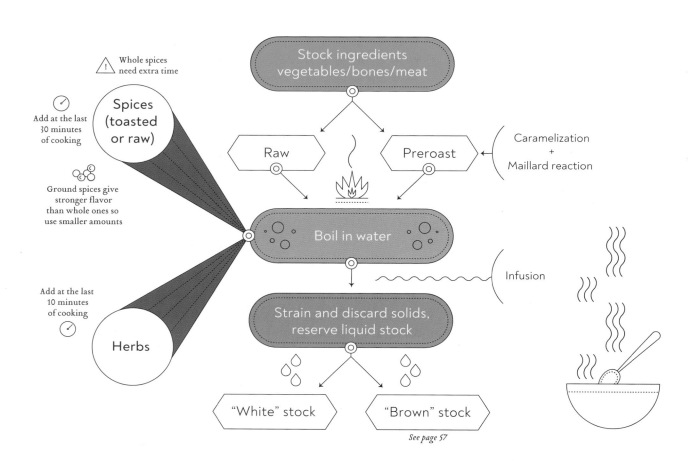

Whole spices need extra time

Add at the last 30 minutes of cooking

Spices (toasted or raw)

Ground spices give stronger flavor than whole ones so use smaller amounts

Add at the last 10 minutes of cooking

Herbs

Stock ingredients vegetables/bones/meat

Raw — Preroast ← Caramelization + Maillard reaction

Boil in water — Infusion

Strain and discard solids, reserve liquid stock

"White" stock — "Brown" stock

See page 57

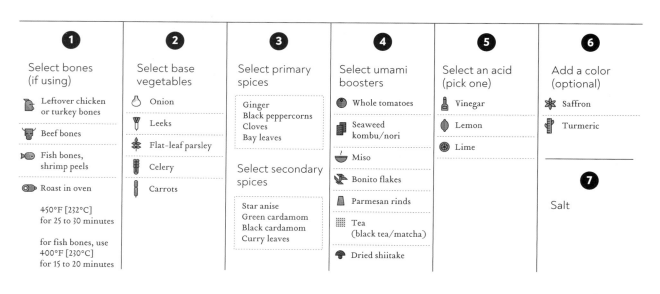

1	**2**	**3**	**4**	**5**	**6**
Select bones (if using)	Select base vegetables	Select primary spices	Select umami boosters	Select an acid (pick one)	Add a color (optional)
Leftover chicken or turkey bones	Onion	Ginger	Whole tomatoes	Vinegar	Saffron
Beef bones	Leeks	Black peppercorns	Seaweed	Lemon	Turmeric
Fish bones, shrimp peels	Flat-leaf parsley	Cloves	kombu/nori	Lime	
Roast in oven	Celery	Bay leaves	Miso		
	Carrots		Bonito flakes		**7**
450°F [232°C] for 25 to 30 minutes		Select secondary spices	Parmesan rinds		
for fish bones, use 400°F [230°C] for 15 to 20 minutes		Star anise	Tea (black tea/matcha)		Salt
		Green cardamom			
		Black cardamom	Dried shiitake		
		Curry leaves			

BASIC UMAMI/SAVORY RICH "BROWN" VEGETABLE STOCK

This is a very simple way to create a vegetable stock with a rich umami taste. There are two parts to building the flavors in this stock. The first involves steeping the dried shiitake in water maintained between 140°F and 158°F [60°C and 70°C] to allow the ribonuclease enzyme to produce the umami nucleotides. The second part is to apply the caramelization and Maillard reactions to the vegetables and sauté them in the absence of any added water or oil over low heat. This produces brown-colored pigments, and the bittersweet and aroma molecules along with the umami molecules give this vegetable stock its rich meaty profile.

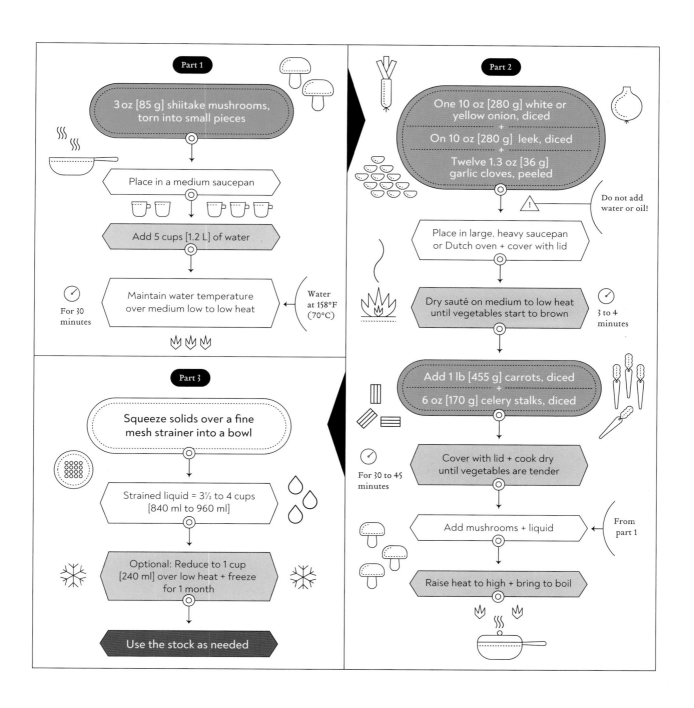

Part 1

3 oz [85 g] shiitake mushrooms, torn into small pieces

↓

Place in a medium saucepan

↓

Add 5 cups [1.2 L] of water

↓

Maintain water temperature over medium low to low heat — Water at 158°F (70°C)

For 30 minutes

Part 3

Squeeze solids over a fine mesh strainer into a bowl

↓

Strained liquid = 3½ to 4 cups [840 ml to 960 ml]

↓

Optional: Reduce to 1 cup [240 ml] over low heat + freeze for 1 month

↓

Use the stock as needed

Part 2

One 10 oz [280 g] white or yellow onion, diced
+
On 10 oz [280 g] leek, diced
+
Twelve 1.3 oz [36 g] garlic cloves, peeled

↓

Place in large, heavy saucepan or Dutch oven + cover with lid — Do not add water or oil!

↓

Dry sauté on medium to low heat until vegetables start to brown — 3 to 4 minutes

↓

Add 1 lb [455 g] carrots, diced
+
6 oz [170 g] celery stalks, diced

↓

For 30 to 45 minutes — Cover with lid + cook dry until vegetables are tender

↓

Add mushrooms + liquid — From part 1

↓

Raise heat to high + bring to boil

1

BRIGHTNESS

ON BUSY HILL ROAD IN BOMBAY, near my grandparents' home, is a sugarcane juice stall. All day long, people of all ages flock there for a glass of freshly squeezed, ice-cold juice. To make the juice, the canes are passed through a series of crushing rollers that free the sweet liquid. For a little extra, I get a whole lime squeezed into my juice. The bright acidity of the citrus adds a tart catch to the sweetness, making this drink the perfect thirst quencher. It epitomizes the sensation of brightness: what I describe, for the purposes of this chapter, as a vibrant flavor, often tartly acidic, that provides contrast to a heavier, sweeter flavor.

To illustrate this principle differently: When my husband and I drove from Washington, DC, to California years ago, we stopped at colorful taco stands. We'd each get a double order of tacos; I'd order the barbacoa with chopped red onion and cilantro leaves, finished with generous squirts of lime juice that brightened the smoky flavor of the rich meat. Once again, in a totally different part of the world, lime juice was used to brighten; in India, to intensify the sweetness of the fruit drinks; in the United States, to contrast the rich meat. In this chapter, we'll explore how, used well, the bright quality of acid can make foods taste crisper, more nuanced, and more alive as our taste buds perceive the acid in addition to all the other flavor sensations.

How Brightness Works

The tongue is covered with specific taste receptors that detect acids in food, even at very low concentrations. When you take a sip of lemonade, the hydrogen ions [H+] in the lemon juice (citric acid and ascorbic acid) interact with the acid taste receptors and relay a signal to the brain, telling us that what we're tasting is sour. Almost all the acids we eat are organic and contain the carboxylic acid group.

Humans can detect the aroma of some acids (acetic and butyric, for example), and we use this skill often as we decide what to eat. Tear open a bag of salt-and-vinegar (acetic acid) potato chips, and the unmistakably sharp odor of vinegar will punch you in the nose as that vinegar smell hits the odor receptors lining the inside of your nose. You immediately anticipate the delicious taste of the sour-salty chips.

This ability to detect the aroma and taste of acids is a product of human evolution; it helped our ancestors avoid and reject foods that were toxic or spoiled. Consider your natural aversion—physically expressed by the wrinkling of your nose, recoiling your body away from the smell—to spoiled milk or a stick of rancid butter. The off-putting odors they emit come from butyric acid produced by harmful bacteria. On the flip side, yogurt, a fermented dairy product produced by beneficial bacteria, creates an opposite reaction, both in our brain and physically—perhaps your mouth waters in anticipation of the creamy tartness of the yogurt. Your nose and mouth signal the sensation of pleasure, telling you this is safe and good to eat.

The key molecules contributing to aroma in spoiled milk are different from those contributing to aroma in yogurt, and they're present in different amounts, which affects our perception of these two products (see the chart on page 62). We also experience different molecules in different acids. While we can smell some of the acids present in foods—such as acetic acid in vinegar and butyric acid in dairy—we can't smell all of them. Take, for example, the acids in lemons and limes (citric and ascorbic acids); we're actually smelling something else. Because acetic and butyric acids (as described in Aroma, page 41) are small molecules, they easily evaporate at room temperature and travel to our nose receptors. But citric acid and most other food acids are composed of larger molecules that don't evaporate as readily. When you cut into a lemon or lime, releasing that citrus smell, you're experiencing a whole different set of aromatic molecules: It's essential oils that give these citruses their singular aromas.

THE PH SCALE

Another useful way to understand the specific qualities of acids is the pH scale. If you've owned fish as pets or grown plants, you've encountered pH in reference to water and the quality of soil. The pH scale—formally known as the *potential of hydrogen* scale—refers to the concentration of hydrogen ions [H+] present in a water-based solution. Depending on its pH number, a liquid is categorized as acidic (pH less than 7.0), basic, a.k.a. alkaline (pH greater than 7.0), or neutral, such as pure water, which is neither acidic nor basic (pH = 7.0).

An acid such as lemon juice has a larger concentration of positively charged [H+] ions; when added to water, it disrupts the balance between acidic and basic, shifting the balance toward the [H+] ions. The pH of an acid will always be less than 7.0, and the stronger the acid, the lower its pH.

Toward the alkaline end of the scale, with higher pH values, are ingredients, such as baking soda, that are rich in negatively charged [OH-] ions. When dissolved in water, these will shift the balance toward the [OH-] ions, and the solution is called basic or alkaline. The pH of a basic solution is always greater than 7.0.

It's interesting to know how pH works to create flavor—to know that what we call sourness or acidity comes from the hydrogen ions in acidic foods interacting with the tongue's taste receptors. Unlike the obvious sour taste of an acid, the taste of alkaline ingredients is harder to describe, because some ingredients, like baking soda, taste soapy and mildly bitter.

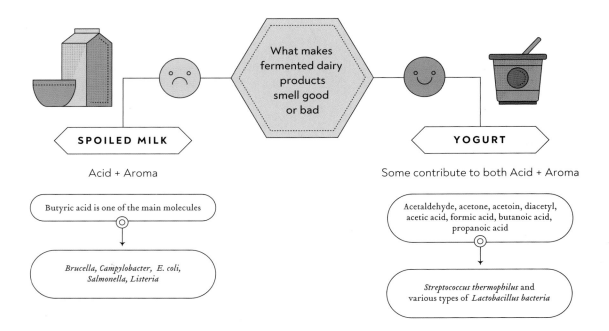

It's useful to understand pH for cooking, because the pH of ingredients plays a very important role in the kitchen. Almost all the ingredients we eat and cook with are acidic; very few are alkaline. Not only is the low pH (high concentration of H+ ions) of acid responsible for the sour taste in food, but we also employ this property when we cook. We rely on bacteria and yeast to break down sugars and produce acids via fermentation to change the physical structure of milk proteins to produce yogurt, paneer, kefir, buttermilk, and cheese as well as soy sauce, kimchi, and miso. We also use the higher pH of other basic ingredients in bagels; commercial bakers dip their bagels in a liquid solution of lye (sodium hydroxide) just before baking to create that chewy golden-brown crust, and my Hot Honeycomb Candy recipe (page 199) relies on baking soda for its signature texture.

Alkalinity affects how a dough's texture and color changes. Consider ramen noodles, a popular dish in Japanese cuisine: The high pH of the *kansui* water (lye—an alkaline salt solution usually made with potassium carbonate and sodium carbonate) used to make ramen affects gluten formation to create a light, springy noodle with a slippery, smooth texture. When my mom cooks beans, she adds a pinch of baking soda to help soften the legumes by breaking down the pectin and make it more palatable (see the effect of baking soda in Dal Makhani, page 292, and Homemade Date Syrup, page 324).

pH is strongly influenced by temperature—the pH of water, for example, changes with temperature—so if you measure the pH of any liquid, make sure you note the temperature. In the pH measurements listed here in the table (facing page) and for brightness boosters (page 70), I measured everything at room temperature in my kitchen. In most instances, when temperature rises, the pH decreases. The pH of water at room temperature (77°F [25°C]) is 7.0, which we refer to as neutral (neither acidic nor basic); in the same sample of water at the boiling point, the pH will drop to around 6.14. This does not mean water has become acidic (there is no change in the number of [H+] or [OH−] ions)—the water sample is still pH neutral—this is simply the new neutral pH at a temperature of 212°F [100°C]. So if you measure the pH of boiling chicken stock or hot tea, you need to note the temperature too, as it will be different when cooled to room temperature.

THE pH SCALE

The pH scale tells us how acidic (sour) or alkaline (basic) a substance is. Water is neutral.
Most foods we eat are acidic (with varying strengths).

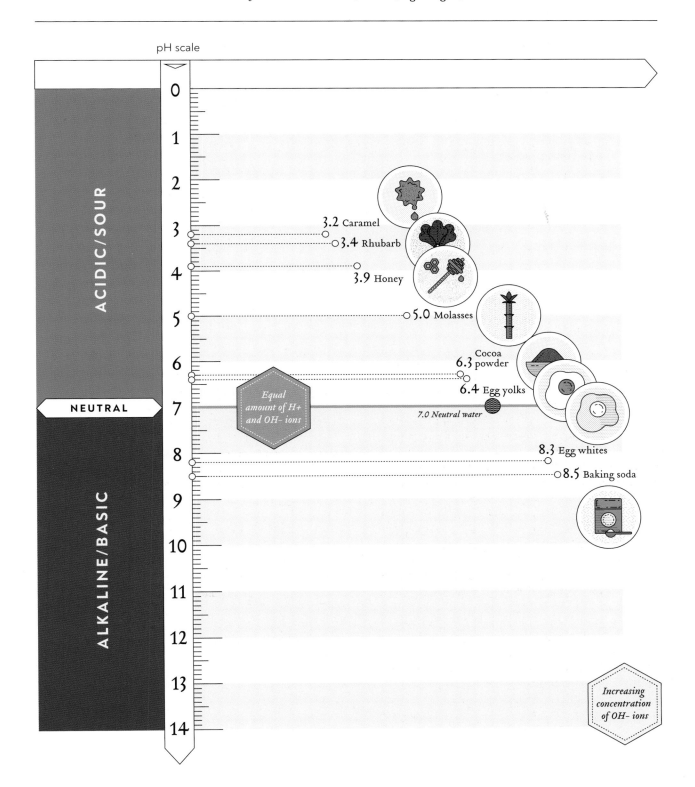

pH scale

ACIDIC/SOUR

0
1
2
3 — 3.2 Caramel
3.4 Rhubarb
4 — 3.9 Honey
5 — 5.0 Molasses
6 — 6.3 Cocoa powder
6.4 Egg yolks

Equal amount of H+ and OH- ions

NEUTRAL — 7.0 Neutral water

8 — 8.3 Egg whites
8.5 Baking soda
9

ALKALINE/BASIC

10
11
12
13
14

Increasing concentration of OH- ions

CASE STUDY: EFFECT OF PH ON
THE COLOR AND TEXTURE OF ONIONS

While writing this book, I did a fun experiment with caramelizing onions to demonstrate the effect of acidity in cooking. I caramelize onions with two different techniques, depending on the texture I need. For soft, jammy onions, I cook them slowly over medium heat for a long time. For crispy caramelized onions, I spread sliced onions in a thin layer on a baking sheet and bake them until crispy in a 300°F [149°C] oven. Onions are rich in sugars such as fructose, fructans (polymers of fructose), and glucose, which reveal their taste on heating. Spreading the onions in a thin layer facilitates evaporation for crispiness.

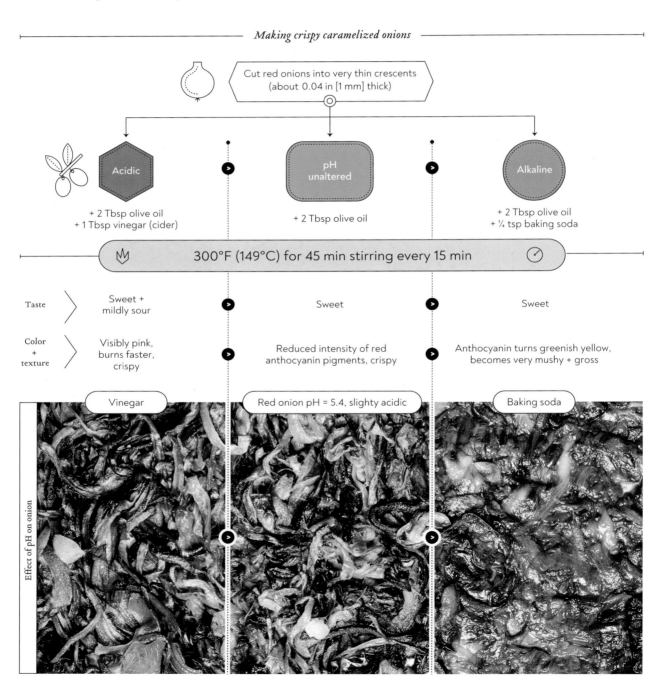

Making crispy caramelized onions

Cut red onions into very thin crescents
(about 0.04 in [1 mm] thick)

Acidic	pH unaltered	Alkaline
+ 2 Tbsp olive oil + 1 Tbsp vinegar (cider)	+ 2 Tbsp olive oil	+ 2 Tbsp olive oil + ¼ tsp baking soda

300°F (149°C) for 45 min stirring every 15 min

Taste	Sweet + mildly sour	Sweet	Sweet
Color + texture	Visibly pink, burns faster, crispy	Reduced intensity of red anthocyanin pigments, crispy	Anthocyanin turns greenish yellow, becomes very mushy + gross

Vinegar	Red onion pH = 5.4, slighty acidic	Baking soda

Effect of pH on onion

Brightness Boosters

If you listed all the foods you eat in a week, you'd find that most contain some kind of acid. Lemons and rhubarb are obvious in their acidity; milk and honey are less intensely acidic. Plants, bacteria, and yeast synthesize most of our cooking acids through the use of biochemical pathways that involve enzymes. Fresh greens, such as spinach, are rich in oxalic acid and will etch the surface of your teeth when eaten raw. Many fruits, such as apples, mangoes, and tamarind, are tart to taste because they contain acids; when unripe they are very sour, but as they ripen the acids dissipate as sugars increase (enzymes convert the acids to sugars). For this reason, unripe fruits are often preferred to ripe fruits when they're used as souring agents.

Certain types of bacteria (lactobacilli) and yeast use the sugars present in fruits, grains, and milk for energy and, through fermentation, produce acids such as acetic acid and lactic acid. Other reactions that occur during cooking, such as caramelization and the Maillard reaction, create acids during cooking and can give foods an acidic taste. You can see this for yourself: If you boil milk with burnt caramelized sugar (if you use molasses or honey to make caramel, the acidity and its effect will be more obvious), the milk can curdle because the acids produced from the sugars during decomposition will cause the milk proteins to denature and coagulate. Adding cream (see Cardamom Toffee Sauce, page 323) instead of milk provides fat, which prevents the milk proteins from coagulating.

The pH and flavor notes can help you gauge how acidic an ingredient is compared to another cooking acid and give you a sense of how to use them. For example, fruity acids from citrus or pomegranate molasses will deliver a much more pleasant taste when paired with fresh salads, vegetables, and fruits. Vinegars have their own distinct aroma, so use them judiciously when cooking, as the aroma can be overpowering to some folks. When curdling milk to prepare cheeses such paneer or tofu, you might use less lemon juice than you would vinegar because lemons are much more acidic (their pH is considerably lower) and the final aroma is more delicate.

These rules aren't set in stone, but they give you a starting point to consider creatively using some of these ingredients. Typically, we use acids at two stages in cooking. *Cooking acids* are the ones added at the start of the recipe to influence the taste and texture; for example, the acids in marinades and the acids added to stews and soups. Sometimes we add the acid at the end, just before the dish is served, such as the fresh lemon or lime juice added to a salad or a plate of roasted carrots just before they go out; this is called a *garnishing acid*.

Here are some of my favorite brightness ingredients and how you can use them in your own cooking.

BUTTERMILK, KEFIR, AND YOGURT

Buttermilk (pH 4.52), *kefir (pH 4.25)*, and *yogurt (pH 4.3)* are all products of milk fermentation. The specific strains of bacteria used to produce these ingredients vary by source and geography. In buttermilk production, added bacteria consume the milk sugar lactose (see Carbohydrates and Sugars, page 331) to produce lactic acid, which in turn reduces the pH of the milk. The protein structure is altered, the milk curdles, and what's left behind is the white coagulated milk proteins and a greenish-yellow liquid called whey.

There are two types of buttermilk: traditional and cultured. Traditional buttermilk (sometimes known as "clabbered") is the liquid left behind after butter is churned from milk. Traditional buttermilk is not sour to taste unless it is made with milk that was already sour. Cultured buttermilk, the kind commercially available in the West, is made by fermenting fresh milk, so it acquires a tangy, sour flavor. I cook most often with cultured buttermilk.

Kefir is a fizzy, tangy, fermented milk drink that originated in the Caucasus Mountains and parts of Eastern Europe. Kefir "grains" containing a special mix of bacteria and yeast are added to fresh milk (or other liquids). The effervescence comes from bubbles of carbon dioxide produced by fermentation. When milk is used, dairy kefir is the product; it is very similar to buttermilk and in most cases works as a fantastic substitute (see Roasted Cauliflower in Turmeric Kefir, page 83, and Blueberry + Omani Lime Ice Cream, page 98). Kefir and buttermilk also add their flavor and tenderizing properties to cakes, pancakes, and batters.

There are nondairy kefirs and yogurts; the microorganisms used to prepare these products are different, and they need to use sugars other than lactose. The consistencies of these products also vary considerably depending on the type of nut or seed used; if you decide to use them, adjust your recipes accordingly. There are some shortcuts to preparing buttermilk by mixing a few tablespoons of vinegar or lemon juice with milk; these work fine in most baking recipes, but I rarely find them successful in recipes where kefir or buttermilk are the focus.

BUTTERMILK SHORTCUT: 1 Tbsp lemon juice or white vinegar + 1 cup milk—mix and let stand at room temperature for 5 minutes, until the liquid is lumpy. (This is an example of protein denaturation—see page 334.)

Because all three of these ingredients contain lactic acid, heating them can cause the milk proteins' structure to change and to separate even further when cooking dishes such as Roasted Cauliflower in Turmeric Kefir (page 83). To avoid this, follow these three tips: (1) start with the freshest possible bottle (the older the bottle, the longer the microbes ferment, leading to more acid accumulation, which causes the proteins to separate faster), (2) add these fermented dairy products toward the end of cooking, and (3) never let them heat beyond a gentle simmer.

AMCHUR AND UNRIPE MANGO

Unripe green mangoes (pH 2.65) are a popular souring agent in India and other tropical countries where they're grown. Both the outer green skin and the pulp are edible. Typically, unripe mangoes can be diced and used fresh in salads, but they can also be cut up and cooked in stews and curries.

In India, unripe mangoes are sun-dried and ground to a fine powder called amchur that is used to add brightness to savory preparations. Amchur is also great in sweet-salty preparations with a bit of chilli; it's used in several types of fresh street-food snacks in India and to enhance the fruity acidity of condiments (see Tamarind-Date Chutney, page 322). Amchur works great as a garnish when sprinkled over fresh salads and fruit, fried or roasted vegetables (see Vegetable Pakoras, page 116, and Tomato Aachari Polenta Tart, page 87), and over grilled or fried seafood; its bright, fruity taste contrasts well with the mellow sweetness of fruit like peaches or apples. Amchur is available as a powder at most Indian grocery stores and specialty spice markets. Green tomatoes, green strawberries, and other unripe fruits are fun to experiment with and provide similar results.

LEMONS AND LIMES

Of the many members of the citrus family, *lemons (pH 2.44)* and *limes (pH 2.6)* are the two most popular souring agents

used in cooking. Though they both contain the same acids (citric and ascorbic acids), their pH is different: limes are much more acidic (5% citric acid in lemons compared with 8% in limes). Lemons are a bit more sweet than limes, which also helps mellow their sourness (2.5% sugar in lemons compared with 1.69% in limes). When a stronger note of brightness is desired, go with a lime.

Among the lemons, the Meyer variety are thin skinned, with a more pronounced floral aroma; they taste slightly sweeter and are slightly less acidic than their Eureka or Lisbon counterparts. For these reasons, I prefer Meyer lemons when making preserves or pickles (page 318), if I can find them.

Omani limes, used in Persian cooking, are dried limes with a smoky perfume. To use one—for example, in a stew or an ice cream base (see Blueberry + Omani Lime Ice Cream, page 98)—simply poke a few holes in the dried lime or crack it and let it steep in a hot or cold liquid. Avoid using a fine-ground powder, because the bitter compounds become much more noticeable and their intensity increases over time.

POMEGRANATE MOLASSES

Pomegranate molasses (pH 1.71) is obtained by heating and concentrating the juice of pomegranates. This thick, dark, brown liquid is sweet, but with a unique fruity acidity. Because of the way in which it is prepared by reduction (the volume is reduced but the acid concentrates), the acidity of pomegranate molasses is much higher than that of pomegranate juice, so a little goes a long way. It works great as a vinegar substitute in salad dressings and is a mainstay in Middle Eastern and Persian kitchens. Use it as a souring agent in savory stews and drizzle it over grilled cuts of meat, especially lamb (and see the chicken wings recipe, page 95). Stir a teaspoon or two into your homemade tomato sauce recipes; you will immediately notice how it brightens while adding a bit of sweetness. I usually store my bottle of pomegranate molasses in the refrigerator, which sometimes causes the sugars to crystallize. If this happens, you can dissolve the crystals by standing the bottle in a bowl of hot water for a few minutes (you can use the same method when your honey crystallizes).

SUMAC

Though they originate from different parts of the world, *sumac (pH 3.10)* is used like amchur: to garnish sweet and savory dishes, in raw salads, and stirred into rice. It's a great option when you want a note of brightness but not the liquid that comes with lemons, limes, and vinegar. The acidity from sumac can be extracted by heating it in water to create a simple syrup; be careful to avoid heating or steeping it for too long, as it contains tannins that will impart a bitter, astringent aftertaste.

TOMATOES

Tomatoes (pH 4.42 fresh, 4.2 paste) are rich in citric acid but also high in glutamates. When ripe, they're sweet, with the added bonus of having an amazing variety of colors, shapes, and sizes to play with. I use fresh tomatoes to eat and cook with, but I find concentrated tomato pastes and sun-dried tomatoes very useful for adding a rich tomato flavor without increasing the liquid volume of a dish. As tomatoes cook, their juices reduce and their acids concentrate, so tomato pastes and canned tomatoes are much more acidic than fresh tomatoes (see Roasted Tomatoes with Curry Leaves, page 153, and Roasted Tomato + Tamarind Soup, page 157). Often in Indian recipes, tomatoes are cooked for a long time to let the flavors concentrate. To save time, I use tomato paste (see Dal Makhani, page 292) instead.

CARBONATED BEVERAGES

I've included *carbonated beverages (pH 4.8)* here because we possess a unique sensing mechanism when it comes to these drinks, and they're also sour to taste. Carbonated beverages are acidic from the carbonic acid produced when carbon dioxide gas in dissolved in water. In liquids such as champagne, the carbon dioxide is a natural byproduct of fermentation; in other beverages, mechanical pressure is applied to force the gas into the water (or other liquid).

For the most part, carbon dioxide gas hates staying in water, and it will do its best to escape in the form of tiny gas bubbles that rise to the surface, the reason why carbonated beverages must be tightly sealed to maintain pressure. When you sip champagne, three things happen. First, your sour taste receptors respond to the change in pH. Second, an enzyme present near the receptors detects the carbon dioxide and tells you how delicious the bubbles taste. Third, the bubbles are sensed by mechanical sensory receptors that line the surface of your mouth. All these reactions make carbonated water a fantastic substitute for baking soda when the volume of the liquid does not matter. Use it to make pancake and waffle batters by using the same volume in place of the original liquid. Carbonation will intensify the acidity of sweetened sour drinks; try it instead of water when diluting the concentrates for the Hibiscus (Ginger Pepper) Refresher (page 266), Lemon + Lime Mintade (page 97), and Grapefruit Soda with Chai Masala (page 120).

TAMARIND

When my mother makes her creamy coconut fish stews (see Caldine, page 301) and *sambhar* (a lentil stew from Southern India), she drops in a small ball of soft *tamarind pulp (pH 2.46)* and lets it work its magic. Worcestershire sauce contains extracts of tamarind, fermented along with a bunch of sweeteners and spices. Though the tamarind tree originated in hot, arid regions of Africa, it made its way to India and other Asian countries, where it quickly became an important souring agent in local cuisines.

It's the pulp of the tamarind fruit pod that is sour; the ripe fruit is sweet. In Indian cooking, unripe tamarind pods are preferred for their acidity; the active ingredient is tartaric acid. Avoid commercial concentrates; instead, look for fresh or frozen pulp or bottled paste. When making broths or stocks, replace the lemon or vinegar with a bit of a tamarind to add a different type of fruity sourness.

To Prepare Tamarind Paste

This makes about 1¼ cups [360 g]. Mix 1 cup [200 g] seedless tamarind fruit pulp in a large, heatproof, nonreactive bowl with 2 cups [480 ml] boiling water. Cover and let sit to soften, about 1 hour. Mash the softened pulp with a fork or potato masher. Set a fine-mesh sieve over a large bowl. Strain the thick, pulpy liquid through the sieve, pressing to collect as much liquid as possible. Discard the fibrous material. The paste in the bowl can be used immediately or stored, refrigerated in an airtight container, for up to 1 month, or frozen for up to 3 months.

NOTE: You can use 8 to 12 whole tamarind pods but remember to peel and discard the outer shell, seeds, and any stringy fibers first.

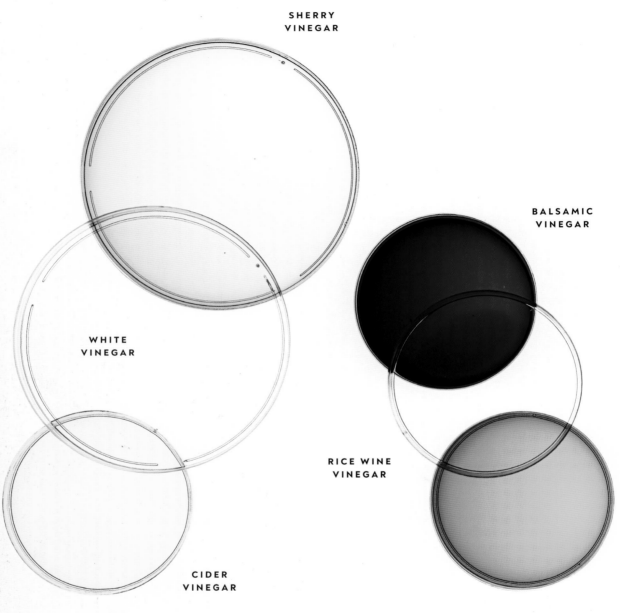

SHERRY
VINEGAR

BALSAMIC
VINEGAR

WHITE
VINEGAR

RICE WINE
VINEGAR

CIDER
VINEGAR

PLUM
VINEGAR

POMEGRANATE
MOLASSES

SUMAC

AMCHUR

TOMATO IN ITS
VARIOUS FORMS

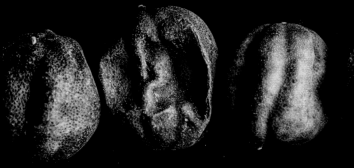

OMANI LIMES

+ Acids can impart visual and textural contrast in dishes and make certain ingredients more palatable.

+ Most fresh or dried berries and fruit like tomatoes, mangoes, and apples will give a pop of acidity and texture when included in a salad.

+ Limes and lemons, and fruit juices such as pomegranate and pomegranate molasses, can be used to finish a dish just before it is served.

+ Acids can change the color of food pigments: Red onions turn a brighter pink when cooked or stored in vinegar (one reason why quick onion pickles made with red onions will be bright pink) (see Sight, page 21).

+ Acids can be used to break down the structure of starch and reduce the thickness of a starch-thickened liquid (see Mouthfeel, page 30, and Manchow Soup, page 255).

+ Acids can change animal and plant tissues, affecting their palatability.

Most marinades for meat are acidic and made with ingredients like lime juice or yogurt. The low pH helps change the protein structure on the surface of the meat so it cooks faster and softens the texture. Because marinades work on the surface, I often poke holes in meat with a fork or make short, deep gashes in chicken to allow the marinade to penetrate the meat.

Vegetables, fruits, and beans get their structure from four types of polysaccharides: pectin, hemicellulose, lignin, and cellulose. A change in pH during cooking will change plant structure. When baking soda is added to beans during cooking, it increases the pH, making the pectin and hemicellulose highly soluble in water (see Dal Makhani, page 292, and the effect of pH on red onions, page 64). The beans and onions will soften and cook faster. Adding an acid like vinegar has the opposite effect: It strengthens the beans' structure, keeping them firmer.

+ When using ground meat to make kebabs, burgers, or koftas, wait until after the meat is cooked to add acid ingredients. The low pH of an acid affects the structure of the muscle proteins in ground meat by denaturing them, so the proteins cannot attract and hold water well. When meat is ground, the exposed area of the surface increases and added acids are more likely to interact with more muscle proteins, so that burger won't be very juicy, and other meat might be dry and tough when cooked.

+ Acidic marinades (Lamb Chops with Scallion Mint Salsa, page 163) help solubilize the collagen in red meat, making the meat less tough; they also increase water retention and tenderization for a moist, toothsome result.

+ Acids can be used in two ways: as a cooking agent or as a finishing touch when garnishing a dish. Sometimes acids are included in marinades (see the grilled chicken salad, page 159) or added to a dish during cooking, such as the malt vinegar used in Spareribs in Malt Vinegar (page 89) to improve texture.

+ Often dishes cooked with acid taste much better after a few days. Try this with Spareribs in Malt Vinegar (page 89): Taste the ribs on the day you make them and again after a few days (if there's any left). In Goan cooking, vinegar is used to make the classic dishes vindaloo and sorpotel. The vinegar not only helps tenderize the pork and build flavor but also acts a preservative. When my family makes these dishes, they store the cooked dish in the refrigerator for several weeks, sometimes even up to a month before it is served. The flavor improves on storage and the high concentration of acid prevents bacterial growth.

+ Acids can be used as a preservative, protecting food from the growth of harmful bacteria as seen in pickles and in fermented foods such as kimchi.

+ When making bone-based broths, add an acid such as lemon juice or vinegar during cooking. The low pH of the acid will help dissolve the calcium of the bones and also help convert the collagen to gelatin, giving it a richer, tastier flavor.

+ Mixing two or more different sources of acidity can enhance brightness. This is employed in the Indian street foods called *chaat*; often lime juice, tamarind, and amchur are used together in the same dish to create different levels of brightness (see Chickpea Salad with Date + Tamarind Dressing, page 74).

+ Adding a souring agent can suppress the intensity of sweetness in food and make it both more palatable and tastier. The presence of acid in a high-sugar wine such as Riesling provides a sourness to counteract the sweetness. Adding a bit of lemon or lime juice to a very sweet fruit or a dessert cuts through the sweetness and adds a flavor dimension.

+ Acids can help suppress bitter taste. The acids in a vinaigrette reduce the intensity of bitterness present in fresh leafy greens such as radicchio, endive, and spinach. Observe the effect of lime juice on the taste of the Roasted Fruit with Coffee Miso Tahini (page 125).

+ Acid can affect the perception of saltiness. A large amount of acid added to a dish will make it taste less salty. A smaller amount of acid will do the opposite and amplify the saltiness. Keep this in mind when you add salt to acidic foods such as salad dressings.

+ Temperature can also affect sourness. Serving food at warmer temperatures can increase the perception of sourness, and chilling will decrease it. You might notice this when you drink a chilled glass of lemonade; when warm, this drink will taste more sour.

+ Fruity, acidic ingredients such as mangoes, pineapples, peaches, and cherries not only work great with sweet fruits and desserts, but when added to barbecue sauces and grilled meats they cut the richness of these foods.

+ To make citrus taste more sour, add the zest along with the juice to get the full effect of their essential oils.

+ The oxalic acid in spinach and rhubarb makes them taste much more acidic when eaten raw. (Notice how the surface of your teeth feels rough? That's the feeling of tooth enamel being etched by the acid.) When heated, the oxalic acid breaks down, and foods that contain it will taste less acidic and sour.

+ Dried ingredients such as amchur, Omani limes, sumac, and dried tomatoes add brightness without increasing the liquid volume. Use these as a garnish over raw vegetables, fruit, or cooked food, or fold them into a seasoning mix. Extract their acidity by using heat and boiling them in water (their acids are water soluble) to make simple syrups (see Hibiscus Refresher, page 266).

+ Acids help reduce the heaviness of fried and oily foods. Pickled onions in a sandwich, vinegar on fries, yogurt on meat, and all sorts of sour add-ons with roasted vegetables provide contrast. Try the Roasted Delicata Squash with Herbed Yogurt Dressing (page 253) with the Gunpowder Oven "Fries" (page 144) and make a note of what you feel and taste.

+ Not all cooking acids behave the same. Raw garlic cloves sometimes turn blue when pickled in vinegar (acetic) acid. Citric acid in the form of lemon juice will prevent the garlic from turning blue.

Grilled Hearts of Romaine with Chilli Pumpkin Seeds

I find grilling to be pure pleasure and one of the most enjoyable acts in cooking. There's the sizzling sound when cold food hits the blazing grate and the aroma of new substances created as it burns and reacts on contact. Romaine lettuce hearts take on a completely new flavor when grilled in this salad. I use a grilling pan, but you can most certainly make this on an outdoor grill.

SERVES 4

For the chilli pumpkin seeds:

¼ cup [35 g] raw pumpkin seeds

1 Tbsp extra-virgin olive oil

½ tsp ground paprika

Fine sea salt

1 tsp red chilli flakes, such as Aleppo, Maras, or Urfa

For the garlic yogurt dressing (makes 1 cup [240 ml]):

¾ cup [180 g] plain, full-fat Greek yogurt

¼ cup [60 g] crème fraîche

2 Tbsp pomegranate molasses

2 Tbsp fresh lime juice

2 garlic cloves, peeled and grated

½ tsp ground turmeric

Fine sea salt

2 Tbsp extra-virgin olive oil, plus extra to brush the grates of the grill

2 hearts of romaine lettuce

1 lime, halved

2 Tbsp shaved Parmesan, for garnish (optional)

THE FLAVOR APPROACH

Grilling the lettuce and lime adds depth via the caramelization and Maillard reactions.

The lime juice and lactic acid from the Greek yogurt offset the rich, creamy texture of fat and proteins.

Parmesan provides a hint of salty and savory, due to its high free glutamate content.

Heat changes the mouthfeel of the lettuce; the leaves will turn a little soft, while the midrib retains its crunchiness.

To prepare the seeds, heat a small skillet over medium heat. In a small bowl, mix the pumpkin seeds, olive oil, and paprika. Season with salt. Add the seeds to the hot pan and sauté until they start to turn golden brown, 1 to 1½ minutes. Remove from the heat, add the chilli flakes, toss to coat well, and spread the seeds out on a plate to cool.

To prepare the dressing, combine the yogurt, crème fraîche, pomegranate molasses, lime juice, garlic, and turmeric in a blender. Pulse for a few seconds until completely smooth. Taste and season with salt.

Heat a grilling pan over medium-high heat. Brush the pan with a little olive oil. Cut the lettuce in half lengthwise and brush the surface of the lettuce and the lime halves with oil. Place the lettuce halves, cut-side down, on the hot pan until the lettuce develops nice char marks, then flip, 2 to 2½ minutes per side. Remove from the heat and season with salt. Place the limes on the hot surface of the grilling pan and sear until they start to develop a few char marks from the grill, about 1 minute.

To serve, place the lettuce on a large serving dish. Drizzle a few tablespoons of the garlic yogurt dressing over the lettuce. Sprinkle the pumpkin seeds and Parmesan, if desired, on top. Place the grilled limes on the side along with the remaining dressing. Serve immediately.

Chickpea Salad with Date + Tamarind Dressing

Street food occupies a celebrated position in India's cuisine, and it is as rich in flavor as it is diverse, from the hot and spicy succulent meat kebabs served on soft *roomali* rotis (a handkerchief-thin flat bread) to the sweet-and-sour tastes of *chaat*. Rather than spending my time eating in restaurants, I make it a point to indulge in street food on every trip. The dressing in this salad is loosely inspired by the ingredients and flavors used in India's street food.

SERVES 2 TO 4

For the dressing:

¼ cup [60 ml] date syrup, homemade (page 324) or store-bought

1 Tbsp tamarind paste, homemade (see page 67) or store-bought

1 Tbsp fresh lime juice

1 tsp ground ginger

Fine sea salt

For the chickpea salad:

One 15½ oz [445 g] can chickpeas, drained and rinsed

1 cucumber (about 12 oz [340 g]), diced

1 shallot (2 oz [60 g]), minced

2 Tbsp fresh dill leaves

2 Tbsp fresh mint leaves

2 Tbsp extra-virgin olive oil

1 tsp red chilli flakes, such as Aleppo

½ tsp amchur powder

½ tsp coarsely ground black pepper

Fine sea salt

THE FLAVOR APPROACH

The acidity comes from sour fruits such as tamarind, lime, and amchur (dried mango powder). Lime juice and tamarind contain two powerful cooking acids—citric and tartaric acids—that add sourness to the dressing along with their fruity notes.

When you taste and season the dressing, make a mental note and observe how much salt you use, as sourness changes the perception of saltiness.

Fresh mint and dill provide a cooler note with their essential oils that act on our nerve endings via chemesthesis. Black pepper, ginger, and the red chillies also act via chemesthesis but provide warmer notes.

For an extra dose of heat, mince and fold in a fresh green chilli.

To prepare the dressing, whisk the date syrup, tamarind paste, lime juice, and ginger in a small bowl. If the dressing is too thick, stir in 1 to 2 Tbsp of water. Taste and season with salt. If making ahead, store in an airtight container for up to 1 week and warm the dressing to room temperature before using.

To prepare the chickpea salad, in a large bowl, toss the chickpeas, cucumber, shallot, dill, and mint with the olive oil, red chilli flakes, amchur, and black pepper. Taste and season with salt. Transfer to a serving plate and drizzle 2 Tbsp of the dressing over the salad; serve the rest on the side. Serve immediately.

Green Beans with Preserved Lemons + Crème Fraîche

I get more excited about preparing the sides and desserts for our Thanksgiving dinner than anything else. Although the base ingredients for our sides remain constant, I change the flavors every year. In this spin on green beans, preserved lemons give a bright pop against the splendid creaminess of crème fraîche. You can make your own preserved lemons (page 318) or pick them up from a Middle Eastern market, and they're now available at most grocery stores. For a bit of added savory salty goodness, garnish the green beans with a generous pinch of bonito flakes just before serving.

SERVES 4

3 shallots (total weight 6½ oz [180 g])

3 Tbsp extra-virgin olive oil

Fine sea salt

1½ lb [680 g] green beans, trimmed

1 tsp black poppy seeds

2 Tbsp preserved lemons, homemade (page 318) or store-bought, diced (see headnote)

8½ oz [240 g] crème fraîche

1 garlic clove, peeled and grated

½ tsp coarsely cracked black pepper

THE FLAVOR APPROACH

The chlorophyll pigment of green beans becomes much more visible and brilliant in intensity after the beans are blanched in boiling water (see Sight, page 21).

Preserved lemons provide a concentrated spot of acid and salt that add contrast to the much more mellow flavors of the green beans and crème fraîche.

Crème fraîche provides fat as well as tang from its lactic acid.

Crunchy textures come from the green beans, crispy shallots, and poppy seeds.

Preheat the oven to 300°F [149°C]. Line a baking sheet with parchment paper.

Trim and discard the ends of the shallots and cut them into thin slices. In a small bowl, toss the shallots with 2 Tbsp of the olive oil and season with salt. Spread the shallots in a single layer on the prepared baking sheet and cook in the preheated oven until the shallots turn golden brown and crisp, 30 to 45 minutes. Stir and redistribute the shallots halfway through cooking to ensure even browning.

Fill a large bowl with ice and cold water and set aside.

Set a large pot of salted water over medium-high heat and bring to a rolling boil. When the water starts to boil, add the green beans and blanch them until the beans turn bright green and are tender but not overly soft, 2 or 3 minutes. Remove the green beans with a slotted spoon and immediately submerge them in the prepared ice water to stop them from cooking further.

Heat a small, dry saucepan or stainless-steel skillet over medium-high heat. Toast the poppy seeds until the seeds just start to get fragrant, 30 to 45 seconds. Remove from the heat and transfer the seeds to a small bowl. Scrape off and discard the pulp from the preserved lemons and rinse the peels under running tap water to remove the excess salt. Pat them dry with a clean kitchen towel to absorb any excess water. Dice the lemon peels and add them to another small mixing bowl. Fold in the crème fraîche, garlic, and black pepper. Taste and season with salt as needed.

Remove the green beans from the ice bath and pat them dry with a clean kitchen towel. Toss the green beans with the remaining 1 Tbsp of olive oil and place them in a serving dish. Add the lemon–crème fraîche dressing and garnish with the crispy shallots and toasted poppy seeds.

Potato + Roasted Corn Herbed Raita

The cooling properties of rich, creamy yogurt mingled with its acidity makes raita an excellent side to accompany a hot and spicy meal. The brilliant green color from the fresh herbs scattered with the blistered kernels of bright yellow sweet corn and dusting of red chilli, along with the soft texture of potatoes, make this raita a colorful portrait of flavor and texture. Serve it chilled with any Indian meal—but truth be told, on days when it's too hot to cook or I feel a bit lazy, I'll eat an entire bowlful as a meal. The potato and corn can be prepared the night before to save time.

SERVES 4 AS A SIDE

1 (6¾ oz [190 g]) Yukon gold potato

Fine sea salt

1 Tbsp grapeseed or other neutral oil

2 ears sweet corn (each approximately 8 oz [230 g]), husked

2 cups [480 g] chilled plain unsweetened Greek yogurt

½ cup [10 g] packed fresh mint leaves plus 1 Tbsp julienned for garnish

½ cup [10 g] packed cilantro

1 green chilli, such as serrano

2 Tbsp fresh lime juice

½ tsp black peppercorns

½ tsp red chilli powder

THE FLAVOR APPROACH

Sweet corn is sweetest the day it is picked, but as it sits in storage, the sugars are converted to starch and its sweetness decreases. For most of us, it's impossible to grab corn from the field; instead, buy it the day you plan to cook or freeze the corn kernels, as freezing stops the enzymes from converting sugar to starch.

A second method to determine the age of the sweet corn is to physically inspect the top pointy tip of the cob. If the top appears slightly dented, dry, and even grayish black, then the sugars are turning into starch and the corn won't be as sweet.

Roasting corn builds new flavor molecules via caramelization and the Maillard reaction. Listen for the corn kernels to sizzle when they grill and char; that's your cue to turn them.

Greek yogurt provides the creamy backdrop of the raita. I've always been a proponent of plain yogurt as the base for raitas; however, over the past few years I've noticed an increasing slimy texture in the whey that arises, due to the addition of stabilizers (which appears to be a trend with commercial brands). Greek yogurt, on the other hand, gives a richer and more luscious texture, since most of the whey has been removed and stabilizers are rarely added.

Scrub the potato and place it in a medium saucepan. Add enough cool water to cover it by 1 in [2.5 cm] and salt. Bring to a rolling boil over high heat, turn the heat to medium-low, and cover. Simmer the potato until completely tender, 25 to 30 minutes.

Carefully drain off the water and allow the potato to cool completely to room temperature. Once the potato is cooled, peel and discard the skin. Flake the potato with the prongs of a fork and season with salt.

While the potato is boiling, prepare the corn. Preheat a grill over medium-high heat and brush the grates with a little oil. Brush the remaining oil over the corn. Sear the corn cobs until they develop deep char marks all over, turning them over with a pair of tongs for 10 to 12 minutes. Remove the cobs from the grill and let rest for 5 minutes to cool. Strip the corn kernels from the cob by slicing with a knife, and discard the cob. Cool completely. The vegetables must be cooled before they're folded into the yogurt because heat can coagulate the dairy proteins.

In a blender, combine the yogurt, mint, cilantro, green chilli, lime juice, and peppercorns on high speed until smooth. If the consistency is too thick, you can add a few tablespoons of chilled water. Taste for salt and adjust. Pour the herbed yogurt into a medium bowl. Fold in the cooled flaked potato and roasted corn. Garnish with the remaining mint and sprinkle with the chilli powder. Serve chilled.

Herb + Paneer Pulao

I find that a pulao, or pilaf, has a lot of advantages; you can serve it as the "fancy" rice to accompany a dinner for guests, or you can tweak it to make it a complete one-pot dish that doesn't require sides—perhaps just a small bowl of plain salted yogurt or a bit of pickle.

SERVES 4 TO 6

2 cups [400 g] basmati rice

4 Tbsp [60 ml] grapeseed or other neutral oil

4 cloves, ground

½ tsp ground green cardamom

½ tsp ground cinnamon

½ tsp ground black pepper

1 medium yellow or white onion (9¼ oz [260 g]), cut in half and thinly sliced

1 in [2.5 cm] piece fresh ginger, peeled and grated

4 garlic cloves, peeled and minced

1 to 2 green chillies such as serrano, minced

Fine sea salt

14 oz [400 g] paneer, homemade (use firm paneer, see case study page 334) or store-bought, cut into ½ in [12 mm] cubes

¼ cup [10 g] packed chopped cilantro leaves or flat-leaf parsley

¼ cup [2.5 g] packed chopped dill leaves

¼ cup [10 g] packed chopped mint leaves

¼ cup [60 ml] fresh lime juice

Lime zest, for garnish (optional)

THE FLAVOR APPROACH

There are a few tips that make this rice dish extremely aromatic. Start with aged basmati (rice that is labeled at least one year old). Grind your spices and chop your herbs just before you cook. Rinsing the rice gently removes the fine dust of starch created as rice grains rub against each other during transport and storage; this starchy powder can cause the grains to stick to each other while cooking. This step, plus frying the rice grains in oil and resisting the urge to disturb the rice too much as it cooks, will give you cooked grains that are separate and delicately tender.

The aromatic spices that give this pulao its perfume are first heated in hot oil to draw out the aromatic substances.

Fresh lime juice is added toward the end of this dish as a garnishing acid. If added early on, the acid will lose its aroma and the flavor will not be as fresh. For increased lime aroma, add a little lime zest before serving.

Halloumi is a good substitute for paneer because it is firm and will hold its shape on heating, but it can be a bit salty, so adjust your seasoning accordingly.

Pick through the rice for any stones or debris, then rinse it in a fine-mesh sieve under cool running tap water until the runoff is clear. Transfer to a large bowl, cover with 4 cups [960 ml] of water, and soak for 30 minutes.

Set up one large and one medium saucepan on the stove. Heat 2 Tbsp of the oil in the large saucepan over medium-high heat. Add the cloves, cardamom, cinnamon, and black pepper and sauté until fragrant, 30 to 45 seconds. Drain the soaked rice and add it to the large saucepan. Fry the rice, stirring until the grains are completely coated in the oil and don't stick to each other, 1 to 1½ minutes. Add the onions and sauté until they just start to turn a light golden brown, 8 to 10 minutes. Add the ginger, garlic, and chilli and sauté until fragrant, about 1 minute. Add 4 cups [960 ml] water and season with salt. Bring the water to

a rolling boil. Lower the heat to a gentle simmer, cover the saucepan, and cook until most of the water has evaporated, 10 to 12 minutes. Remove from the heat.

While the rice is cooking, prepare the paneer. Heat the remaining 2 Tbsp of oil in the medium saucepan over medium-high heat. Once the oil is hot, fry the paneer cubes in batches until they turn golden brown on each side, 8 to 10 minutes. Remove the paneer with a slotted spoon and place them on a plate or tray lined with absorbent paper to absorb any excess oil. Season the fried paneer with salt.

Fold the paneer, cilantro, dill, and mint into the cooked rice. Drizzle with the lime juice, sprinkle with zest, if desired, and serve warm.

Roasted Cauliflower in Turmeric Kefir

This recipe takes advantage of kefir (buttermilk can be substituted) for its bright acidity. I prefer to use a bottle of freshly opened kefir or buttermilk here, because as these liquids age, the lactic acid increases, which not only leaves a strong tart taste but also causes the milk proteins to curdle quickly on heating. If you have leftover kefir, use it to make the Blueberry + Omani Lime Ice Cream (page 98).

SERVES 4

2 lb [910 g] cauliflower, broken into bite-size florets

1 tsp garam masala, homemade (page 312) or store-bought

Fine sea salt

4 Tbsp [60 ml] grapeseed or other neutral oil

5¼ oz [150 g] minced red onion

½ tsp ground turmeric

½ tsp red chilli powder (optional)

¼ cup [30 g] chickpea flour

2 cups [480 ml] fresh kefir or buttermilk

½ tsp cumin seeds

½ tsp black or brown mustard seeds

1 tsp red chilli flakes

2 Tbsp chopped cilantro or flat-leaf parsley

THE FLAVOR APPROACH

Using the acidity of fermented dairy such as kefir and the Maillard reaction creates a bittersweet taste and new aroma molecules in vegetables.

Chickpea flour, which contains starch, acts as a thickener for the base of the sauce.

The sound of the seeds sizzling is a good indicator of how hot your oil is; if the oil is hot enough, they will sizzle immediately and brown quickly.

Preheat the oven to 400°F [204°C].

Place the cauliflower in a roasting pan or baking dish. Sprinkle with the garam masala, season with salt, and toss to coat. Drizzle with 1 Tbsp of the oil and toss to coat evenly. Roast the cauliflower for 20 to 30 minutes, until golden brown and slightly charred. Stir the florets halfway through roasting.

While the cauliflower is roasting, place a deep, medium saucepan or Dutch oven over medium-high heat. Add 1 Tbsp of the oil to the pan. Add the onions and sauté until they just start to turn translucent, 4 to 5 minutes. Add the turmeric and chilli powder and cook for 30 seconds. Lower the heat to low and add the chickpea flour. Cook, stirring constantly, for 2 to 3 minutes. Lower the heat to a gentle simmer and fold in the kefir, stirring constantly. Watch the liquid carefully as it cooks until it thickens slightly, 2 to 3 minutes. Fold the roasted cauliflower into the liquid and remove from the heat. Taste and add salt if necessary.

Heat a small, dry saucepan over medium-high heat. Add the remaining 2 Tbsp of oil. Once the oil is hot, add the cumin and black mustard seeds and cook until they start to pop and the cumin starts to brown, 30 to 45 seconds. Remove from the heat and add the chilli flakes, swirling the oil in the pan until the oil turns red. Quickly pour the hot oil with the seeds over the cauliflower in the saucepan. Garnish with the chopped cilantro and serve warm with rice or parathas (see Parathas, page 297).

Roasted Butternut Squash + Pomegranate Molasses Soup

My favorite formula for a soup is to roast a vegetable, then blend it. This maximizes the way ingredients and flavors interact. This soup is based on my own personal soup philosophy and packs a mighty punch in flavor. Pumpkin can be substituted for squash in this recipe; I recommend using a variety that's not too sweet.

SERVES 4

1½ lb [680 g] butternut squash, peeled and cut into large chunks

1 medium white onion (9¼ oz [260 g]), peeled and diced

4 garlic cloves, peeled

2 Tbsp extra-virgin olive oil, plus extra to drizzle

1 tsp ground black pepper

Fine sea salt

1 tsp Aleppo pepper flakes

½ tsp ground turmeric

2 Tbsp Worcestershire sauce

1 Tbsp pomegranate molasses

¼ cup [30 g] slivered or [25 g] sliced almonds, for garnish

THE FLAVOR APPROACH

Pomegranate molasses gives this soup acidity with a hint of sweetness; if you prefer it a bit more sour, add an additional 1 to 2 tsp of the molasses.

Worcestershire sauce adds to the savory character.

The heat and bright red pigment from the Aleppo pepper flakes and turmeric are extracted in the hot oil.

Heat is used to temper the flavor of turmeric.

Preheat the oven to 400°F [204°C].

Place the butternut squash, onion, and garlic cloves on a large baking sheet. Add 1 Tbsp of the olive oil and the black pepper. Season with salt and toss to coat evenly. Place the baking sheet in the oven and roast until the vegetables are completely cooked and start to turn golden brown, 35 to 45 minutes. (If the garlic starts to burn, remove and set aside.) Remove from the oven and transfer all the contents of the sheet to a blender or a food processor. Add 2 cups [480 ml] of water and pulse on high speed until completely smooth.

Lower the oven temperature to 350°F [177°C].

Heat the remaining 1 Tbsp of olive oil in a large saucepan over medium-low heat. When the oil is hot, add the Aleppo pepper flakes and turmeric and cook for 30 seconds. Stir in the puréed butternut squash, the Worcestershire sauce, and pomegranate molasses. Increase the heat to medium-high and bring to a boil. Lower the heat to a simmer and cook for 5 minutes. Taste and season with salt.

While the soup is cooking, toast the almonds. Line a baking sheet with parchment paper. Spread the almonds in a single layer and toast in the oven until they turn golden brown, 8 to 10 minutes. Transfer to a small bowl.

To serve, ladle the warm soup into a serving bowl. Garnish with toasted almonds, drizzle with olive oil, and serve immediately.

Tomato Aachari Polenta Tart

Aachar is the Hindi word for Indian pickles; *aachari* in this recipe refers to the pickling spices used in their preparation (see Cauliflower Aachar, page 320, to get a sense of how they're different from European-style pickles). In this tart, those spices complement the flavor of ripe summer tomatoes.

MAKES ONE 10 IN [25 CM] TART

2 Tbsp melted ghee or unsalted butter, plus extra to grease the pan

2 or 3 fresh tomatoes (total weight 1.1 lb [500 g])

Fine sea salt

1 tsp black or brown mustard seeds

1 tsp cumin seeds

1 tsp fenugreek seeds

1 tsp nigella seeds

2 Tbsp extra-virgin olive oil

1 cup [140 g] polenta or cornmeal

1 oz [30 g] grated Gruyère

1 oz [30 g] grated Parmesan

1 tsp amchur

1 tsp red chilli flakes, such as Aleppo, Maras, or Urfa (optional)

1 tsp oregano, fresh, or ½ tsp dried

THE FLAVOR APPROACH

A slice of polenta covered with slices of roasted tomatoes, cheese, and spices provides a soft, comforting texture.

Cheese lovers (like me) can add more cheese. The sound of bubbling cheese and its degree of browning is a good index of progress to watch while cooking. If you let it go too dark, it will taste bitter.

The number of tomatoes will vary a little, depending on their width. Take advantage of the colorful heirloom tomatoes that arrive in all sorts of shapes and sizes in summer.

Tomatoes can release a large amount of water, which could make for a soggy tart. Using the principle of osmosis, water is drawn out from the tomato by sprinkling them with a little salt and leaving them to drain on paper towels, which wick the liquid away.

The tomatoes and amchur are the main sources for sourness in the tart.

Grease and line a 10 in [25 cm] circular tart pan with a little melted ghee and a sheet of parchment paper. Place the pan on a baking sheet lined with parchment paper.

Line another baking sheet with two layers of paper towels. Cut the tomatoes into thin slices, sprinkle with a little salt on each side, and place the slices on the prepared baking sheet. Cover with an additional layer or two of paper towels and let rest for at least 30 minutes and up to 45 minutes.

Meanwhile, prepare the spice mix. Toast the mustard, cumin, and fenugreek seeds in a small, dry stainless-steel skillet over medium-high heat until the seeds start to turn fragrant, 30 to 45 seconds. Remove from the heat and transfer to a small plate to cool slightly. Add the cooled toasted spices to a spice mill or grinder and grind to a powder. Stir in the nigella seeds to the ground toasted spice mix.

cont'd

In a large pot, combine 3 cups [720 ml] of water with the olive oil, ghee, and 1 tsp of salt and bring to a rolling boil over medium-high heat. Slowly stir in the polenta, lower the heat to a simmer, and cook, stirring constantly to prevent the polenta from sticking, until completely tender and most of the water has evaporated, 15 to 20 minutes. Remove from the heat and transfer the polenta to the prepared baking tart while it is still warm and pliable. Level the surface with an offset spatula.

Prick the surface of the tart with the prongs of a fork a few times to allow even baking.

Preheat the oven to 400°F [204°C].

Mix together the Gruyère and Parmesan in a small mixing bowl. Sprinkle half over the surface of the polenta. Place the tomato slices on top of the cheese. Sprinkle the ground spice mixture over the tomatoes. Season with salt, if needed. Cover with the remaining cheese and bake until the cheese melts and turns golden brown, 30 to 40 minutes. Remove from the oven and cool in the pan for 5 to 8 minutes. The tart should come out of the pan easily, but if it sticks, run a small paring knife around the edges of the pan to loosen. Place the tart pan over a can or glass and tap gently from the sides to release the ring.

Sprinkle with the amchur, chilli flakes, if using, and oregano. Serve immediately.

Spareribs in Malt Vinegar + Mashed Potatoes

Ribs are an indulgent, messy experience that's oddly relaxing; they're 100% unfussy. Sit back, pour a glass of wine, get your fingers dirty, and dig in. I like my ribs the way they do them in the South, a bit sweet and a bit sour and a lot of spice and heat. Make the mashed potatoes like I do or, if you own a ricer or food mill, by all means go ahead and put it to use. Note: Start this recipe 1 or 2 days before you plan to serve it. My preference is to cut the rack of ribs into individual pieces so it fits into the pan, but you can also ask your butcher to do this and even ask them to cut the ribs in half.

SERVES 4

For the spareribs:

3 lb [1.4 kg] spareribs (pork) with bone left in (see headnote)

Fine sea salt

1 Tbsp extra-virgin olive oil

2 cups [480 ml] dry white wine, such as Pinot Gris

1 cup [240 ml] plus 2 Tbsp malt vinegar

½ cup [100 g] packed jaggery or dark brown sugar

12 black peppercorns

2 tsp ground fennel

½ tsp ground cinnamon

½ tsp ground turmeric

¼ tsp cayenne

For the mashed potatoes:

1¼ lb [570 g] Yukon gold potatoes

¼ cup [60 ml] plus 2 Tbsp extra-virgin olive oil

½ cup [120 ml] warm water at 160°F [71°C]

Fine sea salt

1 tsp nigella seeds

2 garlic cloves, peeled and thinly sliced

2 Tbsp minced chives, for garnish

THE FLAVOR APPROACH

Malt vinegar and white wine tenderize the meat during cooking, and their acids provide contrast against the backdrop of warm spices and sweet jaggery.

Passing the potatoes through the grater and then the fine-mesh sieve gives them a smooth, creamy texture.

To prepare the spareribs, trim off any excess fat and cut them into individual ribs by slicing the meat right between the bones. Pat them dry with clean paper towels and season with salt. Heat the olive oil in a large cast-iron or stainless-steel skillet over medium-high heat. Working in batches, sear the ribs on each side until they turn brown, 5 or 6 minutes. Remove from the heat and place them in a medium heavy-bottomed Dutch oven or saucepan with a lid.

Place the wine, 1 cup [240 ml] of the vinegar, the jaggery, peppercorns, fennel, cinnamon, turmeric, and cayenne in a blender and pulse on high speed for a few seconds, until combined. Season with 1 tsp of salt. Pour the marinade over the ribs, cover, and marinate, refrigerated, for at least 4 hours to overnight.

Preheat the oven to 300°F [149°C]. Cover the top of the Dutch oven with a double layer of aluminum foil and tuck the edges under to seal securely. Cover with the lid and cook for 2 hours. Remove the lid and the foil and cook the ribs for 1 more hour. The meat should be tender and falling off the bones. With a slotted spoon or a pair of kitchen tongs, remove the ribs from the Dutch oven and set them on a plate or tray.

cont'd

Skim and discard the excess fat from the liquid. Return the Dutch oven to the stove and heat the liquid over medium-high heat, stirring to prevent burning, until reduced to a thick syrup consistency, 15 to 20 minutes. Return the ribs with any liquids to the Dutch oven and fold to coat evenly with the sauce. Stir in the remaining 2 Tbsp of malt vinegar. Taste and season with salt if needed. Remove from the heat and serve with the mashed potatoes and garnish with the minced chives.

Note: If you have the time, you can also refrigerate the cooked ribs in the pan overnight and let the fat harden on top, which will make it easier to remove; then proceed with the reduction step.

To prepare the mashed potatoes, place the potatoes in a large pot with enough salted water to cover them by 1 in [2.5 cm]. Bring to a boil over medium-high heat, then lower the heat to medium-low. Cook until the potatoes are completely tender but not mushy, 20 to 30 minutes. Drain the potatoes and set them aside until cool enough to handle.

Peel and discard the potato skins. Grate the potatoes with the fine holes of a grater. Then pass the grated potatoes through a fine-mesh sieve placed over a large mixing bowl. Whisk in ¼ cup [60 ml] of the olive oil and the warm water until smooth and fluffy. Season with salt.

Heat the remaining 2 Tbsp of oil over medium-high heat. When the oil is hot, add the nigella seeds and garlic and cook for 30 to 45 seconds, until they are fragrant and the garlic turns a light golden brown. Pour the seasoned oil over the mashed potatoes and serve warm.

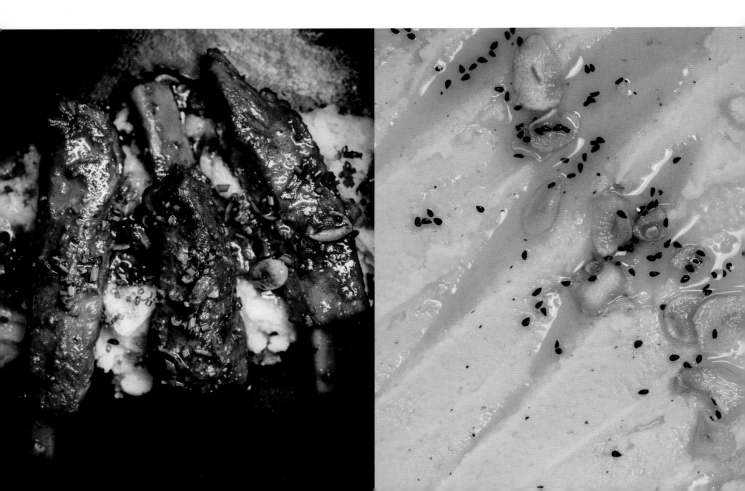

Chouriço Pao (Buns)

Every trip to Goa with my family involves ample consumption of chouriço, or *choriz* as it's more commonly known, a remnant of Portuguese colonial rule. Its fiery flavor combined with vinegar makes it one of the most popular condiments, and you'll see it tossed into pulaos and stuffed into breads such as naan in restaurants, as well as in these buns that my aunts often make. You can substitute a tofu-based chouriço alternative. But be warned: One bun is never enough.

MAKES 12 INDIVIDUAL BUNS

For the dough:

½ cup [120 ml] whole milk

¼ cup [55 g] unsalted butter

¼ cup [50 g] sugar

½ tsp fine sea salt

1 large egg, lightly whisked

2 cups [280 g] all-purpose flour, plus more for dusting

1½ tsp active dry yeast

For the filling:

11 oz [312 g] chouriço

1 medium white onion (9¼ oz [260 g]), diced

1 Tbsp extra-virgin olive oil

1 Yukon gold potato (6¾ oz [190 g]), peeled and diced

1 large egg, lightly whisked with 1 Tbsp of water

2 Tbsp nigella or black sesame seeds

THE FLAVOR APPROACH

Yeast ferments the added sugar (sucrose), the lactose in the milk, and the sugar in the flour to produce carbon dioxide gas that gives the buns their airy texture.

The amylase enzyme comes from three different sources—the yeast, the egg yolk, and the flour. Amylase helps cut the long starch molecules into glucose, which the yeast uses for nutrition but also contributes to the development of the structure of the dough.

Chouriço is a cured sausage and contains acid as well as heat from the chillies used to flavor it.

Note: If you feel your chouriço is lacking a little in the flavor department, do what I do. Because Goan chouriço is nearly impossible to find outside Goa, save for a few people that make it from scratch, I use this formula: For every 1 lb [455 g] of store-bought chouriço, add ¼ cup [60 ml] of coconut or malt vinegar; 1 in [2.5 cm] piece of fresh ginger, peeled and grated; 1 Tbsp of ground Kashmiri chilli; 1 tsp of ground cayenne; 1 tsp of brown sugar or jaggery; 3 cloves, ground; and ½ tsp of ground cinnamon.

Warm the milk, butter, sugar, and salt over medium-low heat to 110°F [43°C], stirring until the butter melts and the sugar dissolves completely. Remove from the heat and stir in the whisked egg.

Place the flour and yeast in the bowl of a stand mixer. With the paddle attachment fixed and the speed set to low, dry whisk just to combine the ingredients. Slowly pour in the milk mixture. Mix until the dough comes together, 5 to 6 minutes. The dough will be sticky. Use a scraper to transfer the dough onto a lightly floured surface. Knead for 1 minute to bring the dough together, shape into a ball, and place it in a lightly greased large bowl.

Cover with plastic wrap and allow to rise in a dark, warm place until the dough doubles in size, 1½ to 2 hours.

cont'd

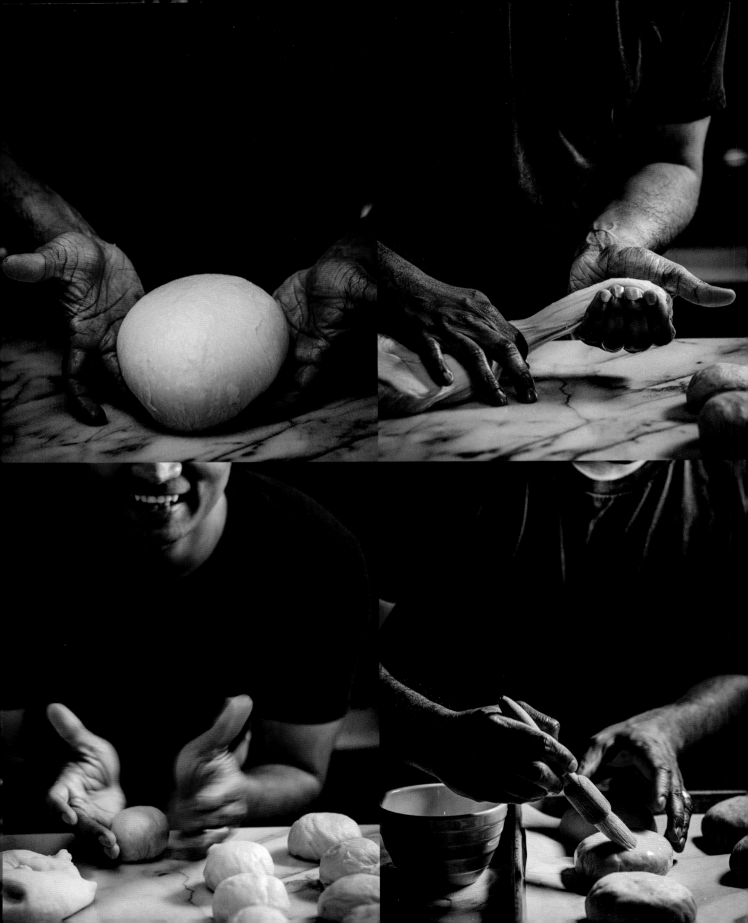

While the dough rests, prepare the filling. Heat a large skillet over medium-high heat. Remove the chouriço from the casing, break it into bits, and add it to the hot skillet. Cook until the meat just begins to brown. Add the onion and sauté until it is translucent, and the sausage is thoroughly cooked. With a slotted spoon, transfer the mixture to a bowl, leaving the fat in the skillet. Add the olive oil and potatoes and cook over medium-high heat until tender, 10 to 12 minutes. Remove from the heat, transfer to the chouriço in the bowl, and discard any excess fat. Fold to mix evenly and let cool completely.

Line a baking sheet with parchment paper and divide the meat mixture into 12 equal parts by weight. Shape each into a ball, place them on the lined baking sheet, and refrigerate.

Once the dough has doubled in size, line two baking sheets with parchment paper. Tip the dough out onto a lightly floured surface, knead it once, and weigh it. Divide the dough into 12 equal parts by weight and shape each into a ball. Pick up one ball of dough and fold by grabbing the underside and stretching it and folding it back on itself. Rotate a quarter turn and repeat three or four times. Flatten the dough to form a small disk, about 5 in [13 cm] across. Place a ball of the refrigerated chouriço filling in the center and wrap the edges of the dough to encase the filling. Gently shape the sides to form a ball and place it on the lined baking sheet. Prepare the remaining buns and divide them equally between the two sheets, leaving about 1½ in [4 cm] between them. Cover the buns loosely with a sheet of parchment paper and let rise for 1 hour until doubled in size.

Preheat the oven to 350°F [177°C]. Brush the buns with the egg and water mixture. Sprinkle a few pinches of nigella over the top of each bun and bake until they are golden brown and springy to the touch and a skewer comes out clean, 25 to 30 minutes. Rotate the pans halfway through baking. Cool on the baking sheets for 5 minutes. Transfer the buns from the baking sheets to a wire rack. Serve warm. Any extra buns can be wrapped in plastic wrap and stored in an airtight container or resealable bag for up to a week in the refrigerator or 2 weeks in the freezer. To reheat, thaw them in the refrigerator overnight, then unwrap and warm them in the oven at 200°F [93°C].

Pomegranate + Poppy Seed Wings

Unlike me, my husband, Michael, is an avid sports fan and watches the Super Bowl every year. My contribution to this annual ritual is preparing all the accoutrements—including these sweet-and-spicy wings that will have you licking your fingers in delight. The recipe for the sauce will give you enough to coat the wings plus a bit extra for dipping.

SERVES 4 AS AN APPETIZER

For the wings:

2 lb [910 g] chicken wings

2 tsp baking powder

Fine sea salt

For the sauce (makes about 1 cup [240 ml]):

¼ cup [55 g] unsalted butter

2 tsp poppy seeds

2 tsp red chilli flakes or ½ tsp ground cayenne

1 tsp ground cumin

1 tsp ground black pepper

¼ cup [60 ml] pomegranate molasses

¼ cup [60 ml] prepared yellow mustard

2 Tbsp dark brown sugar

Fine sea salt

2 Tbsp minced chives, for garnish

THE FLAVOR APPROACH

Moisture and dryness are natural enemies. To make a crispy chicken wing, the water must be drawn to the surface of the skin and wicked away. You can achieve this by using the combined action of salt and exposing the wings to air in the refrigerator. I use Kenji López-Alt's method of applying baking soda to the chicken's skin. Baking soda helps with browning because it increases the pH and, in the presence of heat, facilitates the Maillard reaction.

Pomegranate molasses and the vinegar in prepared mustard is the chief souring agent in this dish.

Adding a sweetener such as dark brown sugar adds sweetness and an earthy character to the sauce, balancing the acidity from the pomegranate molasses.

To prepare the wings, pat them dry with clean paper towels. Place in a medium bowl, sprinkle with the baking powder, and season with salt. Toss to coat evenly. Place a wire rack on a baking sheet; arrange the wings on the rack and leave them in the refrigerator to dry overnight. If you're tight on space, arrange the wings on clean paper towels over smaller plates and refrigerate. You might need to discard and replace the paper towels after 12 hours if they get too wet.

Preheat the oven to 450°F [232°C]. Line a baking sheet with foil and place the wire rack with the wings on the sheet. Bake for 15 to 20 minutes. Flip the wings and bake until the skin starts to get crispy and golden brown, an additional 15 to 20 minutes. The internal temperature of the chicken should read 165°F [74°C] on an instant-read thermometer. Transfer the wings to a large mixing bowl.

To make the sauce, melt the butter in a small saucepan over medium-high heat. When the butter melts, add the poppy seeds, red chilli, cumin, and black pepper. Swirl and cook for 30 seconds until the poppy seeds sizzle. Remove from the heat and stir in the molasses, mustard, and sugar. Taste and adjust with salt.

Pour ½ cup [120 ml] of the sauce over the hot wings and toss to coat evenly. Garnish with the minced chives. Serve the hot wings with the remaining sauce to dip.

Lemon + Lime Mintade

A few years ago, on a flight to India via the Middle East, I drank an exquisite glass of lemon and lime juice garnished with mint. It was refreshing and energizing with its bright citrus flavors and fresh mint aroma. As you might imagine, this was particularly welcome on a sixteen-hour flight. I've re-created that drink here; it's a powerful ode to citrus.

SERVES 6

1 cup [200 g] sugar

Zest of 2 lemons (see The Flavor Approach)

Zest of 2 limes (see The Flavor Approach)

1 bunch fresh mint, leaves and stems (2 oz [55 g]), plus a few extra leaves for garnish

½ cup [120 ml] fresh lemon juice

½ cup [120 ml] fresh lime juice

3 cups [720 ml] chilled club soda or water

THE FLAVOR APPROACH

The aromatic essential oils in the zest of the lemon and lime are added to the hot syrup along with the mint to steep. These oils act on our nerves through chemesthesis (see page 235).

The lime and lemon juice are the main souring agents.

Do not use a Microplane zester to extract the zest of the citrus fruits; instead, use a citrus zester. The zester's larger holes create long strands that are easier to strain and can later double as a garnish. If you prefer the syrup less sweet, reduce the sugar to ½ cup [100 g].

In a medium saucepan, combine the sugar and 1 cup [240 ml] of water and bring to a simmer over medium-high heat, stirring until the sugar dissolves. Remove from the heat and pour the syrup into a large jar with a tight lid. Add the lemon and lime zest to the syrup. Bruise the mint by twisting and crushing the leaves and stems in your hands. Add to the mixture. Cover with a lid and let cool to room temperature. Stir in the lemon and lime juice, cover, and refrigerate for 1 hour.

Strain the liquid through a fine-mesh sieve over a medium bowl. Reserve a few strands of the zest and discard the rest of the zest and leaves left behind in the strainer.

To serve, fill six tall glasses with ice. Pour ½ cup [120 ml] of the syrup into each glass, top with ½ cup [120 ml] of the club soda, and stir. Garnish with the extra mint leaves and reserved zest. Store any leftover concentrate in an airtight container in the refrigerator for up to 1 week.

Blueberry + Omani Lime Ice Cream

This is a wonderfully easy recipe that takes advantage of the smoky flavor of dried Omani limes that are used in Persian and Middle Eastern cooking, and complements the tangy notes of the kefir and the blueberries. Dried Omani limes are sold whole and ground in Persian and Middle Eastern stores as well as spice markets. There is no need to add any salt, since cream cheese is always sold presalted.

MAKES 1QT [1L]

4 whole Omani limes

2 cups [480 ml] kefir or buttermilk

1 cup [200 g] sugar

4 oz [115 g] cream cheese, softened to room temperature and cubed

5 oz [140 g] fresh or frozen blueberries (no need to thaw if using frozen)

THE FLAVOR APPROACH

Because the liquid is cold and the limes are dried, they must be steeped overnight in the refrigerator to extract their acid and citrus aroma.

If ground, the bitter-tasting compounds will get more intense every day in the ice cream.

Sugar, cream cheese, and the pectin from the blueberries help prevent the formation of ice crystals, creating a smooth-textured ice cream.

Lightly crack the Omani limes just enough to open them. Place them in an airtight container and pour the kefir over the limes. Seal and refrigerate overnight to infuse.

Strain the liquid through a fine-mesh sieve over a large bowl. Discard the limes. Transfer the liquid to a blender. Add the sugar and cream cheese. Pulse for a few seconds on high speed until the sugar is completely dissolved and there are no visible flecks of cream cheese. Add the blueberries and pulse for a few seconds on high speed until the blueberries are blended.

Transfer the base to an ice cream maker and churn according to the manufacturer's instructions. Scrape the ice cream into a freezer-safe container, place a sheet of parchment paper cut to size against the surface of the ice cream, and freeze until firm, at least 4 hours.

Alternatively, freeze the ice cream base in a freezer-safe container for 1 hour. Remove the container from the freezer and churn it by hand using a fork, electric hand mixer, immersion blender, or food processor to break the ice crystals, then return it to the freezer. Repeat three or four times at 30-minute intervals. The freezing time will vary a little depending on your freezer.

Leave the ice cream out for about 5 minutes to soften a little before serving. Store the leftover ice cream in the freezer for up to 5 days.

2 BITTERNESS

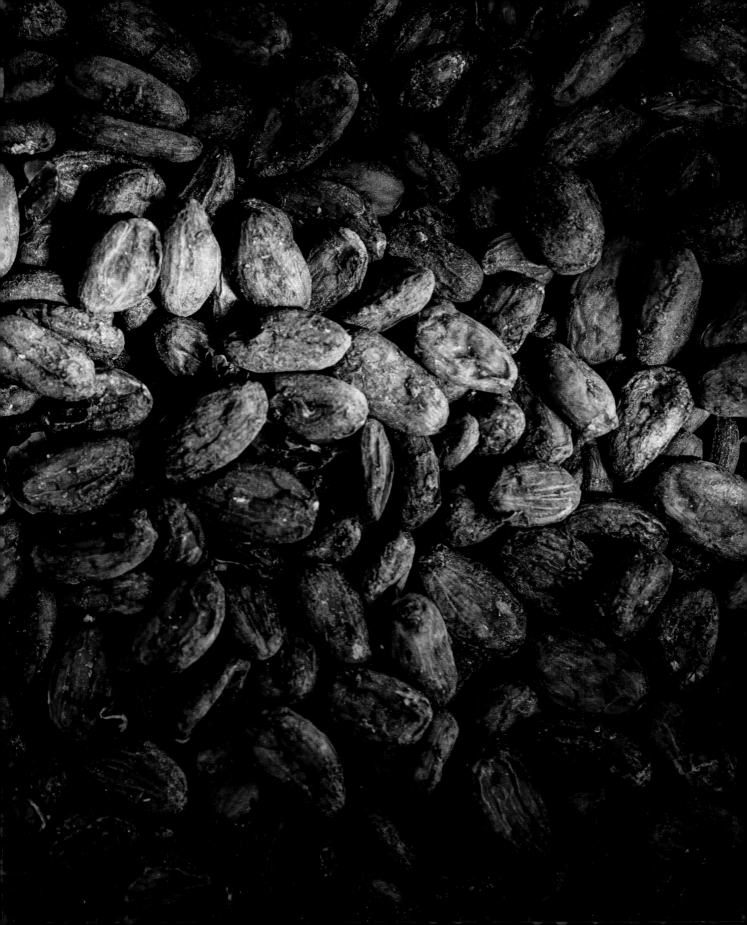

TASTES HAVE PERSONALITIES—or so their usage in language implies—and bitter, rather unfairly, gets the roughest treatment. Nature and experience helped shape our biological behavior, and we've evolved to be bitter-taste averse. Out of the nearly 56,000 recipes I surveyed from online databases, only 0.8% used the word "bitter." With language and nature both priming us against this taste, bitter tastes are indeed harder to sell, and our approach is to treat them just like the bitter medicine pill that must be coated with something sweet to make it more palatable. For most of us, bitterness is the one taste we often try to either remove, mask, or mellow when we cook. When we describe recipes or talk about food, we often tend to describe vegetables such as bitter greens as tasting "sweet" even if this sweetness is extremely mild or unnoticeable to our taste buds, and we are sometimes instructed to massage kale leaves with the goal of making them taste sweet. As a kid, much to the vexation of my parents, I struggled to appreciate the taste of bitter foods like bitter melon—or karela, as it is known in Hindi. But I quickly learned to appreciate the taste of chocolate and coffee as long as they were mixed with some other ingredients, like a sweetener to mellow out their intensely bitter taste.

How Bitterness Works

We are very sensitive to detecting bitter-tasting molecules at extremely low levels. Compared to our ability to taste sugar (detected at 25 μmol/l, or micromole per liter), we can taste bitter compounds at a very low concentration—such as quinine, the active ingredient in tonic water (detected at 10,000 μmol/l); that's a factor of 400! And the perception of bitterness sticks around longer compared to other tastes. Our genetics also make some of us much more sensitive to the taste of bitterness in food (it's unconfirmed, but I think I'm one of them); these people are called supertasters. Due to a variation in the gene that codes for the bitter taste receptor, these folks are bitter averse and will typically prefer the taste of sweet foods.

Bitter-tasting substances are as diverse as one might imagine; unlike acids or sugars, which share similar chemical structures, bitter molecules come in a wide array of shapes. Plant-based phenols, flavonoids, isoflavones, and terpenes are just some of the substances that contribute to bitterness. Remarkably, our bitter-sensing taste receptors (the T2R family) have worked their way around this by being less selective but more sensitive; that is, they don't distinguish between the types of various bitter-tasting substances, but they can detect very low amounts. Once that information is relayed to our brains, we respond to the bitter taste. Some bitter-tasting substances can also create a sensation of astringency, including some of the phenolic compounds present in sumac, cocoa, wine, and cider.

MEASURING BITTERNESS

Plant breeders and food companies spend a lot of time trying to reduce bitterness in foods. They work with many plants, like the *Brassica* family, to select strains that produce low levels of bitterness. In some cases, measurements of these chemicals are used to predict how bitter a vegetable might taste.

Just like the hedonic scales used to measure saltiness, bitterness can be measured by asking tasters to record their experiences. Some ingredients, like beer, have their own bitterness scales; with beer, the amount of the bitter-tasting compound is measured and expressed in terms of a bittering unit scale (International Bittering Units, or IBU). Keep in mind, beer is a complex liquid made up of many other ingredients, such as malt and even acids from fermentation, all of which affect the perception of taste. So even if a beer has a high IBU, it might not taste very bitter depending on what else is present in the drink (see Bitterness Boosters, page 105).

Almost every culture in the world cooks with bitter foods: in India, bitter melon, mustard greens, and fenugreek leaves (*methi* in Hindi); in the West, cardoons, bitter greens, and radicchio are common. However, because our natural response is to be bitter averse, we usually avoid seeking them out. This aversion stems largely from biology and behavior. Most of the bitter-tasting foods we eat originate in plants. To protect themselves from harm or damage by herbivorous animals or insects, plants developed chemical defensive systems by synthesizing bitter-tasting molecules. And the plants' protective strategy affected our evolution; in response, we developed a sensitivity to bitter-tasting molecules. Our brains are hardwired to perceive foods that taste bitter as unpleasant, so we avoid and reject them.

Does this mean all bitter-tasting foods are dangerous? It depends. It's all in the type and quantity of bitter substance present. There are two types of bitter substances: (1) harmful ones, such as some of the bitter alkaloids that are toxic—for example, the alkaloid atropine is present in the nightshade family of plants, which includes chillies, eggplant, tomatoes, and potatoes—and (2) phytonutrients that are considered beneficial. Phytonutrients can potentially protect us against a multitude of diseases, so we're encouraged to eat more leafy greens such as collards, and cruciferous *Brassica* vegetables such as Brussels sprouts, which are rich in phytonutrients. Some alkaloids we've learned to love over time because of their addictive and stimulating effect, such as the caffeine in coffee and tea.

Other bitter foods we've learned to love and consume also provide a stimulant effect, like beer and chocolate. Because the influence of bitterness on consumer choices is highly impactful, plant breeders and the food industry take active steps to reduce bitterness in their plant-based products. As a result, many vegetables taste less bitter than they did several decades ago. Selectively breeding for vegetables and fruits with less bitter taste became an industry standard. In addition, because some bitter compounds can cause health issues—such as the progoitrin in Brussels sprouts—some scientists advocate breeding this chemical out of the *Brassica* species.

Bitterness in foods also comes from bacteria. Some bacteria produce bitter-tasting substances such as the ones present in cheese that arise during the breakdown of milk proteins during fermentation. A third source of bitterness is caramelization and the Maillard reaction, which creates bitter-tasting molecules during cooking of both sweet and savory dishes.

CASE STUDY: DEBITTERING OLIVE AND MUSTARD OILS

The polyphenols present in olive oil and mustard oil are phytonutrients, but they are also responsible for the bitter taste when these oils are used to prepare emulsions such as mayonnaise. To solve this problem, I found a way to extract the polyphenols. Reading through a research document about plant waste, I discovered that the polyphenols present in olive oil are highly soluble in water, and the solubility is at its maximum at the boiling point of water. In the absence of any emulsifiers, when mixed, water and oil eventually separate. The water carries the bitter-tasting molecules away from the oil. This method works with mustard oil too.

METHOD: Mix 1 cup [240 ml] olive or mustard oil with 1 cup [240 ml] boiling water in a large jar or container. Seal with a lid and carefully shake for about 1 minute. Crack the lid to release the pressure and then let the liquid sit until the water and oil separate. Once the liquid separates, discard the water and use the debittered oil to make mayonnaise or aioli. Note: If your debittered oil looks cloudy after you separate the water, warm it up a little over low heat and it will clear up.

Bitterness Boosters

While we typically don't seek to add bitterness in the foods we cook, we do cook and eat foods that feature this taste, and it's more common than you might expect. Several spices, such as cinnamon, taste bitter but we don't notice them because they're used in very small doses and their taste is masked by other dominant tastes in the dish. Flavor reactions like caramelization and the Maillard reaction are used to add a complex note of bittersweet flavor in almost every recipe that uses heat. Let's look at some of the more common ingredients that supply bitterness.

ALCOHOL: BEER AND RED WINE

Beer's bitterness derives from the hop flowers used in the fermentation process. Hops act as a clarifier to remove undesirable proteins, but they also give beer its characteristic taste and aroma. The bitterness in hops comes from a group of chemicals called alpha-iso acids; these undergo changes during beer production. Brewers typically measure individual alpha-iso acids to control the quality of beer. Beer makes a great braising liquid for meat and seafood and pairs well with earthy and woody spices. Beer is also fantastic in desserts: Darker ales, when paired with the sweeteners in cake and even pies such as pumpkin or sweet potato (see Sweet Potato Honey Beer Pie, page 129), give a bittersweet finish.

Wine contains bitter-tasting phenols, quercetin, and tannins, among other substances. In white wines, tannins are low (0.02%); in red wines, the tannins are much higher (0.1% to 0.25% or even higher). However, the taste perception of these bitter molecules is masked by the presence of aroma molecules and the complex mixture of acids and sugars. Tannins are astringent and leave a dry finish in the mouth; this is much more noticeable in red wines. I often use white wines as the basis of my stocks and also to braise meat (see Spareribs in Malt Vinegar + Mashed Potatoes, page 89) or vegetables. Try cooking beans in red wine instead of stock. In general, red wines work better with red meat, less so with fish, but there are exceptions to this rule. In some parts of Europe, red wine is not only served along with fish but also used to cook seafood dishes like *filets de poisson au vin rouge* (fish in red wine sauce).

CACAO AND COCOA

While they both come from the cacao bean, the difference between cacao and cocoa lies in how they're processed and how they taste. Cacao nibs are prepared from fermented cacao beans by roasting and crushing the beans once the shell is removed. The cacao nibs are then ground and most of the fat (cocoa butter) is removed to produce cocoa powder. When cacao nibs are ground and mixed with other ingredients like milk powder and sugar (the cocoa butter removed during the production of cocoa powder is also added), the result is chocolate. Cocoa has a bitter and acidic taste; the addition of milk and sugar in chocolate helps mask some of these tastes. The amount of milk and milkfat added determines whether the chocolate can be labeled as dark or milk chocolate, with white chocolate containing at least 3.39% of milkfat and not less than 12% of milk solids. Dutch or alkalized cocoa is prepared by treating the roasted nibs with an alkali that neutralizes the acids and swells up the starch in cocoa, and the resulting cocoa is a darker shade of reddish brown. Natural cocoa powder often refers to cocoa powder that is not treated with alkalis; it is lighter in color with a fruitier flavor. Theobromine (comes from *Theobroma*—food of the Gods) and caffeine, the active components of cocoa, are contributors to its bitterness along with phenolic substances.

COFFEE

The dark toffee-colored coffee beans in your kitchen jar start out as green beans that are roasted at high temperatures to undergo pyrolysis and the Maillard reaction, which results in the formation of aroma and taste molecules that give this bean its unique flavor. Caffeine is the active component in coffee, which not only acts as a stimulant but also gives the drink a mild bitter taste. Other bitter-tasting components include breakdown products of chlorogenic acids (phenylindanes are the main bitter molecules) and byproducts of the Maillard reaction, among others. Coffee and chocolate pair well; adding a bit of instant coffee or espresso powder to chocolate-based cakes, cookies, and desserts intensifies the chocolate flavor.

BITTER FRUIT: CITRUS, CURRANTS

Fruits and sweetness appear to be synonymous, but many fruits contain bitter elements. Even a ripe plum has a hint of bitterness hidden in its sweet-and-sour flesh. In some fruits, notably citrus family members such as grapefruit, bitterness is more obvious. When extracting the aromatic zest of a lemon, lime, or orange, we're often told to avoid the white pith for its intense bitterness (see also Lemons and Limes, page 66, and Blueberry + Omani Lime Ice Cream, page 98, to see how bitterness played a role in the development of the recipe). Use a Microplane zester or a citrus zester to shave the outer pigmented layer off a citrus fruit; this will give you good control because the blades are short and don't restrip that same spot twice.

There are two additional sources of bitterness in citrus fruits and their intensity varies with the type of fruit. One comes from the seeds, so you should extract the seeds before you use the fruit, especially when blending to make drinks, marinades, chutneys, and sauces that call for a lemon or lime. The other comes from the juice itself. When citrus is squeezed to release its juices and left to stand for a short period, it starts to develop a bitter taste—a phenomenon called *delayed bitterness*. As the small sacs of juice are crushed, the cells release an enzyme that produces a bitter-tasting substance called *limonin*. Commercially, bitter fruit juices are mixed with sweeter juices to blend out the bitterness, but other methods include treating the fruit juice with enzymes or using devices that extract the bitter compounds, as well as selective plant breeding methods. In some instances the bitterness is highly valued, especially for Seville orange (bitter orange) marmalade: The peels are cooked with the pith and seeds (the seeds are also a rich source of pectin that helps thicken the jam) and left to steep overnight to extract as much flavor as possible. When preserving lemons, adding a large amount of salt (see Green Beans with Preserved Lemons + Crème Fraîche, page 76) will mask the bitter taste.

Other bitter-tasting fruits include cranberries, currants, and lingonberries; these fruits are cooked with sugar, acids, and spices to mellow out their bitterness.

TEA

As tea leaves undergo processing through stages of dehydration, withering, oxidation, fermentation, and heating to produce black tea, various new pigments, aroma, and taste molecules form. Green tea is produced in a different way: The enzymes that cause oxidation are inactivated early on to avoid darkening, and the withering and fermentation steps are skipped.

The chemical composition of tea varies considerably depending on the source, age, and processing method, but in general, phenolic substances impart a bitter taste. The

active components in black tea—caffeine (2.5% to 5.5%), theobromine (0.07% to 0.17%), and theophylline (0.002% to 0.013%)—also contribute to taste. Strong brews of tea can also feel astringent, so avoid steeping too much tea and for too long. The water temperature is also important in getting the most out of your tea; typically black teas are steeped at 185°F [85°C] and green teas at 170°F [77°C]. I sometimes grind tea leaves into cake batters with warmer flavors (such as the spiced Masala Chai Apple Cake in *Season*); the bitterness is masked by the mix of sugars and spices in the cake batter.

COOKING FATS AND OILS

Many cooking oils, such as olive and mustard, can taste bitter. These oils are rich in *polyphenols*, bitter-tasting phenolic substances that are phytonutrients, and this bitterness becomes very evident in emulsions like mayonnaise or aioli, in which the polyphenols meet air and water. In the case of olive oil, one key contributor to bitterness is a water-soluble substance called *oleuropein*; when it meets the water component in mayonnaise, it gives it a bitter taste. Phenolic substances also contribute to bitterness in mustard oil; if you make the Curry Leaf + Mustard Oil Mayonnaise (page 316), you might notice a mildly bitter aftertaste. You can avoid this by using a different oil, such as grapeseed, or using pure olive oil (refining reduces the amount of phenols, though this does make it less flavorful), or leaving the olive or mustard oil uncapped on the kitchen counter to "breathe" for a few days; this helps eliminate some of the phenolic substances. In the case of olive and mustard oil, I've developed a method that's quicker and easier (see case study, page 104). In the case of olive oil, the bitter-tasting oleuropein is water soluble, and that solubility rises as the temperature rises, with a maximum amount dissolving at the boiling point of water, 212°F [100°C]. As oil and water will eventually separate, the oil can be separated while the oleuropein stays in the water that can be discarded. While I could not determine which substances made mustard oil taste bitter, the method reproduced the same results, implying that the bitter-tasting substances in mustard oil are also water soluble. This debittered oil can be used to make emulsions such as vinaigrettes or mayonnaise (see Curry Leaf + Mustard Oil Mayonnaise, page 316) while retaining all the flavor characteristics. In condiments like pesto in which there are other stronger flavorful ingredients, bitterness is masked easily and won't be noticed (see also Lipids, page 335).

VEGETABLES AND BITTER GREENS

As with fruit, there are bitter vegetables, including my childhood dinner nemesis, the bitter melon or karela. However, as an adult I've learned to appreciate the bitterness in this knobby-skinned vegetable. Once the vegetable is cut and the seeds extracted, I soak it in a water bath of salt and lemon juice for about 30 minutes to mellow the intensity and then proceed to cook as needed. Some other bitter vegetables with varying degrees of bitterness include Brussels sprouts, eggplants, turnips, and rutabaga. Many of these vegetables are seasoned with salt or cooked with flavorful fats and spices to mask or reduce the perception of bitterness (see Shaved Brussels Sprouts Salad, page 112).

The bitter greens are many: arugula (which also tastes noticeably peppery), cardoons, fenugreek, spinach, endives, and chicories (radicchio). These are often used in salads, where they're coated with a dressing, such as a vinaigrette, or sautéed, so the heat mellows out some of the bitterness. When endives and radicchio are dipped into robust-flavored dips like pesto, hummus (including the various flavored varieties), or even ranch dressing, the perception of bitterness is counteracted and the intensity reduced.

QUICK TIPS FOR BOOSTING FLAVOR WITH BITTERNESS

+ Sprinkle unsweetened cocoa over sweet coffee-based or chocolate desserts, such as brownies, cakes, or truffles; the touch of bitterness complements these desserts. Nuts like hazelnut and walnut pair well with this combination.

+ A hint of instant coffee or espresso powder will intensify the flavor of chocolate, as seen in the Chocolate Miso Bread Pudding (page 133). Add it to your chocolate-based ice creams and cake batters when combining the other ingredients. I don't advise adding leftover coffee from the pot; there are too many variables, especially in the strength of the coffee. Instant powders avoid these issues.

USING BITTERNESS IN THE KITCHEN

+ Caramelization of sugars and the Maillard reaction between amino acids and sugars both produce a complex set of color and taste molecules that leave a bittersweet taste. Slow-cooking alliums like shallots, onions, and even scallions can introduce a pleasant amount of bitterness. Grilling lemon, lime, and orange halves on a hot grate caramelizes the sugars; you can then extract the juice to prepare sweet drinks.

+ Use bitter ingredients like cocoa or coffee beans, including their ground powdered forms, to add texture and a spot of bitterness to desserts and even salads. When I worked as a pastry cook, I used to paint a coffee bean with edible gold dust to put on top of rich chocolate ganache-based cakes. This not only served a decorative purpose but also helped cut through some of that rich taste.

+ Some nuts, like walnuts, taste mildly bitter, from the tannins in the outer skin. Gently toasting walnuts mellows the intensity and brings out their aroma, and you can use them to as a source of crunchiness in salads and desserts (see also How Savoriness Works, page 205).

+ I discuss mustard in the Fieriness chapter as a source for heat, but it merits a special mention here. The heat in mustard comes from a bitter-tasting compound, a type of glucoside called *sinigrin*. When mustard powder is mixed with water, an enzyme converts the sinigrin to its "hot" form, and it is best to let the mixture stand for at least 15 minutes before incorporating it into any recipe. Do not add any type of acid or boiling water; either will kill the enzyme while this reaction occurs, and you will end up with a bitter-tasting substance that lacks that fiery note.

+ The perception of bitterness tends to increase at low temperatures.

+ Adding an acid or salt can help mask bitterness in vegetables and fruits. Salting eggplants and adding vinaigrette to bitter greens in salads hides the intensity of their bitterness.

Warm Kale, White Bean + Mushroom Salad with Chilli Tahini

During the colder months of the year, I often make this quick, flavorful salad. This salad owes its heat to the Chinese condiment Chiu Chow style chilli oil, which comes from the region of Southern China within the Guangdong province. This condiment is prepared from a combination of fresh and brined chillies flavored with garlic, soy sauce, and toasted sesame oil. The most popular brand, and the one that I love, from Lee Kum Kee is available in most grocery stores in the international aisle as well as in Asian markets. Before you use these, give the contents a shake or stir so the flakes are distributed. This can also be served as a one-bowl meal over Plain Rice (page 310) with a generous spoonful or two of the Green Apple Chutney (page 321) or Cauliflower Aachar (page 320).

There are other types of Chinese chilli oil condiments available; the Lao Gan Ma company makes one that is popularly referred to as chilli crisp oil and will also work in this dish. It will taste slightly different because in addition to chillies, garlic, and ginger, it contains Sichuan peppercorns, black cardamom, and cinnamon.

SERVES 4

For the salad:

1 Tbsp extra-virgin olive oil

1 shallot (2 oz [60 g]), thinly sliced

6 oz [170 g] fresh cremini or shiitake mushrooms, sliced

1 small bunch tender kale (about 10 oz [285 g]), such as Lacinato (also called Tuscan or dinosaur kale), midribs stripped, coarsely chopped

Fine sea salt

One 15½ oz [445 g] can white beans, such as cannellini, rinsed and drained

For the chilli tahini:

¼ cup [55 g] tahini

3 Tbsp Chiu Chow style chilli oil (see headnote)

¼ cup [60 ml] rice wine vinegar

Fine sea salt

1 or 2 Tbsp boiling water

THE FLAVOR APPROACH

Tahini carries a mildly bitter taste that is masked by the warmth of the chillies and the acidity of the vinegar.

In addition, tahini provides a layer of creamy texture and fat that coats the kale and beans in this salad.

The bitterness of the kale is offset by the use of fat, acid, and heat.

Chiu Chow style chilli oil provides a complex combination of flavor from the chillies, garlic, soy sauce, and sesame oil.

To prepare the salad, heat the oil in a large saucepan over medium-high heat. When the oil is hot, add the shallot and sauté until it starts to turn golden brown, 4 to 5 minutes. Add the mushrooms and sauté until they start to sear a little, 3 to 4 minutes. Fold in the kale, season with salt, and cook until the leaves turn bright green, 3 to 4 minutes. Remove from the heat. Fold in the cannellini beans. Taste and season with salt. Transfer to a large mixing bowl.

To prepare the chilli tahini, whisk the tahini, chilli oil, and vinegar together in a small bowl. Taste and season with salt. If the mixture is too thick, stir in 1 or 2 Tbsp of the boiling water.

Pour the tahini dressing over the kale in the mixing bowl and toss to coat evenly. Serve warm.

Shaved Brussels Sprouts Salad

I was once asked if I could recall something I tasted for the first time after I moved to the United States. It's Brussels sprouts. I can't recollect the exact dish and how it was cooked, but I remember they reminded me of strange Lilliputian cabbages. Brussels sprouts are spectacular when shaved into shreds for a salad or roasted. Because some folks, especially my husband, love a bit more dressing or sauce with everything they eat, this recipe makes a little more to give you that option.

SERVES 4 TO 6

For the salad:

3 shallots (total weight 6½ oz [180 g])

2 Tbsp extra-virgin olive oil

Fine sea salt

1 lb [455 g] Brussels sprouts

1¾ oz [50 g] chopped walnuts

½ cup [24 g] thinly sliced scallions, both white and green parts

2 Tbsp chopped mint leaves, for garnish

1 tsp red chilli pepper flakes, such as Aleppo or Maras, for garnish

For the dressing:

2 garlic cloves, peeled

1 cup [240 g] crème fraîche

2 Tbsp fresh lemon juice

1 tsp ground black pepper

Fine sea salt

THE FLAVOR APPROACH

The dressing's combination of acid, fat, salt, and herbs provides textural contrast to the crunchy walnuts and Brussels sprouts, and offsets their mild bitterness.

Submerging the cut or shredded bits of the vegetable in a bowl of ice-cold water helps reduce their sulfurous smell.

Mint and crème fraîche create a cooling sensation via chemesthesis.

Crispy shallots and walnuts add a crunchy mouthfeel.

To prepare the salad, preheat the oven to 300°F [149°C]. Line a baking sheet with parchment paper.

Trim and discard the ends of the shallots and cut the shallots into thin slices. Toss with the oil and a little salt in a small bowl. Spread the shallots on the prepared baking sheet and bake until golden brown and crisp, 30 to 45 minutes, stirring occassionally to ensure even browning.

Meanwhile, trim the stalk ends off the Brussels sprouts and cut them into fine shreds. Place the shredded Brussels sprouts in a bowl of salted ice-cold water for 10 minutes.

Toast the walnuts in a small skillet over medium-low heat until they start to brown and release a toasty aroma, 4 to 5 minutes. Remove from the heat and transfer to a small bowl.

To make the dressing, smash the garlic cloves using the flat side of a knife until you get a smooth purée. Transfer to a small mixing bowl. Fold in the crème fraîche, lemon juice, and black pepper. Taste and add salt as needed.

To assemble the salad, drain the Brussels sprouts. Spread them out on a clean kitchen towel to absorb any excess liquid. Transfer them to a large mixing bowl. Add the scallions, walnuts, and half the crème fraîche dressing, and fold to coat evenly. Transfer to a serving bowl. Garnish with the mint, chilli flakes, and crispy shallots and serve with the remaining dressing on the side. The salad will be good for up to 2 days if refrigerated in an airtight container. Before serving, let it warm to room temperature.

Charred Asparagus with "Gunpowder" Nut Masala

This asparagus dish is an explosion of aroma and taste. If you have a bit of smoked salt at home, use it here to amplify and enhance the effect of grilling. This is an excellent side to serve at a barbecue or to accompany any grilled vegetable or meat dish. I sometimes serve this for lunch with a plain omelet and a bowl of Plain Rice (page 310).

SERVES 4

4 Tbsp [60 ml] extra-virgin olive oil plus a little extra to brush the pan

1 lb [455 g] asparagus, tough ends trimmed and discarded

1 Tbsp fresh lime juice

1 tsp lime zest

Sea salt flakes

1 Tbsp My "Gunpowder" Nut Masala (page 312)

1 Tbsp chopped cilantro or flat-leaf parsley

1 lime, cut into quarters (optional)

THE FLAVOR APPROACH

During charring, the mildly bitter taste of asparagus is reduced, and it takes on an entirely new set of flavors, including some caramelization and the Maillard reaction.

Salt is not added at the start during grilling because salt flakes are used as a finishing salt.

Observe how the green color of the asparagus gets brighter once cooked.

Heat a grill pan or cast-iron skillet over medium-high heat. Brush the grates with a little oil.

Place the asparagus on a large plate or baking sheet. Drizzle with 1 Tbsp of the oil and rub to coat well.

Add the asparagus to the hot pan and cook for 5 to 6 minutes, turning with a pair of kitchen tongs, until they turn bright green and develop charred spots or grill marks. Transfer the asparagus to a serving dish. Drizzle the remaining 3 Tbsp of oil and the lime juice over the asparagus. Sprinkle with the lime zest, salt flakes, "Gunpowder" Nut Masala, and cilantro and serve immediately with the quartered limes on the side, if desired.

Vegetable Pakoras

My mother's favorite breakfast is pakoras. Often on weekends, she wakes up early to fry a large batch. Pakoras can get soft after they cool, so I changed things up a bit. I limit the water and instead allow the water inside the vegetables to dissolve the dry ingredients. Tempura batter flour bumps up the level of crispiness. There are several fantastic condiments to serve with hot pakoras: Maggi Hot and Sweet Tomato Chilli Sauce (available at Indian grocery stores), Mint Chutney (page 322), Pumpkin Seed Chutney (page 323), and Tamarind-Date Chutney (page 322). You can also pop a few pakoras into a toasted bun and sprinkle with either of the condiments to make it a sandwich.

SERVES 4

For the vegetables:

1 medium russet potato (7½ oz [215 g])

1 small bunch Lacinato kale (about 10 oz [285 g]), midribs stripped, coarsely chopped

1 medium red onion (9¼ oz [260 g]), halved and cut into thin slices

1 in [2.5 cm] piece fresh ginger, peeled and minced

1 green chilli, minced

2 Tbsp cilantro leaves (optional)

For the batter:

¾ cup [90 g] chickpea flour

¼ cup [40 g] tempura batter flour

1 tsp garam masala, homemade (page 312) or store-bought

1 tsp ground turmeric

½ tsp ground black pepper

½ tsp fine sea salt

3 cups [720 ml] grapeseed or other neutral oil

1 Tbsp amchur

THE FLAVOR APPROACH

Mechanically breaking down some of the cells of the vegetables by massaging them gently releases the water trapped inside their cells, which helps bring the dry ingredients together to form a batter.

Achieve maximum crispiness by using minimal water plus a combination of chickpea flour and tempura batter flour.

Since the oil is maintained at a temperature of 350°F [177°C], use an oil with a smoke point way above this number, such as grapeseed.

To prepare the vegetables, peel the potato and grate it on the coarse blades of a grater into a large mixing bowl. Add the kale, onions, ginger, chilli, and cilantro to the mixing bowl.

To prepare the batter, whisk together the chickpea flour, tempura batter flour, garam masala, turmeric, black pepper, and salt in a medium bowl. Sift the flour mixture through a fine-mesh sieve over the vegetables in the mixing bowl and dump any bits of the black pepper left behind over the vegetables. Massage the ingredients together until the vegetables are completely coated with the batter, 3 to 4 minutes. If it needs a bit of water to help bind the ingredients, sprinkle on 1 or 2 Tbsp.

Heat the oil in a small, heavy cast-iron pot or saucepan over medium-high heat until the oil reaches 350°F [177°C]. Set a wire rack on a baking sheet lined with parchment paper. Once the oil is hot, test a small batch by dropping in 1 Tbsp of batter; the batter should float to the surface. To shape and fry the pakoras, use two dinner spoons—one to scoop the batter and the second to help shape and transfer the batter to the hot oil. Fry the pakoras in batches. The pakoras are cooked when they turn golden brown all over, 3 to 4 minutes. Remove the pakoras with a slotted spoon and transfer them to the prepared baking sheet to drain any excess oil. Sprinkle the hot pakoras with the amchur and serve them immediately with chutney on the side, if desired.

Collard Greens, Chickpea + Lentil Soup

I like tangy flavors in all my soups; it's a constant in most of the soups I cook or write about. The bitterness of collard greens is tamed by the acids in the tamarind and tomatoes. Red lentils cook quickly, so you don't have to soak them like green or brown lentils, but I still do; it's a habit I learned from my family in India. Soaking seeds and legumes in water changes their chemical composition and makes them more digestible. If you're running low on time, skip the soak and just cook them. Depending on where you buy your red lentils, you might notice some differences in their thickness and diameter. Indian red lentils are wider and thicker than the ones sold in American grocery stores; consequently, you will need to increase your cooking time accordingly and add a little more water if you notice the liquid all being absorbed.

SERVES 4

½ cup [100 g] red lentils

2 Tbsp extra-virgin olive oil

1 medium white or yellow onion (9¼ oz [260 g]), diced

4 garlic cloves, peeled and sliced

1 in [2.5 cm] piece fresh ginger, peeled and grated

2 in [5 cm] piece cinnamon stick

1 tsp ground black pepper

½ to 1 tsp red chilli powder

½ tsp ground turmeric

2 Tbsp tomato paste

1 medium tomato (5 oz [140 g]), diced

1 bunch collard greens (about 7 oz [200 g]), midribs removed, coarsely chopped

One 15½ oz [445 g] can chickpeas, drained and rinsed

1 qt [960 ml] vegetable stock, "brown" vegetable stock (page 57), or water

1 Tbsp tamarind paste, homemade (page 67) or store-bought

Fine sea salt

2 Tbsp chopped flat-leaf parsley

2 Tbsp chopped cilantro

Buttered bread or naan, for serving

THE FLAVOR APPROACH

Tamarind and tomato provide a sour backdrop for bitter greens and vegetables in this soup.

Pick over the lentils for any stones or debris, rinse in a fine-mesh sieve under running tap water, and transfer to a small bowl. Cover with 1 cup [120 ml] of water and soak for 30 minutes.

Heat the olive oil in a large saucepan over medium-high heat. Once the oil is hot, add the onion and sauté until translucent, 4 to 5 minutes. Add the garlic and ginger and cook until fragrant, about 1 minute. Add the cinnamon, black pepper, red chilli, and turmeric and sauté until fragrant, 30 to 45 seconds. Stir in the tomato paste and cook until it just starts to brown, 2 to 3 minutes.

Stir in the diced tomato and collard greens and sauté until the leaves turn bright green, 1 to 2 minutes. Drain the soaked lentils and add along with the chickpeas and vegetable stock. Bring to a boil, lower the heat to a simmer, and cook until the lentils are tender and completely cooked, 25 to 30 minutes. Stir in the tamarind paste. Taste and season with salt.

Before serving, stir in the chopped parsley and cilantro. Serve hot with toasted slices of warm buttered bread or naan.

Grapefruit Soda with Chai Masala

My husband loves grapefruit, so one year I surprised him with a dwarf Ruby Red Grapefruit plant. The little plant is housed in a big pot only a few feet high but bears impressively large, orb-like yellow citrus that are extremely fragrant when sliced. Sometimes I collect the juice and stir it into a simple syrup made with chai masala (tea spices). I infuse whole spices rather than ground into the simple syrup to get a lighter flavor that delicately complements the citrus.

SERVES 8

½ cup [100 g] sugar

2 in [5 cm] piece fresh ginger, peeled and cut into thin slices

1 in [2.5 cm] piece cinnamon stick

10 whole black peppercorns

2 whole green cardamom pods, lightly cracked

1 star anise

2½ cups [600 ml] fresh grapefruit juice (from 2 to 3 large pink grapefruit)

One 4⅓ cup [1 L] bottle club soda, chilled

THE FLAVOR APPROACH

The bitterness of grapefruit is complemented by a combination of spices.

Aroma and taste molecules in the whole spices are extracted using a combination of heat and water.

Club soda and grapefruit juice both provide acidity, while the soda's carbonation adds the textural effect of fizz by playing with our receptors (see Carbonated Beverages, page 67).

The added sugar and the sugars present in grapefruit soda help temper the bitter tastants in the grapefruit juice.

Combine 1½ cups [360 ml] of water and the sugar in a medium saucepan. Add the ginger, cinnamon, peppercorns, cardamom, and star anise. Bring to a boil over medium-high heat and immediately remove from the heat. Cover with a lid and steep for 10 minutes. Strain the simple syrup through a fine-mesh sieve placed over a bottle or jug. Discard the spices. You should have 1½ cups [360 ml] of simple syrup. Refrigerate the syrup until chilled.

In a large pitcher, combine the chilled simple syrup and grapefruit juice. Fill eight tall glasses with ice. Pour ½ cup [120 ml] of the syrup mixture into each glass, top with ½ cup [120 ml] of the club soda, and stir. Store any leftover syrup in an airtight container in the refrigerator for up to 1 week.

Spiced Coffee Kulfi

When I was in high school in India, a street-food vendor would drop by the school every afternoon during our lunch break. Attached to the back of his bicycle was a large metal box filled with chunks of ice and metal containers of frozen kulfi. I'm hesitant to call kulfi an Indian ice cream, because it really isn't that; it's a type of frozen dessert. Unlike ice cream, in which ice crystals are a negative trait, a kulfi will contain a certain amount of ice crystals and is a little firmer than a soft ice cream. Kulfi is one of the easiest treats to make at home. Make ahead of time to allow ample time to freeze.

SERVES 6

1 cup [240 ml] heavy cream

One 14 oz [400 g] can evaporated milk

One 14 oz [400 g] can sweetened condensed milk

1 Tbsp instant espresso or coffee

¼ tsp fine sea salt

2 green cardamom pods, cracked

2 in [5 cm] piece cinnamon stick

1 or 2 star anise

1¼ oz [35 g] ground toasted hazelnuts, (optional; see Hazelnut Flan, page 126, for instructions on toasting hazelnuts)

THE FLAVOR APPROACH

The flavor molecules in the whole spices are extracted into the milk fat for a more delicate flavor to complement the coffee. For a stronger dose of spice, add ½ tsp of ground spices directly to the milk. If you want to reduce the flavor of coffee, use ½ Tbsp.

The use of instant coffee helps in two ways: It dissolves very easily, and it provides a very concentrated dose of coffee flavor without increasing the liquid volume, which would otherwise pose a problem in achieving the correct frozen texture. Excess water will cause a higher proportion of ice crystal formation by changing the ratios of the ingredients involved such as fat, proteins, and sugars.

Evaporated milk acts as a shortcut here; it provides the taste of caramelized lactose, a characteristic feature of kulfis made in India. See the Polenta Kheer (page 185) for a more detailed explanation of the use of evaporated milk and its concentrated flavor in Indian desserts.

Stir together the heavy cream, evaporated milk, condensed milk, instant espresso, salt, cardamom, cinnamon, and star anise in a medium saucepan over medium-high heat, until the espresso dissolves and the liquids are combined. Bring to a boil and remove from the heat. Press a piece of plastic wrap against the surface of the mixture to prevent a skin from forming on the surface and let the mixture steep for 1 hour at room temperature. Remove the whole spices and discard. Pour the liquid into 6 freezer-safe ramekins or kulfi molds. Wrap the tops with plastic wrap or top with kulfi lids. Transfer to the freezer and let firm for at least 6 hours, preferably overnight.

The kulfi can be served directly in the ramekins. If using kulfi molds, run the metal mold under water for a few seconds, flip, and tap gently to release the kulfi. Garnish with the toasted hazelnuts.

Roasted Fruit with Coffee Miso Tahini

This combination of coffee and miso with tahini might seem a bit unusual, but stick with me; it works, creating a somewhat butterscotch-like taste. I prefer fruit-based desserts. No matter when you make them and how many times you repeat them, fruit always tastes different depending on variety, ripeness, and provenance. This dessert is a good choice for a light and sweet finish to a heavy meal. Use it as a topping over vanilla or cardamom ice cream, or over a bowl of lightly sweetened Greek yogurt. To add a bit of a kick, fold in a few tablespoons of crystallized ginger. A little bit of this dressing goes a long way. Serve it on the side.

SERVES 4

For the roasted fruit:

2 Tbsp unsalted butter, plus extra for greasing

12 oz [340 g] blueberries, fresh or frozen (no need to thaw if using frozen)

12 oz [340 g] fresh figs, sliced in half lengthwise

2 Tbsp fresh lime juice

2 Tbsp maple syrup

½ tsp ground black pepper

¼ tsp fine sea salt

For the coffee miso tahini (makes ¾ cup [180 ml]):

2 Tbsp shiro or sweet white miso

¼ cup [85 g] maple syrup or honey

¼ cup [55 g] tahini

¼ tsp instant espresso or coffee powder

Fine sea salt

THE FLAVOR APPROACH

White or shiro miso provides a welcome salty and savory character to the bitter taste of coffee and tahini. This combination works well with fruit and dishes that are sweet with a bold sour character.

Roasting the fruit in their juices helps introduce a bunch of new flavor molecules via the caramelization and Maillard reactions.

Unlike red cabbage, which loses its bright anthocyanin colors on heating, blueberries retain their color. One reason is the presence of blueberry pectin, which is used in the food industry as a stabilizer for anthocyanins. Blueberry pectin can bind some types of anthocyanins and form a complex that is stable in the presence of heat and even acidic pH.

To prepare the fruit, preheat the oven to 375°F [190°C].

Grease a rectangular 8 by 10 in [20 by 25 cm] baking dish with a little butter and place it on a baking sheet lined with parchment paper to catch any of the juices that might bubble over. Place the blueberries and figs in a medium mixing bowl. Drizzle the lime juice and maple syrup over the fruit. Add the black pepper and salt and toss to coat well. Transfer the fruit with the liquids to the baking dish and spread in an even layer. Dot the fruit with the butter and roast until the figs start to caramelize and the fruits release their juices, 25 to 30 minutes. Remove from the oven.

While the fruit is roasting, prepare the coffee miso tahini. Whisk the miso, maple syrup, tahini, ¼ cup [60 ml] of water, and the espresso powder in a small bowl until smooth. Taste and season with salt.

To serve, drizzle a few tablespoons of the sauce over the warm fruit and serve the rest on the side. You can also serve this over scoops of ice cream or Greek yogurt.

Hazelnut Flan

When summer turned searing hot and humid in Bombay, we would eat chilled bowls of flan (we call it caramel pudding in India). Sometimes we made it from an instant mix, and sometimes we made it from scratch. Here I celebrate one of my favorite childhood desserts through flavors I've learned to love as I grew older. The bittersweet taste of cara-melized sweet jaggery is offset by the creaminess of the flan and the aroma of hazelnuts. You have two options for this recipe, depending on the time you have available. You can infuse milk with hazelnuts by yourself (which I highly recommend) or skip that and use a good-quality hazelnut extract or creamer. Note: Making your own infused milk must be done a day or two in advance.

MAKES ONE 8 IN [20 CM] ROUND FLAN

⅛ tsp cream of tartar

¾ cup [150 g] sugar

2 cups [480 ml] whole milk or hazelnut-infused milk (recipe follows)

One 14 oz [400 g] can sweetened condensed milk

1 tsp hazelnut extract or 2 Tbsp hazelnut creamer (if using whole milk)

¼ tsp fine sea salt

4 large eggs

THE FLAVOR APPROACH

Cream of tartar is acidic, which prevents the caramel from crystallizing by helping the sucrose "invert" and produce glucose and fructose from the sucrose. The glucose and fructose interfere with sucrose crystallization, and the caramel remains in liquid form.

A bain-marie, or water bath, is used to gently coagulate the egg proteins to form the structure of the pudding. The aromatic molecules of hazelnuts are intensified by toasting the nuts and then infusing them into the milk.

While bubbles do not affect the taste of the flan (I'll happily devour the pudding), some consider them a textural flaw. To minimize introducing air bubbles in the batter, don't whisk the eggs; instead, gently stir and fold them using a spatula.

A second source for bubbles is the infused hazelnut milk. I took a tip from Stella Parks, author of *BraveTart* and pastry whiz at Serious Eats, who recommends heating the custard base for the flan to get rid of most of the air bubbles.

Preheat the oven to 325°F [163°C].

Combine ¼ cup [60 ml] of water and the cream of tartar in a small sauce-pan. Pour the sugar into the center of the saucepan so it does not stick to the sides. Cook, without stirring, over medium-high heat until the sugar starts to caramelize and turn dark brown, 6 to 8 minutes. Pour the liquid into an 8 in [20 cm] round cake pan and rotate to coat evenly.

cont'd

THE FLAVOR EQUATION

In a medium saucepan over medium-high heat, combine the milk, condensed milk, hazelnut extract (if using plain milk), and salt, using a spatula to gently stir. Heat until hot but not boiling. Remove from the heat.

Crack the eggs into a large mixing bowl. Using a silicone spatula, slowly break the yolks and stir the eggs gently until combined. Avoid whipping, whisking, or aggressively folding the eggs, or you will incorporate air. While mixing the eggs, slowly add ½ cup [120 ml] of the hot milk mixture to the eggs. Continue to stir the eggs and add another ½ cup [120 ml] of the hot milk. Repeat until all the milk is incorporated into the eggs. Pass this custard base through a fine-mesh sieve over a medium jug or bowl with a spout to remove any lumps.

Hold the flat end of the spatula right over the layer of caramel in the prepared baking pan. Slowly pour the custard base over the flat surface of the spatula, to prevent disturbing the layer of caramel. Cover the top of the pan with a double layer of foil.

Fill a kettle with water and bring it a boil. Place a deep, wide baking dish or pan large enough to accommodate the round baking pan in the oven. Place a circular wire rack inside the dish or make a thick, 8 in [20 cm] ring with aluminum foil to prevent the baking pan from touching the base of the baking dish.

Carefully place the prepared baking pan over the rack or ring in the center of the larger dish. Pour boiling water from the kettle into the space between the baking pan and the

large dish and fill it to about a ½ in [12 mm] from the top of the baking pan. Cook the custard in the oven until it is almost set and the center jiggles slightly, 45 to 50 minutes. Carefully remove the baking pan from the oven, place it on a wire rack, and let it cool completely to room temperature. Refrigerate the flan overnight to set.

The next day, remove the foil cover. Run a small, sharp knife around the inside edge of the flan. Place a large serving plate over the baking pan. Holding them tightly, flip the pan and the plate and tap gently to release the flan onto the plate. Scrape any extra caramel liquid over the flan. Serve chilled or cold. Refrigerate any leftovers in an airtight container for up to 3 to 4 days.

Hazelnut-Infused Milk

This step adds an extra day, but it is well worth the gorgeous, rich flavor of hazelnut and is my preferred method. On the first day, prepare the hazelnut milk; on the second day, use this infused milk in place of the milk and hazelnut extract or creamer and proceed as indicated in the recipe. Be careful to avoid introducing air bubbles when stirring in the hazelnuts.

MAKES 2 CUPS [480 ML] INFUSED MILK

7 oz [200 g] raw hazelnuts

2 cups [480 ml] whole milk

Preheat the oven to 350°F [177°C].

Line a baking sheet with parchment paper. Place the hazelnuts on the sheet and toast in the oven until they start to turn golden brown and fragrant, 12 to 15 minutes. Remove the nuts from the oven, transfer them to the bowl of a blender or food processor, and pulse for a few seconds, just long enough to break the whole nuts

apart. Do not overgrind to a powder or it will incorporate air bubbles.

Pour the milk into a large jar with a lid. Gently stir in the toasted hazelnuts. Seal the jar and leave to infuse overnight in the refrigerator. You can steep the milk for 24 or 48 hours for a richer flavor.

On the day you plan to prepare the flan, line a fine-mesh sieve with a

piece of wet cheesecloth and place it over a medium bowl. Strain the hazelnut-infused milk through the cloth and discard any solids left behind in the cheesecloth. If your milk volume is slightly under 2 cups [480 ml], add enough milk to bring it back to the original volume. Use this infused milk in the recipe and skip adding the hazelnut extract or creamer.

Sweet Potato Honey Beer Pie

Sweet potatoes are on a monthly rotation in my household; even my dog, Snoopy, loved them. The different components of the pie can be prepared on different days. Here's a suggested order of steps you might find useful, especially if you make this for Thanksgiving. Day 1: Roast sweet potatoes, reduce the beer, and prepare the pie crust, but don't blind bake (partially bake). Day 2: Blind bake the pie crust, prepare the sweet potato custard, and bake the pie. Of course, you can also do this all in one day.

MAKES ONE 9 IN [23 CM] PIE

For the crust:

¼ cup [55 g] unsalted butter, cubed and softened to room temperature, plus extra for greasing the pan

¼ cup [50 g] packed dark brown sugar

1 large egg, lightly whisked

7 oz [200 g] almond flour (blanched or unblanched)

½ tsp fine sea salt

For the filling:

1 lb [455 g] sweet potatoes, preferably an orange-fleshed variety such as Garnet or Jewel

One 12 fl oz [360 ml] bottle dark beer

½ cup [100 g] packed dark brown sugar or jaggery

¼ cup [85 g] honey

3 large eggs plus 3 yolks

2 tsp ground ginger

1 tsp ground green cardamom

½ tsp ground turmeric

¼ tsp fine sea salt

½ cup [120 ml] whole milk

½ cup [120 ml] heavy cream

1 Tbsp cornstarch

THE FLAVOR APPROACH

Heat plays a very important part in this recipe: The bitterness of beer is concentrated through reduction by evaporating the water. When the nuts in the crust are heated, a whole new set of flavor molecules is produced, which will vary depending on the type of nut used. Heat also helps the egg, nuts, and sugar bind together to form the structure of the pie.

When sweet potatoes are heated, the enzyme amylase breaks down the starch stored in the vegetable's cells to release sweet-tasting sugar molecules, making a roasted sweet potato taste much sweeter than a raw one. This is why roasting sweet potatoes is a superior method for producing not just sweetness but also a beautiful fragrance. Research shows that roasting produces at least seventeen more aromatic molecules than are achieved through boiling or microwaving, and most of them in higher concentrations. Roasting also helps with caramelization of sugars and the Maillard reaction.

To prepare the crust, line the base of a 9 in [23 cm] round tart pan with parchment paper and grease lightly with a little butter.

Place the butter and sugar in the bowl of a stand mixer and beat with the paddle attachment on medium-low speed until the mixture is a uniform pale brown and fluffy, 4 to 5 minutes. Stop the mixer and scrape down the sides of the bowl with a silicone spatula. Add the egg and whisk on medium-low speed until combined, 1 minute. Add the almond flour and salt and mix on medium-low speed until it comes together to form a ball of dough, 3 to 4 minutes. Scrape the dough from the bowl directly into the prepared pan.

Using a small, flat-bottomed bowl or the base of a flat measuring cup (with parchment paper covering the dough if you wish), spread and level the dough until it covers the base and

cont'd

the sides in an even layer. Wrap with plastic wrap and freeze for at least 1 hour until firm. The crust can be prepared in advance and frozen, wrapped and sealed in a resealable bag, for up to 2 weeks.

To partially bake the crust, at least 1 hour before it will be filled with the custard, preheat the oven to 350°F [177°C] and set a rack in the lower one-third position. Line a baking sheet with parchment paper. Place the crust on the baking sheet. Dock the surface by pricking it all over with a fork. Cover with a large sheet of parchment paper and weigh it down with pie weights. Bake until the sides just start to brown, 15 to 20 minutes. Transfer to a wire rack and cool for 5 minutes.

Remove the weights and the parchment paper.

To prepare the filling, preheat the oven to 400°F [204°C]. Rinse the sweet potatoes to remove any dirt and pat them dry with paper towels. Place the sweet potatoes in a baking dish or on a baking sheet lined with aluminum foil. Roast until completely tender, 35 to 45 minutes. Cool completely before handling. Peel the sweet potatoes, discard the skins, and purée the flesh in a food processor. You should have about 12 oz [340 g] of sweet potato purée. Once the purée is completely cooled, proceed with the filling or refrigerate overnight in an airtight

container. This can be done a day or two in advance.

When ready to complete the filling, pour the beer into a medium, deep, heavy-bottomed saucepan and bring to a boil over medium-high heat. Watch carefully to avoid overflowing as the liquid foams on heating. Lower the heat to low and cook until the liquid reduces to about ¼ cup [60 ml], 20 to 30 minutes. Cool to room temperature before using.

Preheat the oven to 350°F [177°C]. In a large mixing bowl, whisk together the reduced beer, sweet potato purée, sugar, honey, eggs, yolks, ginger, cardamom, turmeric, and salt. Slowly whisk in the milk and heavy

cream until the sugar completely dissolves. In a small bowl, whisk the cornstarch and 1½ Tbsp of water to form a slurry. Pour the slurry into the custard and whisk until combined. Alternatively, add the ingredients to a high-speed blender and pulse on high speed briefly until you get a smooth slurry (this is my preferred method to obtain a silky-smooth filling).

Transfer the custard to a large saucepan and heat over medium-low heat, stirring constantly, scraping down the sides, until the mixture reaches 165°F [74°C] on an instant-read thermometer and begins to noticeably thicken, 10 to 12 minutes. Quickly remove from the heat. Set a fine-mesh sieve over a large measuring

pitcher and strain the custard to remove any lumps.

Pour the custard into the prebaked crust and bake until the custard is set and an instant-read thermometer reads 185°F [85°C] when inserted into the center of the custard, 25 to 30 minutes. The custard should be firm on the sides but slightly jiggly in the center. Transfer to a wire rack and let the pie cool to room temperature before serving.

NOTES:

You can use the same recipe to make a pumpkin pie, using 15 oz [430 g]

unsweetened pumpkin purée in place of the sweet potatoes. Feel free to use a different crust, homemade or store-bought.

Most pie crusts tend to absorb a bit of water from the filling; nut-based crusts are notorious for this, because nuts release their fat on cooling and also absorb moisture from air (most nuts, including almonds, are hygroscopic). I've tried "waterproofing" pie crusts with egg whites, but that's never worked for me. Here's a method that does work: Melt 3 Tbsp of white or dark bittersweet chocolate and paint the surface of the pie with a pastry brush. Let the chocolate set and harden before you pour in the custard and bake.

Chocolate Miso Bread Pudding

This pudding has all my favorite things in one dish. Since this pudding is rich, I prefer to serve it by itself, warm and gooey, but I wouldn't refuse a big scoop of vanilla or green cardamom ice cream on top. If your local bakery makes a challah or brioche topped with poppy or sesame seeds, go for it. I love the extra crunchy texture the seeds add to the pudding. Note that it's best to start a day ahead so the bread can really soak up the liquid.

SERVES 8 TO 10

1 lb [455 g] challah or brioche

2 Tbsp unsalted butter, cut into small cubes, plus extra for greasing the pan

9 oz [255 g] bittersweet chocolate (70% cacao), chopped

1 tsp instant coffee or espresso

3 oz [85 g] dried tart cherries

1½ cups [360 ml] heavy cream

¼ cup [40 g] shiro or sweet white miso

1½ cups [360 ml] whole milk

¾ cup [150 g] sugar

3 large eggs plus one yolk, lightly whisked

¼ tsp fine sea salt (optional)

THE FLAVOR APPROACH

Chocolate's flavor is enhanced by the addition of coffee. You can introduce deeper smokier notes depending on the type of chocolate and coffee used and the quality of the roast (both the coffee and chocolate beans are roasted).

Miso gives this dish a boost of salty and sweet notes. You don't need to add salt, because miso contains salt.

Tart cherries give a welcome spot of sourness to this sweet dessert.

If your bread is not stale, preheat the oven to 200°F [93°C]. Set a wire rack on a baking sheet. Cut the bread into 1 in [2.5 cm] cubes and arrange them on the rack. Dry the bread cubes in the oven until completely dry, 45 minutes to 1 hour. You can also dry the bread cubes overnight, on your kitchen counter at room temperature.

Butter a 9 by 12 by 2 in [23 by 30.5 by 5 cm] rectangular baking pan. Add the bread cubes.

Chop the chocolate and transfer half to a large mixing bowl with the instant coffee. Sprinkle the remaining chocolate and the cherries over the bread in the baking pan and fold in. Avoid leaving the bits of chocolate and cherries on top; they might burn during baking.

Warm the cream in a small saucepan over medium-high heat. When the cream just starts to bubble, pour it over the chocolate in the large mixing bowl. Whisk until the chocolate mixture is completely melted and smooth. Transfer ½ cup [120 ml] of the chocolate mixture to a small mixing bowl. Add the miso and whisk until completely smooth, with no lumps. Pour the miso mixture into the large bowl with the chocolate mixture. Whisk in the milk, sugar, eggs, yolk, and salt until smooth. Pour the liquid over the bread cubes in the baking pan. Cover with plastic wrap and let it sit for 1 hour, or preferably overnight, in the refrigerator.

When ready to bake, preheat the oven to 325°F [163°C]. Unwrap the baking pan and discard the plastic wrap. Dot the surface of the pudding with the butter, then bake until the top is crisp and the pudding is firm, about 1 hour. Serve warm or at room temperature.

3 SALTINESS

THE WORD "SALT" IS an umbrella term that includes a large group of molecules. In chemistry, a salt is produced from the union of an acid and an alkali; it will contain a positively charged ion and a negatively charged ion. To most cooks, salt represents the tiny white crystals we sprinkle on our food when we cook and just before we eat. But salts are present everywhere in our kitchens. When vinegar (acetic acid) is mixed with baking soda (sodium bicarbonate), they react. The liquid left behind contains a salt called sodium acetate. When baking powder is added to a cake batter, salts are produced by the reaction that occurs between its active components. The marble counters in some of our kitchens is made of a salt called calcium carbonate.

Salt is a key ingredient with which we achieve balance in taste. (Note: We don't really appreciate saltiness until we're four to six months old, as it takes some time for our salt receptors to fully mature.) Without salt, food will simply taste bland. Too much salt can overwhelm the taste buds. Sometimes we add more salt than normal, as when preserving vegetables or fruit such as olives or making preserved lemons (page 318). Here you will learn about what salt does for taste, the different kinds of salt that will enhance your cooking, and how to use it judiciously.

How Saltiness Works

Every crystal of table salt is made up of a metal, sodium [Na+], and a gas, chlorine [Cl-]; together, they form the salt we eat, sodium chloride [NaCl]. Salt is an important source of sodium, which helps give our bones their structure (along with other metals like calcium). The sodium and chlorine in salt also carry electric charges and act as electrolytes in our body.

Pure salt (NaCl) tastes like sea water, but unlike sea water, it has no smell, since sodium chloride has no aroma. The distinct, unmistakable smell we associate with the ocean actually comes from ocean algae that produce a volatile substance called dimethyl sulfide that is released into the atmosphere. For us to taste salt, it must be dissolved in water. Even the flaky bits of salt sprinkled on a salad or a slice of buttered toast must first dissolve in the water present in our saliva. When the salt dissolves, the positively charged sodium and negatively charged chlorine molecules separate and split, and their electric charges come into play. Our nerves and brains communicate via electric currents, and salt is one of the major contributors to this electricity. This currency also enables us to taste the salt in our food.

While it is a universally accepted truth that pure salt will taste salty, there is a slight deviation from this perception of taste. Depending on the concentration of salt in water, tasters report other tastes. At low concentrations, some describe it as mildly sweet; at high concentrations, it starts to taste bitter and sour. Water might be responsible for this perception of sweetness at low concentrations, while at high concentrations, the bitter and sour taste receptors are activated by sodium. There is a reason for this: We need salt to maintain the electrolyte balance of our body, but too much salt is harmful. Sweetness evolved as a response to tell us which foods are nutritive; bitter and sour tastes arose as a way to signal foods that could be toxic. The sweet taste of salt at very low concentrations encourages us to consume more salt, while the bitter and sour tastes at high concentrations help protect us by creating an aversion.

Salts other than sodium chloride create a variety of taste perceptions in addition to saltiness. Sodium acetate and sodium diacetate used in salt-and-vinegar flavored potato chips taste both salty and sour—the salty taste comes from the sodium and the sour from the acetic acid (vinegar).

THE SALTINESS SCALE

Depending on the source and the goals, the quantity of salt can be measured in a few different ways. In the lab where I worked, I used an electrolyte analyzer that directly read out numerical values on a computer screen from my research samples. It gave me a sense of how much sodium and chlorine were present.

But to measure saltiness or how salty a dish might taste, researchers use a subjective measure called a hedonic scale. This tool takes into account whether the taster likes or dislikes a taste and by how much. Similar to the way in which a judge decides what jam or marmalade will win a competition at a food fair, a group of people are selected to taste a variety of food samples, and they rate their responses on a questionnaire. Their responses can be converted to a numerical score, which makes it easier for food scientists and researchers to analyze. Some researchers also record facial reactions of taste testers and report these observations in their studies.

Common Salt and Varieties

Since there was no airport close to my dad's hometown, we always took the train to visit his family in the northern Indian state of Uttar Pradesh. I always picked the berth closest to the window and spent the journey staring out at the passing landscape. As we left the confines of the big city, the landscape would change from lush green hills to sandy deserts. Along this part of the western coast, we'd see large spans of flat land, divided into big squares. Some held water and others mounds of white, dried salt. These were the salt pans of India, where the water was cordoned off and left to dry to produce salt.

Most of the salt we consume is sourced from the ocean, but salt originates in the rocks on land. As rainwater mixes with carbon dioxide in the air, it becomes mildly acidic, and as it falls on rocks, the rainwater dissolves salts and other minerals. This water, rich with leached salts, makes its way to the ocean, where the salt content accumulates. Our salt is extracted from ocean water, marshes, salt lakes, and even salt mines and rocks; the water in which it dissolved is evaporated, heated, or vacuumed off to yield the stuff that makes its way to grocery stores and kitchens.

Some salts undergo several rounds of cleaning and purification to remove all the extra minerals to produce the purest form of salt, called refined salt, which is what most of us are familiar with growing up. But the variety available has exploded in recent years. The spice aisle of my local grocery store has an entire section devoted to salt, a wide variety in different shapes and colors. Some are infused with flavors. You don't need to buy all of them; some will be more beneficial to your cooking than others.

This is how I categorize my salts.

BASIC SALTS

These salts are the ones that I use while I'm cooking. They dissolve quickly, some faster than others.

Table Salt

Table salt is what you see in little glass shakers on restaurant tables: tiny cubic crystals of salt that flow smoothly through the perforated holes of the lid when the shaker is tipped over. Most table salt comes from underground salt mines and is purified to remove any other materials. Because the crystals are minuscule, they dissolve quickly in water.

Because salt by nature is hygroscopic—absorbing water from air, the crystals get wet and coalesce—this salt is mixed with some type of anticaking agent (due to laws and regulations, the chemicals vary by country). You'll sometimes notice uncooked rice grains or coffee beans added to saltshakers or larger jars of salt.

In some countries, as a public health measure, salt is fortified with iodine or fluoride. Should you use iodized or fluorinated salt? I don't, and unless your diet or drinking water (fluoride is added to drinking water in some places to strengthen and protect teeth) is severely lacking in either of these ingredients or your physician recommends it, you don't need to either.

Coarse Salt

As the name suggests, coarse salt has larger crystals than fine table salt. It's best to grind these down with a mortar and pestle or a grinder and sprinkle them over food when seasoning or finishing a dish. When making Preserved Lemons (page 318), I prefer to use coarse salt because it takes longer for the salt to dissolve and the process of extracting the bitter compounds proceeds more steadily. You can also use it to season soups and broths while they're simmering and sprinkle it over fish or meat while grilling.

Rock Salt

Like table salt, rock salt comes from salt mines. I use this salt when I cook oysters Rockefeller, like my version in *Season*. The heat transfers evenly as the oysters sit in their shells on top of a thick bed of rock salt. You can use it to cook whole fish or vegetables such as potatoes and beets.

As the salt heats, it forms a crusty layer around the food, creating a protective seal that traps the moisture inside, resulting in a tender texture. Before serving, the salt crust is broken and discarded before the food is eaten.

Another use for rock salt is in the classic manual ice cream makers, in which salt is mixed with water to lower the freezing temperature. A smaller bucket containing the ice cream base is placed in this water bath and churned until frozen. I do not use this salt to flavor food.

Fine Sea Salt

This is by far my top choice for cooking or baking, savory or sweet. Tiny crystals dissolve quickly, and it's comparatively inexpensive and readily available. Containing nothing but ocean water salt obtained by evaporation, sea salt is unrefined unless the label indicates otherwise; this means there are trace minerals.

Kosher Salt

Kosher salt is a special type of coarse salt that's extremely popular with chefs and many cooks because it dissolves quickly and its texture makes it easier to reach in and grab a quantity with the fingers. The crystals are light, flat, large, and flaky, which helps it stick to food well. Because these flakes occupy a larger volume than regular salt, it is less dense and you actually end up using less salt as you season and cook, which reduces the risk of oversalting a dish.

This is my second top choice of cooking salt for two reasons: The quality of kosher salt varies dramatically by brand (Morton and Diamond Crystal are the two popular brands in North America), and it's not readily available across the globe, so I prefer to use fine sea salt when I develop my recipes.

FANCY SALTS

These salts have intrinsically interesting textures, colors, and flavors, so they're better used as a finishing touch than to provide basic seasoning while cooking—although as you'll see, they have their uses in cooking, too.

Flaky Salt

This is a wonderful salt with large thin, crystals—they look like snowflakes—that can be used to cook with as well as for a finishing salt. I keep a box of Maldon salt flakes in my pantry; the flaky, crunchy crystals create a fantastic texture when sprinkled over chocolate chip cookies or brownies.

Maldon is prepared by collecting the seawater from estuaries in Essex County, England, and drying it out in large salt pans. The salt crystallizes into flakes, which are removed and then dried in an oven.

Several other types of sea salts are popular with chefs, such as *fleur de sel* and *sel gris*. Fleur de sel is harvested from young salt crystals that form during evaporation on the surface of seawater under specific weather conditions. It is also one of the most expensive salts. Sel gris (gray salt) gets its grayish hue from the minerals present in clay that lines the base of the salt pan. To appreciate the full flavor, appearance, and texture of these salts, use them to finish a dish.

Kala Namak or Indian Black Salt

Kala namak—"black salt" in Hindi—is obtained from salt mines and salt lakes in the northern parts of India, Nepal, Bangladesh, and Pakistan. This salt is highly valued for its sulfurous aroma. Though it's called black, the chunky crystals are a deep, dark shade of red. When ground to a powder, the salt is pink.

The salt is mined, then heated in a kiln for several hours to develop color and flavor. This salt owes its unique flavor and color to the presence of iron sulfur compounds. In Indian cooking, kala namak is often used as a finishing salt on street-food snacks, as well as stews and vegetables; I sprinkle it over grilled meats and vegetables and add it to barbecue sauces in place of table salt. The sulfurous aroma does not last in a dish; it dissipates after 30 minutes, so add it just before serving. It works well with spicy and hot flavors and in Spiced Fruit Salad (page 164). This salt is increasingly popular and can be found in many specialty spice stores and Indian grocery stores.

Infused Flavored Salts

There are many types of flavored salts available, some infused with spices and aromatic ingredients such as vanilla or lemon peel, some with naturally occurring flavor and beautiful colors. Hawaiian sea salts come in the red alaea variety and the Hiwa Kai black variety. Volcanic red clay imparts a reddish hue and earthy flavor to the alaea salt, which is used in the preparation of the famous Kalua pork of Hawaiian cuisine. Hiwa Kai gets its color and flavor from charcoal.

Another salt from India, Himalayan pink salt, or *sendha namak*, is noted for its light pink color, which comes from minerals. This salt has become popular for unproven health benefits, but it's a delicious salt with a pretty pink hue that's good for general use.

There is a wide array of choices when it comes to smoked salts depending on what is used for smoking. The crystal sizes range from flaky to fine, and they're helpful when you want to add a bit of smoky flavor without actually smoking the food. Use this on grilled meats or vegetables.

Foods preserved in salt or brine, such as olives, sardines, and pickles, will add saltiness to a dish, so when you include them you'll need to use less salt than you normally would. All the varieties of miso are salty to taste (in addition to their rich savoriness), and you can use this to your advantage (see the Chocolate Miso Bread Pudding, page 133). Unsalted and low-sodium versions of many pantry staples give us greater control over our seasoning during cooking; for this reason I use low-sodium chicken stock, low-sodium soy sauce, and unsalted butter when I cook.

USING SALTINESS IN THE KITCHEN

+ Salt adds texture when sprinkled on as a finishing detail, adding crunch to sweet and savory dishes. Sprinkle on top of savory pastries, fruits, or chocolatey desserts to provide texture and contrast.

+ Salt can affect the solubility of proteins; some will dissolve better in a concentrated solution of salt while others will fall out of solution and precipitate. When salt dissolves in water, it splits into its positively and negatively charged components, and the negatively charged Cl- ions will increase the negative charge on the proteins (proteins have a negative charge), causing changes in the protein's structure. Applying salt to the surface of meat by sprinkling it on or through liquid brines makes some of the muscle protein, myosin, more soluble. As the meat is cooked, the soluble and insoluble parts of the muscle proteins stick together and trap water molecules, making the meat juicy and tender. In the case of ground meat, salt dissolves myosin and encapsulates the fat and water to increase tenderness and juiciness. Keep this in mind when making burgers and ground meat kebabs; add the salt when you're ready to cook, or the meat will lose it juiciness.

+ Salt loves water. It is hygroscopic. When sprinkled over the surface of fruits and vegetables, it pulls the water out by the process of osmosis. As salt dissolves in the water on the surface of a cut vegetable, it creates a highly concentrated solution of salt. Now there is an imbalance between the high salt concentration on the outside of the vegetable and the salt inside its cells. As a result, the water inside the vegetable's cells will start to move outward, trying to correct this imbalance. Cooks can take advantage of this by using salt to draw out the water from vegetables. In the case of pickled vegetables, such as the Cauliflower Aachar (page 320), this helps achieve a firm texture, and in the case of the Tomato Aachari Polenta Tart (page 87), it prevents the crust from getting soggy.

+ Adding salt to a pot of boiling water when cooking vegetables quickens the process by which the hemicellulose that gives structure to vegetable fibers falls apart. In addition, there is a significantly reduced loss of nutrients from the vegetables by osmosis than would happen with pure water. Starchy vegetables like potatoes need more salt when cooked in boiling water, as the starch binds sodium well and reduces the perception of salty taste. When cooking pasta, add a bit more salt than you normally would. Salt helps prevent pasta from getting too sticky by reducing the gelatin-like layer that forms on the surface of pasta as it cooks.

+ The principle of osmosis also applies to meat. Cured meats like salami and gravlax are prepared by adding salt (and in some cases sugar) to draw out the excess moisture and change the structure of the proteins over a long period. The water that comes to the surface evaporates. The reduced water availability and the high concentration of salt prevents the growth of harmful microbes and imbues the meat with flavor.

+ Here's a handy conversion for the weights of different types of salt:
1 tsp fine sea salt = 5.7 g
1 tsp Diamond Crystal kosher salt = 3.3 g
1 tsp Morton's kosher salt = 6.2 g
1 tsp coarse salt = 6.2 g

+ While I can give you some guidance on how to salt your food, how much salt you add depends on your preference and taste. I cannot emphasize this rule enough: Taste your food as you cook, whenever possible. This helps you develop a sense of how much salt works for you. In cases where it is not possible to taste as you cook, such as raw meats and the batter and dough for baked sweets, I provide measurements for how much salt to add. Foods and ingredients that already contain a lot of salt will probably need little to none added. In the case of dishes such as the Chicken Lollipops (page 243), the marinade and flour are salted before the chicken is cooked; I taste one lollipop first to decide if I need to add any more salt to the final coat of sauce applied to the cooked lollipops just before they're served.

+ Use flavored salts or salts infused with food pigments, such as the red color of beets or red or black lava salts, to rim a drink. To do this, spread some of the infused salt on a small plate (you can even add a few sugar crystals, if it works with the flavors). Lightly moisten the mouth of an empty glass with water, lime, or lemon juice, and then invert the glass and press the mouth into the salt.

+ Some condiments that are preserved in salt—such as olives, egg yolks, canned sardines, and lemon and lime preserves—are used to add a spot of saltiness to food. Because they can be quite salty, I recommend tasting the dish after the salty condiment is added, then seasoning with salt as needed.

+ Sodium can displace the calcium present in pectin, which is naturally present in plant-based foods. This, in turn, will help ingredients like beans and potatoes cook faster and become more tender (see Dal Makhani, page 292, and Gunpowder Oven "Fries," page 144).

SALT AND TASTE INTERACTIONS

+ We add a bit of salt to everything, be it savory or sweet, to round out the various flavors. How much salt you add depends on your sensitivity. If you typically add less salt to your food, your taste buds are acclimated to sensing lower amounts of salt. You are more inclined to notice the natural saltiness present in foods. For this reason, it is always best to taste as you cook and add salt as needed.

+ When I cook plain basmati rice, I never add salt. When salt is added to an aromatic rice like basmati, its aroma disappears. The absence of salt does not affect the taste of plain basmati; in fact, it makes the cooked rice taste better. However, if I make a pulao (Goan Shrimp, Olive + Tomato Pulao, page 220; Herb + Paneer Pulao, page 80) or a biryani, I do add salt because several other ingredients including aromatic spices and herbs are added, and they need salt to maximize their flavor.

+ Fish, preserved fish, brined olives, or tomatoes may contain higher levels of salt, so use caution when salting dishes with these ingredients.

+ Salt reduces the intensity of bitterness by masking it. In India, when my parents cooked eggplant, they first salted the vegetable, letting it rest for 30 minutes. Water was wicked off and discarded and bitter molecules were masked.

+ Starch-rich ingredients bind the sodium in salt and decrease our perception of saltiness. When a stock or soup is too salty, you can drop a few chunks of potato or a ball of wet dough in it to absorb the excess salt (discard before serving). When cooking starch-thickened sauces such as roux or Roasted Cauliflower in Turmeric Kefir (see page 83), increase the salt for the same reason.

+ Adding a cooking acid like lemon juice or vinegar enhances the perception of saltiness in food. Use this principle when you want to reduce the amount of salt during cooking.

+ Umami-rich ingredients boost the perception of saltiness. You can test this yourself when using a low-sodium soy sauce or tamari during cooking.

+ Salt affects sweetness. High concentrations of salt reduce the perception of sweetness in food. Sprinkle a bit of salt over an extremely sweet, overripe piece of fruit, such as a peach or mango, and pay attention to how the sweetness pales. Think of how salt offsets the sweetness of caramel candies and chocolate, a recent popular trend.

+ Too much salt can destroy the flavor of fat by breaking it down. Too much salt also causes the red hemoglobin pigment in meat to turn brown as it ages.

"Pizza" Toast

By no means is this a classic pizza in any way, shape, or form, but rather a throwback to a breakfast dish I grew up with. Once I started to get comfortable in the kitchen, I would make breakfast on Sundays, and this "pizza" toast was in constant rotation. It's the sauce that makes it perfect.

MAKES 4 TOASTS

¼ cup [55 g] unsalted butter or
¼ cup [60 ml] extra-virgin olive oil

4 slices sandwich bread

¼ cup [60 ml] My Quick Marinara (page 316) or store-bought pizza sauce

½ cup [40 g] shredded sharp cheddar

1 medium (7 oz [200 g]) bell pepper

1 medium tomato (5 oz [140 g])

Fine sea salt

Fresh coarsely ground black pepper

2 Tbsp chopped cilantro or flat-leaf parsley

1 tsp red chilli flakes, such as Aleppo

THE FLAVOR APPROACH

The major contributor to saltiness in this dish is the tomato sauce, followed by the cheese.

The vegetables provide different textural counterpoints to the toast and the sauce.

Preheat the oven to 350°F [177°C]. Line a baking sheet with parchment paper and set a wire rack on top.

Butter each slice of bread with 1 Tbsp of butter and place them on the wire rack. Spread 1 Tbsp of the marinara sauce on each slice. Sprinkle 1 Tbsp of the cheese over each slice. Cut the bell pepper and tomato into thin rings; reserve 4 and save the rest for another purpose. Place a slice of bell pepper and a slice of tomato on each bread slice. Season with salt and pepper. Sprinkle the remaining cheese over the vegetables on the bread slices. Bake until the cheese is melted and the bread is toasted, 10 to 12 minutes. Remove from the heat. Garnish each toast with ½ Tbsp of the cilantro and some red chilli flakes. Serve immediately.

Gunpowder Oven "Fries" with Goat Cheese Dip

These aren't technically fried, but the slender matchstick cuts deliver the same finger-food experience, and the ghee gives them a comforting nutty perfume. Be generous with the gunpowder masala; you can use more than I recommend in the instructions or serve extra on the side. The idea behind the technique came from a principle used in blood collection, using citric acid and sodium citrate as *chelators*—agents that can bind and hold ions like calcium and magnesium—which in this case improves texture.

MAKES 2 TO 4 SERVINGS

For the fries:

¼ cup [60 ml] fresh lemon juice

1 tsp fine sea salt, plus more as needed

¼ tsp baking soda

⅛ tsp ground turmeric (optional)

Three large russet potatoes (total weight 2 lb [910 g])

2 Tbsp melted ghee

2 Tbsp My "Gunpowder" Nut Masala (page 312)

For the dip:

5 oz [140 g] soft goat cheese or fromage blanc, at room temperature

2 Tbsp full-fat plain Greek yogurt

1 Tbsp chopped flat-leaf parsley

1 Tbsp fresh lemon juice

1 tsp lemon zest

1 garlic clove, peeled and grated

½ tsp ground black pepper

Fine sea salt

THE FLAVOR APPROACH

The ghee provides the oleogustus "taste for fat" that we love in fried foods. Both goat cheese and fromage blanc are salted during their preparation from milk and provide a salty counterpoint to the warm temperature and spices of the potato fries.

Ghee is a fat with a high smoke point, above 450°F [232°C], unlike grapeseed or canola, which would degrade at this high temperature.

A floury or starchy potato, such as the russet, is a good choice for fries because the water content is lower than in the waxy kind (low-starch potatoes). Yukon gold potatoes will also work well here. When a floury potato is cooked, it loses a small quantity of water, so the result is a fuller, denser fry. A waxy potato will release a large quantity of water when cooked, leaving empty space inside the fries.

When the potato strips are partially cooked in water, the starch will gelatinize on the surface, helping to form a crispy shell.

The sodium in the salted water displaces the calcium present in pectin inside the potato, which in turn separates the potato cells to give a soft and creamy interior.

Citric acid in lemon juice also works on pectin and binds the calcium released by sodium, improving the texture. Citric acid also prevents excessive browning by the Maillard reaction, a quality that is considered undesirable in french fries.

Baking soda reacts with the citric acid to produce sodium citrate, which binds and holds calcium and improves texture.

Turmeric is used for color.

To make the fries, in a medium sauce-pan, mix 4 cups [960 ml] of water with the lemon juice, salt, baking soda, and turmeric, if using. The liquid will foam a little.

While the potatoes boil, preheat the oven to 425°F [218°C]. Move the racks in the oven to the center. Line two baking sheets with foil and place a wire rack over each sheet.

Peel the potatoes and cut them into approximately ⅜ by 3½ in [1 by 9 cm] matchsticks. Place the potatoes in the saucepan with the lemon-water

mixture. Place the pan over high heat and bring to a rolling boil. Lower the heat and simmer for 1 minute, until the potatoes are just tender but not falling apart. Carefully drain off the water and place the potatoes in a large bowl. Toss them gently with the melted ghee and season with salt.

Divide the potatoes between the prepared baking sheets, spreading them out in a single layer and leaving enough space between them to cook evenly. Bake until lightly golden brown, 20 to 25 minutes, rotating the sheets and flipping the potatoes with

a spatula or kitchen tongs halfway during cooking. The fries should be soft on the inside and crispy on the outside. Remove them from the oven and sprinkle with the masala, 1 Tbsp per baking sheet.

To prepare the dip, in a small bowl, whisk the cheese, yogurt, parsley, lemon juice, lemon zest, garlic, and pepper. Taste and season with salt, if needed.

Serve the hot fries with the dip.

Paneer + Beet Salad with Mango-Lime Dressing

There is an incomparable joy that I find difficult to express in words when I eat ripe Indian mangoes. During ripening, the starch transforms and gives way to a soft pulp that's sweet and sour, carrying an aroma that reminds me of warm summer holidays in Goa. While mangoes are delicious as a sweet treat, they also make an excellent addition to savory applications. The fruity, sweet flavor of mangoes with lime gives this beet salad a refreshing taste. Try to use a good ripe mango without a chalky aftertaste. It's no surprise that I recommend Indian mangoes, but champagne mangoes are a good option. You'll find paneer in the cheese section at Indian grocery stores as well as most regular food markets.

SERVES 4 PLUS 1½ CUPS [360 ML] DRESSING

For the marinade:

1 cup [240 ml] plain unsweetened kefir, buttermilk, or yogurt

2 tsp fine sea salt

½ tsp ground cumin

½ tsp ground turmeric

½ tsp red chilli powder

½ tsp freshly ground black pepper

14 oz [400 g] firm paneer, homemade (see case study, page 334) or store-bought

For the beets:

4 medium beets (total weight 1 lb [455 g]), ideally a mixture of red and yellow

2 Tbsp extra-virgin olive oil, plus extra for greasing the pan

Fine sea salt

For the mango-lime dressing:

5 oz [140 g] diced ripe mango

½ cup [120 ml] kefir or buttermilk

¼ cup [60 ml] grapeseed or debittered extra-virgin olive oil (see case study, page 104)

1½ Tbsp fresh lime juice

1 Tbsp prepared yellow mustard

¼ tsp freshly ground black pepper

¼ tsp red chilli powder

Fine sea salt

For serving:

7 oz [200 g] arugula leaves

1 Tbsp extra-virgin olive oil

1 tsp freshly ground black pepper

Fine sea salt

2 tsp amchur

cont'd

Paneer is not a salty cheese, so the marinade must contain a bit more salt for the cheese to absorb.

The salad dressing provides a second layer of flavor as well as salt.

While paneer is one of the easiest cheeses you can make at home, I prefer the store-bought variety in this application, where shape and structural integrity are important. It takes the pressure of an extremely heavy weight to bring together the protein molecules in the paneer and force them to coalesce, producing a firm, compact paneer that can hold its shape when cut and cooked. Commercial producers have equipment that generates sufficient pressure; it's a little tricky to do this at home but I've developed a method that you can use (see case study, page 334); otherwise store-bought is perfectly fine.

Whisk the kefir, salt, cumin, turmeric, chilli powder, and black pepper in a small bowl. Taste and season with more salt if needed. Pour the marinade into a large resealable bag.

Cut the paneer into approximately 1 by 2 by ½ in [2.5 cm by 5 cm by 12 mm] cubes and place them in the bag with the marinade, seal, and gently shake to coat evenly. Let the paneer marinate for 1 hour at room temperature. If you need to marinate it longer, leave it in the refrigerator.

Preheat the oven to 400°F [204°C].

While the paneer marinates, prepare the beets. Peel, trim the ends, and cut into quarters. Place the beets in a baking dish or roasting tray, drizzle with the olive oil, and season with salt. Roast for 30 to 45 minutes, until they are tender on the inside and a knife slides through the center with ease. Remove from the oven and let them rest for 10 minutes.

While the beets roast, prepare the dressing. Place the mango, kefir, oil, lime juice, mustard, pepper, and chilli powder into a blender and pulse on slow speed until combined and smooth. Taste and season with salt.

Grill the paneer just before you're ready to assemble the salad. Heat a cast-iron grill pan or a medium nonstick saucepan over medium-high heat and brush the surface with a little olive oil. With a pair of kitchen tongs, carefully lift the paneer out of the bag and cook it in batches in the hot pan until it turns golden brown and is slightly seared, 2 to 3 minutes per side.

To serve, toss the arugula in a large mixing bowl with the olive oil. Add the pepper and season with salt. Add the warm grilled paneer pieces. Drizzle with a few tablespoons of the salad dressing. Sprinkle with the amchur just before serving. Serve the remaining salad dressing on the side.

Green Olives + Chouriço Stuffing

I love the concept of stuffing; it's a blank slate waiting to be painted in flavors that depict who you are. Green olives are my ode to California, while the chouriço, saffron, and vinegar speak for the India I grew up in.

SERVES 8 **TO** 10

1 lb [455 g] ciabatta or sourdough bread

½ cup [110 g] unsalted butter, plus extra for greasing

20 strands saffron

Fine sea salt

11 oz [310 g] chouriço

1 leek (10½ oz [300 g]), ends trimmed and thinly sliced

1 medium yellow onion (9¼ oz [260 g]), thinly sliced

4 garlic cloves, peeled and thinly sliced

2 Granny Smith or other firm, tart baking apples (each about 7 oz [200 g]), cored and diced

3 oz [85 g] dried tart cherries

½ cup [60 g] walnut halves

¼ cup [60 ml] apple cider or malt vinegar

One 6 oz [170 g] can medium green olives, drained and halved

3 cups [720 ml] low-sodium chicken stock

2 large eggs, lightly whisked

2 Tbsp chopped cilantro, for garnish

2 Tbsp chopped flat-leaf parsley, for garnish

THE FLAVOR APPROACH

Salty brined green olives provide a strong taste counterpoint to the bold flavors of the chouriço. To boost the flavor of your chouriço, see Chouriço Pao (page 91) for tips.

Apples and cherries add a pop of sweetness and mild sourness.

Saffron is ground to a fine powder using a little salt as an abrasive. Grinding saffron extracts more color and flavor than would be achieved by using the strands directly.

Drying the bread helps dehydrate it, aids the caramelization and Maillard reactions, and makes the bread behave like a sponge to absorb the liquid on soaking.

The stuffing is first cooked covered, to let the egg proteins change their shape, forming a protein meshwork that binds together the different ingredients and flavor molecules. It is then uncovered to finish cooking at a lower temperature, which helps create a crunchier top surface and reduces the risk of burning.

Preheat the oven to 200°F [93°C] and line a baking sheet with parchment paper. Cut or tear the bread into ½ in [12 mm] cubes, spread them out in a single layer on the baking sheet, and dry in the oven, about 1 hour. Remove and let cool completely. Transfer to a large mixing bowl.

Increase the oven heat to 350°F [177°C]. Grease a 9 by 13 by 2 in [23 by 33 by 5 cm] ceramic or glass baking dish with a little butter.

Grind half of the saffron to a fine powder with a little salt and set aside. Remove and discard the casing from the chouriço and break the sausage into small bits. Heat a medium saucepan over low heat and sauté until the sausage starts to brown, 8 to 10 minutes. Add the butter and stir until it melts. Increase the heat, add the leek and onion, and sauté until they start to turn translucent, 4 to 5 minutes. Add the garlic and sauté for 1 minute. Add the whole and ground saffron strands.

cont'd

Add the apples, cherries, and walnuts and sauté until the cherries get plump, 1 minute. Add the vinegar and remove from the heat. Gently fold in the olives, followed by the dried bread. Season with salt. Transfer the mixture to the prepared baking dish.

In a medium bowl, whisk 1 cup [240 ml] of the stock with the eggs, then whisk in the remaining stock. Pour the liquid over the bread mixture in the baking dish and fold in gently to distribute. At this stage, you can let the baking dish sit for 30 minutes before baking, or cover it with plastic wrap and refrigerate overnight.

When ready to bake the stuffing, discard the plastic wrap. If chilled, leave the baking dish out on the kitchen counter to warm to room temperature, about 15 minutes. Cover the baking dish snugly with a sheet of aluminum foil to form a tight seal and bake for 40 minutes. Lower the heat to 300°F [149°C], remove the foil, and continue to bake, uncovered, until the top is golden brown and crispy and the liquid has completely evaporated, 20 to 30 minutes. A skewer or knife inserted into the center should come out clean. Remove from the oven and let cool for at least 10 minutes. Garnish with the cilantro and parsley and serve warm.

Roasted Tomatoes with Curry Leaves

My first formal introduction to gardening came when we got our backyard in Oakland. I grow all sorts of things—ingredients that are harder to find at grocery stores and the foods I love to eat. Tomatoes fall right into this last category. Sometimes my tomatoes ripen well and sometimes they do fairly okay; this recipe arose out of a need to use the semi-ripe ones or the ones with weaker flavor. I serve this as an appetizer with slices of warm, toasted sourdough and extra salt and pepper on the side. The oil develops a delicious flavor as it gets infused with the curry leaves and garlic, which makes it the ideal candidate to sop up with bread. For an added layer of flavor, use a smoked flaky salt. As for the tomatoes, you can use any kind and color: cherry and grape varieties, or even some of the small and medium ones; larger tomatoes must be halved before they are roasted. If you can get your hands on them, tomatoes ripened on the vine look very attractive in this dish.

MAKES JUST UNDER 2 LB [910 G]

½ cup [120 ml] extra-virgin olive oil

2 lb [910 g] small tomatoes

4 garlic cloves, unpeeled

3 or 4 sprigs fresh curry leaves

1 Tbsp coriander seeds, coarsely cracked

1 tsp coarsely cracked black pepper

Coarse sea salt or flaky salt

Toasted bread, for serving

THE FLAVOR APPROACH

This recipe is an experiment in using heat to concentrate and infuse flavor molecules. As the tomatoes roast in the olive oil, the juices evaporate, which concentrates the salt, sugars, glutamate, and other flavors.

The aromatic flavor molecules in the curry leaves and spices are released on heating, and, thanks to their higher solubility in fats and oil, are absorbed by the oil.

Preheat the oven to 320°F [160°C]. Pour the olive oil into a rectangular 9 by 12 in [23 by 30.5 cm] roasting pan.

Rinse the tomatoes carefully under tap water to remove any dirt. Pat them dry and place them in the roasting pan. Smash the garlic cloves with their paper on and toss them into the pan. Add the curry leaves, coriander seeds, pepper, and salt. Fold to coat well.

Roast for about 1 hour, until the tomatoes have burst and lightly caramelized. Remove the pan from the oven and allow to cool before serving. The tomatoes can be stored, covered, for up to 2 weeks in the refrigerator. Serve warm or at room temperature with the toasted bread.

Couscous with Sesame-Roasted Carrots + Feta

While filming a documentary for PBS in Oakland, my friend Jessica Jones (who produced the video) brought in a delicious couscous salad studded with roasted carrots and a bunch of fresh green herbs. At the time, we had just moved into our home and the furniture hadn't arrived yet, so we squatted on the bare wood floors and ravished that dish rather quickly. It ranks as one of the most flavorful meals I've eaten. I might be a little biased because I think Jessica is absolutely wonderful. This couscous dish, inspired by Jess's couscous, is also simple yet elegant.

SERVES 4 AS A SIDE

For the couscous:

1 lb [455 g] carrots, peeled and cut in half lengthwise

8 garlic cloves, peeled

3 Tbsp extra-virgin olive oil

1 tsp black sesame seeds

1 tsp white sesame seeds

1 tsp red chilli flakes, such as Aleppo, Maras, or Urfa

Fine sea salt

½ tsp ground black pepper

1 cup [240 ml] low-sodium chicken stock, "brown" vegetable stock (page 57), or water

2 bay leaves

¾ cup [135 g] couscous

2 Tbsp chopped cilantro or flat-leaf parsley

¼ cup [30 g] crumbled feta

2 Tbsp chopped mint

For the dressing:

¼ cup [60 ml] rice wine vinegar

2 Tbsp toasted sesame oil

1 Tbsp maple syrup or 2 tsp honey

½ tsp red chilli flakes, such as Aleppo, Maras, or Urfa

Fine sea salt

1 shallot (2 oz [60 g]), thinly sliced

THE FLAVOR APPROACH

Observe how vinegar affects the perception of salt in the shallot and sesame oil dressing. Acids increase the perception of saltiness, and you will end up using less salt than you would otherwise.

The shallot is cut thinly enough to pickle quickly when submerged in the acid in the vinegar. Notice how the pinkish-red anthocyanin pigments in the shallots turn a little more intense once they're in the vinegar. The low pH helps intensify the color.

To prepare the couscous, preheat the oven to 425°F [218°C].

Place the carrots in a roasting pan or baking sheet with 4 of the garlic cloves. Add 1 Tbsp of the olive oil, the black and white sesame seeds, and the red chilli flakes and rub with your fingers to coat the carrots and garlic. Season with salt and the black pepper. Roast for 25 to 30 minutes, until the carrots are crispy on the outside and thoroughly cooked and tender on the inside. Watch carefully to prevent the garlic from burning;

it should be just slightly roasted and charred. Remove the cloves with a pair of kitchen tongs if they're cooking too quickly.

Meanwhile, place the stock and the remaining 2 Tbsp of olive oil in a medium saucepan over medium-high heat. Smash the remaining 4 garlic cloves and toss them into the stock along with the bay leaves. Season with salt and bring the stock to a boil. Stir in the couscous, remove from the heat, cover with a lid, and let stand until the couscous absorbs

the stock and swells up, about 5 minutes. Fluff the couscous with a fork.

To make the dressing, combine the vinegar, sesame oil, maple syrup, and chilli flakes in a small bowl. Season with salt. Fold in the shallots and let sit for 15 minutes.

To serve, fold the cilantro into the couscous. Place the roasted carrots and garlic on top. Garnish with the feta and mint. Pour the dressing on top and serve warm or at room temperature.

Roasted Tomato + Tamarind Soup

On a cold day or when you're feeling a bit under the weather, this is a peppery tomato soup you'll want to have in your repertoire. This is a soup of contrasting flavors that goes well with a sharp cheddar or salty feta on buttered toast. Kashmiri chilli powder is a mild, bright-red chilli that can be purchased at Indian grocery stores as well as international markets and specialty spice stores.

SERVES 4

1½ lb [680 g] large ripe tomatoes, quartered

4 garlic cloves, peeled

1 tsp black or brown mustard seeds

1 tsp coriander seeds

1 tsp cumin seeds

1 tsp ground turmeric

1 tsp whole black peppercorns

¼ tsp asafetida

2 Tbsp extra-virgin olive oil

Fine sea salt

1 tsp red chilli powder

1 tsp dark brown sugar or jaggery, plus extra as needed

1 Tbsp tamarind paste, homemade (see page 67) or store-bought

Extra-virgin olive oil or mustard oil, for garnish

Coarsely ground black pepper, for garnish

Warm buttered toast, for serving

THE FLAVOR APPROACH

Tomatoes are a rich source of different taste molecules including salt; preroasting tomatoes concentrates the salts and also creates new flavor molecules in addition to the salt, sugars, and glutamate already present in the tomatoes.

Tamarind provides sourness to complement the sweet, sour, and savory taste of the tomatoes.

Adding a bit of sugar helps reduce the impression of acidity from the tomatoes and tamarind.

Taste this soup when warm and compare with chilled leftovers to observe how the perception of salt and acid changes with temperature. For a hotter feel to the soup, replace the Kashmiri chilli powder with ¼ tsp to ½ tsp of cayenne and a generous pinch of quality red chilli flakes.

Preheat the oven to 425°F [218°C].

Quarter the tomatoes and place them on a baking sheet or roasting pan. Add the garlic, the mustard, coriander, and cumin seeds, turmeric, black peppercorns, and asafetida. Drizzle with olive oil, toss, and season with salt. Roast the tomatoes cut-side up until they start to brown, about 30 minutes. If the garlic starts to burn, remove and set aside. Remove from the heat and transfer the contents of the pan to the bowl of a blender or a food processor.

Add the red chilli powder, sugar, 3 cups [720 ml] of water, and the tamarind. Pulse until completely smooth and combined. Taste and season with salt and/or sugar if needed.

To serve, portion the hot soup into four bowls. Drizzle each with a few drops of olive or mustard oil and a generous sprinkling of black pepper. Serve with warm buttered toast.

Grilled Spiced Chicken Salad with Amchur

This is my weekday afternoon salad. The salad itself is very simple—a splash of lime juice and a bit of amchur for a dose of acidity—but it's the chicken that carries the strongest punch of flavor. You can also use this chicken in sandwiches for a brunch or picnic menu, served with a little mayonnaise. Depending on what I have at home, I sometimes add 2 Tbsp of fresh herbs such as mint, cilantro, or tarragon. Both breast and thigh meat from the chicken work here.

You will need to plan a few hours in advance to marinate the chicken. Here's a kitchen trick that I use at home to plan ahead for the week: I marinate the chicken for 1 hour in the refrigerator, then freeze it with the marinade in small batches in resealable bags. Whenever you're ready to cook the chicken, thaw it in the refrigerator overnight or leave it out on the kitchen counter and then cook it.

SERVES 4

4 boneless, skinless chicken thighs (total weight about 1 lb [455 g])

¼ cup [60 ml] plus 2 Tbsp extra-virgin olive oil (you can use debittered; see case study, page 104), plus extra for greasing

¼ cup [60 ml] red wine vinegar

1 tsp ground coriander

1 tsp ground cumin

1 tsp red chilli powder

1 tsp fine sea salt, plus more as needed

½ tsp freshly ground black pepper, plus more as needed

2 heads butter lettuce (total weight 14 oz [400 g]), leaves separated and torn

3 shallots (total weight 6½ oz [180 g]), thinly sliced

12 oz [340 g] cherry tomatoes, sliced in half

2 Tbsp fresh lime juice

Fine sea salt

Freshly ground black pepper

1½ to 2 tsp amchur

THE FLAVOR APPROACH

The marinade for the chicken acts as a flavor booster and also as a brining solution.

The salt and acid present in the vinegar in the brine create favorable conditions for the salt to diffuse and other ingredients to flavor the meat. Together salt and acid affect protein structure and increase the water retention capacity of the chicken breast. The result is a chicken breast that's juicier and more tender.

Pat the chicken thighs dry with clean paper towels and place them in a resealable bag. In a medium bowl, combine the ¼ cup [60 ml] of olive oil, the vinegar, coriander, cumin, red chilli powder, salt, and black pepper. Pour over the chicken in the bag, shake to coat evenly, and seal. Refrigerate the bag to marinate for at least 4 hours and up to 8 hours. When ready to cook, bring the bag out and leave on the kitchen counter for at least 15 minutes to warm to room temperature.

Heat a grill pan over medium-high heat. Brush the grates with a little oil. Take the chicken thighs out of the bag with a pair of kitchen tongs, tapping them on the side of the bag to get rid of any excess liquid. Place the chicken on the hot grates and grill until they are completely cooked (165°F [74°C] on an instant-read thermometer) and develop grill marks on each side, 4 to 5 minutes per side. Transfer the chicken to a plate and let rest for 5 minutes. Cut the chicken into strips.

Place the lettuce leaves, shallots, and cherry tomatoes in a large bowl. Whisk the lime juice and remaining 2 Tbsp of olive oil in a small bowl and pour it over the vegetables in the bowl. Season with salt and black pepper and toss to coat evenly. To serve, place the chicken on top of the salad and sprinkle the amchur on top.

Beef Chilli Fry with Pancetta

This is my take on a classic Goan dish that I grew up eating, served over a bowl of warm, Plain Rice (page 310). The classic method does not use pancetta; however, I find it adds a nuanced note of flavor. If you're a meat-and-potatoes type person, this one is for you. The Braised Cabbage with Coconut (page 291) is a good accompaniment to this dish.

SERVES 4

4 oz [115 g] diced pancetta

2 Yukon gold potatoes (total weight 15½ oz [445 g]), peeled and diced into ½ in [12 mm] cubes

Fine sea salt

2 Tbsp extra-virgin olive oil

2 yellow onions (total weight 18 oz [500 g]), cut in half and thinly sliced

6 garlic cloves, peeled and minced

1 in [2.5 cm] piece fresh ginger, peeled and grated

6 cloves, ground

1 tsp ground black pepper

1 tsp ground cinnamon

1 tsp ground turmeric

1 lb [455 g] flank steak

2 Tbsp malt or apple cider vinegar

¼ cup [10 g] fresh cilantro, chopped

2 or 3 fresh chillies, minced

THE FLAVOR APPROACH

Pancetta is a type of cured pork that develops flavor substances during the curing process. When the pancetta is cooked, it acts as a flavor booster by adding a layer of fat and salt that's released by heat.

The flavor boosters are heated in hot oil to extract their fat-soluble fiery molecules. The onion's pungency is tamed by cooking it for a few minutes, which helps make the taste of their sugars more obvious and softens the impact of heat in every bite.

Heat a large stainless-steel or cast-iron saucepan over medium-low heat. Add the pancetta and sauté until the fat renders and the meat starts to brown, 5 to 8 minutes. Add the potatoes and season with salt. Cook until the potatoes turn golden brown and are completely cooked but crispy on the outside, about 30 minutes. Remove the potatoes and pancetta and transfer to a medium bowl.

In the same saucepan, heat the oil over medium-high heat. Add the onions and sauté until they turn translucent, 4 to 5 minutes. Add the garlic and ginger and sauté until fragrant, about 1 minute. Add the ground cloves, black pepper, cinnamon, and turmeric and cook until fragrant, 30 to 45 seconds. Transfer the onions with the spices to a small bowl and leave the saucepan on the stove over medium-high heat.

Pat the steak dry with paper towels. Cut the steak against the grain into ½ by 1 in [12 mm by 2.5 cm] cubes. Season with salt and add the steak to the hot saucepan. Cook until the beef is tender and medium-rare (130°F [54°C] on an instant-read thermometer), 4 to 5 minutes. Turn the heat to low and scrape the bottom of the pan to mix the drippings with the beef. Fold in the cooked potatoes, onions, and pancetta. Sprinkle with the vinegar. Taste and season with salt if needed. Transfer from the heat to a serving dish, garnish with the cilantro and chillies, and serve immediately.

Lamb Chops with Scallion Mint Salsa

The seasoning on these lamb chops envelops them in a jacket of flavor, while the scallion and mint salsa is the bright green scarf that makes it all dressed up for a fancy dinner party. Halve the amount of garlic for a milder flavor. Toum (page 315) is a great alternative or accompaniment to the salsa.

SERVES 4

For the lamb:

8 lamb rib chops (total weight 2 lb [910 g])

¼ cup [60 ml] fresh lemon juice

4 Tbsp [60 ml] extra-virgin olive oil

1 tsp amchur

1 tsp ground black pepper

1 tsp red chilli powder

1 tsp fennel seeds, coarsely cracked

2 tsp kala namak, or more as desired

**For the salsa
(makes 1½ cups [360 ml]):**

½ cup [120 ml] extra-virgin olive oil

¼ cup [60 ml] fresh lemon juice

1 bunch fresh mint (2 oz [55 g]), chopped

4 scallions, both white and green parts, thinly sliced

4 garlic cloves, peeled and minced

1 tsp ground black pepper

1 fresh green chilli, minced

Fine sea salt

THE FLAVOR APPROACH

Kala namak, or Indian black salt, acts as the brining salt and also as a flavoring agent for the meat.

The combination of salt and acid in the marinade changes the lamb's protein structure. In the case of red meat, the tough collagen starts to solubilize, and the tissue swells as it retains water and is tenderized. The cooked meat will be tender and juicy.

To prepare the lamb, pat the chops dry with clean paper towels and place them in a large resealable bag. In a small bowl, mix the lemon juice, 2 Tbsp of the olive oil, amchur, black pepper, chilli powder, fennel, and kala namak and pour it over the lamb chops in the bag. Seal the bag and shake to coat the chops well. Leave the chops to marinate in the refrigerator for at least 2 hours, preferably 6 hours.

An hour before you're ready to cook, prepare the salsa. In a lidded bowl, mix the olive oil, lemon juice, mint, scallions, garlic, black pepper, and chilli. Taste and season with salt. Cover and let stand until ready to serve.

When you're ready to cook the chops, leave them in the plastic bag out on the kitchen counter for at least 15 minutes to warm to room temperature.

Cook the marinated chops in batches. Heat 1 Tbsp of olive oil in a large stainless-steel or cast-iron skillet over medium-high heat. When the pan is hot, lift 4 chops out of the bag with a pair of kitchen tongs and place them on the hot pan for 3 to 4 minutes per side for rare and 5 to 6 minutes per side for medium-rare (on an instant-read thermometer, 145°F [62.8°C] for rare and 160°F [71°C] for medium-rare). Repeat with the remaining 1 Tbsp of olive oil and the remaining chops. Transfer the chops to a plate, tent loosely with foil, and let rest for 5 minutes before serving.

Before serving, garnish the lamb with the scallion mint salsa. Serve warm.

Spiced Fruit Salad

Most recipes capture a point of view in time and are versions of other versions; they reveal how ideas evolve. I originally created a version of this recipe for my column at the *San Francisco Chronicle*, which was inspired by the fruit chaats of India.

SERVES 4

1 yellow nectarine or peach (9¼ oz [260 g]), ripe but still firm

1 plum (3 oz [85 g]), ripe but still firm

14 oz [400 g] mixed grapes

12 fresh mint leaves

2 Tbsp lime juice

¼ cup [60 ml] maple syrup

2 Tbsp pomegranate molasses

1 tsp red chilli flakes, such as Aleppo, Maras, or Urfa

½ tsp fennel seeds, lightly cracked

½ tsp freshly ground black pepper

½ tsp kala namak, or more as desired

THE FLAVOR APPROACH

Kala namak, or Indian black salt, complements the spices by releasing its unique sulfurous aroma as soon it meets water.

The salt and sweeteners help draw out the juices from the fruit through the combined mechanisms of osmosis and maceration.

Cut the nectarine in half and discard the stone. Cut each half into thin slices and place them in a large mixing bowl. Repeat with the plum. Add the grapes to the fruit in the bowl. Add the mint.

Whisk together the lime juice, maple syrup, pomegranate molasses, and red chilli flakes in a small mixing bowl.

Toast the fennel seeds in a small dry skillet over medium-high heat until they just start to turn brown and get fragrant, 30 to 45 seconds. Quickly transfer to a mortar and pestle, crush to crack the seeds, and add them to the fruit. Add the pepper and kala namak and fold gently to coat. Taste and add more kala namak if needed. Cover the bowl with a lid and allow to sit in the refrigerator for at least 30 minutes before serving.

4

SWEETNESS

WHEN I WORKED AS A PASTRY COOK at Sugar, Butter, Flour, my responsibilities included preparing large batches of frostings in addition to assembling the various pastries and cakes. Large tubs of various types of sugars were neatly labeled to avoid the risk of a mix-up. Unfortunately, one day somehow the lids got switched and I ended up using a large quantity of cornstarch instead of confectioner's sugar to make a frosting. You can imagine what happened next—a tasteless, chalky-textured mass of cream. There was no option but to clean up and start from scratch. Carbohydrates are the main energy source for humans, and our ability to taste the sweetness of sugars evolved as a guide to help us seek foods that provide energy for our metabolic needs. Sugars are also responsible for several food textures that we want in baked foods such as breads and cakes. We also rely on sugars as the main source of energy for bacteria and yeasts during fermentation to produce acids like vinegar, alcohols such as wine, and ingredients like bread and yogurt.

How Sweetness Works

When you take a bite out of a ripe plum, lick the scoop of ice cream in a cone, or eat a spoonful of honey, you taste sweetness. The sugars present in these foods are responsible for this sweet taste (see Carbohydrates and Sugars, page 331), but some proteins and other substances (see Amino Acids, Peptides, and Proteins, page 333) can also create that taste. When we eat sweet foods and beverages, the sugar molecules dissolve in our saliva and travel directly to our taste receptors. More complex carbohydrates like starch are broken down to individual sugars like glucose by the enzyme amylase, which we then taste as sweet. (This is an extremely mild level of sweetness in the mouth that you can try out for yourself. Refrain from eating or drinking water for at least 30 minutes, then put a small piece of bread on your tongue; you'll pick up a mild hint of sweetness.) These sweet-tasting ingredients will travel and bind the sweetness receptors (T1R2 and T1R3; T=taste, R=receptor) with varying degrees of strength, which in turn sends a signal to our brain that tells us our food is sweet, and also how sweet.

THE SWEETNESS SCALE

To create the sweetness scale that can be used to gauge the relative intensity of sweetness of various ingredients, the taste of various sweeteners is compared to table sugar (sucrose). The less sweet a substance, the lower its value. Most sugar substitutes, whether natural like stevia or artificial like sucralose, are extremely sweet when compared to table sugar.

Keep in mind that many of the sweeteners listed in the table here are sold in a solid or liquid form and can behave differently in recipes for cakes and ice creams, and several sweeteners like lactose, honey, maple syrup, molasses, and agave have their own intrinsic aromas and tastes, which will affect the final flavor of the food.

Pure, refined sugar is sweet to taste, but it has no characteristic aroma.

Sugar	% Sweetness*
Starch	0
Cellulose	0
Lactose	20
Maltose	30
Galactose	35
Maple syrup	60
Glucose	70
Molasses	70
Honey	97
Sucrose (table sugar)	100
High-fructose corn syrup	120
Agave	140
Fructose	170
Aspartame	180
Stevia	250
Saccharin	300
Sucralose (Splenda)	600

*Compared to sucrose

Sweetness Boosters

Several types of liquid and solid sugars are used as sweeteners. Some, like white sugar, have no unique flavor profiles other than sweetness but are valued for the neutral taste profile against which other flavors in the recipe can stand out and the reliability they provide in recipes such as baked goods. The information in the following tables will give you an appreciation for the different sugars—what they are and what they do.

NONCARBOHYDRATE-BASED SWEETENERS AND SUGAR SUBSTITUTES

Some amino acids and proteins can taste sweet. A few years ago, my friend Jessica introduced me to miraculin—the protein from the miracle berry—and I found its effect on taste astonishing. Miraculin can change the taste of any sour ingredients like vinegar and limes and make them appear sweet. You can try it for yourself: Start out by chewing the berry, wait for a few minutes, and then take a slice of a raw lemon. The lemon will not taste sour; it will taste sweet.

There are several sugar substitutes available in the market; some come from plants, such as stevia, while others are synthetics produced in laboratories, like aspartame. These substances provide sweetness, carry few to no calories, and are not metabolized like sugar in the body, but when it comes to baking, they simply do not work very well.

Because many of these substitutes are chemically different from sugars, they do not replicate the textures of a cake or cookie very well, as they cannot leaven or make a cake tender. Of all the sweeteners, saccharin and sucralose are heat stable. Most other substitutes are unstable in high baking temperatures. In addition, most sugar substitutes are also several times sweeter than table sugar (see The Sweetness Scale, page 169), so the amounts must be adjusted accordingly, and a few of them leave an aftertaste that might be noticeable and affect the final taste of a dish. As they aren't sugars, they cannot contribute to the flavor and color developing reactions, such as caramelization or the Maillard reaction, so a cake might not brown as expected.

OTHER SOURCES OF SUGAR IN OUR FOOD

Most fruits are sweet, to varying degrees. As fruits ripen, the cells convert some of the stored starch to sweet sugars such as glucose and fructose. Vegetables contain modest amounts of glucose and fructose (0.3% to 4%) and sucrose (0.1% to 12%). In dairy milk, the main source of sugar is lactose, which can vary between 4% and 6% depending on the animal and the breed (cow's milk is approximately 4.8%, varying a little by breed).

QUICK TIPS FOR BOOSTING FLAVOR WITH SWEETNESS

+ Sprinkle jaggery or one of the darker raw sugars such as muscovado over grilled or broiled fruit and when baking sweet breads or desserts. They also work great in upside-down cakes.

+ For drinks and cocktails, moisten the mouth of the glass with a bit of citrus juice (depending on your drink, the choice of citrus can vary to complement the flavor of your drink) and press the glass gently over a plate containing raw sugar with a few salt flakes.

+ When making caramel, replace the plain sugar with jaggery, brown sugar, or dark raw sugars for a more interesting taste. Pay careful attention when caramelizing the sugar, as these darker sugars can heat faster and the transition to the deep caramel color occurs quickly.

+ Maple syrup and honey can be paired and infused with a variety of spices, such as black pepper, cinnamon, coriander, fennel, and green cardamom, as well as aromas like orange blossom, lavender, pandan, and turmeric leaves. For dried spices, crush and toast them gently for 30 to 45 seconds, then toss them into the syrup. For aromatic infusions when using flowers and leaves, warm the liquid sweetener first and then let them steep for a few hours before using.

+ Make scented sugars by grinding peels of citrus fruits or leaves of makrut limes or the curry plant, and spices such as vanilla beans and green cardamom. These can be stored indefinitely in airtight containers and used as a garnish just before serving a sweet treat or a drink.

+ A drizzle of maple syrup, honey, or golden syrup on a stack of pancakes is a welcome blend of textures.

+ Garnish hot broiled or roasted fruit with a sprinkling of powdered jaggery or panela for texture and sweetness.

+ Glaze baked buns with golden syrup (see Chouriço Pao, page 91), honey, or maple syrup for a sweet finish and shine.

+ Dusting confectioner's sugar and a layer of sweet frosting on cakes provides visual detail, contrast, and texture.

+ Coarse sugar crystals that do not dissolve easily can provide a textural contrast in gingersnap cookies (and in my favorite childhood chocolate cookie sandwich, the Bourbon cookie).

In baking, sugar plays several important roles in addition to providing sweetness:

+ In breads raised with yeast and bacterial fermentation, sugar acts as a source of energy for the microbes to create carbon dioxide and acid, helping give the bread its airy texture.

+ Sugars participate in the caramelization and Maillard reaction to produce golden-brown colors and a variety of flavor molecules that we inhale and taste.

+ Sugar acts as a humectant, attracting and binding moisture, which helps prevent foods from getting dry and stale.

+ Sugar is an important contributor to leavening in cakes and breads because it helps maintain air bubbles.

+ When flour is mixed with sugar, the sugar interferes with the gluten formation that could otherwise make a cake or pastry's mouthfeel tough and unpalatable.

+ Maceration: Sugar, like salt, is hygroscopic and attracts water. When sugar is sprinkled onto thin-skinned fruit such as berries or over cut slices of thick-skinned fruit such as apples, the water inside the fruit's cells begins to travel outward to the exterior, bringing with it some of the aroma and taste molecules. As the water exits, the cells soften and the fruit juices that collect make a delicious fruit syrup. You can also macerate fruit with flavored liquids such as wine, liqueurs, vinegar, and sweetened water mixed with spices. The pickled nectarines (page 319) and the fruit salad (page 164) employ this principle. Sometimes heat is applied to hasten the process of drawing out the flavor molecules from ingredients, as seen in the simple syrup infused with ginger in the Hibiscus (Ginger Pepper) Refresher (page 266).

+ Warm temperatures can increase the perception of a sweetener in a dessert, whereas low temperatures, as in sorbets and ice creams, reduce the perceived level of sweetness.

+ Pastry chefs and candy makers know how to manipulate sugar to form all sorts of delicious and exciting confectioneries because they know how sugar behaves when heated. When a saturated solution of sugar (one in which no more sugar will dissolve in that specific volume of water at a specific temperature) is heated, sugar's molecules undergo changes in their physical properties. Depending on the temperature, you can use sugar to make soft candies such as Peppermint Marshmallows (page 196) or hard candies such as lollipops. Sugar has a tendency to crystallize when heated; to avoid this, chefs use acidic ingredients such as cream of tartar or lemon juice or add an invert sugar such as corn syrup.

+ It's important to know the right amount of sweetener to use when cooking because too much can spoil the taste and inhibit the perception of the various other tastes in the dish.

+ Sugar can make acids more palatable. Adding a sweetener mellows the sourness of acidic ingredients like lemons in lemon curd or lime in a glass of limeade.

+ Sugar can mask bitterness. When sugar is stirred into a cup of coffee, it directly interacts with the bitter molecules and suppresses their bitter taste. The bitter taste of brassica vegetables, such as cabbage, is also reduced when sugar is added to raw cabbage. When sugar is caramelized by heating, it produces a combination of bitter and sweet taste molecules that we seek out when we cook onions over low heat for a long time or make caramel (see Hazelnut Flan, page 126) for sweets.

+ A small amount of sugar can enhance the savory notes of a dish, but I find salt does a better job.

+ Sometimes recipes that involve the use of hot, fiery ingredients like chillies will call for the addition of a tiny amount of sugar to help reduce some of the heat intensity. Many classic Goan recipes in India (and even some Thai curry recipes) call for palm jaggery to suppress some of the heat.

+ Sweet cooking wines, such as Shaoxing and mirin, can be used to enhance the meaty flavors of braised meats and stir-fries. The sugars in these wines also participate in the flavor, creating effects such as caramelization and the Maillard reaction.

+ Sweeteners that boast rich, earthy profiles—like molasses, jaggery, raw sugars, and brown sugar—work great in barbecue sauces and roasts because they create deeper, more complex flavor notes (see the ribs, page 89).

Sweetener	Color and Texture	Aroma and Taste	Description	Uses	Kitchen Notes
Jaggery/Gur	Jaggery comes in various color grades from light brown to dark. The palm variety has a dark, molasses-like color. Sold as a solid block or as a powder. Always store it in a dry, airtight container away from light, as it can absorb moisture quickly from the air.	Less sweet than sugar with a mineral and slightly salty taste. Jaggery obtained from palm sugar has a very different taste, with hints of caramel.	An unrefined sugar obtained from raw sugar cane juice or unfermented palm tree (coconut) sap by boiling the liquid in large pans.	A sweetener often used in Indian cuisine. Use it as you would sugar for a finishing touch on desserts or bread, or incorporate into baking and ice cream recipes. It can be substituted for brown sugar in most recipes.	I prefer the ground, pre-powdered stuff sold in jars in Indian stores because it is much easier to work with. Fresh blocks of jaggery can be chopped with a knife and stored in a sealed container or bag. If too hard, the block can be grated or broken into small pieces with a heavy tool.
Panela	A hard solid that is available in a lighter color, called *blanco*, and a darker variety, called *oscuro*.	The taste is similar to molasses; the oscuro variety has a much stronger flavor.	An unrefined sugar obtained by concentrating sugarcane juice.	A sweetener used in Central and South American cuisines. The names vary by the country and the language (*piloncillo/chancaca/rapadura*). It's a bit firmer than jaggery and is usually sold in cone-shaped blocks.	Use as a substitute for brown sugar. Grate or chop with a serrated knife before using. If it is too hard, warm it for a few seconds in a microwave to soften.
Brown sugar	Brown-colored sugar crystals that come in two grades: light and dark.	It has a distinct molasses-like flavor. The dark grade brown sugar has a richer molasses flavor.	A refined sugar prepared by adding molasses to sugar.		Store in a dry container because it absorbs moisture easily. Can be used in sweet and savory preparations.
Raw sugar	A purified form of sugar available in different varieties: Demerara is white sugar with added molasses; Barbados/Muscovado is moist, dark, with fine-textured grains; Turbinado has light-brown crystals; Sucanat is a branded product, with small brown grainy crystals.	Demerara: toffeelike flavor. Barbados/Muscovado: deep, rich, molasses flavor. Turbinado: mild caramel flavor. Sucanat: intense, smoky molasses taste	The various grades of raw sugar are obtained from purified sugarcane residues during processing of the juice.		Muscovado is a close substitute for jaggery in flavor. Sucanat does not dissolve in liquids quickly and might need to be ground to a powder before use.
White sugar	Pure white, available in crystals of various sizes—coarse to superfine.	Pure sweetness, without aroma.	A refined sugar obtained from sugarcane or sugar beets.		Superfine sugar dissolves quickly and works great in baking and dessert recipes; it is my go-to baking sugar for almost all my dessert recipes. Used in sweet and savory recipes.
Confectioner's sugar, powdered sugar, 10x sugar, icing sugar	A white powder, fine as dust.	No unique aroma or taste, other than sweetness.	Obtained by powdering refined white sugar and mixing it with a small amount of cornstarch to prevent clumping in the presence of moisture.		Used to garnish by sifting over desserts, but do this right before serving, as sugar can absorb moisture quickly and get sticky. It can thicken sauces quickly because the sugar dissolves quickly and also contains a small amount of cornstarch. The presence of cornstarch and the small size of the sugar particles can affect the final shape and texture of cookies and cakes when baking.
Golden syrup, light treacle	A thick, pale golden-yellow liquid.	A noticeable buttery flavor.	Obtained from sugar (sugarcane) but is an invert sugar.	Used in British cuisine, especially in baking.	Used as a sweetener for desserts but also to brush onto the surface of baked breads.

Sweetener	Color and Texture	Aroma and Taste	Description	Uses	Kitchen Notes
Molasses, black treacle (UK)	A thick, viscous, dark-brown liquid.	Sugar cane molasses: First Molasses/Grade A/cane syrup/light molasses/Barbados is the sweetest. Second Molasses/Grade B/dark molasses has a mild bitter taste. Third Molasses/Grade C/blackstrap molasses is less sweet, due to a very low sugar amount, but with a noticeable bitter flavor. Sulfured molasses is obtained by treating the sugarcane with sulfur dioxide fumes, which leaves behind a distinct chemical flavor. Always use unsulfured molasses. Sugar beet molasses is obtained at the final stage. Because of its flavor, unpalatable to humans, it's typically used in cattle feed.	An unrefined sweetener obtained during the production of sugar from sugarcane or sugar beets.	Used in North American and European cuisines in both sweet and savory preparations.	For both savory and sweet cooking, use either light molasses, dark molasses, or black treacle. Never use blackstrap molasses unless specified in a recipe; it has an intense bitter taste and a much lower sugar content, which often leads to undesirable outcomes in both texture and flavor.
Honey	Usually sold in a thick liquid form. Honey powder is a solid form of honey obtained by dehydrating and then grinding honey to produce a fine powder. Raw honey is unpasteurized honey.	Aromas and taste can vary depending on the source of the honey. Some sources include orange blossom, clover, and manuka.	Honey is produced by bees from the nectar they harvest from flowers.		Used in sweet and savory preparations.
Maple Syrup	Usually sold in liquid form. Maple syrup powder is obtained by removing the water through dehydration. Grade A Maple Syrup classified by color: Light Amber (golden) Medium Amber Dark Amber Very Dark	Grade A Maple Syrup Light Amber: Delicate taste Medium Amber: Rich taste Dark Amber: Robust taste Very Dark: Very strong taste	An unrefined liquid obtained from the sap of maple trees in North America.		Used in sweet and savory preparations.
Corn syrup	Sold in liquid form. Comes in three grades: light, dark (caramel food coloring is added), and high-fructose corn syrups.	Light corn syrup is flavored with vanilla; dark syrup is flavored with caramel.	Obtained during the processing of cornstarch.		Baking and savory preparation. They are valuable in the preparation of ice creams because they prevent the crystallization of sugars.
Date syrup (*silan*; page 324), date molasses	Usually sold in a viscous liquid form; has a dark caramellike color.	Toasty, fruity, molasses-like, mildly acidic taste.	An unrefined sweetener prepared by extracting the sugar from dates in boiling water, followed by concentration.	Used in Persian, Middle Eastern, and North African cuisine.	Used in sweet and savory preparations.
Pekmez	Usually sold in a thick liquid form.	Fruity, molasses-like taste varies depending on the fruits used.	Obtained by concentrating a variety of sugar-rich fruits such as grapes, figs, mulberries, and/or dates.	Used in Turkish, Azerbaijani, and Greek cooking.	Used in sweet and savory preparations.
Malt syrup and extract	A thick, viscous brown liquid.	Has a malt-like aroma.	An unrefined sweetener obtained from germinated whole grains such as barley.	One of the earliest sweeteners known to man.	Used in baking and in sweet and savory preparations.

Baked Sweet Potatoes with Maple Crème Fraîche

We all adore certain pantry staples. Kefir and crème fraîche are two of my favorites. I've been testing new ways to improve on roasting sweet potatoes in the oven, and I found that a combination of steaming and roasting works great for a dish like this for both the texture and the extra set of aroma molecules that comes through. The first step, partial steaming, keeps the moisture inside the sweet potato while cooking, and the second step, uncovered roasting, helps create a robust flavor profile. I recommend using fragrant nuts. Toasted hazelnuts are a good substitute for the peanuts.

SERVES 4

For the sweet potatoes:

4 sweet potatoes (each 7 oz [200 g]), preferably a yellow-fleshed variety such as Garnet or Jewel

2 Tbsp unsalted butter, at room temperature

Fine sea salt

For the dressing:

½ cup [120 g] crème fraîche or sour cream

1 Tbsp maple syrup or honey

1 Tbsp fresh lime juice

2 tsp fish sauce (optional)

½ tsp ground black pepper

Fine sea salt

For garnish:

2 Tbsp thinly sliced scallions, both green and white parts

2 Tbsp roasted peanuts

1 tsp red chilli flakes, such as Aleppo, Maras, or Urfa

½ tsp lime zest

THE FLAVOR APPROACH

Butter works as the fat of choice here due to its higher smoke point. As the butter melts, it separates into its constituents—fat, water, sugars, and milk solids—which undergo caramelization and the Maillard reaction.

The sugars concentrate as the water evaporates during cooking.

Fish sauce adds a spot of umami to the sauce, but you can use vegan fish sauce as an alternative.

The peanuts and scallions provide crunch against the softer textures of the potato and the dressing.

To prepare the sweet potatoes, preheat the oven to 400°F [204°C].

Rinse and scrub the sweet potatoes under running tap water. Slice them lengthwise and place them in a roasting pan, cut side facing up. Brush with the butter and season with salt. Cover the pan with a sheet of aluminum foil and press around the edges to seal snugly. Bake for 20 minutes. After 20 minutes, remove the foil, flip the sweet potatoes, and cook, uncovered, for 20 minutes more, until the sweet potatoes are cooked thoroughly and are tender; a knife inserted into the center of the sweet potato should slide through easily. Remove from the heat and let rest for 5 minutes.

To prepare the dressing, in a small bowl, combine the crème fraîche, maple syrup, lime juice, fish sauce, if using, and pepper. Taste and season with salt.

To serve, top the warm roasted potatoes with a few tablespoons of the maple crème fraîche dressing. Sprinkle with the scallions, peanuts, red chilli flakes, and lime zest. Serve with the extra dressing on the side.

Crispy Carrots with Garlic + Mint Tahini

Go for the rainbow variety of carrots if available. Their colors shimmer through the sequined crust of crumbs, making a visual treat full of crunchy goodness. If you love garlic and want a bigger punch of flavor, add a few more cloves. Use either Rice Crumbs (page 310) or breadcrumbs to coat the carrots. Both amchur (ground dried unripe mango) and kala namak (Indian black salt) can be obtained in both crystal and ground form from Indian grocery stores and specialty spice stores. These carrots are also wonderful served with Herbed Yogurt Dressing (page 253).

SERVES 4

For the garlic + mint tahini:

¼ cup [55 g] tahini

¼ cup [60 ml] boiling water

2 Tbsp fresh lemon juice

1 garlic clove

1 tsp dried peppermint, ground

¼ tsp ground cayenne

Fine sea salt

For the carrots:

2 large eggs

2 tsp ground black pepper

½ tsp ground cayenne

Fine sea salt

7 oz [200 g] rice crumbs, homemade (page 310) or store-bought

½ cup [120 ml] extra-virgin olive oil

1 lb [455 g] young carrots, cut in half lengthwise

1 Tbsp amchur

1 tsp kala namak

THE FLAVOR APPROACH

Beyond the natural sweetness of carrots, this recipe is about sound and texture. The sizzling sound of crumb-coated carrots frying in hot oil, the fragrant steam that escapes, and the "crunch" of crisped rice crumbs lend unique audio and mouthfeel.

There are two main types of mint sold: peppermint and spearmint. I prefer to use peppermint over spearmint because it contains a few different aromatic substances (menthol, menthone, menthyl acetate, and 1, 8-Cineole) that give it a stronger flavor. If you prefer a milder flavor, use spearmint.

Kala namak is added at the end for unique flavor and saltiness.

To prepare the Garlic + Mint Tahini, in a small bowl, whisk together the tahini, boiling water, lemon juice, garlic, peppermint, and cayenne to form a thick sauce. Taste and season with salt. This sauce can be prepared a day ahead of time and stored in the refrigerator in an airtight container.

To prepare the carrots, line a baking sheet with newspaper or paper towels and set a wire rack on top.

Set up two medium shallow plates or wide bowls large enough for the carrots to comfortably fit in. In one, whisk the eggs with the black pepper and cayenne, and season with salt. In the second plate, spread out the rice crumbs, season with salt, and mix.

Heat the oil in a medium saucepan over medium-high heat to 350°F [177°C].

Meanwhile, dip the carrots in the whisked egg, coating them evenly. Tap to remove any excess liquid and carefully press them into the rice crumb mixture, coating evenly. Shake gently to remove excess crumbs.

Shallow fry the carrots in batches until golden brown on each side, 3 to 4 minutes. The carrots should be completely cooked in the center. Using a slotted spoon, transfer the fried carrots to the wire rack to drain off any excess oil. While still hot, place them on a serving plate. Sprinkle with the amchur and kala namak. Serve hot with the Garlic + Mint Tahini on the side.

Honey + Turmeric Chicken Kebabs with Pineapple

I've always been fascinated with kebabs. I love to watch them being cooked with panache, rotating over a hot charcoal grill or tandoor. Experience, intuition, aroma, and texture all come into play to determine when they're ready. The role of the fruit and vegetables on the skewer is twofold: They add flavor and color, but also secure the meat in place as it cooks. Serve the kebabs with Mint Chutney (page 322) and Masala Parathas (page 297).

SERVES 4 TO 6

For the marinade:

¼ cup [60 ml] fresh lime juice

¼ cup [60 ml] extra-virgin olive oil

8 garlic cloves, peeled and grated

2 Tbsp honey

2 tsp ground black pepper

2 tsp ground coriander

2 tsp red chilli powder

2 tsp ground turmeric

2 tsp fine sea salt

For the kebabs:

1½ lb [680 g] boneless, skinless chicken breast, cut into 1 in [2.5 cm] cubes

1 lb [455 g] ripe pineapple

1 large red onion (10½ oz [300 g])

1 medium green bell pepper (7 oz [200 g])

1 medium red bell pepper (7 oz [200 g])

1 medium yellow bell pepper (7 oz [200 g])

4 Tbsp [60 ml] extra-virgin olive oil

½ tsp ground black pepper

Fine sea salt

For garnish:

2 Tbsp cilantro leaves

1 lime, cut into quarters or sixths

THE FLAVOR APPROACH

Both honey and pineapple provide a sweet counterpart to the warmer flavors in this dish.

The pineapple and chicken are kept separate until they are threaded onto the skewers. Raw pineapple contains bromelain, an enzyme that breaks down protein molecules into smaller peptides by a process called *proteolysis*. If the chicken and pineapple were kept together in the marinade, the proteins in the chicken breast would be broken down by the enzyme, eventually affecting the texture of the chicken; once cooked, it will appear crumbly on the surface. However, once heated on the skewers, the bromelain loses its ability to break down proteins.

To prepare the marinade, combine the lime juice, olive oil, garlic, honey, black pepper, coriander, chilli powder, turmeric, and salt in a small bowl.

To prepare the kebabs, pat the chicken dry with clean paper towels and place in a resealable bag. Pour the marinade into the bag, seal, and shake to coat the chicken well. Let the chicken marinate in the refrigerator for at least 4 hours, preferably overnight.

When ready to grill, remove the bag from the refrigerator and let the chicken come to room temperature for at least 15 minutes.

Cut the pineapple, onion, and bell peppers into quarters and place them in a large bowl. Add 2 Tbsp of the olive oil and the black pepper. Season with salt and toss to coat evenly.

Thread a skewer with the onion, bell peppers, and pineapple, alternating with the marinated pieces of chicken. Pour the leftover marinade over the kebabs.

Heat a grill over medium heat and oil the grates with a little bit of the remaining oil. Cook the kebabs in batches, turning and basting with the reserved marinade and remaining oil. The kebabs will be ready when the vegetables and chicken are thoroughly cooked and tender, appearing browned and charred in spots, and the internal temperature of the chicken reaches 165°F [74°C], 10 to 12 minutes. If some kebabs start to cook before the others, move them to the cooler part of the grill to continue cooking. Transfer the kebabs to a plate, cover with a tent of foil, and let cool slightly, 2 to 3 minutes, before serving.

Garnish with the cilantro and serve with the lime wedges on the side.

Masala Cheddar Cornbread

I'm the type of person who adds extra cheese to pizza, so this cornbread is a tribute to my love for cheese. It's a riot of flavor, with sharp cheddar; sweet, tiny nuggets of corn that burst in your mouth; and a little fire from the red chilli flakes.

SERVES 4 TO 6

½ cup [120 ml] melted ghee or unsalted butter, plus a little extra to grease the baking dish

2 cups [280 g] all-purpose flour

2 cups [280 g] medium-grind cornmeal

1 Tbsp baking powder

1 tsp ground coriander

1 tsp ground fennel

1 to 2 tsp red chilli flakes, such as Aleppo or Maras

½ tsp ground turmeric

¼ tsp ground cayenne

1½ cups [120 g] grated sharp cheddar

1 cup [144 g] sweet corn kernels, fresh or frozen (if frozen, thaw before use)

¼ cup [50 g] packed dark brown sugar or jaggery

¼ cup [85 g] honey

4 large eggs, at room temperature

2 cups [480 ml] whole milk, at room temperature

2 tsp fine sea salt

THE FLAVOR APPROACH

Adding sweet corn kernels to the mixture of flour and cornmeal adds a depth of sweetness.

Dark brown sugar and honey contribute sweetness as well as help with the structure of the bread as it bakes. They also participate in the caramelization and Maillard reaction and introduce new flavor molecules.

Dairy fats, including ghee and cheddar, as well as the lipids in the yolks provide fat in the cornbread, which boosts texture, taste, and aroma.

Turmeric's chief role in this cornbread is as a pigment to increase the rich yellow.

Fennel seeds amplify the perception of sweetness.

Preheat the oven to 400°F [204°C]. Grease a 9 by 12 in [23 by 30.5 cm] baking dish with a little ghee.

In a large bowl, whisk together the flour, cornmeal, baking powder, coriander, fennel, red chilli flakes, turmeric, and cayenne. Reserve 3 Tbsp of the dry mixture.

Toss 1 cup [80 g] of the cheddar and the corn kernels with the reserved 3 Tbsp of the dry mixture in a medium mixing bowl.

In a large bowl, whisk together the melted ghee, brown sugar, honey, eggs, milk, and salt until combined and the sugar is completely dissolved.

Make a well in the center of the dry ingredients in the large mixing bowl. Pour the liquid mixture into the well and whisk until the ingredients are completely combined and there are no visible flecks of the dry ingredients. Using a spatula, fold in the cheddar-corn mixture. Pour the mixture into the greased baking dish and level the surface with the spatula. Sprinkle the remaining ½ cup [40 g] of cheddar over the surface. Bake until the sides are golden brown, and a skewer or knife comes out clean when inserted into the center, 25 to 30 minutes. Serve warm.

Polenta Kheer

On the streets of Mathura in northern India, sweet (*mithai*) makers stir large pans of boiling milk over hot gas stoves. Most of the water evaporates out of the milk and concentrates the flavor, and the milk sugar (lactose) slowly caramelizes to give the milk a delicious flavor. This forms the basis of many milk-based desserts in India, including the rice pudding *kheer*. Here, a can of evaporated milk provides that same caramel flavor and also reduces the cooking time significantly. Rice is the classic grain of choice, but polenta gives a similarly wonderful, comforting texture.

SERVES 4 TO 6

For the kheer:

½ cup [100 g] packed dark brown sugar

20 strands saffron

¼ tsp fine sea salt

1 cup [140 g] coarse-ground polenta

1 cup [240 ml] whole milk

One 12 oz [355 ml] can unsweetened evaporated milk

½ tsp ground green cardamom

½ tsp rose water

For the topping:

2 Tbsp ghee or unsalted butter

½ cup [85 g] diced dried apricots

¼ cup [35 g] raw whole cashews

2 Tbsp raisins

½ tsp ground black pepper

¼ tsp ground green cardamom

¼ tsp fine sea salt

THE FLAVOR APPROACH

Sweetness tends to dominate this dish, accentuated by rose water and cardamom. To balance this, I find it helpful to add a bit of black pepper and salt to the topping.

Lightly frying the dried fruit and nuts with the spices draws out the flavorful essential oils, and the heat helps the sugars participate in the caramelization and Maillard reaction, giving you a much more flavorful topping than you would achieve if they were just folded into the milk and boiled.

To prepare the kheer, place 3 cups [720 ml] of water in a large heavy-bottomed saucepan. Grind 2 Tbsp of the brown sugar with 12 of the saffron strands to a fine powder using a mortar and pestle or in a spice grinder. Add the ground powder along with the remaining sugar, whole saffron strands, and salt to the water in the saucepan. Bring to a boil over medium-high heat. Add the polenta and lower the heat to a gentle simmer. Stir occasionally to prevent burning and sticking to the bottom of the saucepan and cook until the mixture is thick and the polenta completely tender, 30 to 40 minutes. Increase the heat to medium-high, stir in the milk, evaporated milk, and cardamom, and bring to a boil. Remove from the heat and stir in the rose water. Transfer to a serving bowl.

To prepare the dried fruit and nut topping, melt the ghee in a medium saucepan over medium-low heat. When the ghee is hot, add and fry the apricots, cashews, and raisins until the fruits are plump and the nuts are a light golden brown, 2 to 2½ minutes. Add the pepper and cardamom and season with salt. Sauté for an additional 30 seconds and immediately transfer to a medium bowl. Just before serving, garnish the kheer with the dried fruit and nut topping. Serve the pudding warm or at room temperature.

Cherry + Pepper Granola Bars

A good dose of black pepper gives these granola bars a little warmth. I sometimes crush these granola bars and sprinkle them over scoops of ice cream or roasted fruit (such as Roasted Fruit with Coffee Miso Tahini, page 125).

MAKES THIRTY-TWO 1 BY 2 IN [2.5 BY 5 CM] BARS

2 Tbsp olive oil, plus extra to grease the pan and your hands

2 cups [200 g] old-fashioned rolled oats

½ cup [70 g] raw cashews

½ cup [70 g] raw pistachios

7 oz [200 g] dried cherries, preferably the sour variety

1 tsp fresh coarsely ground black pepper

½ tsp ground green cardamom

½ tsp fine sea salt

½ cup [120 ml] maple syrup

¼ cup [60 ml] date syrup, homemade (page 324) or store-bought

THE FLAVOR APPROACH

For these bars, I played with different types of sweeteners. Maple syrup is mostly sucrose with very little fructose and glucose; date syrup contains glucose and fructose (in ascending order of concentration).

This recipe uses twice as much maple syrup as date syrup by volume. When the resulting syrup reaches 252°F [122°C] (hard ball stage), the sucrose starts to crystallize as most of the water is removed by evaporation and the sugars are concentrated. This ensures that the sugar will harden as the bars cool off, which prevents the bars from falling apart.

Preheat the oven to 325°F [163°C]. Grease an 8 by 8 by 2 in [20 by 20 by 5 cm] baking pan with a little olive oil and line with parchment paper.

Heat a medium saucepan over medium heat and add the olive oil. When the oil is hot, add the oats and cook until they start to turn light brown, 5 to 6 minutes, stirring occasionally. Add the cashews and pistachios and cook for an additional 2 minutes. Transfer the oat mixture to a large mixing bowl. Fold in the cherries, pepper, cardamom, and salt.

In a medium saucepan, whisk together the maple and date syrups. Heat the saucepan over medium heat, stirring occasionally, until the mixture reaches 252°F [122°C] on an instant-read thermometer (hard ball stage), 8 to 12 minutes. Quickly pour the hot liquid over the oat mixture in the bowl and fold with a silicone spatula to coat the ingredients well. Transfer the mixture to the prepared pan and, using the spatula, spread and firmly press the oat mixture down in an even layer. Bake until it turns a darker shade of golden brown, 15 to 20 minutes. Remove the pan from the oven, set it on a wire rack, and let cool completely to room temperature in the pan. Once it has cooled, run a knife around the edges of the pan and flip the granola onto a cutting board. Peel and discard the parchment paper. Cut into 1 by 2 in [2.5 by 5 cm] bars. Store the granola bars in an airtight container, with parchment paper between the layers to prevent sticking, for up to 2 weeks.

Raspberry + Stone Fruit Crisp

My mother in-law introduced me to the bright, sweet world of cobblers, crisps, and other delicious fruit-based desserts. I love their unfussy nature compared to pies, whose crusts usually require a bit of extra planning ahead—and kitchen work.

SERVES 4 TO 6

For the fruit:

3 ripe peaches (total weight 1½ lb [680 g])

3 ripe nectarines (total weight 1 lb [455 g])

3 ripe plums (total weight 9 oz [255 g])

12 oz [340 g] raspberries

¾ cup [150 g] jaggery or dark brown sugar

¼ cup [40 g] crystallized ginger

¼ tsp fine sea salt

1 vanilla bean

2 Tbsp fresh lime juice

2 Tbsp cornstarch

For the topping:

1 cup [100 g] old-fashioned rolled oats

1 cup [100 g] sliced almonds, with the skin on

¾ cup [150 g] jaggery or dark brown sugar

¼ tsp fine sea salt

¼ cup [55 g] unsalted butter

1 tsp fresh lime zest

1 tsp ground cinnamon

THE FLAVOR APPROACH

Butter is heated to produce brown butter, in which the milk proteins and sugars undergo the Maillard reaction and caramelization.

Cinnamon and lime zest are added to the hot fat to dissolve and extract their essential oils.

Stone fruits release a lot of water when heated, which can eventually end up making the crisp topping soggy. To avoid this, cook the fruit and crisp separately, and assemble just before you are ready to serve and eat.

To prepare the fruit, preheat the oven to 350°F [177°C]. Line two baking sheets with parchment paper.

Cut the peaches, nectarines, and plums in half. Remove and discard the center stones and cut the halves into slices. Place in a 9 by 12 by 2 in [23 by 30.5 by 5 cm] baking pan and gently fold in the raspberries, jaggery, ginger, and salt. Cut the vanilla bean in half lengthwise and scrape the tiny seeds out with the tip of a knife. Add the seeds and bean to the fruit. Add the lime juice and gently fold to distribute. Sift the cornstarch over the fruit and fold once again to coat evenly. Set the dish on one of the baking sheets. Bake for 45 to 60 minutes, until the fruit juices are bubbling in the center. Remove from the oven and keep warm.

To prepare the topping, combine the oats, almonds, jaggery, and salt in a medium mixing bowl. Melt the butter in a small saucepan over medium-low heat until the milk solids separate and start to turn reddish brown, 5 to 8 minutes. Remove from the heat and stir in the lime zest and cinnamon. Scrape the bottom of the saucepan to dislodge any milk solids, pour the hot fat over the oat mixture, and mix with a spatula to coat evenly. Spread the oat mixture out over the parchment paper on the second baking sheet. Bake for 10 to 12 minutes, until the oats and nuts are golden brown. Remove from the oven and let cool for 15 to 20 minutes. Crumble by hand. The crisp topping can be prepared ahead of time and, once cooled completely, stored in an airtight container for up to 1 week.

When ready to serve, top the warm fruit in the baking dish with the warm crisp and serve immediately. You can also serve it warm with scoops of vanilla ice cream. To reheat and serve, preheat the oven to 350°F [177°C] and warm the fruit and crisp.

Semolina Coconut Cookies (Bolinhas)

Coconut fans, this cookie is for you. I like these with a cup of hot, sweetened, milky black tea. *Bolinhas*, as they are called in Goa, are crunchy and crisp, full of coconut aroma and sweetness. You may notice that this cookie uses pound cake ratios to come together. I strongly recommend using a brand of desiccated coconut with a strong coconut aroma, or use a good-quality coconut extract. I use the fine-grade (No. 1) semolina flour; the smaller particle size eliminates the need to soak the cookie batter before baking as is classically done with the coarser variety used in India.

MAKES APPROXIMATELY 24 COOKIES

3 cups + 2 Tbsp [250 g] unsweetened shredded desiccated coconut (see The Flavor Approach)

1½ cups + 1 Tbsp [250 g] fine-grade semolina flour

1¼ cups [250 g] sugar

2 Tbsp ghee or unsalted butter

¼ tsp fine sea salt

1½ to 2 tsp ground green cardamom

1 tsp coconut extract (optional)

3 large egg yolks plus the white of one large egg, lightly whisked together

All-purpose flour, for shaping the cookies

THE FLAVOR APPROACH

The aromatic molecules in the ground green cardamom and coconut help amplify the perception of the cookie's sweetness. You can apply this trick to other sweets too when you want to accentuate the sweetness without increasing the amount of sweetener; use aromatic ingredients and spices, such as cinnamon, nutmeg, orange blossom water, or rose water, that we commonly associate with sweets.

The classic bolinha uses fresh coconut ground to a paste, which yields a smooth texture. I prefer the texture of shredded coconut, so I use a combination of ground and shredded.

You can toast the desiccated coconut before it meets the semolina (see instructions, Coconut Milk Cake, page 306), but remember to cool it before you add it.

Place half of the coconut in the bowl of a food processor and grind it into a fine powder. Mix the ground coconut and remaining shredded coconut with the semolina in a large mixing bowl.

Prepare a simple syrup by combining 1 cup plus 2 tsp [250 ml] of water and the sugar in a medium saucepan and bringing to a boil over medium heat. Stir until the sugar dissolves. Add the ghee and salt and stir until the fat melts. Remove from the heat, pour the hot liquid over the semolina and coconut, and fold with a spatula until evenly combined. Cover with plastic wrap and let cool to room temperature.

Once the semolina mixture is cooled, sprinkle on the cardamom and coconut extract, if using, and fold to combine. Add the whisked egg yolks and fold into the mixture until combined. Cover the mixture and refrigerate for at least 4 hours and up to 8 hours to let the dough firm up and absorb the flavors.

cont'd

When ready to bake, preheat the oven to 350°F [177°C] and line two baking sheets with parchment paper.

You can store the wrapped cookie dough for up to 2 weeks in the freezer. When ready to use, leave it out on the kitchen counter for about 15 minutes, until soft enough to be pliable.

To assemble the cookies, work in batches. Lightly dust your hands with a little flour to help prevent the dough from sticking to the surface of your palms. Take about 2 Tbsp of the dough and shape it into a 1 in [2.5 cm] round patty. Evenly space about 12 patties on each baking sheet. Take the blunt end of a knife and press gently to make three equally spaced parallel cuts in the center of the cookie patty. The cuts do not need to be very deep or go all the way across the diameter of the cookie. Rotate the tray and repeat to create three perpendicular cuts, creating a crosshatch pattern.

Bake two sheets at a time for 25 to 30 minutes, until the cookies turn brown on the edges and light golden brown on top and are firm, rotating the sheets halfway through baking. Remove the sheets from the oven and transfer the cookies to a wire rack to cool completely. Repeat with the remaining cookie dough. The cooled cookies can be stored in an airtight container for up to 1 month in the refrigerator; just remember to bring them to room temperature before serving.

Saffron Swirl Buns with Dried Fruit

When I wanted to pursue my dream of baking, I envisioned owning a tiny little bakery selling only buns. Buns of all sorts, sizes, shapes, and flavors, sweet and savory. Life had different plans for me, but I still bake a lot of buns, sharing them with my friends and neighbors.

Cookbook author and baker extraordinaire Edd Kimber, who writes the blog *The Boy Who Bakes*, first introduced me to the delicious nature of golden syrup; I now use it to brush all my sweet breads. In the United States, you can find Lyle's Golden Syrup online or anywhere British foods are sold. If you can't find it, use the substitution I've provided. Note: The paddle attachment at low speed does a much better job of mixing this sticky dough than the dough blade.

MAKES 12 INDIVIDUAL BUNS

For the dough:

20 strands saffron

¼ cup [50 g] sugar

½ cup [120 ml] whole milk

¼ cup [55 g] unsalted butter, cubed, plus extra for greasing

½ tsp fine sea salt

1 large egg, lightly whisked

1½ tsp active dried yeast

2 cups [280 g] all-purpose flour, plus extra for dusting

For the filling:

3½ oz [100 g] sliced almonds, with skins left on

3 oz [85 g] dried apricots, chopped

3 oz [85 g] dried blueberries

3 oz [85 g] dried figs, chopped

¼ cup [55 g] unsalted butter, plus extra for greasing

1 tsp ground cinnamon

1 tsp ground green cardamom

1 tsp fresh lemon zest

¼ cup [50 g] packed dark brown sugar

½ tsp fine sea salt

1 large egg

¼ cup [80 g] golden syrup or
¼ cup [85 g] honey mixed with
1 tsp lemon juice

THE FLAVOR APPROACH

Unlike cakes and cookies, this basic bun dough calls for a smaller amount of sugar—just enough to provide energy to the yeast for fermentation and leave behind a trace of mild sweetness.

The sweetness in this dessert comes chiefly from the dried fruit filling and the coating of golden syrup.

Yeast gives the bread its light and airy structure through fermentation of the sugars in the dough.

The enzyme amylase from the yeast and flour helps break down the starch into smaller molecules that the yeast utilizes for energy.

To make the dough, grind the saffron with 2 Tbsp of the sugar to a fine powder using a mortar and pestle, then transfer to a small saucepan. Add the remaining sugar and the milk, butter, and salt and warm over medium-low heat to 110°F [43°C], stirring until the butter melts and the sugar dissolves completely. Remove from the heat and stir in the whisked egg and yeast.

Lightly flour a work surface and grease a large bowl. Place the flour in the bowl of a stand mixer and make a well in the center. With the paddle attachment fixed and the speed set to low, slowly pour in the milk mixture. Mix until the dough comes together, 5 to 6 minutes. The dough will be sticky. Using a bowl scraper, turn out the dough onto the floured surface. Knead for 1 minute to bring the dough together, then transfer it to the greased bowl. Cover with plastic wrap and let rise in a warm spot until the dough doubles in size, 1½ to 2 hours.

cont'd

While the dough rises, prepare the filling. Place the almonds and dried fruit in a medium bowl. Melt the butter in a small saucepan over medium-high heat, swirling until the butter melts and the milk solids separate and turn reddish brown, 4 to 5 minutes. Remove from the heat and add the cinnamon, cardamom, and lemon zest. Scrape loose the solids at the bottom of the saucepan with a spatula, then pour the liquid over the almonds and dried fruit. Add the brown sugar and salt and fold to coat evenly. Cover with a lid and let sit for at least 30 minutes.

To assemble the buns, once the dough has doubled in size, line a half sheet pan with parchment paper and lightly dust it with flour. Turn the dough out onto the sheet and roll it out with a small rolling pin to cover the entire surface.

Sprinkle the dough with the fruit-and-nut mixture and press it in gently. Using the parchment paper as a support, starting from the longer side of the dough, roll up the dough and filling to form a log. Refrigerate the log on the baking sheet for 30 minutes to firm up.

Grease a rectangular 9 by 12 in [23 by 30.5 cm] baking dish with a little butter and line it with parchment paper. Take the baking sheet with the log from the refrigerator and cut the dough with a sharp knife perpendicular to its length into 1 in [2.5 cm] thick sections. Place the sections on the prepared baking dish, spacing them about 1 in [2.5 cm] apart. Cover loosely with parchment paper and let rise for 1 hour, until they double in size.

Preheat the oven to 350°F [177°C].

Whisk the egg in a small bowl and brush it over the surface of the buns. Bake the buns until they're golden brown, 25 to 30 minutes, turning the sheet halfway through baking. Remove from the oven and dab the buns with the golden syrup all over. Let cool in the baking dish for 15 minutes, then transfer the buns to a wire rack to cool. Serve warm or at room temperature. These buns are best eaten the day they're prepared but can also be wrapped with plastic wrap and stored in an airtight bag for 3 days and rewarmed in the oven at 200°F [93°C].

Peppermint Marshmallows

Come December, we'd dust my grandparent's large wooden dining table with a mixture of cornstarch and confectioner's sugar, and on this we'd roll out logs of marshmallows. I'd joyfully play with the soft pillow-like logs, my arms and face becoming covered in white powder. I've reworked my grandmother's original recipe by adding cream of tartar. Back then in India, corn syrup (glucose) wasn't readily available, so she relied on lime juice to achieve the same result.

MAKES EIGHTEEN 1 **IN [2.5 CM] SQUARES**

¼ cup [35 g] cornstarch

¼ cup [30 g] confectioner's sugar

¾ oz [21 g] granulated gelatin

10½ oz [300 g] superfine sugar

⅛ tsp cream of tartar

2 large egg whites, at room temperature

½ to 1 tsp peppermint extract

Red food coloring or 1 tsp beet powder mixed in 2 Tbsp water

Neutral oil, for greasing

THE FLAVOR APPROACH

For the Cherry + Pepper Granola Bars (page 186), a higher temperature ensures sugar crystallization, desirable for firm bars that hold together. For marshmallows, sugar (sucrose) must be heated to a lower temperature to prevent crystals from forming.

The acidic cream of tartar also helps prevent sugar crystallization by "inverting" some of the sucrose, which splits into glucose and fructose. Glucose and fructose interfere with sugar crystal formation.

Gelatin is a protein derived from collagen. When mixed with hot water, the granules of gelatin begin to absorb water and swell and form a gel. When combined and whisked with the egg white proteins and sugar, the proteins start to unfold and bond and produce a meshwork that gives the marshmallows their soft texture and airy shape.

The mixture of cornstarch and confectioner's sugar acts like talcum powder; it creates a thin layer over the marshmallows that prevents them from sticking and absorbing moisture from air.

Sift the cornstarch and confectioner's sugar with a fine-mesh sieve over a small mixing bowl. Sift 2 Tbsp of this mixture over a 9 by 9 by 2 in [23 by 23 by 5 cm] baking pan. Reserve the rest.

Pour ½ cup [120 ml] of water into a large, wide, medium heatproof mixing bowl; this will increase the surface area of water available and reduce the chances of the gelatin clumping. Sprinkle the gelatin over the surface of the water and let sit undisturbed until the gelatin swells and absorbs the liquid, 5 to 6 minutes.

Pour another ½ cup [120 ml] of water into a medium saucepan and add the sugar and cream of tartar. Cover with a lid and heat over medium-low heat until the sugar is completely dissolved and the temperature reaches between 238°F and 240°F [114°C and 115°C] on an instant-read or candy thermometer (soft ball stage).

While the sugar cooks, place the egg whites in the bowl of a stand mixer fitted with the whisk attachment and whisk on medium-high speed until the egg whites turn foamy and eventually produce stiff peaks, about 5 minutes. Set aside.

Once the sugar syrup reaches 238°F to 240°F [114°C to 115°C], pour it slowly into the gelatin, directing a thin stream down the side of the mixing bowl. It will start to foam, and this slow method prevents it from foaming over. Stir with a fork to dissolve the gelatin in the syrup until completely smooth with no undissolved clumps. While whisking the egg whites on medium-high speed, add the hot sugar-gelatin syrup in a thin, steady stream. Once

the syrup is added, continue to whisk for 1 additional minute, then increase the speed to high and whisk until the foam is shiny and satiny white and will hold stiff peaks, 8 to 10 minutes. Add the peppermint extract and whisk for 1 minute on high speed. Stop the mixer and add a few drops of the coloring and whisk for 3 to 4 seconds, just long enough to create a few swirls. Resist the urge to over-mix or it will turn uniformly pink.

Lightly grease a small offset spatula with a little neutral oil. Remove the bowl from the mixer and use a sili-cone spatula to quickly transfer the mixture to the prepared baking pan; it starts to set quickly once it begins to cool. Use the greased spatula to level the surface. Cover the pan and

allow it to rest for at least 4 hours and preferably 6 hours. The marsh-mallow is ready once it is completely cooled and spongy to the touch in the center.

To cut, dust a clean surface with a little bit of the reserved cornstarch mixture. Run a small knife around the edges of the pan to release the marshmallow. You might need to gently pull it from the sides to help release it. Cut into 1 in [2.5 cm] squares with a sharp serrated knife (you can grease the knife with a little neutral oil to prevent sticking). Dust the squares with a little bit of the cornstarch mixture and store in an airtight container for up to 1 week.

Hot Honeycomb Candy

Honeycomb candy (also called cinder toffee) is a marvel of science and ingenuity, and it's very easy and fun to make. I've added a pinch of cayenne to give it a little kick of heat. You might notice some darker brown spots; these are normal, indicating greater caramelization wherever the baking soda is a little more concentrated, so the pH is higher.

MAKES 10 ½ OZ [300 G] CANDY

Neutral oil, for greasing

1¼ tsp baking soda

½ tsp ground cayenne

1 cup [200 g] sugar

½ cup [170 g] honey

THE FLAVOR APPROACH

Honey, an invert sugar, prevents the crystallization of sugar as it heats to the hard crack stage.

The irresistible spongy-crunchy texture of the honeycomb candy is created by bubbles of carbon dioxide produced when the baking soda (sodium bicarbonate) is added to the hot syrup. Sodium bicarbonate breaks down at 176°F [80°C] to sodium carbonate and carbon dioxide, and the acids in the honey, such as gluconic acid, contribute to a minor degree as they react with the sodium bicarbonate.

Adding cayenne to the hot sugar infuses it with capsaicin, which gives the candy a "hot" taste. If you like it hot, use more cayenne.

A second way to achieve heat in this candy is to use a chilli-infused honey and skip the cayenne.

Grease an 8 in [20 cm] square baking pan with a little oil. Line the bottom and sides with a sheet of foil big enough to allow for a generous overhang on at least two sides; fold this down against the outside of the pan.

Mix the baking soda and cayenne together in a small bowl.

Place the sugar, honey, and ¼ cup [60 ml] of water in a medium saucepan over medium-high heat, stirring with a wooden spoon, until the sugar reaches 300°F [149°C] on a candy thermometer, 8 to 10 minutes. Working quickly, stir in the baking soda mixture with a whisk; the mixture will foam. Pour the foaming mixture out onto the prepared pan and tilt the pan slightly so the mixture evenly covers the entire bottom. Resist the urge to level it or you will lose the bubbles. Let the pan sit undisturbed to cool completely and harden at room temperature, about 2 hours. Once the candy is set and hard, lift it out of the pan with the help of the overhanging foil around the sides and peel it away. Break the candy into chunks or cut with a sharp serrated knife. It will keep in an airtight container for 3 to 4 days.

No-Churn Falooda Ice Cream

Summers in India are extremely hot and humid, and people find ingenious ways to stay cool. Falooda, which originates from the Persian *faloodeh,* is a chilled milk drink. In its simplest form, it's made with sweetened rose syrup, basil seeds, and vermicelli noodles. Because chia seeds behave just like basil seeds when soaked in water, developing a soft gel-like cloud around each tiny black seed, they make the perfect substitute. The seeds might settle, so I usually stir the ice cream once it's partially frozen to redistribute them.

I first came across no-churn ice creams that use heavy cream and condensed milk in Nigella Lawson's now-classic masterpiece *How to Eat,* which forms the backbone of this recipe.

**MAKES
APPROXIMATELY 6 CUPS [1.4 L]**

1¼ cups [300 ml] heavy cream

One 12 oz [355 ml] can evaporated milk

1 tsp rose water

½ tsp ground green cardamom

½ tsp beet powder or a few drops of red food coloring

One 14 oz [400 g] can sweetened condensed milk

2 Tbsp chia seeds or sweet basil seeds

¼ cup [30 g] chopped pistachios

THE FLAVOR APPROACH

Here, heavy cream provides the structure for the ice cream's texture, which works beautifully in this rendition of falooda.

The chia seeds are soaked in heavy cream; they absorb the water but also get surrounded by a coat of dairy fat, which prevents them from freezing in the ice cream. Consequently, the chia seeds retain their chewiness as well as their crunch.

In this ice cream, sweetness comes from the sugar in the condensed milk as well as the caramelized lactose in the evaporated milk.

Whip 1 cup [240 ml] of heavy cream with a whisk in a large bowl until soft peaks form.

In a small bowl, mix 2 Tbsp of the evaporated milk with the rose water, cardamom, and beet powder to form a smooth mixture. There should be no visible specks of the red beet powder. Pour this liquid along with the remaining evaporated milk and the condensed milk into the heavy cream and whisk until the liquid is thick, 2 to 3 minutes. Transfer to a freezer-safe container, cover with plastic wrap, and freeze for 1 hour. Mix the remaining ¼ cup [60 ml] of heavy cream with the chia seeds in a

small bowl to swell. Cover and let sit in the refrigerator until ready to use.

Remove the container from the freezer; the mixture will have started to freeze around the edges of the container. Fold in the chia seeds and stir the liquid with a fork. Cover the container with plastic wrap and return it to the freezer. After 2 hours, stir the ice cream with a fork to redistribute the chia seeds and break up any ice crystals. Freeze until the ice cream is firm, at least 4 hours.

When ready to serve, leave the ice cream out for 5 minutes to soften. Garnish with a few chopped pistachios.

5

SAVORINESS

NOT FAR FROM MY PARENTS' HOME in Bombay is the fishing village of Chimbai. The catch is spread over large mats or hung over long strings attached to bamboo poles—fish such as the Bombay duck (actually a fish, also called *bombil* or *bummalo*) and shrimp. The air smells briny with the unmistakable scent of fish. The fish and shrimp are added to curries and stews and also cooked with chillies and vinegar to form hot pickles with a distinct savory taste.

Savoriness—or the now more commonly used Japanese word, umami—is the taste most recently inducted into the group of canonical tastes. Savoriness or umami will remind you of meaty and bone brothlike tastes. Glutamate, one of the most well-known sources for savoriness, was discovered in 1908 by the Japanese scientist Kikunae Ikeda in a seaweed, kombu. This discovery led researchers on a path of discovery of gathering data to demonstrate that the response to this ingredient was indeed unique and satisfied the necessary criteria to qualify as a taste (see Qualifications to Be a Taste, page 50).

While it took time to uncover the exact mechanism by which savoriness occurs, we all play with it in various ways when we cook, and we've been doing it for years. Cooking onions, ginger, and garlic together in meat curries or stir-fries; a generous shaving of Parmesan over pasta; a splash of soy sauce over a bowl of warm egg drop soup; even cooking with tomatoes in savory dishes—all help to create the taste of savoriness in our food.

How Savoriness Works

Several substances in our food create the taste of umami or savoriness. Aging and fermentation also help increase the concentration of these savory-tasting molecules (think: cheese and soy sauce). These substances are usually amino acids such as glutamate and nucleotides, which are a part of our nucleic acids; for example, DNA and RNA. Glutamate in our diet acts as an energy source and gets metabolized by the body to synthesize various other substances that it needs to function. At present, there are several candidates that might function as umami taste receptors. Based on experimental studies, some of these receptors respond to only glutamate; others respond to both glutamate and the nucleotides.

GLUTAMATE

Glutamate is the salt form of the amino acid glutamic acid, discovered in the seaweed kombu. When a salt of glutamate is dissolved in water, it splits into two parts: the cation sodium [Na+] and its anion or "free glutamate" [Glutamate -]. Glutamic acid by itself tastes sour, but free glutamate is what's responsible for the savory taste in food. Glutamate is also present in proteins, but because it is attached to other amino acids in the peptide chains and not free, we can't taste this glutamate. Glutamate is not easily broken down by heat; this stability is valuable for cooking purposes.

NUCLEOTIDES

The nucleic acids DNA and RNA are composed of molecules called nucleotides (see Nucleic Acids, page 336); of these, adenosine triphosphate (ATP) and guanosine triphosphate (GTP) from RNA give rise to two of the umami-tasting molecules in our food.

5'-INOSINATE (IMP)

Within the first few months of moving to the Bay Area, I went out on a tasting spree at food spots that locals loved and recommended. Namu Gaji (now Namu Stonepot) was one of them. The kimchee okonomiyaki, a savory pancake, came topped with a layer of bonito flakes. Every bite was pure savory delight. Bonito flakes, or katsuboshi, a fermented dried product obtained by processing and fermenting skipjack tuna, owes its savoriness to 5'-inosinate. Just like glutamate, 5'-inosinate is not easily broken down during heating.

5'-GUANYLATE (GMP)

I often use dried shiitake mushrooms to bump up the savory notes of a stock. When the cells of a food are alive, the nucleic acid, RNA, is kept hidden away from an enzyme called ribonuclease that specifically works to break it down. When cells dry, as in these mushrooms, they lose their structural integrity and break, bringing the enzyme into direct contact with the RNA, and they produce 5'-guanylate.

OTHER FOOD CHEMICALS

Green tea is rich in an amino acid called *theanine* and glutamate, both of which contribute to the savoriness of the tea. Because black tea is produced by a different method (green tea undergoes less oxidation), the amount of theanine is considerably lower. You can take advantage of this by steeping tea in hot water to extract the theanine, adding it to a vegetarian stock (see Percentage of Umami Substances in Common Ingredients, page 341). Several other molecules can elicit an umami response: aspartate from the amino acid aspartic acid; some organic acids, like the lactic acid in cheese; and several tiny peptides in cheese, garlic, and onions (see Proteins, page 333).

UMAMI SYNERGISM

Synergism is a special phenomenon that occurs when two or more substances come together and produce a greater effect combined than they would alone.

If you taste food rich in monosodium glutamate with either of the 5'-nucleotides (inosinate or guanylate), you will find the umami taste much stronger than if you consumed them separately. By themselves, the 5'-nucleotides don't have as much umami taste compared to glutamate; you can use this property when selecting ingredients to make richer savory notes. Combine a seaweed like kombu or nori with shiitake mushrooms to create a stock or broth with a powerful note of savoriness. You can test this quickly for yourself when you sear the peppers in Blistered Shishito/Padrón Peppers with Bonito Flakes (page 213). Taste it first with the soy sauce and again after you sprinkle them with bonito flakes: the umami intensity will be more powerful.

How Savoriness Is Measured

Glutamate, 5'-nucleotides, and other umami-tasting substances are measured using specific assays to give a sense of the food's possible savory potency (see the table on page 341).

Savoriness Boosters

There are several vegetarian and nonvegetarian options for boosting the savory profile of dishes. Some come from the ocean, and many are produced through fermentation that allows the breakdown of proteins via enzymes. Other ingredients, like tomatoes, get their umami taste through ripening.

MONOSODIUM GLUTAMATE (MSG)

In some of the Chinese and Japanese cookbooks I inherited from my mother, often a pinch of MSG (or *ajinomoto*, as it sometimes is colloquially referred to in India) shows up in ingredient lists. The Ajinomoto company in Japan was one of the earliest companies to commercially produce taste enhancers after the discovery of glutamate and its relationship to umami; in 1909 they introduced their first umami seasoning, called Aji-No-Moto, which contains monosodium glutamate, a purified salt of glutamic acid. By itself, when dissolved in water, it doesn't have a strong umami taste, but the presence of the other 5'-nucleotides amplifies it. In the 1960s, controversial reports surrounding the safety of MSG in food arose, creating what was called the "Chinese restaurant syndrome." This claim has been debunked several times, and several scientific studies demonstrate the safety of MSG. For one, glutamate is ubiquitous in living organisms; it is naturally present in most of the food we eat, and the human brain is one of the richest stores of glutamate in the body. When food is labeled as "MSG free," typically 5'-nucleotides are used to contribute to the umami flavor.

ALLIUMS

Members of the *Allium* family of plants, such as garlic, leeks, onions, and shallots, when fresh, are not as rich in glutamate when compared to ingredients such as miso or anchovies, but they are easily accessible. Dried, powdered onion and garlic are often used in seasonings because they contain more glutamate than fresh. When paired with ingredients like ginger and soy sauce, they amplify the savory profile. Black garlic is a special form that is slowly fermented under controlled heat for several days; it has a mellow flavor and can be used like regular garlic in recipes when you want to avoid the pungency but boost the savory profile of a dish.

ANCHOVIES AND FISH SAUCE

Anchovies are a tiny, oily fish sold either fresh, preserved in salt, or packed in oil. The preserved fish are also rich in glutamate, which gives them their rich umami flavor. They are featured in the Italian tomato sauce puttanesca, as well as in the classic Caesar salad dressing and in some of the fish-based sambals of South Asia. To use, cook the anchovies in a bit of hot olive oil; the fish will fall apart as if melting and can then be used to form the base of a sauce or any recipe. I use anchovies to increase the glutamates in My Quick Marinara (page 316).

Fish sauce is one of the most potent sources of savoriness; a little bit goes a long way. Produced by fermenting fish, it has a funky odor and is rich in glutamates. There are several types of fish sauce: The ancient Romans' version was *garum*; in Asia, the Vietnamese use *nuoc nam*, the Thai use *nam pla*, and the Indonesians use *kecap ikan*. Asian fish sauces are prepared by the fermentation of anchovies in a mixture of salt and water. Ancient recipes for garum used anchovies, mackerel, and even eel. A splash of fish sauce in a salad dressing (Cucumber + Roasted Corn Salad, page 287), soup, or braised vegetables can remarkably improve the savory character.

BONITO FLAKES

Katsuobushi are thin, paperlike pieces of dried, fermented, and smoked skipjack tuna. When the fish bonito, a cheaper alternative, is used, they are called *bonito flakes*. The fish is dried in the sun and left to age for several months to years. This renders the flesh as hard as wood, and the flakes are prepared by shaving the hard, dried fish on a special shaving tool (very similar to the way in which wood shavings are made). Bonito is used traditionally in the preparation of the Japanese stock *dashi*; it was studies of this ingredient by Japanese scientists that led to the discovery of the umami-tasting nucleotide 5'-guanylate. Because bonito is prepared by drying and the umami substances are concentrated early on in processing, you don't need to cook bonito flakes for very long to extract their savoriness; that's why most Japanese recipes

NUTRITIONAL YEAST

WALNUTS

SHIITAKE

BONITO FLAKES

for dashi call for only a few minutes to steep the flakes. You can quickly boost the savory taste of your broths or soups by sprinkling in bonito flakes. Bonito flakes also provide a unique texture, and because they move in the presence of wind and steam, they give the illusion of being "alive." Use them to top omelets and roasted vegetables, and even as a garnish (see Crab Tikka Masala Dip, 284).

MISO

Miso, a type of fermented soybean paste, is sold in little tubs at almost all grocery stores across the country, including Asian markets. In the miso-making process, first the koji (*kōji* in Japanese, *qu* in Chinese, *nurukgyun* in Korean)—the mold *Aspergillus oryzae*, inoculated in rice, barley, or soybeans—is added to steamed soybeans along with salt and left to ferment for anywhere from several months to years in cedar barrels. Miso is the salty fermented paste that results. Miso can be classified by color (*akamiso* or the darker red, a medium-light color miso, and *shiro* or white miso), taste (*amakuchi*, sweet, or *karakuchi*, salty), or the type of koji used (rice, barley, or soybean). The type of soybean used determines the color; malt determines the sweet taste. Add white or red miso to your soups and stews to bump up their savory notes, and use white miso in sweet desserts such as Chocolate Miso Bread Pudding (page 133) and brownies. I sometimes stir in a small amount of white miso or shiro into dulce de leche to add a bit of salty and umami tastes.

MUSHROOMS

Mushrooms such as shiitake are a wonderful ingredient to boost the savory taste in a dish. Fresh mushrooms contain glutamate; dried mushrooms, when mixed with cold water, produce 5'-guanylate by an enzyme. I keep a stash of dried shiitake in my kitchen pantry. I first steep the mushrooms in cold water, then use the liquid in my stocks and sauce recipes when I need to quickly bump up the savory profile. Use mushrooms in conjunction with other glutamate-rich ingredients to take advantage of the umami synergism.

PARMESAN

Parmesan is the term for hard cheeses made in the United States and other countries outside Italy that emulates the Italian hard cheese licensed as Parmigiano-Reggiano. To make it, fresh cow's milk is collected in the evening and left to rest. The fat that rises to the top is skimmed off and used to make butter; the skimmed milk is mixed with rennet (a protein-coagulating enzyme used to make cheese) and added to large copper cauldrons. Leftover whey (lactic acid) from the previous batch of fermented milk in the cauldrons helps with the milk protein coagulation. The milk proteins denature (see Proteins, page 333) and are then physically broken down into smaller-size particles. The liquid is heated to help the proteins denature further, and they stick together to form a large clump. This falls to the bottom and is then collected, wrapped in cloth, and pressed in a mold to give it its round shape. The cheese is soaked in saltwater and then left to age for at least 12 months. Parmesan gets its savoriness from the high content of glutamate that arises during the aging of the cheese, as well as some other organic acids such as lactic acid.

SEAWEED

On returning to Japan from overseas, the scientist Kikunae Ikeda noticed a familiar taste in dashi made from dried kombu; it reminded him of the tomatoes, cheese, and meat he'd eaten during his years spent working in Germany. This led him to the discovery of glutamate—and the savory taste of umami. The amount of glutamate can vary depending on the type of seaweed, but in kombu and nori it is relatively high. They're sold in dried sheets in most grocery stores as well as in Asian markets. Because they're dried and already concentrated, just like bonito, they release their glutamate easily, and you don't need to spend too much time infusing; simply let the sheets steep in simmering water or broth for a few minutes. You can chop up the dried sheets and use them for flavor and texture over seafood, vegetables, and even rice as is done with the Japanese seasoning *furikake*. Two other Japanese-based seasonings that I keep on hand are *shichimi togarashi* and *gomasio*. Like furikake, these are exquisite flavor and texture boosters for roasted vegetables and seafood. You can also incorporate chopped bits of dried seaweed when making savory crackers and breads such as scones.

SOY SAUCE AND TAMARI

Soy sauce, a staple in many Asian cuisines, is prepared by the fermentation of soybeans and wheat by the koji, either *Aspergillus oryzae* or *Aspergillus sojae*, mold. The mixture is then treated with saltwater and allowed to ferment. During fermentation, the mold uses enzymes to break down proteins and glutamate levels rise. The resulting liquid is dark brown, with a noticeably salty and meaty taste.

Though tamari tastes and looks similar to soy sauce, its production is quite different. To prepare tamari, very little to no wheat is used (if you are sensitive to gluten, check the label to see if it is gluten-free). Miso paste is the basis for tamari, and the taste is usually less salty and much more rounded compared to soy sauce. Both soy sauce and tamari can be used interchangeably in most recipes; be sure to factor in the amount of salt when seasoning (see Roast Chicken Thighs + Vegetables, page 225, or Manchow Soup, page 255).

TEA

Tea is rich in a special type of amino acid, theanine (5-N-ethylglutamine), which has an umami taste. You can use mild brews of black tea, especially smoked teas like lapsang souchong, to build on savory flavors in soups and broths. Green tea and matcha are also rich in this amino acid, and you can use them in savory applications.

TOMATO

As a tomato ripens on the vine, the glutamate concentration begins to rise; it increases by a whopping 480%, or a 5.84-fold increase, making it a rich source of umami for cooking. You might also notice that the inner pulp, which contains the seeds, has a much stronger umami taste compared to the outer flesh; this is where the glutamate and the umami-tasting nucleotides are much more concentrated. Don't discard that gel-like pulpy mass of seeds the next time you cook—umami goodness is stored there.

When I prepare a dish that needs tomatoes' umami flavor, but not necessarily the flavor of a fresh tomato—such as preparing the base for a soup, stew, stock, or even a curry (Dal Makhani, page 292)—I opt for tomato paste. Tomato paste is prepared by concentrating puréed tomatoes, and a few tablespoons can dramatically enhance the umami taste, with the added advantage of not introducing more liquid. Sundried Tomatoes + Red Bell Pepper Spread (page 314) and dehydrated tomato powder are additional options for umami boosters.

YEAST EXTRACT

One of the most popular sources for cheese-like flavorings among people who consume an exclusively plant-based diet is yeast extract. This is produced from leftover dead yeast cells after fermentation; these are heated and then processed to produce yeast extract. A combination of enzyme-based reactions such as proteolysis helps boost the umami taste of this product. It can be sprinkled on top of pasta, chips, popcorn, or vegetables and stirred into soups and stocks, much like bonito flakes, to add a rich umami note. Marmite, a byproduct of beer brewing, and Vegemite, a byproduct of brewers' yeast, both contain yeast extract with other flavoring ingredients and are usually eaten as a spread on toast or sandwiches.

FISH SAUCE

SOY SAUCE

+ Umami-infused salts are a great way to add and increase the perception of savoriness in food. You can use them as a cooking salt and even as a finishing salt just before serving.

+ Most fermented food products, such as kimchi, fish and shrimp pickles and aachars, and hot sambals are rich in savoriness, fieriness, and other tastes. Serve them as condiments on the side with a meal; use them in sandwiches or wraps to add a layer of flavor. If possible, try to incorporate them into mayonnaise or dips for added depth. For example, grind a few tablespoons of kimchi to make a purée, and incorporate that into sauces.

+ The Indo-Chinese Condiments (page 317) provide heat, saltiness, acidity, and savoriness. The Indo-Sichuan Sauce (page 318) is extremely versatile; at home I serve it with almost any appetizer. In India, many restaurants serve the potato chops from my book *Season* with this condiment.

+ Steep ingredients like kombu, nori, tea leaves, matcha, or bonito in hot liquids to make flavorful stocks. Since most of these ingredients are dried, it makes it much easier to draw out their umami-tasting substances than with other foods in a short period of time, usually a few minutes.

+ A spoonful of miso can impart a bucketload of flavor. I usually use white miso or shiro for sweeter applications (see Chocolate Miso Bread Pudding, page 133) and the darker red akamiso for savory dishes.

+ Diced sundried cherry tomatoes and tomato powder are a great way to boost the savory factor in a meal. Blend them into vinaigrettes to make salad dressings or into sauces for braised or roasted vegetables and meat.

USING SAVORINESS IN THE KITCHEN

+ When making kitchen stocks with ingredients rich in IMP, such as bonito, add the cooking acids once the stock is prepared, not during cooking. Acids tend to decrease the amount of IMP when heated.

+ Bring texture to your food by sprinkling a generous tablespoon or two of bonito flakes over hardboiled eggs, inside sandwiches, and even as a garnish over soups.

+ Shavings of Parmesan over sweet and tart fruits, such as pears, peaches, and apples, in salads with a few toasted nuts provide a spot of savory and salty all rolled into one.

+ Salt-cured egg yolks (see recipe in Pantry Essentials, page 312) are rich in glutamate, which provides a strong umami taste. Grated, they taste like salted cheese. Use as a garnish wherever you would use grated cheese.

+ Nuts such as walnuts are rich in glutamate and can also provide a crunchy texture.

+ Our sensitivity to umami decreases as the temperature drops. Consequently, serving umami-rich dishes at warmer temperatures will increase the perception of savoriness. A cold broth will not taste as delicious as it would when warm for this very reason.

+ Cooking techniques like roasting will enhance the perception of savoriness. You can try this trick to improve on the flavor of tomatoes when they aren't in season or they just don't taste as good (which sometimes happens even when I grow them in summer) (see Roasted Tomatoes with Curry Leaves, page 153).

+ Savoriness can enhance the perception of saltiness. You can take advantage of this when you want to cut back on the amount of salt in a dish; for example, by adding fish sauce. Several brands of fermented food products, such as soy sauce, are now commercially available in a low-sodium version (see Baked Sweet Potatoes with Maple Crème Fraîche, page 177, and

Shepherd's Pie with Kheema + Chouriço, page 226).

+ A pinch of salt on a slice of tomato or sautéed mushrooms will bump up the note of savoriness (see "Pizza" Toast, page 143, and Goan Shrimp, Olive + Tomato Pulao, page 220).

+ A tiny bit of sugar or sweetener such as honey can enhance the perception of umami. While most foods are a blend of various flavors, you might notice this sweet touch in many South Asian recipes. Sometimes, a pinch of sugar is added to curries such as my beloved Massaman to enhance the savory taste. Besides sweeteners, some curries will often call for ingredients that contain a small amount of sugar such as coconut milk and even tamarind.

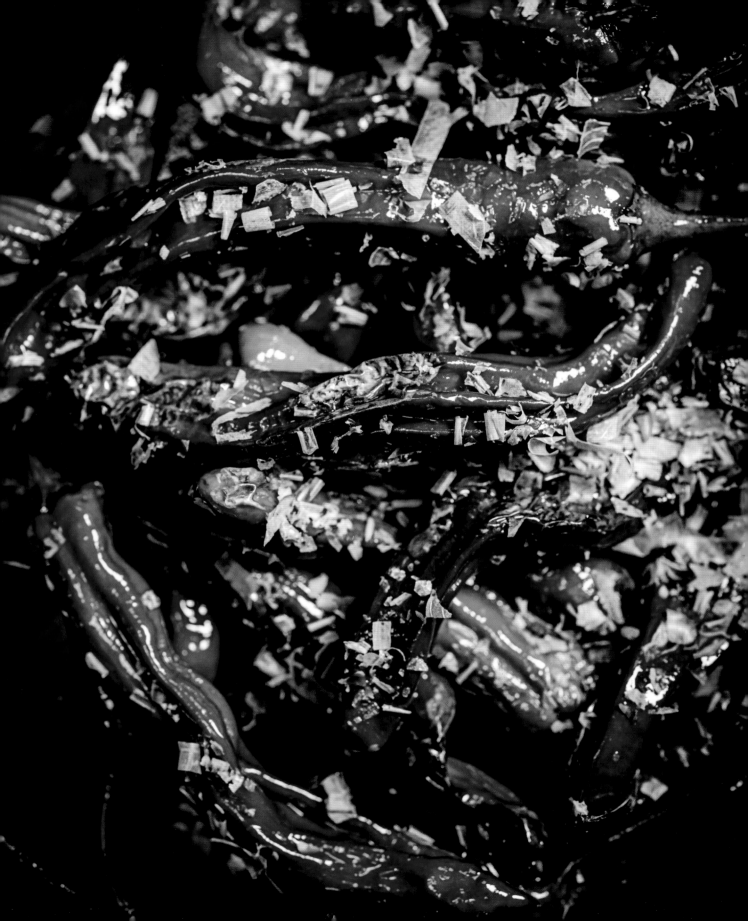

Blistered Shishito/Padrón Peppers with Bonito Flakes

The excitement in eating shishito or padrón peppers is the gamble; you never know which pepper out of the lot will be blazing hot. Full disclosure: I eat only the tame ones but cautiously take a tiny bite every time. Typically, one or a few out of a batch of these curvy peppers will taste fiery. You can easily double this recipe to serve a larger group.

SERVES 4

2 Tbsp extra-virgin olive oil

12 oz [340 g] shishito/padrón peppers

2 Tbsp low-sodium soy sauce

Flaky sea salt

3 to 4 Tbsp bonito flakes

THE FLAVOR APPROACH

The synergistic effect of soy and bonito flakes comes together in this dish. Try tasting the dish before and after you add the bonito flakes to see for yourself how umami synergism works.

Using a low-sodium soy sauce gives you more control over the amount of salt to use.

Salt helps enhance the umami.

Heat the oil in a medium skillet over medium-high heat. When the oil is hot, add the peppers and sear, turning occasionally, until they develop a few blisters on each side, 2 to 3 minutes. Drizzle with the soy sauce and toss to coat evenly, cooking for 30 seconds. Remove from the heat and transfer the peppers to a serving dish. Sprinkle generously with the salt and bonito flakes. Serve immediately.

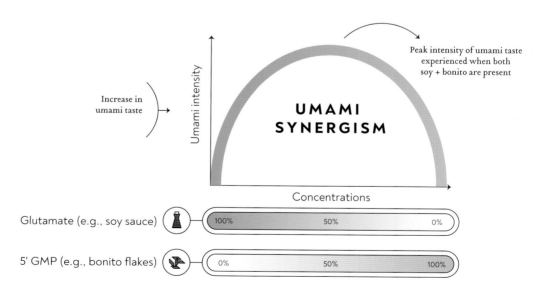

Adapted from Yamaguchi S., Ninomiya K. "Umami and food palatability." *Journal of Nutrition* 130, 4S (2000).

Roasted Broccolini + Chickpea Pancakes

Besan chilla, chickpea pancakes—or chickpea omelets, as my dad calls them—are best eaten as soon as they come off the hot pan. Smear the pancake generously with the Indo-Sichuan Sauce (page 318), throw in a couple of roasted broccolini stalks, wrap, and take a big bite.

SERVES 4

For the broccolini:

2 bunches broccolini (total weight 1 lb [455 g])

2 Tbsp extra-virgin olive oil

½ tsp ground black pepper

Fine sea salt

For the pancakes:

2 cups [240 g] chickpea flour

½ tsp red chilli powder

½ tsp ground turmeric

½ tsp fine sea salt

2 Tbsp chopped cilantro

1 green chilli, minced

4 Tbsp [60 ml] extra-virgin olive oil to fry

½ cup [97 g] Indo-Sichuan Sauce (page 318)

THE FLAVOR APPROACH

Broccoli and many other brassicas are rich in glutamates, which gives them a savory aspect that becomes much more apparent on roasting. To increase the umami taste, splash 1 Tbsp of soy or tamari sauce on the broccolini once they're cooked, and swap the fine salt out for an umami-infused salt.

Using a wire rack allows air circulation and prevents the broccolini from sitting in a pool of its own liquid and turning soggy. The broccolini are spread out between two baking sheets to prevent overcrowding. This gives the broccolini a crispy, roasted texture.

Variation: To make a lighter, airier pancake, like the classic American-style pancake, add 1 tsp baking powder along with ½ tsp baking soda and 1 Tbsp of apple cider vinegar to the batter.

To prepare the broccolini, preheat the oven to 425°F [218°C]. Line two baking sheets with aluminum foil and place a wire rack on top of each.

Trim the ends of the broccolini stalks. Rub them with the olive oil, black pepper, and salt. Divide and spread the broccolini over the two baking sheets. Roast the broccolini in the oven for 15 to 20 minutes, until the tops are slightly charred and crispy.

To prepare the pancakes, whisk the flour and 1½ cups [360 ml] of water to form a smooth batter. Whisk in the chilli powder, turmeric, and salt. Fold in the cilantro and chilli.

Heat 1 Tbsp of the olive oil in a cast-iron or stainless-steel skillet over medium-high heat. Stir the batter and pour ¼ cup [60 ml] into the pan, swirling to spread the batter. Cook until the pancake starts to release from the bottom, about 2 minutes. Flip and cook again until the pancake is completely cooked, slightly firm, and golden brown, about 2 minutes. Prepare the remaining pancakes similarly. Transfer to a serving plate and top with some of the roasted broccolini and Indo-Sichuan Sauce.

Chicken Hakka Noodles (Indo-Chinese)

Indo-Chinese food differs quite a bit from familiar Chinese food; to many, it bears little resemblance. But this special cuisine is an integral part of Indian cuisine and is highly celebrated all over the country. Born out of innovation by the original Hakka immigrants who first moved to Kolkata (Calcutta) and by local Indian chefs, an array of recipes that use spices lavishly and defy any rules gave rise, unexpectedly, to a whole new genre of Indian cuisine. It's not that easy to find some of these recipes in restaurants outside India, save for a few large metropolitan areas, and it's even rarer to see them mentioned in Indian cookbooks. Chicken hakka noodles are delicious on their own and really require no other accompaniment besides the Chilli-Soy Vinegar Sauce and the Indo-Sichuan Sauce (pages 317 and 318).

SERVES 4

12 oz [340 g] chow mein stir-fry noodles

Fine sea salt

2 Tbsp sesame oil

2 Tbsp grapeseed oil or other neutral oil

2 garlic cloves, minced

One 1 in [2.5 cm] piece fresh ginger, peeled and minced

1 green chilli, minced

1 medium onion (9¼ oz [260 g]), halved and thinly sliced

1 bunch scallions (about 4 oz [115 g]), both white and green parts, thinly sliced

1 tsp ground black pepper

1 tsp ground cumin

½ tsp red chilli powder

7 oz [200 g] green cabbage, shredded

1 medium green bell pepper (7 oz [200 g]), thinly sliced

5½ oz [155 g] green beans, thinly sliced

5½ oz [155 g] carrots, sliced into 1 in [2.5 cm] matchsticks

7 oz [200 g] shredded rotisserie chicken, skin and bones discarded

2 Tbsp low-sodium soy sauce

2 Tbsp rice wine vinegar

2 tsp amchur

THE FLAVOR APPROACH

The fruity sour taste of amchur is what really makes this noodle dish's flavors stand out against the savory soy and the warmth of the scallions, garlic, and ginger.

Select an oil with a high smoke point if you don't have grapeseed oil (see table of oils and smoke points, page 336). The temperature of the wok should be at about 350°F [177°C] when you stir-fry (I use an infra-red surface thermometer to measure the temperature). At this temperature, the oil starts to shimmer and will be hot enough to cook.

Cook the noodles in a large pot of salted water according to the package instructions. The noodles will be cooked in 3 to 4 minutes, once they are just tender. Drain, rinse under running tap water, and drain again. Place them in a large bowl and drizzle immediately with the sesame oil. Toss to coat the noodles evenly and prevent sticking. Season with salt.

Heat the grapeseed oil in a wok or saucepan over medium-high heat. Add the garlic, ginger, and chilli to the hot oil and sauté until fragrant, 30 to 45 seconds. Add the onions and sauté until they turn translucent, 4 to 5 minutes. Add the scallions and sauté for 1 minute, until they just start to soften. Add the black pepper, cumin, and red chilli powder and cook until fragrant, 30 to 45 seconds.

Add the cabbage, bell pepper, green beans, and carrots and stir-fry until the vegetables are tender-crisp, 3 to 4 minutes. Season with salt. Add the chicken and cook for 1 minute. Transfer the vegetables and chicken to the noodles in the large bowl.

Combine the soy sauce, vinegar, and amchur in a small mixing bowl. Pour the liquid over the noodles in the large bowl and toss to coat evenly with a pair of kitchen tongs. Serve warm.

Stir-Fried Cabbage

This is a simple side dish, yet one that packs savoriness in vegetables. Every ingredient here works in concert to support the umami notes in the cabbage.

SERVES 4 AS A SIDE

1¾ lb [800 g] green cabbage

1 Tbsp grapeseed oil or other neutral oil

1 garlic clove, peeled and smashed

½ tsp ground black pepper

Fine sea salt

1 Tbsp low-sodium soy sauce

1 Tbsp toasted sesame oil

THE FLAVOR APPROACH

Another brassica that's rich in glutamate is cabbage, which benefits from the addition of soy sauce as well as toasted sesame oil.

Be sure the cabbage leaves are dried after washing (a salad spinner is helpful); too much water will end up braising the cabbage rather than stir-frying, as the water will cool the wok down considerably.

Select an oil with a high smoke point if you don't have grapeseed oil (see table of oils and smoke points, page 336). The temperature of the wok should be at about 350°F [177°C] when you stir-fry (I use an infra-red surface thermometer to measure the temperature). At this temperature, the oil starts to shimmer and will be hot enough to cook.

Cut the cabbage into large chunks and separate the leaves.

Heat the grapeseed oil in a wok or large stainless-steel saucepan over high heat until it starts to shimmer. Add the garlic and cook until it just starts to brown, 30 to 45 seconds. Add the cabbage and stir-fry until the leaves begin to wilt and get slightly seared, 10 to 12 minutes. Add the pepper and season with salt. Drizzle in the soy sauce and sesame oil and toss to coat. Remove from the heat, transfer to a serving dish, and serve immediately.

Goan Shrimp, Olive + Tomato Pulao

Growing up on the coast, you quickly learn to appreciate the sea and all it offers. Shrimp, both fresh and dried, is a popular staple in Goan cuisine. This is a one-pot dish that really doesn't need anything but a salad on the side. My grandmother used to make this dish by cooking the shrimp with the rice, but there is the added risk of the shrimp overcooking and turning rubbery. Adding the shrimp toward the end avoids this. You can use fresh or frozen shrimp here, but stay away from precooked shrimp because it will leave an unpleasant aftertaste (similar to the reasons why the taste and aroma of fish change when cooked twice).

SERVES 4

2 cups [400 g] basmati rice

1¼ lb [570 g] white onions, cut in half and thinly sliced

4 Tbsp [60 ml] extra-virgin olive oil

Fine sea salt

Two 2 in [5 cm] cinnamon sticks

4 cloves

1 tsp ground green cardamom

4 garlic cloves, peeled and thinly sliced

One 2 in [5 cm] piece fresh ginger, peeled and cut into 1 in [2.5 cm] matchsticks

¼ tsp ground cayenne

¼ cup [55 g] tomato paste

4 cups [960 ml] low-sodium chicken stock or "brown" vegetable stock (page 57)

1½ lb [680 g] medium shrimp, peeled and deveined, tails left on

2 Tbsp fresh lemon juice

One 6 oz can [170 g] large pitted black olives, cut in half, for garnish

2 Tbsp scallions, both white and green parts, thinly sliced, for garnish

Plain unsweetened Greek yogurt, for serving

THE FLAVOR APPROACH

The concentrated savory taste comes from the combination of tomatoes, olives, and shrimp, and salt helps enhance that effect.

I typically prepare this pulao with chicken stock; however, you can opt to use the "brown" vegetable stock (page 57) for a richer punch of umami.

Preheat the oven to 300°F [149°C]. Set a rack in the upper one-third position. Line a baking sheet with parchment paper.

Check the rice for any debris and soak it in enough water to cover for 30 minutes.

Toss the onions with 2 Tbsp of the oil, season with salt, and spread them out in a single layer on the prepared baking sheet. Roast in the oven until they turn crisp and golden brown, stirring occasionally to redistribute and ensure even browning, about 1 hour. Watch them carefully to prevent them from burning. If the oven is too hot, cook them at mid-level in the oven.

About 5 minutes before the rice soaking time is up, heat the remaining 2 Tbsp of olive oil in a medium saucepan or Dutch oven over medium-high heat. Fry the cinnamon, cloves, and cardamom until fragrant, 30 to 45 seconds. Add the garlic, ginger, and cayenne and sauté until they just start to turn light brown and become fragrant, 1 minute. Stir in the tomato paste and cook for 4 minutes, stirring constantly, until the tomato paste just starts to brown and stick to the pan bottom. Drain the rice, add it to the pan, and fry carefully, stirring and taking care to avoid breaking the grains, until the rice starts to stick to the pan, 2 to 3 minutes.

cont'd

Pour in the stock, increase the heat to high, and bring to a boil. Lower the heat to a simmer, cover with a lid, and cook without stirring till the liquid at the base of the saucepan almost evaporates, 15 to 20 minutes. Season the shrimp with salt and layer the shrimp on top of the rice in the pan. Cover the pan with the lid and continue to cook till the shrimp turn pink, 3 to 4 minutes, and the water evaporates completely.

Sprinkle with the lemon juice. Remove from the heat and let sit for 5 minutes before serving. Fluff the rice with a fork, fold the shrimp in carefully, and transfer to a serving dish. Garnish with the olive halves and scallions and serve warm with yogurt.

Chicken Kanji

The Sanskrit *kanji* refers to the thick, starchy water that's left behind when rice is cooked for a while; it is also the origin for congee, which is also eaten in other parts of Asia where rice is a staple. While this is the dish my mother always served me when I was unwell (she cooked it with bits of chicken), I've given it a bit of a makeover and brought in a few spices.

SERVES 4

For the kanji:

½ cup [100 g] rice

4 chicken thighs (about 1½ lb [680 g]), bone-in and skin left on

Fine sea salt

1 Tbsp grapeseed oil or other neutral oil

½ tsp ground black pepper

4 cloves

2 bay leaves

3 shallots (total weight 6½ oz [180 g]), thinly sliced

2 Tbsp extra-virgin olive oil

For the chutney:

2 Tbsp [60 ml] extra-virgin olive oil

½ cup [20 g] chopped cilantro leaves

¼ cup [60 ml] fresh lime juice

2 garlic cloves, peeled and minced

½ tsp red chilli flakes such as Aleppo, Maras, or Urfa

THE FLAVOR APPROACH

You can use any kind of rice here; both short-grain and long-grain work well. Unlike the pulaos or other recipes in which long-grain basmati rice is left undisturbed while it cooks, here the rice must be stirred occasionally. This helps break up the grains as they soften, creating a thicker consistency.

The savory character of this porridge-like soup comes from the chicken, which is first seasoned and seared to build flavor molecules through the Maillard reaction.

Lime juice provides the necessary touch of sourness to the taste of the congee.

The crunchy shallots and the sour notes of the chutney provide a much-needed contrast to the smooth and soft texture of this simple dish.

To prepare the kanji, clean and pick through the rice for any debris. Rinse the rice in a fine-mesh sieve under running tap water. Transfer the rice to a small bowl, add enough water to cover, and let soak for 30 minutes.

Use clean paper towels to wipe the chicken and pat dry. Season both sides with salt. Heat the grapeseed oil in a medium saucepan or Dutch oven over medium-high heat. Sear the chicken on each side until the skin turns golden brown, 3 to 4 minutes. Add the black pepper, cloves, and bay leaves and cook until fragrant, 30 to 45 seconds. Drain the rice, add it to the pan with the chicken, and stir in 2 cups [480 ml] of water. Bring to a boil over medium-high heat, then lower the heat to low and let simmer until the chicken is completely cooked, the rice is falling apart, and the liquid is thickened, 45 minutes to 1 hour. Stir occasionally to break the rice grains. The liquid should have a thick, soupy consistency. Add more water if needed.

Once the chicken is cooked, remove the thighs with a pair of kitchen tongs and separate the meat from the bones. Shred the meat and discard the bones.

While the chicken and rice cook, prepare the shallots. Preheat the oven to 300°F [149°C]. Line a baking sheet with parchment paper.

Trim and discard the ends of the shallots and cut them into thin slices. Toss the shallots with the olive oil in a small bowl and season with salt.

Spread the shallots in a single layer on the prepared baking sheet and cook until the shallots turn golden brown and crisp, 30 to 45 minutes. Stir them occasionally during cooking to ensure even browning.

To prepare the chutney, in a small bowl, whisk together the olive oil, cilantro, lime juice, garlic, and red chilli flakes. Taste and season with salt.

When ready to eat, serve the kanji warm or hot topped with chicken, shallots, and chutney on the side.

Roast Chicken Thighs + Vegetables

A quick, flavorful chicken recipe with minimal effort. If you have time to marinate the chicken overnight, the flavor will benefit. For a strong dose of umami, use an umami-flavored salt; it will give this a whole new dimension of taste.

SERVES 4

For the chicken:

4 chicken thighs (total weight about 2 lb [910 g]), bone-in and skin left on

For the marinade:

2 garlic cloves, peeled

One 1 in [2.5 cm] piece fresh ginger, peeled

2 Tbsp white vinegar

2 Tbsp Worcestershire sauce

2 Tbsp extra-virgin olive oil

1 tsp fine sea salt

½ tsp black peppercorns

For the roasted vegetables:

1 lb [455 g] new potatoes

8 oz [230 g] sliced mushrooms

1 cup [120 g] fresh or frozen peas (no need to thaw)

1 Tbsp extra-virgin olive oil

½ tsp coarsely ground black pepper

Fine sea salt

For garnish:

2 Tbsp chopped chives

1 fresh green or red chilli such as bird's eye chillies, thinly sliced

THE FLAVOR APPROACH

Worcestershire sauce acts as the savory booster for the marinade that seasons the chicken.

The fat in the chicken is released during roasting and renders, adding a second component of flavoring to the vegetables in the pan.

Garlic, ginger, peppercorns, and fresh chillies provide the "heat" molecules that act via chemesthesis.

To prepare the chicken, dry it with clean paper towels and place in a large resealable bag.

To prepare the marinade, blend the garlic, ginger, vinegar, Worcestershire sauce, olive oil, salt, and peppercorns on high speed for a few seconds until combined. Pour the marinade over the chicken, seal the bag, shake to coat, and let marinate in the refrigerator for at least 2 hours, preferably overnight.

When ready to cook, set the bag with chicken on the kitchen counter to reach room temperature, about 15 minutes.

Preheat the oven to 400°F [204°C].

To prepare the vegetables, toss the potatoes, mushrooms, and peas in a large bowl with the olive oil and pepper and season with salt. Spread the vegetables out in a large baking pan or roasting dish.

Remove the chicken from the bag and arrange the thighs, skin side up, over the vegetables. Pour any leftover marinade over the chicken thighs. Roast in the oven until the skin on the thighs is browned and crispy and the potatoes are soft and tender, 55 to 60 minutes. The chicken is ready when the internal temperature reaches 165°F [74°C] on an instant-read thermometer. Remove the pan from the oven and let sit for 5 minutes.

Garnish with the chives and chillies and serve.

Shepherd's Pie with Kheema + Chouriço

Though our family served this only on special holidays such as Christmas or Easter, this is comfort food all the way. I usually use small or medium potatoes, as they take less time to cook than larger ones. Ground beef can be substituted for lamb.

SERVES 6 TO 8

For the lamb kheema:

1 Tbsp extra-virgin olive oil

1 medium white onion (9¼ oz [260 g]), diced

4 garlic cloves, peeled and minced

1 in [2.5 cm] piece fresh ginger, peeled and minced

1 green chilli, minced

¼ cup [55 g] tomato paste

2 tsp garam masala, homemade (page 312) or store-bought

1 tsp ground turmeric

1 tsp red chilli powder

8 oz [230 g] peas

8 oz [230 g] carrots, cut into 1 in [2.5 cm] matchsticks

6 oz [170 g] chouriço

2 lb [910 g] ground lamb

2 Tbsp all-purpose flour

¼ cup [60 ml] malt or apple cider vinegar

¼ cup [10 g] chopped cilantro leaves

1 tsp fish sauce

For the mashed potato topping:

1 medium russet potato (1 lb [455 g])

5 oz [140 g] crème fraîche or sour cream

¼ cup [55 g] unsalted butter, cubed, at room temperature

1 tsp ground black pepper

Fine sea salt

½ cup [25 g] panko crumbs

THE FLAVOR APPROACH

Kheema, or minced meat, appears in several variations throughout India; in this version, chouriço adds a pop of sourness and heat to the savory profile of the meat.

A tiny splash of fish sauce amplifies the umami nature of the filling.

Vinegar adds sourness to balance the stronger flavors from the spices and meat.

Tomato paste adds to the savory character of the meat.

The mashed potatoes retain moisture and stay soft due to the addition of fat.

Panko crumbs provide a layer of crunchiness.

Preheat the oven to 400°F [204°C].

To prepare the lamb kheema, heat the oil in a large skillet over medium-high heat. Add the onion and sauté until it turns translucent, 4 to 5 minutes. Add the garlic, ginger, and green chilli and sauté for 1 minute. Add the tomato paste, garam masala, turmeric, and red chilli powder and cook until the spices are fragrant, 30 to 45 seconds. Add the peas and carrots, and sauté until tender, 8 to 10 minutes. Remove the chouriço from the casing and break it into small bits. Add it to the skillet and cook until the sausage starts to brown, 4 to 5 minutes. Break the lamb into chunks and add it to the skillet. Sauté until the lamb starts to brown, 4 to 5 minutes. At this stage, you can remove some of the excess fat using a large spoon and discard. Sift the flour over the meat and fold it in to coat evenly. Add the vinegar and cook, stirring, over low heat until the liquid has almost completely evaporated. Remove from the heat and stir in the cilantro and fish sauce. Transfer the meat to a large baking dish and level with an offset spatula.

Rinse and scrub the potatoes under running tap water. Place the potatoes in a large pot with enough salted water to cover them by 1 in [2.5 cm]. Bring to a boil over medium-high heat, then lower the heat to medium-low. Cook until the potatoes are completely tender but not mushy, 20 to 30 minutes. Drain the potatoes and set them aside until cool enough to handle.

Peel the potatoes and discard the skins. Mash the potatoes in a large bowl with the crème fraîche, butter, and pepper until smooth. Taste and season with salt. Spoon the mixture onto the meat in the baking dish. Level with an offset spatula. Sprinkle the panko over the layer of mashed potatoes and bake until the top is golden brown, 20 to 25 minutes. Remove from the oven and let rest for 10 minutes before serving.

Coffee-Spiced Steak with Burnt Kachumber Salad

Kachumber is an Indian condiment type of salad (we often serve our salads on the side as part of a larger meal) made with cucumber, onions, and tomatoes. In this version I've reconstructed it, roasting the onions and tomatoes, then adding bits of fresh cucumber—being rich in water, the cucumber is not heated. This "burnt" version pairs well with the grilled steak. Note: The salad can be made a few hours ahead of time.

SERVES 2

For the burnt kachumber salad:

12 oz [340 g] cherry or grape tomatoes, cut in half

1 medium red onion (9¼ oz [260 g]), peeled and cut in half

1 green chilli, cut in half

3 Tbsp extra-virgin olive oil

1 cucumber (12 oz [340 g]), diced

2 Tbsp chopped cilantro

2 Tbsp fresh lemon juice

½ tsp ground black pepper

Fine sea salt

For the steak:

2 Tbsp coarsely ground coffee beans

1 Tbsp coriander seeds, cracked

1 Tbsp red chilli flakes, preferably Urfa

1 Tbsp fine sea salt

1 tsp ground green cardamom

Two 1 in [2.5 cm] thick rib eye steaks (1 lb [455 g] each)

2 to 4 Tbsp melted ghee or extra-virgin olive oil

THE FLAVOR APPROACH

Coffee is bitter to taste, but when added to meat in this spice blend, it enhances the savory character.

Urfa biber has a chocolate-like aroma that pairs well with the ground coffee in the steak seasoning.

As the tomatoes and onions cook in the oven, they not only change their flavor, but the tomatoes begin to fall apart and release their juices, which concentrate and create a salsa-like texture that makes it worthy to coat each slice of steak. The tomato flavor molecules concentrate on heating, which adds to the umami profile of the steak.

I've included the steak flipping method as an option in the instructions; this method lets the juices redistribute as the meat cooks by reducing the time for the juices to settle; consequently the risk of the meat drying out is reduced, as explained by Harold McGee in *On Food and Cooking*.

To prepare the kachumber, preheat the oven to 425°F [218°C]. Line a baking sheet with aluminum foil.

Toss the tomatoes, onion, and chilli with 1 Tbsp of the oil. Place the baking sheet on the top rack of the oven and roast for 15 to 20 minutes, until the vegetables just start to get charred and the tomato juices bubble. Turn the oven to the medium broil setting and cook for an additional 5 to 8 minutes, until the vegetables develop deeper dark char marks and are slightly burnt. Do not overdo it or they will turn very bitter. Remove from the heat and let cool for 10 minutes. (If making ahead of time, store in an airtight container in the refrigerator for up to 2 days, then proceed with the recipe.)

cont'd

Once the vegetables are cool, chop them coarsely and place them with the cucumber and cilantro in a medium mixing bowl. Add the lemon juice, the remaining 2 Tbsp of olive oil, and the pepper and season with salt. Toss to coat. Keep covered and let rest for at least 30 minutes before serving.

To prepare the steaks, mix the coffee, coriander, red chilli flakes, salt, and cardamom together in a small bowl.

Pat the steaks dry with paper towels and press the spice mixture generously onto the surface of both sides and let sit at room temperature for at least 45 minutes and up to 1 hour.

When ready to cook, preheat the grill to high and brush the grates with a little ghee. Drizzle about 1 Tbsp of ghee on each side of the steaks. Place them on the hot grill, close the lid, and cook the steaks 3 to 4 minutes per side for rare (120°F [49°C] on an instant-read thermometer) and 5 to 6 minutes per side for medium-rare (130°F [55°C]). Or, if using a grill pan, heat 2 Tbsp of the ghee over high heat until it smokes and cook the steaks one at a time. If you don't care about the aesthetic of grill marks, flip the steaks as they cook over the hot pan every 30 seconds till they're cooked. Flipping the steaks often allows the juices to redistribute and the meat does not dry out. Transfer the steaks to a plate, tent loosely with foil, and let rest for 5 minutes before serving.

Serve with the burnt kachumber salad on the side.

6 FIERINESS

I CAN'T TOLERATE HOT foods the way the rest of my family can. My dad eats fresh tiny green chillies as a side with his meals, and my mother throws generous handfuls of hot dried chillies into the blender when she makes her fish curries. I don't think I would survive either.

As a kid, I wanted to cook everything out of my parents' cookbooks, so I attempted the classic Punjabi samosa. The recipe calls for a lot of freshly ground black peppercorns and green chillies. I assembled and fried the pastries—but they were too hot to eat. They tasted pungent. My mouth and ears were on fire. It taught me that our individual ability to handle heat varies; what works for some might not work for others. I began to pay attention to how much heat could work as a middle ground for me and the people I fed—what types of chillies fit with specific dishes. Alongside the salt on my table at home is a range of hot sauces so those I feed can add as much heat as they need.

How Fieriness Works

Fieriness isn't one of the five canonical tastes. It's not a literal spike in temperature inside our mouth. This is an illusion; the "heat" is a sensation. Scientifically, it's a phenomenon called *chemesthesis*: the body's response to irritation. Throughout our body, including our mouth and nose, are sensory receptors that constantly scan our environment for changes in temperature (thermoreceptors), pain, and pressure (mechanoreceptors). When you take a bite out of a fresh or dried chilli or a black peppercorn, specific chemicals in these ingredients attach to these sensory receptors, which get irritated and trick the brain to produce a sensation of heat and pain. You feel a desire to drink water to wash away the feeling of intense heat. Over time, by gradually introducing hotter foods, you can develop a tolerance as your pain receptors adjust. Many of us have learned to love this perception of heat and associate it with deliciousness.

Many common ingredients work through chemesthesis: cinnamon, for example, produces a warming sensation, while cardamom "tastes" cool.

FIERINESS SCALES

There are several different types of scales used to compare the level of heat produced by some of the fire-boosting ingredients. Since no machine can actually measure the human perception of taste, most measurements are based on responses from people in taste test groups. The pyruvate scale is calculated based on measured amounts of specific components.

THE SCOVILLE SCALE

A chilli's heat can vary considerably for a few reasons, mainly genetics and environment. The plant's genetic makeup will affect how much capsaicin is produced; this also differs between varieties. For example, the Kashmiri chilli produces very little heat and clocks in at 1,000 to 2,000 Scoville Heat Units (SHU), but the fiery cayenne chilli registers at 30,000 to 50,000 SHU.

Soil, water, climate, and other environmental factors affect the amount of capsaicin produced; for example, if a low-heat-producing chilli plant is grown under stressful conditions, the plant will adapt and produce hotter chillies.

The Scoville values for a chilli are obtained by determining how much sugar it takes to dilute a chilli extract until the taste is no longer detectable by a group of tasters. The more sugar it takes, the hotter the chilli. Because the Scoville method is based on taste perception by people, it is imprecise. Chilli experts will complement the information from the scale by scientifically measuring capsaicin to quantify a chilli's heat.

PYRUVATE SCALE FOR ALLIUMS

When an allium, such as onion or garlic, is cut open, the cells break and a series of reactions leads to the formation of the flavor molecules that give these vegetables their pungent aroma and taste, and in the case of the onion make us cry. The pungency is expressed indirectly by measuring the amount of pyruvic acid formed as a byproduct of these reactions. The scale runs from 1 to 10 units, and the general assumption is that the lower the number, the sweeter the taste. These foods can vary in pungency depending on the type of plant and how it grew. Usually, plants grown in hot weather and dry soil rich in sulfur produce the strongest flavor.

There are various ways to add fieriness to food. Here are some of the ingredients I turn to most often.

Pepper and Pepper Varieties

The three most common forms of pepper you will encounter are black peppercorns, long peppers, and cubeb, each of which contain a group of related "heat" producing chemicals, the most well-known being piperine (see Black Pepper Chicken, page 260).

Peppercorns start out as unripe green berries on a pepper vine. They're harvested at different stages of development and undergo treatments to produce the peppercorns we buy, which vary in color, heat, and aroma. In general, black peppercorns have the strongest bite; green and white ones are much more mellow. Green peppercorns are often sold pickled, and these can be blended into sauces, stews, and salad dressings. Within black pepper are many varietals, each with their own aroma and flavor. Decorticated peppercorns are produced by mechanically rubbing the skin off; these are milder than black pepper.

The pink peppercorns sometimes mixed into jars labeled as "rainbow peppercorns" are not true peppercorns. Not only are they physically different in appearance, but they lack piperine and contain a chemical called cardanol. These tiny fruits come from Peruvian and Brazilian pepper trees and are surprisingly sweet in taste. Heat drastically reduces their flavor, so use them raw, lightly cracked, and sprinkled over cheese or salads.

Long pepper looks like an elongated pinecone. I use it to infuse drinks and grate it into ice creams and desserts (see Gingerbread Cake with Date Syrup Bourbon Sauce, page 268) for its distinct floral aroma. In appearance it is almost identical to black peppercorn. You will find it in the *markout* semolina pastries of Morocco and in the spice blend *ras el hanout* as well as in the *gulés* (curries) of Indonesia.

With so many different varieties of peppercorns now available in markets and specialty stores, you can experiment by cooking with one type of peppercorn at a time to understand its full flavor potential before moving on to the next.

SICHUAN PEPPERCORNS

These aren't really peppercorns; instead, this popular spice used in Chinese cuisine grows on the prickly ash tree. They create a numbing sensation on the tongue via a chemical called *hydroxy-alpha-sanshool*. The outer pink shell carries all the flavor, so use the husk and not the inner black seed.

There are a couple of different ways to extract the hydroxy-alpha-sanshool. You can toast the peppercorns over medium-high heat until fragrant, 30 to 45 seconds, then crush and add to hot oil. A second method (see Burrata with Chilli Oil + Thai Basil, page 283) involves cold infusion—the peppercorns resting overnight in cold oil—followed by a warm infusion in oil after the oil is slowly warmed up to draw out the hydroxy-alpha-sanshool.

CHILLIES (FRESH AND DRIED)

While chillies are perceived as synonymous with Indian cooking and culture, they were actually brought by the Portuguese from Mesoamerica and quickly absorbed into the local cuisine.

Chillies are the fruit of the capsicum plant and owe their heat to the capsaicin molecules that are heavily concentrated in the placenta (the pale, soft fleshy area close to the stem) and the seeds; removing these two components of the chilli will help reduce some of the intensity. The Scoville Scale (page 238) will give you a good idea of how hot some chillies are compared to others. Dried chillies will always be hotter than fresh ones, as the removal of water by dehydration helps concentrate the capsaicin. Some chillies are renowned for their bright red color, like paprika, Aleppo, and the Kashmiri chillies used in Indian cooking; others, like cayenne and bird's eye, are renowned for their fiery heat; some, like the chipotle (obtained by drying fresh jalapeños) and the Turkish Urfa biber, are distinctly smoky.

You can get greater relief from the burning heat of chilli by consuming dairy, like a glass of milk or yogurt, than by drinking water. The milk protein casein prevents the capsaicin molecules from interacting with sensory receptors and takes away some of the burning. If you visit an Indian restaurant, you'll often see yogurt or raita on the menu; these not only cool but also counteract the heat from the chillies used in the food.

When I moved to the United States, I struggled with the various names for chillies (in this book I'm using the Indian spelling, chilli): peppers, chillies, chiles. Harold McGee and Alan Davidson explain the word comes from the South American Nahuatl *chilli*, and it came to be associated with the word "pepper" when their taste reminded Spanish explorers of Old World black peppercorns.

GINGER

Prized for its aroma and heat, ginger is one of the most used spices. Along with garlic and onions, ginger forms part of the triad of ingredients added to many meat dishes in India and Asia. Ginger comes in various forms; the fresh rhizome can be grated or pulped for sauces, stews, and curries. The fibrous flesh must be chopped into bits before putting it in the blender or food processor.

Young ginger has a thin skin that does not need to be removed; it is milder in flavor and best in simple syrups for drinks or in desserts. Ginger (and young ginger) juice can be used as a flavoring agent for drinks such as chai or syrups, but keep in mind that the juice is acidic and will curdle dairy. Dried ginger is sometimes sold as a whole root that can be tossed into broths and soups; more commonly, it's powdered and used in baking. Fresh and dried ginger are very different in aroma and flavor, and I don't find them interchangeable in recipes.

Finally, crystallized or candied ginger is a form of cooked ginger used to add a pop of sweetness and heat in ginger-snap cookies and cake (see Gingerbread Cake with Date Syrup Bourbon Sauce, page 268). Galangal, popularly used in Thai, Lao, and Indonesian cooking, is related to ginger. Dried galangal can be used to infuse stocks and broths. For making curry paste, stick with fresh.

ALLIUMS: GARLIC, ONIONS, AND MORE

Within the allium plant family are garlic, onions, shallots, scallions, scapes, ramps, leeks, and chives, all of which contain sulfuric compounds (alk[en]yl-L-cysteine sulfoxides, or ACSOs) that give them their distinctive flavor. When an allium is cut or bruised, the ACSOs are released from the plant's cells and undergo a series of chemical reactions to produce flavor compounds that we can smell and taste. The raw bite of an onion in a salad might seem harsh when compared to fresh scallions, but when onion slices are slipped on top of a burger, they create a delightful burst of heat. Garlic has four ACSOs while an onion has three. This is why they taste unique but familiar.

HORSERADISH AND WASABI

Although their flavors are similar, horseradish and wasabi do not come from the same plants. They both contain the highly volatile chemical allyl isothiocyanate, which instantaneously travels from the mouth to the nose, where it aggravates the sensory receptors and burns—that searing sensation you feel when you eat sushi daubed with wasabi, or prime rib dolloped with horseradish sauce. Both are best eaten raw and are usually prepared by finely grating the roots. The pungency begins to dissipate quickly with exposure to air, so use them soon after grating. Because hot temperatures destroy the enzymes that create the fiery heat of these ingredients, it is best to avoid heating horseradish or wasabi.

MUSTARD AND MUSTARD OIL

The mustard family of plants includes cabbage and the plant from which we get mustard seeds and mustard oil. The three types of mustard seeds—black, brown, and white—contain pungent components called *glucosinolates*, found in many plants we associate with fieriness, including horseradish. The different varieties of seed range in their pungency, with black and brown mustard seeds being a bit more intense than the white variety because they produce different types of isothiocyanates that create different degrees of heat. Black seeds are crushed to produce and release a cooking oil that is used extensively in North India, where it is celebrated for its deliciously pungent flavor and high smoke point. Black mustard seeds are often added to hot oil or ghee, where they "pop" and release their flavor into the oil by a technique called *tadka*; this oil with the seeds is then drizzled over food as a finishing touch. In this preparation, the high cooking temperatures destroy the enzyme that produce pungency, so the result is nutty instead of sharp.

Mustard powder is made by drying and grinding a mixture of black and white seeds; this powder is used to make the popular condiment mustard. The leaves of the mustard plant are edible and are used raw in salads, stir-fried, or sautéed.

OLIVE OIL

While olive oil makes an appearance in Richness (page 278), like mustard oil it deserves a short mention in this section. One unexpected thing I learned at an olive oil taste testing was that olive oil can create a burning sensation in the mouth. A bottle of fresh olive oil will leave a burning, peppery taste at the back of your mouth due to the presence of oleocanthal, a compound that irritates the sensory receptors. The fresher the oil, the stronger the sensation.

CHILLI HEAT SCALE

Total scale runs from 0 to 16 million Scoville Heat Units (SHU).

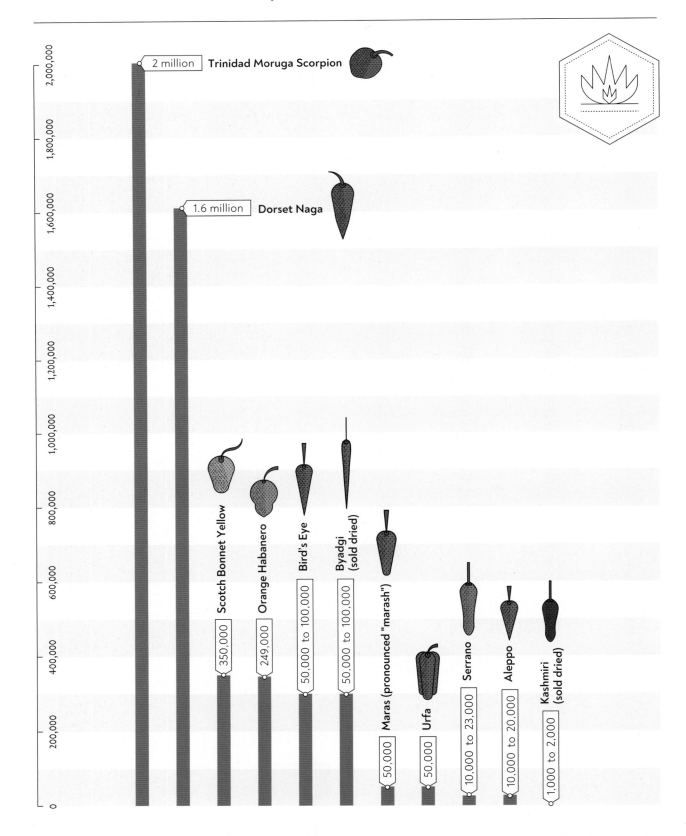

2 million — **Trinidad Moruga Scorpion**

1.6 million — **Dorset Naga**

350,000 — Scotch Bonnet Yellow

249,000 — Orange Habanero

50,000 to 100,000 — Bird's Eye

50,000 to 100,000 — Byadgi (sold dried)

50,000 — Maras (pronounced "marash")

50,000 — Urfa

10,000 to 23,000 — Serrano

10,000 to 20,000 — Aleppo

1,000 to 2,000 — Kashmiri (sold dried)

+ Crack black or cubeb peppercorns or grate long pepper with a Microplane zester over cheese; fresh, broiled, or grilled fruits; vegetables; and even eggs. Coarser grinds will give you a stronger pop of heat.

+ Sprinkle bright chilli powder over raita (pages 78 and 288) or generously drizzle a deep red chilli oil over a salad or savory dish just before serving.

+ Chopped chives, fried slices of garlic, slices of fresh green chillies, or *sil-gochu* (thin threads of red chillies used in Korean cuisine) make fantastic garnishes.

+ Warm mustard oil infused with spices drizzled over a raita, dal, or savory dishes can add a pleasant touch of pungency.

+ Warm temperatures tend to amplify the effect of fiery ingredients like chillies and black pepper in food (try the Manchow Soup, page 255, both warm and chilled and you'll notice the difference). If you drink a glass of cold water while eating hot food, it will instantaneously yet temporarily provide a moment of respite from the heat of the chilli, which returns as the water is swallowed; cold milk or yogurt will do a much better job of cooling you off (see why on page 236).

+ When used in excess, the heat from chillies and peppers can temporarily distract from the appreciation of other tastes and might mask them, so keep this in mind when judging how much to use.

+ Most of the heat-inducing chemicals dissolve better in alcohol or fats; you can take advantage of this when making infusions to flavor drinks or savory dishes. In the case of chillies, extracting them in hot oil or an alcohol like vodka gives you a stronger punch, while water will give you a milder dose.

+ Some of the heat-producing chemicals are temperature sensitive and will break down when cooked. Onions and garlic, for example, lose their potent pungency as they cook and become sweeter in taste.

+ Mustard oil can be used in place of oils in vinaigrettes, mayonnaise, and other condiments (see Curry Leaf + Mustard Oil Mayonnaise, page 316). You can also use it as an oil to fry and flavor fish, meat, and vegetables.

+ Olive oil's pungency is best tasted in raw salads; it's noticeably reduced by heating and aging. I recommend keeping olive oil for no longer than a year.

+ In cocktails, you can take advantage of some of these fiery, pungent molecules by infusing in alcohol to extract the hot flavor. Alcohol will also extract a variety of aroma and taste molecules from these ingredients. For more intense heat, pulverize or crush the chillies rather than using them sliced or whole.

+ Adding fresh or dried chillies to hot oil extracts their heat and color (in the case of dried chillies), and the capsaicin acts as an antioxidant to protect the oil from the oxidation that occurs during heating.

QUICK TIPS FOR BOOSTING FLAVOR WITH FIERINESS

+ Brush whole, skin-on garlic heads or small onions with a little olive oil, wrap in foil, and roast in the oven at 400°F [204°C] for 45 minutes to 1 hour. Squeeze the cloves out and use the flesh to flavor mayonnaise, spread it on warmed bread with olive oil or butter, or add it to meats and stews for a nutty flavor.

+ Caramelized onions are a fantastic topping or sweet-savory addition to any dish. They lose their pungency on heating.

+ Fry thin slices of garlic in olive oil carefully, over low heat until they just turn golden brown; season with a bit of fine sea salt. Use this toasted garlic oil as a garnish on savory dishes.

+ Grate a fresh clove of garlic or a teaspoon of horseradish and stir it into a cup of plain unsweetened Greek yogurt with a bit of salt and pepper to use as a dip with roasted vegetables.

+ Warm up olive oil and sprinkle with a generous teaspoon or two of a bright red chilli such as Aleppo, Maras, or Urfa and a teaspoon or two of crushed coriander seeds or cumin. This flavorful oil can then be drizzled over breakfast eggs (fried, boiled, or poached), vegetables, or meats to add a bit of warmth. For a warmer note, use mustard oil.

+ Cut ginger into thin matchsticks and fry them in a bit of olive oil or grapeseed oil and use as a flavor and texture booster over savory dishes such as dal (see Dal Makhani, page 292), curries, or stews.

+ As with ginger, drop whole dried chillies in hot oil for a few seconds to draw out their flavor and red color. Pour this oil over savory dishes. This forms the basis of the Indian tadka technique, in which hot oil is used to draw out the color and flavor molecules from ingredients.

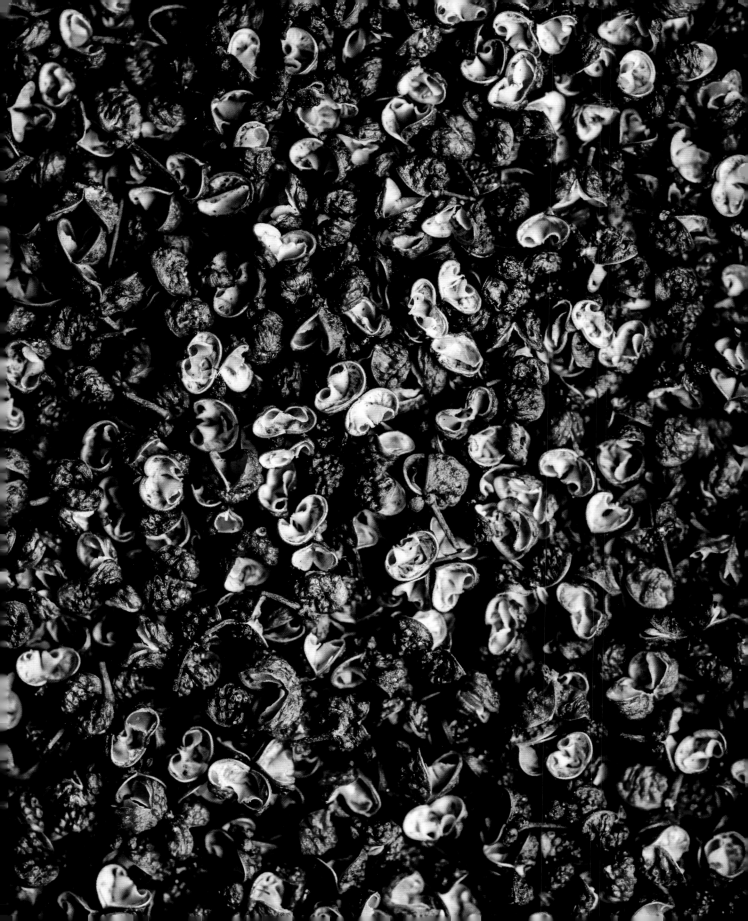

Chicken Lollipops

A few years ago, I introduced my husband, Michael, to this marvelous hot-and-spicy appetizer. It's become so popular in India that it's not only served at Indo-Chinese restaurants; it's also sold at some of the local bakeries near my parents' home in Bombay. The Indo-Sichuan Sauce (page 318) is the mandatory accompaniment to these lollipops. In many ways, I think of them as India's answer to chicken wings, and I think this is why Michael is so fond of them. And yes, you can adapt this recipe to make chicken wings (use 2 lb [910 g] of chicken wings)—skip the lollipop shaping step and proceed according to the recipe.

SERVES 4

For the chicken:

12 chicken drumettes (total weight 1 to 1½ lb [455 to 680 g])

For the marinade:

2 Tbsp low-sodium soy sauce

2 Tbsp sambal oelek

2 Tbsp rice wine vinegar or apple cider vinegar

8 garlic cloves, peeled and grated

2 in [5 cm] piece fresh ginger, peeled and grated

1 tsp ground black pepper

½ tsp fine sea salt

¼ tsp cayenne powder

1 large egg white, lightly whisked

4 cups [960 ml] grapeseed oil or other neutral oil, for frying

¼ cup [35 g] all-purpose flour

2 Tbsp cornstarch

1 tsp beet powder or red food coloring

¼ tsp fine sea salt

For the final coating sauce:

1 Tbsp grapeseed oil or other neutral oil

2 Tbsp sambal oelek

2 Tbsp low-sodium soy sauce

4 garlic cloves, peeled and grated

1 in [2.5 cm] piece fresh ginger, peeled and grated

Fine sea salt, as needed

1 cup [194 g] Indo-Sichuan Sauce (page 318)

THE FLAVOR APPROACH

Heat comes to these lollipops from a few different places: the fermented sambal oelek, black pepper, garlic, ginger, and cayenne.

Beet root provides the bright red color. The outer crust of flour and egg gives a nice crunchy texture when fried.

Since the marinade and the flour contain salt, I recommend tasting one lollipop to determine if you need to season the final coat of sauce with salt.

To prepare the lollipops, take each drumette by the bone end and make an incision around the exposed bone to release the skin and, using the edge of your blade, push it all the way toward the end. Using the knife tip, tuck the skin into the gap between bone and flesh. You can also remove the skin if you prefer. Nip any ligaments or tendons that are attached to the bone. The result should resemble a lollipop with all the meat gathered at one end. Place the lollipop in a large bowl and repeat with the remaining drummettes.

cont'd

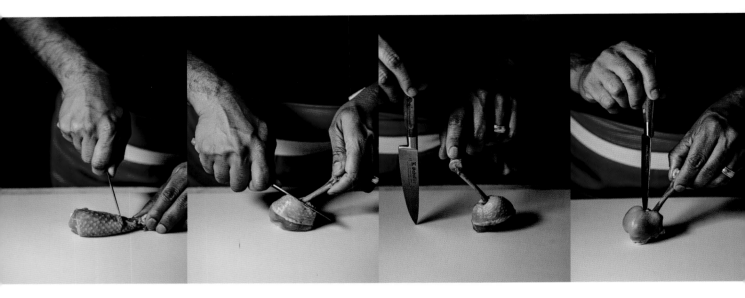

To prepare the marinade, mix the soy sauce, sambal oelek, vinegar, garlic, ginger, black pepper, salt, and cayenne in a small bowl. Pour this over the chicken lollipops and stir gently to coat evenly. Cover and let rest at room temperature for 30 minutes or in the refrigerator overnight. When ready to fry the lollipops, warm them to room temperature by leaving them out on the kitchen counter for about 15 minutes.

Pour the lightly whisked egg white over the marinated lollipops and turn to coat evenly.

Warm the oil in a heavy-bottomed saucepan or Dutch oven over medium heat and maintain the temperature at 350°F [177°C].

While the oil warms, dry whisk the flour, cornstarch, beet powder, and salt. Sift this over the chicken and massage all over to coat well, especially over the meat.

Fry the chicken in batches until it reaches an internal temperature of 165°F [74°C] on an instant-read thermometer, 5 to 6 minutes. The outer surface will have a deep red crust. Transfer the chicken to a plate

lined with paper towels to drain the excess oil, then transfer them to a large bowl.

To prepare the final coating of sauce for the lollipops, heat the oil over medium-high heat in a small skillet. Add the sambal oelek, soy sauce, garlic, and ginger and cook until the spices are fragrant and the juices bubbling, 1½ to 2 minutes. Lightly season with salt (since the chicken is already seasoned with salt) and pour this mixture over the hot chicken lollipops. Turn to coat well and serve them hot with the Indo-Sichuan Sauce.

Fried Eggs with Masala Hash Browns + Seared Tomato Green Peppercorn Chutney

This was my breakfast on weekends all through grad school, the one meal that I consistently made in my tiny apartment. It works because it contains the proven mathematical combination of crunchy potatoes, fried eggs, and a salty tomato sauce that seems to be appropriate for a lazy Sunday just before the long week starts to rear its head. The seared tomato green peppercorn chutney is something I think you might want to make in a large batch; it is quick to make and pairs well with many different types of savory dishes—try it with roasted butternut or pumpkin slices. This chutney gets better with age.

SERVES 4 WITH 1 CUP [240 ML] SAUCE

For the hash browns:

3 Tbsp ghee

1 lb [455 g] Yukon gold potatoes, diced into ½ in [12 mm] cubes

1 medium yellow or white onion (9¼ oz [260 g]), diced

2 tsp garam masala, homemade (page 312) or store-bought

¼ tsp cayenne powder

Fine sea salt or kala namak

1½ to 2 tsp amchur

2 Tbsp fresh cilantro leaves, for garnish

For the chutney:

12 oz [340 g] cherry tomatoes

1 Tbsp extra-virgin olive oil

1 Tbsp apple cider vinegar

1 garlic clove, peeled

2 Tbsp brined green peppercorns, crushed

1 fresh green chilli

Fine sea salt

For the eggs:

4 Tbsp [55 g] ghee

4 large eggs

Fine sea salt or kala namak

Coarsely ground black pepper

THE FLAVOR APPROACH

I've built and layered heat in different ways into the different components of this dish. The warm spices in garam masala work in concert with the cayenne to create heat in the potatoes.

The acidity of amchur makes the heat even more prominent. For a tangier note, use more amchur.

The quality of your cherry tomatoes and the degree of charring will make the flavor of this chutney. Using a large skillet provides a larger surface area for the tomatoes to cook and prevents overcrowding, helping the steam escape.

The tomato chutney gets a mild dose of heat from the brined green peppercorns; the fried eggs get theirs from black pepper.

Additionally, this dish is served warm, which intensifies the chemesthetic quality of these ingredients.

cont'd

To prepare the hash browns, melt the 3 Tbsp ghee in a large cast-iron or stainless-steel skillet over medium-low heat. When the ghee is hot, add the potatoes and onion. Sprinkle on the garam masala and cayenne and season with salt. Cook until the potatoes are completely tender, turning them every 6 to 8 minutes until they are evenly browned, 25 to 30 minutes. Remove from the heat and season with the amchur. Taste and season with salt. Garnish with the fresh cilantro.

While the hash browns cook, prepare the chutney. Heat a large, dry stainless-steel skillet over high heat until smoking, 3 to 4 minutes. When the pan is hot, add the tomatoes and cook until they are seared and develop slight char marks all over and the skins start to split, 4 to 6 minutes. Transfer the tomatoes to the bowl of a blender or a food processor. Add the oil, apple cider vinegar, garlic, peppercorns, and chilli and pulse for a few seconds until combined and the peppercorns are broken into bits. The sauce can be slightly chunky or smooth. Taste and season with salt.

To prepare the eggs, heat the ghee in a small cast-iron or stainless-steel skillet over medium-high heat, swirling to coat. Turn the heat to low. Crack an egg into a small bowl, tip it into the skillet, and cook until the egg white sets and the edges turn crispy, about 1½ minutes. Transfer the egg to a serving plate. (If you want the white to set on top of the yolk, cover the skillet while you cook the egg.) Repeat with the remaining eggs. Season with a little salt and pepper and serve immediately with the warm hash browns and the tomato green peppercorn chutney on the side.

Potato Pancakes

Potato pancakes are the best side to any dish; served warm, their crispy, crunchy texture is perfection. Served as a side with a meal, they work well with Beef Chilli Fry with Pancetta (page 160) or the dal recipes (Garlic + Ginger Dal with Greens, page 256, or Dal Makhani, page 292). I sometimes serve this at lunch with Roasted Eggplant Raita (page 288) and a bowl of Plain Rice (page 310).

SERVES 4 TO 6 AS A SIDE

1½ lb [680 g] Yukon gold potatoes, peeled

1 medium onion (9¼ oz [260 g])

2 fresh chillies, minced

2 Tbsp minced cilantro

1 tsp amchur

1 tsp ground coriander

½ tsp ground cumin

Fine sea salt

2 large eggs, lightly whisked

1 Tbsp plus 1 tsp ghee, melted

THE FLAVOR APPROACH

Fresh chillies give this pancake its fiery note.

The protein in the eggs denature on heating and form a network that binds and holds the ingredients together to form the pancake.

Squeezing the grated potato and onion helps get rid of excess water that would otherwise affect the formation of the egg pancake.

Preheat the oven to 350°F [177°C].

Grate the potato and onion using the large holes on a grater. Over a fine-mesh sieve, squeeze and discard as much liquid as possible out of the potatoes and onion. Place these in a large mixing bowl. Add the chillies, cilantro, amchur, coriander, and cumin and season with salt. Stir gently with a fork to combine evenly. Add the eggs and stir again to combine.

Pour 1 Tbsp of the ghee over the surface of a 10 in [25 cm] oven-proof cast-iron or stainless-steel skillet over medium-high heat. Spread out the potato mixture to form an even layer, drizzle the remaining 1 tsp of ghee over the surface, and cook until the base just starts to set, 3 to 4 minutes. Remove from the heat and transfer the skillet to the oven. Bake until the top is crispy and golden brown and the potatoes are completely cooked, 15 to 20 minutes.

Slice and serve warm or at room temperature.

New Potatoes with Mustard Oil Herb Salsa

This salsa, a cross between Mexican salsas and Indian chutneys, is my love letter to the wasabi lover. If mustard oil is unavailable, use a good-quality extra-virgin olive oil with a strong, pungent flavor. To make this a more wholesome salad, I sometimes add a chopped shallot, bits of chopped smoked salmon, and even a soft- or hard-boiled egg or two. Note: The nuts must be cooled before they meet the mint, or the mint will turn black.

SERVES 4 PLUS 1 CUP [256 G] SALSA

For the potatoes:

2 lb [910 g] new potatoes

Fine sea salt

For the salsa:

½ cup [60 g] raw pistachios, coarsely chopped

½ cup [20 g] packed chopped mint leaves

½ cup [20 g] packed chopped cilantro or flat-leaf parsley

½ cup [120 ml] mustard oil or extra-virgin olive oil (see The Flavor Approach)

4 or 5 garlic cloves, peeled and minced

2 Tbsp fresh lime juice

½ tsp ground black pepper

Fine sea salt

THE FLAVOR APPROACH

The pungent flavors of mustard oil and garlic work together to give the potatoes a pop of heat, while the oil brings the fat-soluble taste molecules together.

Lime juice helps embolden the coolness of the fresh herbs.

Potatoes absorb salt very well, so you will need to taste them after they're coated with the salsa and decide if you want to season them further.

If you prefer a milder dose of wasabi flavor, then prepare a mixture with equal parts mustard oil and extra-virgin olive oil and use that.

To prepare the potatoes, scrub them under running cold tap water to remove any dirt. Place them in a medium saucepan with enough water to cover them by 1½ in [4 cm]. Add salt and bring the water to a rolling boil over medium-high heat. Turn the heat to low and let simmer until the potatoes are completely cooked and tender, 15 to 20 minutes. Your cooking time might vary depending on the size of the potatoes and the variety. Drain the potatoes and pat them dry with a clean kitchen towel.

When the potatoes are cool enough to handle, cut them in half and place them in a large mixing bowl.

To prepare the salsa, toast the pistachios in a small skillet over medium-low heat until they just start to brown, 1½ to 2 minutes. Transfer to a small mixing bowl and let cool completely. Add the mint, cilantro, mustard oil, garlic, lime juice, and black pepper. Fold and season with salt.

Add the salsa to the potatoes and toss gently to coat evenly. Taste and season with salt. Serve warm or at room temperature.

Roasted Delicata Squash with Herbed Yogurt Dressing

Delicata is one of the thin-skinned squashes that you do not need to peel before you eat it. Roasting it in oven tenderizes the flesh as well as the skin, making the vegetable easy to eat. This dish is the perfect balance of warm and cool flavors but also temperature.

SERVES 4 AS A SIDE

For the squash:

2 delicata squash (total weight 2 lb [910 g])

2 Tbsp extra-virgin olive oil

½ tsp ground black pepper

Fine sea salt

For the herbed yogurt dressing (makes about 1¼ cups [300 ml]):

1 cup [240 g] plain unsweetened Greek yogurt, chilled

1 bunch [75 g] cilantro

1 shallot (2 oz [60 g]), diced

4 garlic cloves, peeled and minced

1 in [2.5 cm] piece fresh ginger, peeled

1 green chilli

2 tsp fresh lemon juice

Fine sea salt

For serving:

2 Tbsp raw pepitas (pumpkin seeds)

½ cup [120 ml] Tamarind-Date Chutney (page 322, optional)

2 Tbsp thinly sliced scallions

THE FLAVOR APPROACH

To make this sauce less allium intense, I've used a shallot, but if you want to tone it down even more, sauté the shallot and garlic (you can also sauté the ginger) in 1 Tbsp of ghee until translucent, then blend it with the rest of the ingredients.

Temperature plays an important role in appreciating the flavors of this dish. The squash is served warm, the Herbed Yogurt Dressing is chilled, and the Tamarind-Date Chutney can be served chilled or at room temperature. This results in different sensations on the surface of the tongue, as your taste receptors are simultaneously sampling and experiencing flavor molecules at different temperatures.

To prepare the squash, preheat the oven to 350°F [177°C]. Line two baking sheets with parchment paper.

Trim the squashes and cut in half lengthwise. Hollow each half out with a spoon to remove and discard the seeds. Cut the squash halves into ⅜ in [1 cm] thick crescents and place them in a medium bowl. Drizzle with 1 Tbsp of the olive oil, sprinkle with the pepper, and season with salt. Arrange the squash on the baking sheet in a single layer and roast until the squash is tender and golden brown, 25 to 30 minutes. Remove from the oven and transfer to a serving plate.

To prepare the dressing, place the yogurt, cilantro, shallot, garlic, ginger, green chilli, and lemon juice in a blender. Blend on high speed until combined. Taste and season with salt. Keep chilled.

Toast the pepitas in a small dry skillet over medium-high heat for 2 to 3 minutes, until they just start to brown. Remove from the heat and transfer to a small bowl.

When ready to serve, garnish the squash slices with some of the scallions. Drizzle a few tablespoons of the dressing and the Tamarind-Date Chutney over the squash slices and serve with the remaining dressing and chutney, pepitas, and scallions on the side.

Manchow Soup

This hot and fiery soup is seen only in the Indo-Chinese restaurants of India. When the weather is cold or I'm feeling unwell, I often make this soup. To boost the protein, you can add bits of leftover rotisserie chicken or tofu. Serve this with rice wine vinegar, Chilli-Soy Vinegar Sauce (page 317), or Indo-Sichuan Sauce (page 318) on the side.

SERVES 4

2 Tbsp grapeseed or other neutral oil

8 garlic cloves, peeled and minced

2 in [5 cm] piece fresh ginger, peeled and minced

2 green chillies, minced

5¾ oz [160 g] cabbage, finely chopped

5¾ oz [160 g] mushrooms, thinly sliced

3½ oz [100 g] green beans, finely sliced

3½ oz [100 g] carrots, finely diced

3½ oz [100 g] green bell pepper, finely diced

3 Tbsp low-sodium soy sauce

1 tsp ground black pepper

3 Tbsp cornstarch

2 large eggs, lightly whisked (optional)

Fine sea salt

3 scallions, both white and green parts, finely chopped

2 Tbsp finely chopped cilantro leaves

4 oz [115 g] fried noodles, store-bought

Rice wine vinegar, for serving

Chilli-Soy Vinegar Sauce (page 317), for serving

Indo-Sichuan Sauce (page 318), for serving

THE FLAVOR APPROACH

Using fat extracts the heat from the capsaicin of the chillies as well as the gingerol in ginger and the allium products from the garlic.

Umami-rich flavor boosters like garlic, ginger, and soy sauce are used to take advantage of the synergism effect.

Cornstarch is added at the end at 140°F [60°C] to thicken the soup. Don't add the vinegar until just before serving; added sooner, it would destroy the gel-like structure created by the cornstarch.

Heat a carbon-steel wok or large stock pot over high heat. When the wok is hot, add the oil and stir-fry the garlic, ginger, and chillies for 1 minute.

Add the cabbage, mushrooms, green beans, carrots, and bell pepper and stir-fry until the cabbage just starts to wilt, 2 minutes. Add the soy sauce, black pepper, and 2½ cups [600 ml] of water. Bring to a boil. Remove from the heat and let cool to 140°F [60°C].

Whisk the cornstarch with ½ cup [120 ml] of water in a small bowl to form a slurry, and slowly stir this into the soup. Return the wok to the stove and let it simmer. Cook until the soup thickens, stirring slowly and gently. If you're running low on time, don't cool the soup. Remove the wok from the stove and stir the cornstarch slurry directly into the hot soup. Return the wok to the stove and let it simmer until it thickens.

Slowly pour in the eggs, if using, while gently stirring the soup; it will form ribbons. Taste and season with salt. Remove from the heat. Stir in the scallions and cilantro.

To serve, divide the hot soup among four bowls and top each with 1 Tbsp of the fried noodles. Offer rice wine vinegar, Chilli-Soy Vinegar, and Indo-Sichuan Sauce on the side.

Garlic + Ginger Dal with Greens

The trick to cooking dal (as with cooking rice) is to leave the lentils alone as they simmer and avoid disturbing them too much. In this case, the lentils will cook slowly and will be creamier in texture when you whisk them gently. There are lots of fun things to do with this dal. Fry a chopped tomato or use fresh green chillies instead of the dried red powder in the tadka. Make it your own!

SERVES 4 TO 6

1 cup [212 g] red lentils

½ tsp ground turmeric

2 Tbsp ghee or a neutral oil

1 cup [60 g] packed chopped kale or spinach leaves

Fine sea salt

1 in [2.5 cm] piece fresh ginger, peeled and cut into matchsticks

2 garlic cloves, peeled and thinly sliced

¼ tsp red chilli powder

¼ tsp asafetida (optional)

Rice or flatbread, for serving

THE FLAVOR APPROACH

The fat-soluble heat-creating substances in the garlic, ginger, and dried chilli powder are drawn out by heating them in hot oil. This infusion, or tadka, is then poured over the dal as the final garnish.

In addition, the oil also takes on the fat-soluble red pigment from the chillies.

Asafetida (sold as *hing* in Indian stores) is used as an allium substitute in Indian cooking; here it complements the garlic.

Pick through the lentils and remove any stones or debris. Place the lentils in a fine-mesh sieve and rinse under running tap water. Cover the lentils with 2 cups [480 ml] of water in a medium bowl and soak for 30 minutes.

Place the lentils and the soaking water with the turmeric in a medium sauce-pan and bring to a boil over medium-high heat. Turn the heat to low and let simmer for 10 to 15 minutes, until the lentils are cooked and completely tender. Resist the urge to stir the lentils while they're cooking. If you notice the water getting too low while cooking, add a little more boiling water from a kettle, about ½ cup [120 ml] at a time. If the dal feels too watery, simmer a little longer to cook off some of the liquid. Remove from the heat and lightly whisk the lentils to break them apart. The dal will start to thicken.

Melt 1 Tbsp of the ghee in a separate medium saucepan over medium-high heat. Add the kale and season with salt. Sauté until the leaves start to wilt slightly, 3 to 4 minutes. Fold the kale into the dal. Taste the dal and season with salt.

Next, make the tadka. In a medium saucepan, heat the remaining 1 Tbsp of ghee over medium-high heat. Once the ghee is hot, sauté the ginger and garlic until they just start to turn golden brown, 45 to 60 seconds. (Be careful not to let them burn or they will taste bitter. If that happens, discard and start over.) Remove from the heat and add the chilli powder and asafetida, if using. Pour the hot oil with its contents over the dal. Serve the dal warm with rice or flatbread.

Masala Shrimp

On a trip to Auckland to visit my cousins, we decided to rent out a *bach* (a beach house) and spend Christmas at the beach. We grilled all week and ate a lot of ice cream, as one does in New Zealand. Because shrimp cooks quickly, it became the appetizer of choice to eat while our food cooked on the grill. This dish brings back fond memories of that special holiday.

SERVES 4 TO 6 AS AN APPETIZER

1 lb [455 g] raw medium shrimp, peeled and deveined, tails left on

2 Tbsp extra-virgin olive oil

2 garlic cloves, peeled and grated

1 in [2.5 cm] piece fresh ginger, peeled and grated

2 Tbsp tomato paste

1 Tbsp fresh lime juice

1 tsp garam masala, homemade (page 312) or store-bought

½ tsp ground cayenne

¼ tsp ground cinnamon

Fine sea salt

2 Tbsp minced chives, for garnish

1 lime, quartered, for serving

THE FLAVOR APPROACH

The heat from the cayenne and spices in the garam masala are amplified by the addition of the lime juice.

Lime juice also helps denature the proteins in the shrimp, which cook even faster once heated, so do not over-marinate the shrimp, or they will get rubbery.

Rinse the shrimp under cold running water, pat dry with clean paper towels, and place in a large bowl.

Combine 1 Tbsp of the oil and the garlic, ginger, tomato paste, lime juice, garam masala, cayenne, and cinnamon in a small bowl. Add the shrimp, season with salt, and fold to coat evenly. Let sit for 5 minutes.

Heat the remaining 1 Tbsp of oil in a medium stainless-steel or cast-iron skillet over medium-high heat. Add the shrimp with the liquids in the bowl to the hot oil and sauté until they turn pink, 3 to 4 minutes. The tomato paste and shrimp might make it tricky to determine the pink color, so cut a piece of the shrimp in half; the flesh inside should be completely tender and white in addition to the outer surface and tail turning pink.

Transfer the shrimp to a serving plate. Garnish with the chives. Serve immediately with the lime quarters on the side.

Black Pepper Chicken

Before chillies arrived in India, black pepper was an important ingredient that provided heat in cooking. There are a few different versions of black pepper chicken, some dry and some with a more gravy-like sauce. If you prefer a drier chicken, use half the amount of coconut milk indicated in the recipe.

SERVES 4 TO 6

2 Tbsp black peppercorns

1 tsp coriander seeds, ground

1 tsp fennel seeds, ground

2 tsp ground turmeric

2 Tbsp fresh lime juice

Fine sea salt

3 lb [1.4 kg] boneless, skinless chicken thighs

2 Tbsp coconut oil

2 large onions (total weight about 1¾ lb [800 g]), cut in half and thinly sliced

4 garlic cloves, peeled and grated

2 in [5 cm] piece fresh ginger, peeled and grated

One 13.6 fl oz [403 ml] can full-fat unsweetened coconut milk

2 Tbsp chopped cilantro, for garnish

Plain Rice (page 310), for serving

THE FLAVOR APPROACH

The heat in this dish comes from the pepper. For a more pronounced aroma and taste, use Tellicherry peppercorns, inspired by the South Indian stew of the same name.

Fennel seeds and slow-cooked onions provide sweetness to counteract the heat. Onions contain long chains of fructose molecules called *fructans* that break down on heating to release the sweeter-tasting fructose molecules.

Coconut milk is an emulsion of water, fat, proteins, and sugars that provides creaminess.

Use a fragrant coconut oil to get the full impact of coconut fragrance and flavor in this dish.

Grind the peppercorns to a coarse powder. In a small dry skillet or saucepan, toast the pepper, coriander, and fennel until they just turn fragrant, 30 to 45 seconds. Immediately transfer to a small bowl. Stir in the turmeric and lime juice and season with salt to form a paste.

Place the chicken in a large bowl and massage it with the spice paste. Transfer to a large resealable bag or wrap the bowl with plastic wrap and refrigerate for at least 4 hours, preferably overnight, to marinate.

When ready to cook, set the chicken on the kitchen counter to reach room temperature, about 15 minutes.

Heat the coconut oil in a large saucepan over medium-high heat. Add the onions and sauté for 4 to 5 minutes, until they just turn translucent. Add the garlic and ginger and sauté until fragrant, about 1 minute. Add the marinated chicken with any liquid and the coconut milk, bring to a boil over high heat, then turn the heat to low and cook for 10 to 15 minutes, until the chicken is completely cooked and the liquid becomes a thick sauce. Stir occasionally to prevent burning. Remove from the heat, taste, and season with salt. Garnish with the cilantro and serve with warm rice.

Spiced Roast Chicken

This is an aromatic, colorful, flavorful roast chicken that I make often at home. I shred and store the leftover chicken and use it in wraps or salad. Serve the chicken with Quick Pickled Nectarines with Mint + Serrano (page 319) or Green Apple Chutney (page 321) and Roasted Eggplant Raita (page 288).

SERVES 6

¼ cup [60 ml] extra-virgin olive oil or melted unsalted butter

4 large garlic cloves, peeled and grated

2 tsp ground coriander

2 tsp dried oregano

1 tsp ground black pepper

1 tsp ground turmeric

1 tsp smoked red paprika

1 tsp ground Kashmiri chilli

1 tsp kosher salt, plus extra as needed

One 4 lb [1.8 kg] whole roasting chicken

Fine sea salt

2 cups [480 ml] low-sodium chicken stock

1 lemon, cut into wedges, for serving

THE FLAVOR APPROACH

Placing the chicken on a wire rack set over a roasting pan allows the chicken juices to drip down into the pan, and the chicken skin cooks evenly.

Turmeric and paprika provide both color and flavor.

Paprika and Kashmiri chilli both add a mild yet delicious aroma of smokiness to the meat.

Chicken stock provides moisture and flavor. As the chicken cooks and the juices drip into the pan, the liquid's flavor is enriched, making it a strong basting liquid.

Prepare the seasoning by mixing the olive oil, garlic, coriander, oregano, black pepper, turmeric, paprika, chilli, and salt in a small bowl.

Pat the chicken dry with clean paper towels. Place the chicken on a wire rack set over a large roasting pan or a large, deep baking dish wide enough to hold the chicken comfortably. Slip your fingers between the skin and flesh to loosen the skin. Rub the spice mixture all over the meat and the skin. Sprinkle a little salt over the chicken. Refrigerate the chicken, uncovered, for at least 1 hour, preferably overnight.

Position a rack in the lower third of the oven and preheat the oven to 400°F [204°C]. Place the chicken on the rack and pour the broth into the pan. Roast the chicken for at least 70 to 80 minutes, basting it with the broth from the pan every 15 to 20 minutes, until the internal temperature registers 165°F [74°C] on an instant-read thermometer and the skin turns golden brown. During roasting, if the liquid in the pan starts to evaporate, add a bit more water, about 1 cup [240 ml]. Remove the chicken from the oven, tent it loosely with foil, and let sit for 10 minutes. Carefully transfer the chicken to a serving platter. Collect any juices that remain in the pan, spoon off the excess fat, and transfer to a small serving bowl.

Serve the chicken warm with the cut lemon wedges on the side and the reserved juices.

Lamb Koftas in Almond Gravy

Koftas are to India what meatballs are to the West. They can be made with any type of ground meat and can be either baked in the oven or fried on the stove. Koftas are typically served in some kind of sauce or gravy. The koftas in this recipe are served with a golden-yellow turmeric sauce thickened with almond flour. My accompanying carbohydrate of choice is the Parathas (page 297) or a bowl of Plain Rice (page 310) with the Cucumber + Roasted Corn Salad (page 287). I often make a large batch of koftas and freeze them, uncooked, on a large plate or tray and then transfer them to a resealable bag and freeze for up to 2 months. When you plan to cook, thaw them overnight in the refrigerator and proceed as instructed in the recipe. I treat koftas like meatballs and sometimes add them (without the almond gravy) to my sandwiches as well as to pizza.

SERVES 4

For the koftas:

1 lb [455 g] ground lamb or beef

1 medium white onion (9¼ oz [260 g])

1 tsp ground turmeric

1 tsp ground coriander

1 tsp red chilli powder

4 garlic cloves, peeled and minced

1 in [2.5 cm] piece fresh ginger, peeled and grated

1 green chilli, minced (optional)

1 large egg, lightly whisked

1 tsp fine sea salt

¼ cup [60 ml] extra-virgin olive oil (if frying)

For the gravy:

2 Tbsp ghee, extra-virgin olive oil, or neutral oil

1 medium white onion (9¼ oz [260 g]), minced

2 garlic cloves, peeled and minced

1 in [2.5 cm] piece fresh ginger, peeled and grated

1 tsp ground coriander

½ tsp ground turmeric

½ tsp red chilli powder

½ cup [30 g] almond flour, blanched or unblanched

2 Tbsp white vinegar or lemon juice

Fine sea salt

1 Tbsp fresh mint, for garnish

Parathas (page 297) or Plain Rice (page 310), for serving

THE FLAVOR APPROACH

Almond flour is used to thicken the sauce; this can occur through the combined action of carbohydrates as well as the fiber in the almonds.

For a silkier texture, blend the sauce at high speed in a blender just before the meatballs are added. Blanched almond flour gives a smoother texture than unblanched because the skins are removed.

To prepare the koftas, line a baking sheet with parchment paper or foil.

Place the lamb in a large mixing bowl. Add the onion, turmeric, coriander, chilli powder, garlic, ginger, green chilli, egg, and salt. Fold to combine evenly. Divide the meat into 12 equal portions by weight and shape into balls using your hands. Place the koftas on the lined baking sheet.

If baking the koftas, preheat the oven to 400°F [204°C]. Bake for 20 minutes, until the koftas turn golden brown all over and are completely cooked, with the internal temperature reaching 160°F [71°C] on an instant-read thermometer. It's

completely fine if the meatballs are slightly pink in the center. Remove from the oven and reserve any collected juices on the baking sheet.

If frying the koftas, set a wire rack on a baking sheet. Warm the oil in a medium saucepan over medium heat. Fry the koftas in batches until they turn golden brown all over and are completely cooked, 8 to 10 minutes, with the internal temperature reaching 160°F [71°C] on an instant-read thermometer. It's completely fine if the meatballs are slightly pink in the center. Using a slotted spoon, transfer the koftas to the wire rack to drain any excess oil.

To prepare the gravy, heat the ghee in a medium saucepan or Dutch oven over medium heat. Add the onion and sauté until translucent, 4 to 5 minutes. Add the garlic and ginger and sauté for 1 minute, until aromatic. Add the coriander, turmeric, and chilli powder and cook for 30 to 45 seconds, until fragrant. Stir in the almond flour and cook for 1 minute. Stir in 1 cup [240 ml] of water and add the koftas along with any juices. Bring to a rolling boil over high heat, then reduce to a gentle simmer, cover with a lid, and cook for 5 minutes. Stir in the vinegar. Taste and season with salt. Remove from the heat and garnish with fresh mint. Serve with parathas or plain rice.

Hibiscus (Ginger Pepper) Refresher

This is a wonderful drink to enjoy when the weather gets warm, but I'll admit that I've made it in the cold winter too (it works well with Christmas colors).

SERVES 8

8 oz [230 g] fresh ginger, preferably young

2 cups [400 g] sugar

½ cup [40 g] packed dried edible hibiscus petals

5 or 6 long peppers, lightly cracked

¾ cup [180 ml] chilled water or club soda

THE FLAVOR APPROACH

Hibiscus petals, when steeped in hot water, impart a glorious deep red from their anthocyanin pigments, as well as their aroma and their innate acidity, to create a bold statement.

Hibiscus petals also contain acids, which give this drink a sourness that works with the combination of heat and sweetness. In addition, the low pH of the acids keeps the anthocyanins red in the drink.

Long pepper and ginger provide a subtle note of heat and aroma. If you can't find long pepper, use 1 Tbsp whole black peppercorns and crack them gently before steeping.

Rinse and gently scrub the ginger to remove any traces of dirt. If the ginger is young with a thin skin, leave the skin on; otherwise peel it. Cut into thin slices.

In a medium saucepan, combine the ginger, sugar, and 2 cups [480 ml] of water. Bring to a boil over medium-high heat. Turn the heat to low, add the hibiscus petals and long pepper, and boil for an additional 5 minutes. Remove from the heat, cover, and let it cool completely to room temperature. You can also leave it overnight in the refrigerator to cool, for a stronger flavor.

Line a fine-mesh sieve with a layer of cheese cloth and set it over a small bowl. Strain the liquid through it, and squeeze the solids left behind in the cloth to extract as much liquid as possible. You can reserve a few teaspoons of the petals to use as a garnish for the drink; discard the remaining solids.

To serve the drink, fill eight tall glasses with ice. Pour ¼ cup [60 ml] of the concentrate into each glass, top with the chilled water, and stir. Garnish with the reserved hibiscus petals. Store any remaining hibiscus syrup in an airtight container in the refrigerator for up to 1 week.

Gingerbread Cake with Date Syrup Bourbon Sauce

I'm of the opinion that all gingerbread cakes must have ginger in both the ground spice form and a bit of the crystallized form. The Date Syrup Bourbon Sauce gives it that extra edge of smooth richness and is inspired by one of the top-ten desserts I've eaten: the date cake with whiskey sauce at Gjelina in Los Angeles. Use a Microplane zester for the lime zest to get a fine grate.

SERVES 12 / MAKES ONE 9 IN [23 CM] SQUARE CAKE AND 2 CUPS [480 ML] SAUCE

For the cake:

¾ cup [165 g] unsalted butter, at room temperature, plus extra for greasing

1 Tbsp ground ginger

1 tsp ground black pepper

1 tsp ground green cardamom

1 tsp lime zest

2½ cups [350 g] all-purpose flour

1½ tsp baking soda

½ tsp fine sea salt

2 oz [55 g] crystallized ginger, chopped

¼ cup [50 g] sugar

¼ cup [85 g] honey

1 cup [320 g] unsulfured molasses or sorghum

½ cup [120 g] crème fraîche

2 large eggs, at room temperature

1 cup [240 ml] water warmed to 158°F [70°C]

For the date syrup bourbon sauce:

2 Tbsp unsalted butter

1 cup [240 ml] date syrup, homemade (page 324) or store-bought

1 cup [240 ml] heavy cream

2 Tbsp honey bourbon or whiskey

¼ tsp fine sea salt

For serving:

Lightly sweetened crème fraîche

Fresh lime zest

THE FLAVOR APPROACH

Ginger and black pepper give this cake its warmth.

The aromatic molecules in the spices and lime zest are extracted into the butter, where they are highly soluble, before they are incorporated into the cake batter.

There are a few ways to tell if a cake is done: You can insert a skewer through the center, and it should come out completely clean. But you can also tell if a cake is done by gently pressing the surface; it should spring back to its original form in a few seconds. If the cake isn't done, it will remain depressed after the pressure is removed, as the flour has not yet formed the necessary structure.

Grease a 9 in [23 cm] square baking pan with a little butter and line with parchment paper. Grease the parchment paper.

Melt the butter in a small saucepan over medium heat. Remove from the heat and stir in the ginger, black pepper, cardamom, and lime zest. Let steep for 10 minutes.

Sift the flour, baking soda, and salt through a fine-mesh sieve into a large bowl. Reserve 2 Tbsp of the flour

mixture in a small bowl, add the crystallized ginger to it, and toss to coat well.

Preheat the oven to 325°F [163°C]. Place the sugar, honey, and molasses in the bowl of a stand mixer. Scrape out the melted butter from the sauce-pan with a silicone spatula and add it to the mixer bowl. Using the paddle attachment, mix on medium speed until it turns a toffee-brown color, 4 to 5 minutes. Stop the mixer and scrape the sides of the bowl, add the crème fraîche, and mix on low speed until combined, 1 minute. Stop and scrape down the bowl. Mix in 1 egg at a time on medium speed until combined. Add the sifted dry ingredients and mix on low speed until combined,

about 30 seconds. Stop and scrape down the sides of the bowl. On low speed, add the water and mix until combined. Remove the bowl from the mixer and scrape the sides. Fold in the crystallized ginger and transfer the cake batter to the prepared baking pan. Bake until the cake is golden brown on the surface and a skewer inserted in the center comes out clean, 50 to 60 minutes. Remove from the oven and let cool completely in the pan. Run a knife along the edges of the pan to release the cake and transfer to a serving plate.

To prepare the date bourbon sauce, melt the butter in a small saucepan over medium-high heat. Swirl the butter in the saucepan until the milk

solids start to turn red. Whisk in the date syrup and bring to a boil. Remove from the heat and whisk in the cream, followed by the bourbon and the salt. Transfer to an airtight jar and refrigerate until ready to use. You can make this sauce 2 days ahead of time.

To serve, cut the cake into slices and serve with sweetened crème fraîche, a little lime zest, and a generous drizzle of the date bourbon sauce.

7 **RICHNESS**

FAT MAKES FOOD TASTE DELICIOUS; it gives it *richness*. A spoonful of full-fat yogurt is creamy and luscious. The taste of fried chicken with its crispy skin is incomparable.

In cooking, fats provide texture and taste and, when used sparingly, they can also add nutrition. Fats are the richest sources of energy for our body's cells. They help our bodies absorb fat-soluble vitamins. For example, the vitamin A in carrots is more easily absorbed when those carrots are cooked in a fat. In this way, when used correctly, fats can provide both flavor and nourishment.

In the kitchen, we use fat in myriad ways. We use fat to build texture and mouthfeel characteristics such as "creamy" and "crispy." We use fat to release both the flavor of fat-soluble substances, like the fiery hot capsaicin inside a chilli, as well as the color of fat-soluble pigments, like the bright red color of a chilli pepper. We also use it to extract the aromatic essential oils in lemon peels. And, perhaps most commonly, we use fat as an ingredient to transfer heat to food while cooking.

IS FAT A TASTE?

While the idea that fat might be a taste in and of itself isn't new, it has become more widely researched in recent years. Scientists have gathered data that identifies potential taste receptors for fat as well as mechanisms to explain how fat might be the sixth primary taste, called *oleogustus*. Our taste system evolved as a way for us to detect nutrients and toxins, so it wouldn't be surprising if fat was one day deemed a canonical taste. While scientists debate the role of fat and whether it should be considered an official taste group, we as cooks are constantly working with fat to build flavor in our food, which is why I felt it necessary to include a chapter in this book devoted to the use of fats in our kitchens. I recommend reading the section on Lipids (page 335), to familiarize yourself with some of the terms used here; it will help give you an understanding of why fats behave the way they do.

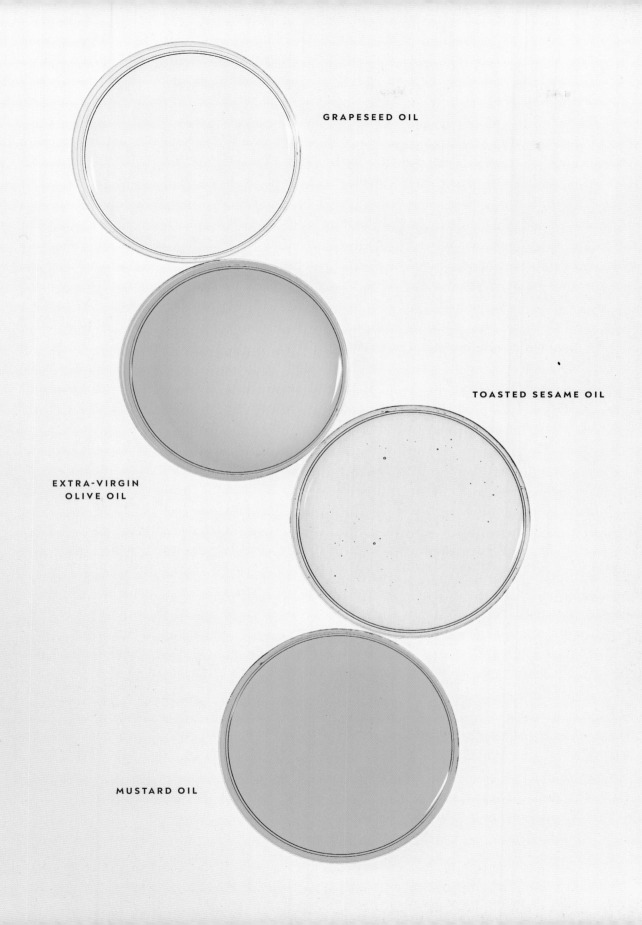

GRAPESEED OIL

TOASTED SESAME OIL

EXTRA-VIRGIN
OLIVE OIL

MUSTARD OIL

SOLID FATS VERSUS LIQUID OILS

In biochemistry, fats include both the solids we typically call fats, such as butter and coconut oil, as well as liquid oils, such as olive oil and canola oil. Some of them have distinct aromas and taste profiles, like pungent mustard oil and the nutty, sweet perfume of coconut oil. Others, like grapeseed oil, are categorized as neutral because they won't contribute any noticeable flavor when you cook with them.

FATS = SOLID FATS + LIQUID OILS

Fats and oils are composed of triacylglycerols or triglycerides in which three fatty acids—either an unsaturated or saturated fatty acid, or both—are attached to an alcohol molecule called *glycerol*. Solid fats have a higher proportion of saturated fatty acids, which makes them behave like solids at room temperature; oils are richer in unsaturated fatty acids, which makes them behave like liquids at room temperature. Of the unsaturated fatty acids, the monounsaturated fatty acids (MUFAs) are relatively stable to oxidation, take a longer time to turn rancid, and are considered healthier (for example, olive oil is rich in MUFAs). The second type of unsaturated fatty acids is the polyunsaturated fatty acids (PUFAs), which are unstable; these include the omega-6 and omega-3 fatty acids (see Lipids, page 335).

The composition of these saturated and unsaturated fatty acids in a fat or oil can vary depending on the plant or animal source. For example, butter produced from cow's milk has a different fatty acid composition than butter produced from buffalo's or sheep's milk. In addition, the diet of the animal can change the fatty acid profile of the fat. In plants, the climate and soil conditions can affect the fatty acid profile of the oils they produce.

UNREFINED AND REFINED FATS AND OILS

Depending on the extraction method, fats and oils fall into two categories: Unrefined fats and oils are extracted using minimal to no heat, whereas refined oils are subjected to heat as well as other physical and chemical treatments. Unrefined fats and oils are sometimes lightly filtered. You might notice a bit of cloudy sediment at the bottom of the bottle, which isn't bad—it's simply the leftover materials from the seeds or nuts. Unrefined fats and oils almost always have a richer color and flavor profile, but their shelf life is shorter. To take maximum advantage of these oils,

avoid using them in high-heat applications such as frying. Instead, use them to sauté at low temperatures, or as flavoring agents when you make salad dressings or mayonnaise.

Fats and oils can be refined using gentle, natural methods like passing them through filters, mildly heating them, or both. Sometimes harsher chemicals or extremely high temperatures are used to refine fats and oils. Again, try to avoid these products whenever possible. Because refining is essentially a cleaning process used to increase the stability and life of the fat or oil, a lot of nutrients and flavor molecules are lost in the process. However, some of these nutrients and flavor molecules are unstable at high temperatures and might change. They can impart a distinct taste to the fat or oil and, consequently, any food it comes into contact with. Therefore, refined fats and oils are often recommended for frying or cooking at very high temperatures.

HYDROGENATED OILS

Liquid oils that are rich in unsaturated fatty acids are sometimes subjected to hydrogenation to convert them into solid fats. This gives the fat a higher melting point, which is useful in cooking, frying, and baking. Hydrogen fills up and saturates the double bonds in some of the unsaturated fatty acids to create a saturated fatty acid, but it can also lead to a side effect; sometimes it will partially saturate the double bond and make the molecule change its structure to produce a trans-fatty acid. As a result, there will be a mixture of saturated and trans-unsaturated fatty acids in the hydrogenated fat. Avoid cooking with hydrogenated and partially hydrogenated fats; numerous studies have demonstrated the role of trans-fatty acids in heart disease.

NEUTRAL FATS AND OILS

Some fats and oils—such as olive, mustard, sesame, coconut, and ghee—carry distinct aroma and taste profiles that define their flavor. Any food cooked with these ingredients will reflect their flavor—which can be desirable or undesirable. On the other end of the spectrum are the neutral oils, such as grapeseed and cottonseed oil, which have no detectable aroma or taste. Use these oils when you do not want the flavor of the fat or oil to affect the final outcome of your recipe.

STORAGE OF FATS AND OILS

Exposure to light, air, moisture, and even some metals can degrade the quality of a fat or oil over time. Store fats and oils in a cool, dark spot in tightly sealed bottles or jars.

RANCIDITY AND DEGRADATION OF FATS AND OILS

In fats and oils, unsaturated fatty acids are attached to glycerol to form triglycerides. Typically, you only see these unsaturated fatty acids in their "free form" (that is, unattached to the glycerol) when some kind of degradation of the fat or oil occurs, such as oxidation. Oxidation is a process in which oxygen reacts with the unsaturated fatty acids in a fat or oil. Unlike hydrogenation, which is used to increase the stability of a fat or oil (see page 337), oxidation does the opposite, creating off-flavors such as rancidity, which is how you know degradation has occurred.

It's also important to store oil out of contact with water and other foods. The presence of moisture degrades fats by a process called *hydrolysis*, and some foods contain enzymes called peroxidases and lipases, both of which degrade fat. Store fat-rich foods such as whole nuts, ground nut flours, and even grain flours in the colder sections of the refrigerator to help reduce degradation of flavor substances as well as of fatty acids from enzymes and warmer temperatures. If left out at room temperature, the fats and oils will eventually turn rancid and create off-putting odors and tastes.

Cooking with Fats and Oils

When selecting a fat or oil to cook with, you must consider how temperature affects its stability. A fat or oil might have a lot of wonderful health or taste attributes, but if it starts to burn and give off smoke at a low cooking temperature, it's probably not a good choice for that particular cooking method. Getting a sense of temperature and its relationship with the fat or oil in question is a very useful tool in the kitchen.

TEMPERATURE

The way fats and oils behave at various temperatures plays a very important role in cooking. Fats are usually solids at room temperature and colder, while most oils behave as liquids. Thus knowing the melting point of a cooking oil will give you an idea of whether it will harden when added to the cool ingredients of a salad. Knowing the temperature at which a fat or oil will start to smoke indicates how much heat you can subject it to without affecting the flavor of the oil and whether it will work for a high-heat application like frying.

Pour Point and Cloud Point: The pour point refers to the temperature at which a fat or oil can be poured; the cloud point refers to the temperature at which a fat or oil starts to turn turbid or cloudy. These two temperatures are typically not critical for cooks when working with fats and oils, but they give you an idea of how to store your fat or oil for easy, everyday usage. For example, if kept in the refrigerator, ghee and olive oil will quickly turn cloudy and stiff to the point of being unpourable; thus they are best kept on the counter (but out of direct sunlight and away from the stove).

Melting Point: At this temperature, the fat or oil exists as a liquid. This temperature is important because it gives a sense of how the fat or oil can be used. Solid fats usually have a higher melting point than oils, so they're often used in baking (with a few exceptions, as seen in olive oil– or walnut oil–based cakes). Oils have lower melting points and, as we've discussed, will behave like liquids, so they're better used for recipes like salad dressings and vinaigrettes.

Smoke Point: At this temperature, wisps of smoke start to come off the fat or oil as it heats. This indicates the heat is beginning to break down the fat or oil. Oils with a high smoke point are useful to deep-fry and stir-fry food because they can withstand higher temperatures. Keep in mind, the smoke points listed in the table on page 336 can serve as a general guide, but smoke points for the same type of oil can vary. For example, different olive oils will vary in their smoke points depending on the blend of olive varieties and even their age.

When cooking, never heat oil to the following high temperatures!

Flash Point: At this temperature, a fat or oil will briefly catch fire.

Fire Point: At this temperature, the fat or oil will continue to burn for at least 5 seconds.

Frying food in a hot fat or oil creates crispiness, a texture that we value in foods such as french fries, fried chicken, doughnuts, meat, and fish. Typically, food is dipped directly into a pot of hot fat or oil and left for a couple of minutes, until it is cooked completely on the inside and develops a crispy exterior. Fats and oils act as the medium to transfer heat to the food. Because most fats and oils can be used to transfer heat at significantly higher temperatures well beyond the boiling point of water (212°F [100°C]), a whole range of new textures and flavors develops in food that is deep-fried rather than cooked in water.

The fat or oil also undergoes change as it heats. Polymers form between the unsaturated fatty acid molecules, and the liquid becomes more viscous. This becomes obvious when the same batch of cooking oil is repeatedly used to fry food; the oil becomes thick as it cools. You can use this to your advantage when seasoning a cast-iron pan, for example. When heated to a high temperature, hot oil will form a layer of polymers that fill up the tiny depressions on the surface of the metal in the pan, making the surface smooth. This prevents sticking and makes it easy for foods such as fried eggs to slide out of the pan.

There are other reactions taking place: The oxygen from air reacts with water, causing oxidation of the fat. Even the water present inside food will affect the aroma and taste of the oil because it can react with oil to produce various substances that will affect the quality of the oil.

Finally, fats and oils act as solvents—they dissolve the flavor molecules present in food and spices that accumulate in the fat or oil with every use. These flavor molecules can transfer to other foods, so it's important to not use the same fat or oil to fry or cook a different dish. Avoid too much repeated usage of the same fat or oil for the same dish and discard it as soon as you start to notice any changes in its color, viscosity, or smell.

Richness Boosters

There are abundant options for cooking fats and oils—some flavorful, some neutral; some animal-based, some plant-based.

Most animal fats used in cooking carry unique aromas and tastes that can help build flavor. Let's take a look at some of the common ones found in our kitchens.

Butter and Ghee

Butter is an emulsion composed of milk fat, proteins, sugars (lactose), and water; it is available salted or unsalted. Use unsalted butter for cooking; it gives you more control in seasoning your food. You can also buy cultured butter (both salted and unsalted options are available), a special type with a slightly tangy taste from the acids produced by bacteria in the butter. This can be used to cook and bake with but is also great over a slice of warm toast with a spoonful of marmalade. As a general rule, to save on space in my refrigerator, I typically buy unsalted butters and add a sprinkling of sea salt if I need to.

Ghee is a favorite cooking fat in India, produced by using heat to separate and extract the fat from churned cream or butter. It has a high smoke point, ideal for deep-frying food. And because ghee lacks any proteins, sugars, or water, it can be stored for several months. In flatbreads such as the paratha, it adds flakiness as well as flavor, and I particularly love it for crispy fried eggs.

In India, my mother prepares ghee by skimming off the top layer of cream on the surface of store-bought milk (milk there is usually sold unhomogenized, so the creamy layer of fat rises to the top over time). As soon as she's gathered enough, she churns the cream to separate the butter from the water and slowly cooks it over a hot stove. The water is boiled out and the milk solids (proteins and sugars) undergo the Maillard reaction. The caramelization reaction produces flavor substances that give this fat a nutty aroma. The bright golden liquid fat is then separated from the milk solids by filtering it through a piece of cheesecloth. Because of the way its prepared, ghee is free from lactose and milk proteins and water, which gives it an extremely long shelf life.

At home, I skip a lot of these steps by starting out with blocks of butter when I make my own ghee, heating the butter directly on the stove. I typically make a batch, keeping one out at room temperature in my pantry and storing the extra jars in the refrigerator.

Lard and Other Animal Fats

When a fatty cut of meat such as bacon or pancetta is heated, the fat starts to melt and separate from the tissue; this is also called *rendering*, and rendered pig fat is also known as *lard*. The fats from different animals each carry their own unique aroma and taste. You can collect and save the rendered fat and use it to cook with and as a flavoring agent. I usually strain the hot fat through a fine-mesh sieve lined with dry cheesecloth over a glass jar and use it as needed. Store the fat in a cool, dark place away from heat and light. Fat extracted from chicken and duck skin can be used to add flavor to roasted vegetables and will add a whole new dimension of flavor to your eggs and french fries. I sometimes replace ghee with chicken and duck fat in recipes when I make my pilafs, to play with flavor. I once ate a slice of chocolate cake that had a little bit of smoked duck fat incorporated into the cake batter; the flavor combination gave it a delicious edge.

PLANT-BASED FATS

Many of our cooking fats and oils come from fruits, nuts, and seeds. Cooking fats and oils are typically expeller pressed by mechanically pressing the fruit, nuts, or seeds. In some cases, mechanical pressure is all that is needed to release the oil, as is the case with softer foods like olives and walnuts. These oils are often identified on the bottle label as "cold-pressed." However, some seeds, such as soy, can be rather resilient and tough to break, in which case expeller extraction is augmented with heat in the form of steam. Occasionally, chemical solvents, which help release the fat in the seed, are also applied to help extract oils. Avoid these chemically extracted oils; they don't taste as good as pressed oils, and they've lost most of their flavors and nutritional quality.

Nuts and Seeds

Nuts and seeds are naturally rich sources of fats. They can be soaked in water to soften, then ground into thick pastes with a rich, creamy texture. Almond, cashew, and sunflower seed butters are now as common as peanut butter and are often used as a dairy substitute. Tahini, made from sesame seeds, is another relatively common plant-based fat. Several cooking oils, such as walnut and sesame, are extracted by expelling the oil under pressure. Toasting seeds or nuts before they're ground or pressed adds a whole new dimension of taste and aroma. All these plant-based fats are delicious options for garnishing a dish, preparing a salad dressing, or whipping into mayonnaise when you want to build more complex flavors into a recipe.

Coconut Oil

Coconut oil is rich in saturated fats and consequently behaves as a solid at room temperature but liquefies when warmed. Unrefined coconut oil has a strong coconut aroma; I like to use it as a flavoring agent in dishes where I want the coconut flavor to dominate. Refined coconut oil and deodorized coconut oil are odorless and neutral to taste. Coconut cream and full-fat coconut milk give off a tropical, nutty aroma; they are used in desserts and in the preparation of savory stews and curries. It's best to keep coconut oil away from hot surfaces in your kitchen, as repeated temperature fluctuations will cause it to melt and reharden, which degrades the oil and can make it go rancid. Coconut oil can be refrigerated; I do this during the hotter summer months.

Mustard Oil

In certain northern states of India and in Pakistan and Bangladesh, mustard oil has long taken center stage as a cooking fat. Its wasabi-like flavor gives it a unique edge of heat, and it is often used as the main oil in many Indian pickles or aachars (see Cauliflower Aachar, page 320). Its high smoke point also makes it a popular choice for cooking seafood. However, until recently, the sale of mustard oil for culinary purposes was banned in America and parts of Europe. This was based on a few experimental studies in animal models demonstrating that erucic acid—a monounsaturated fatty acid that makes up nearly half of mustard oil—might play a role in heart disease. However, the practice of using mustard oil in cooking is centuries old in India. Some studies demonstrate that diets rich in mustard oil may lower the risk of heart disease. Mustard oil is found in Indian grocery stores, labelled for "external usage."

Fortunately, the Australian company Yandilla has produced the first ever FDA-approved mustard oil from a special non-GMO-bred strain of mustard plant that is erucic acid–free. You can purchase Yandilla mustard oil in specialty markets and grocery stores as well as online.

Olive Oil

Olive oil is a spectacular oil; it is flavorful, it can carry a fiery bite, and it has a bitterness that becomes noticeable in emulsions. Olive oil comes in a wide array of types, from extra-virgin to various blends.

A popular question concerning olive oil is whether one can use it for deep-frying. The answer is yes—and no. Folks in the Mediterranean region cook exclusively with olive oil and use it to fry their food. Determining the smoke point of olive oil can get a little confusing. Extra-virgin olive oil has a higher smoke point than most refined olive oils and is great for deep-frying, but as it ages, the smoke point will start to drop. The amount of free fatty acids present also affects the heat stability of olive oil. Olive oil extracted from fresh olives will have a lower amount of free fatty acids and a higher smoke point. Olive oil contains two types of antioxidants: the fat-soluble tocopherols and the more water-soluble polyphenols. Together these antioxidants help protect the oil from degradation at room temperature. When olive oil is heated to 350°F [177°C] or higher, the tocopherols are destroyed but the polyphenols are stable and protect the oil from degradation. A younger, brand-new bottle of olive oil is rich in these antioxidants and is better equipped to protect itself from degradation. As the oil ages, the amount of these antioxidants decreases, the stability of the oil starts to decline, and so does the smoke point.

You might have noticed that olive oil often solidifies when kept in the refrigerator. The exact temperature varies depending on the harvest of olives and the blend of oils. For a while this was touted as a way to determine the quality of olive oil, but this is a myth; hardening in the refrigerator is not related to the oil's quality. Refrigerating olive oil is a great way to increase its shelf life.

Sesame Oil

Sesame oil is a popular cooking oil in Chinese cuisine. It is rich in an antioxidative substance called lignan. There are two varieties: a milder, lighter-flavored one, and a dark, heavy, and intensely aromatic oil extracted from toasted sesame seeds. I usually use both as finishing oils when I cook. Drizzle a few drops over cooked noodles (see Chicken Hakka Noodles, page 216) or use it to infuse the flavor of spices (see the Sichuan peppercorn infusion in Burrata with Chilli Oil + Thai Basil, page 283). In Indian cooking, a light golden sesame oil (or *gingelly*, as it is commonly known) is used to cook and fry food, as well as in the preparation of Indian pickles or aachars.

Neutral Oils

Oils such as grapeseed and canola have no detectable aroma or taste, making them excellent choices as cooking fats when you don't want the flavor of the oil to affect the final outcome of your food. At home, depending on what I'm cooking, I usually use grapeseed or canola as my neutral oil.

Canola oil is obtained from the rapeseed plant, a relative of the mustard family was specifically bred to remove an unsaturated fatty acid called erucic acid that has been implicated in heart disease. Some folks notice a strange, rancid, "fishy" taste after the oil is heated, which is probably due to the breakdown of unsaturated fatty acids during heating.

How to Prepare Ghee

Ghee is a clarified fat prepared by boiling out the water from butter or churned cream. It takes advantage of caramelization and the Maillard reaction to produce new flavor molecules from the milk sugar lactose and the amino acids in milk proteins.

Line a fine-mesh sieve with a few layers of cheesecloth and place over a clean, dry 1 pint [480 ml] jar with a tight-fitting lid. In a heavy, medium saucepan over medium-high heat, melt 1 lb [455 g] unsalted butter, stirring occasionally with a large metal spoon. As the butter starts to melt, skim off and discard any foam that rises to the surface. Cook until all the water in the butter boils off, and the fat stops sizzling and turns a deep golden yellow. The milk solids at the bottom of the pan will be reddish brown. The entire process should take 12 to 15 minutes. Remove the saucepan from the heat and pour the liquid through the cheesecloth-lined sieve into the jar. Seal the jar and store in a cool, dark place for up to 3 months, or indefinitely in the refrigerator. Makes approximately 1¼ cups [250 g].

QUICK TIPS FOR BOOSTING FLAVOR WITH RICHNESS

+ Should you always use neutral oils when you make mayonnaise or condiments, especially when there are so many other options available? To that, my answer is no. Experiment with other oils; start with milder-flavored oils, such as sesame or walnut, or go for something bolder, like mustard oil. Mayonnaise (page 316) takes on a whole new flavor when the wasabi-like heat of mustard is incorporated into the emulsion.

+ Many different flavorful oils can be used as finishing or garnishing oils. A generous drizzle over a dish just before it is served can elevate it to a whole new level. In most cases, the warmer the temperature of the food, the stronger the aroma released—and savored.

+ Refrigerate or freeze your olive oil in small batches in an ice tray when you infuse them with spices or dried herbs. This not only lengthens their shelf life and preserves their quality of flavor, but it also makes it convenient to pop out an "oil cube" and use just the amount you need. It will warm up and liquefy quickly once brought to room temperature.

+ Store your oil in dark amber bottles if possible and keep them away from exposure to light. This increases their shelf life.

+ When making crispy fried eggs, use a fat or oil with a high smoke point, such as ghee. Ghee also gives the egg a lovely nutty taste. Other fats to consider are duck and chicken fat.

+ Sometimes when I want a batch of plain rice to accompany lunch or dinner, I'll boil the rice with a spoonful of chicken or duck fat to add more richness and flavor. If my jar of chicken fat is empty, I'll add a chicken thigh with the skin still attached and boil it with the rice.

+ Finally, a tip for cooks that doesn't concern flavor: Red beets are notorious for staining everything they come into contact with. Fortunately, betalain, the red pigment in beets, is not fat-soluble. To prevent the color from staining your skin or kitchen surfaces, spray the surface of your cutting board with a little neutral oil and lightly grease your hands before handling beets. The red pigment is insoluble in fat, so it will slide right off your kitchen surfaces and skin.

BUTTER

CREAM

GHEE

Burrata with Chilli Oil + Thai Basil

There are two methods for extracting the flavor from Sichuan peppercorns. The first involves toasting for a few seconds, then infusing them into hot oil. The second, and the one that I share here, is from the exemplary Chinese cooking textbook *Phoenix Claws and Jade Trees* by Kian Lam Kho. Here the peppercorns are left to infuse in cold oil for several hours, after which the oil is warmed, keeping it below its smoke point.

To garnish the burrata, I prefer the smaller baby leaves of the Thai basil plant, but you can use the larger leaves; just tear them up into smaller bits.

SERVES 2 TO 4 AS AN APPETIZER

1 Tbsp Sichuan peppercorns

¼ cup [60 ml] sesame oil

1 tsp coriander seeds

1 tsp red chilli flakes, such as Aleppo or Maras

8 oz [230 g] burrata cheese

1 tsp fresh baby Thai basil leaves

Flaky sea salt

Toasted slices of sourdough bread or flatbread, for serving

THE FLAVOR APPROACH

In my opinion, using both cold and hot infusions gives a stronger punch of flavor.

Sesame oil carries a nutty aroma. The dairy fats in cheese provide creaminess.

The textures here are a combination of soft, crunchy, smooth, and luscious.

Gently crush the Sichuan peppercorns with a mortar and pestle. Place the peppercorns and sesame oil in a small jar or bowl. Cover with a lid, shake, and leave in a cool, dark place for at least 8 hours, preferably overnight.

Transfer the oil with the peppercorns to a small saucepan. Crush the coriander with a mortar and pestle to form a coarse powder and add it with the chilli flakes to the oil. Heat the saucepan over low heat and bring to 250°F [121°C]. Remove from the heat and let it cool completely to room temperature. Transfer to a small bowl.

Place the burrata on a serving plate. Drizzle 2 to 3 Tbsp of the flavored oil with the spices over the burrata. Garnish with the Thai basil leaves and sprinkle generously with flaky salt. Serve with slices of toasted bread.

Crab Tikka Masala Dip

This is a playful take on tikka masala; it's not as hot or spicy as the usual dish, but still has that edge of flavor that makes this seasoning unique. You can also serve this with a bit of hot sauce on the side; just make sure you eat this while it is warm.

SERVES 6 TO 8

1 Tbsp extra-virgin olive oil

2 shallots (total weight 4¼ oz [120 g]), minced

2 garlic cloves, peeled and grated

1 in [2.5 cm] piece fresh ginger, peeled and grated

2 tsp ground paprika

2 tsp Kashmiri red chilli powder

1 tsp ground coriander

1 tsp ground cumin

1 tsp ground black pepper

½ tsp grated nutmeg

¼ cup [55 g] tomato paste

8 oz [230 g] cream cheese, at room temperature

5 oz [140 g] crème fraîche

Fine sea salt

1 lb [455 g] precooked jumbo lump crab meat

2 Tbsp fresh lime juice

1 green or red chilli, minced (optional)

2 Tbsp thinly sliced scallions, for garnish

Crackers, toasted slices of naan, or sourdough, for serving

THE FLAVOR APPROACH

The generous amount of paprika and chilli powder (along with the tomato paste) provides color. If you decide to substitute a different red chilli powder, keep the level of heat in mind; Kashmiri chilli powder is extremely mild, so you'll need to reduce substitute amounts accordingly.

Cream cheese and crème fraîche provide the fat necessary to give this dish its rich mouthfeel.

Observe how the combination of fat and dairy in this dish reduces the intensity of heat.

Heat the oil over medium-high heat in a medium saucepan. When the oil is hot, sauté the shallots until they turn translucent and just start to brown, 5 to 6 minutes. Add the garlic and ginger and sauté for 1 minute. Lower heat to low. Add the paprika, chilli powder, coriander, cumin, black pepper, and nutmeg and cook until fragrant, 30 to 45 seconds. Stir in the tomato paste and sauté until the tomato paste just starts to brown, 2 to 3 minutes.

Stir in the cream cheese and crème fraîche. Season with salt and fold to combine. Remove from the heat and fold in the crab meat, lime juice, and fresh chilli, if using. Taste and adjust the seasoning if necessary. Transfer to a serving bowl and garnish with the scallions. Serve warm with crackers, toasted slices of naan, or sourdough.

Cucumber + Roasted Corn Salad

A good cucumber salad for summer, this also works well for a barbecue meal. Watch the mustard seeds carefully; if they fry for too long, they will turn bitter. If that occurs, discard and repeat. If you don't want to cook the corn on a cast-iron skillet, you can cook the corn over a grill as done in the Potato + Roasted Corn Herbed Raita (page 78).

SERVES 4

For the salad:

1 sweet corn cob (8 oz [230 g])

1 Tbsp extra-virgin olive oil

1 English cucumber (12 oz [340 g]), diced

1 shallot (2 oz [60 g]), thinly sliced

2 Tbsp cilantro or flat-leaf parsley leaves

2 Tbsp pepitas (pumpkin seeds)

For the dressing:

¼ cup [60 ml] extra-virgin olive oil (can be debittered, see case study on page 104)

1 tsp black mustard seeds

¼ cup [60 ml] sherry vinegar

1 tsp fish sauce

1 tsp honey

1 tsp red chilli flakes, such as Aleppo, Maras, or Urfa

½ tsp ground black pepper

Fine sea salt

THE FLAVOR APPROACH

Extra-virgin olive oil provides the backdrop for the fish sauce that gives this salad a bold kick of umami.

Sweet corn and honey add a pop of sweetness.

Fish sauce adds an umami character to the dressing.

To prepare the salad, heat a large cast-iron skillet over medium-high heat. Cut the corn cob in half cross-wise to its length. Coat the skillet with half of the oil and brush the remaining oil over the corn halves. Sear them until they develop deep char marks all over, turning them around in the pan with kitchen tongs every 4 to 5 minutes, 15 to 20 minutes total. Remove the cob halves from the pan and let rest for 5 minutes to cool. Strip the corn kernels from the cob by slicing with a knife, and discard the cob. (For an alternative method, see Potato + Roasted Corn Herbed Raita, page 78). Place the corn kernels in a large mixing bowl with the cucumber, shallot, and cilantro.

Toast the pepitas in a small skillet over medium-high heat until they just start to brown, 1 minute. Add the pepitas to the mixing bowl.

To prepare the dressing, heat 1 Tbsp of the oil over medium-high heat in a small skillet. Add the mustard seeds and fry until the seeds start to sputter and get fragrant, 30 to 45 seconds. Remove from the heat and pour the liquid into a small mixing bowl. Add the remaining oil, sherry vinegar, fish sauce, honey, red chilli flakes, and black pepper and whisk to emulsify. Taste and season with salt. Pour the dressing over the ingredients in the large mixing bowl and toss to coat evenly. Serve immediately.

Roasted Eggplant Raita

I'm a strong advocate for grilled vegetables and fruits in raitas; you end up with a big boost of flavor. This raita makes an excellent side and could be a meal in itself.

SERVES 4

SERVES 4

1 medium eggplant (13 oz [370 g])

1 Tbsp extra-virgin olive oil

Smoked sea salt or fine sea salt

3 shallots (total weight 6½ oz [180 g]), minced

1 green chilli, minced

2 Tbsp chopped cilantro

2 Tbsp chopped mint

½ tsp freshly ground black pepper

1 cup [240 g] plain unsweetened Greek yogurt, chilled

¼ cup [60 ml] water, chilled

1 tsp fresh lime juice

2 Tbsp grapeseed oil or other neutral oil

1 tsp black or brown mustard seeds

1 tsp cumin seeds

1 tsp red chilli flakes, such as Aleppo

THE FLAVOR APPROACH

Smoked sea salt amplifies the perception of smokiness in the roasted eggplant.

For a kick of heat, use mustard oil instead of grapeseed oil when tempering the spices. These oils, unlike ghee or coconut oil, remain liquids at low temperatures and will not congeal on the yogurt.

Heating the spices in the hot oil of the tadka helps extract and infuse their flavor molecules into the oil and also adds a crunchy texture.

Preheat the oven to 425°F [218°C].

Cut the eggplant in half lengthwise. Brush the cut surfaces with the olive oil and arrange them in a baking dish or roasting pan, cut side facing up, and roast until the tops are golden brown and slightly charred and they're completely cooked on the inside, about 45 minutes. Remove from the heat, cover with aluminum foil, and let cool completely. Once cooled, remove and discard the skin and chop the flesh. Place the eggplant flesh in a large bowl and season with salt.

Add the shallots, chilli, cilantro, mint, and black pepper.

In a separate bowl, whisk the yogurt with the water and lime juice. Pour the mixture over the vegetables in the large mixing bowl and stir to combine. Taste and season with salt.

In a small, dry saucepan, make the tadka. Heat the grapeseed oil over medium-high heat. Once the oil is hot, add the mustard and cumin seeds and fry until the cumin turns brown and the spices are fragrant, 30 to 45 seconds. Remove from the heat. Add the red chilli flakes and swirl to mix. Pour the hot oil with the spices over the raita and serve.

Braised Cabbage with Coconut

As a young child, I ate very few different vegetables. In fact, I restricted my vegetable intake to potatoes and cabbage. This was a constant source of frustration for my parents, who tried their best to make me love vegetables. At least once a week, I'd request cabbage *foogath*, in which slender shavings of cabbage leaves are braised and then finished off with a generous sprinkling of soft fresh coconut. (*Foogath* is the Konkani word for braising; the Portuguese name for this dish is *fugad de repolho*.) Serve this dish as a side with rice or bread and a bowl of warm stew or curry. You can also fry a few curry leaves with the spices for added aroma.

SERVES 4 TO 6

2 lb [910 g] green cabbage, shredded

2 Tbsp grapeseed oil or other neutral oil

1 tsp black mustard seeds

1 tsp red chilli flakes

1 medium yellow onion (9¼ oz [260 g]), thinly sliced

2 garlic cloves, peeled and minced

½ tsp freshly ground black pepper

Fine sea salt

3 Tbsp grated fresh or thawed unsweetened coconut, for garnish

2 Tbsp chopped cilantro, for garnish

1 green or red chilli, thinly sliced, for garnish

THE FLAVOR APPROACH

The greener parts of the leaves turn brighter as the cabbage cooks, as the breakdown of cell material makes the green pigment appear more intense.

The water trapped inside the cells of the cabbage leaves provides the liquid needed to braise the vegetable. Use a cabbage with thick, firm leaves for this dish; the thinner varieties release a lot of water when braised and fall apart quickly.

The softer texture of fresh coconut pairs well with the tender texture of the braised cabbage leaves.

Coconut is added at the end as a garnish rather than fried or toasted. In this dish, I find fresh and frozen coconut works best; the drier texture of desiccated coconut simply doesn't work as well.

Rinse the cabbage and remove any excess water by patting it dry with clean kitchen towels or using a salad spinner.

Heat the oil in a large saucepan over medium-high heat. When the oil is hot, add the mustard seeds and chilli flakes and cook until the seeds start to pop and sizzle, 20 to 30 seconds. Add the onions and sauté until they turn translucent, 4 to 5 minutes. Add the garlic and sauté for 1 minute. Add the cabbage and black pepper and season with salt. Lower the heat to medium-low, cover with a lid, and cook, stirring occasionally, for 10 to 12 minutes, until the leaves are tender but not falling apart. Remove from the heat. Taste and season with salt if needed. Garnish with the coconut, cilantro, and chillies. Serve warm.

Dal Makhani

In India, the word *dal* is an all-encompassing term that includes not only the dish but also lentils and some beans. Dal is a staple in many Indian homes across the world; it's easy to make, comforting, and a great source of protein. One of the things I love about dal is that regardless of the lentil or bean you cook it with, it's a blank slate for flavor. You can use my simple flavor guide to build and layer flavors into your own dal recipes at home; feel free to tweak it and make your own combinations of flavors. Technically, urad dal is not a lentil but the bean of the *Vigna mungo* plant, sometimes sold as black gram. You will need to plan a day in advance to soak the beans.

SERVES 4 TO 6

1 cup [200 g] whole urad beans with skin

½ cup [60 g] kidney beans (optional)

⅛ tsp baking soda

1 medium white onion (9¼ oz [260 g])

6 garlic cloves, peeled

2 in [5 cm] piece fresh ginger, peeled and cut in half

¼ cup [55 g] ghee or unsalted butter

1 tsp garam masala, homemade (page 312) or store-bought

½ tsp ground turmeric

¼ cup [55 g] tomato paste

¼ tsp cayenne powder

Fine sea salt

2 Tbsp heavy cream or crème fraîche

2 Tbsp loosely packed chopped cilantro leaves, for garnish (optional)

THE FLAVOR APPROACH

Presoaking provides several benefits. The seeds soften and plump up to almost twice their original volume, and their chemical composition changes. The amount of sugars and starches decreases, which helps with cooking, palatability, and digestion.

Adding baking soda to the beans softens the fiber by acting on the pectin and hemicellulose and drastically reduces the cooking time, from several hours to 30 to 45 minutes. Use filtered water if you live in an area with hard water or it might take a bit longer to cook.

Dal makhani is one of the creamiest dals; it leaves a luxurious texture on your tongue imparted by the cream and butter but also by the soft beans. For an extra-rich flavor, top the dal with a few small dabs of salted butter before you add the garnish.

This comfort food contrasts pleasingly with plain rice or flat bread like paratha, and yogurt or raita on the side provide cool contrast.

This dal is special because it gets it unique fiery flavor from the large amount of garlic and ginger used; if you prefer a milder dose of heat, reduce their quantities by half. The hint of cayenne in this dal adds a third note of heat.

The dhungar method of smoking utilizes the principle of smoking fat and infusing it into food by entrapping the smoke in a small enclosed space.

cont'd

Pick through the beans and discard any dirt or stones; transfer to a medium bowl and rinse under running tap water, then add enough clean water to cover the beans by 1 in [2.5 cm] and soak overnight.

The next day, discard the water. Place the beans in a medium saucepan or Dutch oven. Add 4 cups [960 ml] of water and the baking soda and bring the contents to a rolling boil over high heat. Lower the heat to a simmer, cover with a lid, and cook for 30 to 45 minutes, until the beans are tender and almost falling apart. Remove from the heat and transfer the beans with the liquid to a large bowl. Rinse the saucepan and wipe it dry.

Quarter the onion and add it with the garlic in a blender. Mince half of the ginger, add it to the blender, and pulse until it forms a smooth paste. If needed, add a bit of the water from the dal to the blender to help things move around.

Melt 2 Tbsp of the ghee in the saucepan over medium-high heat. Add the garam masala and turmeric and cook for 30 to 45 seconds, stirring constantly, until the spices start to release their aroma. Add the tomato paste and sauté for 2 to 3 minutes. Turn the heat to medium-low, stir in the onion mixture, and cook for 10 to 15 minutes, stirring occasionally, until most of the liquid has cooked away and the ghee separates from the mixture. Return the cooked beans

with their liquid to the saucepan and stir in the cayenne. Season with salt. Increase the heat to high and bring the contents to a boil. Stir occasionally to prevent the beans from sticking to the bottom of the saucepan. Lower the heat to a gentle simmer. Stir in the cream and remove from the heat.

Make the tadka. Melt the remaining ghee in a small, dry saucepan over medium-high heat. Cut the remaining ginger into matchsticks and fry them in the hot ghee for about 1 minute, until the strips just start to turn golden brown. Pour the fried ginger and ghee over the dal. Garnish with the cilantro, if using, and serve hot.

The Dhungar Method

This method is used by some to add a smoky aroma to the dal (and other dishes). Do this after the cream is added to the dal, then proceed with fried ginger step. Don't forget to switch the stove off while doing this. The density of the dal will keep the onion or bowl afloat, and it won't sink.

A small, shallow metal bowl or a medium onion, hollowed out in the center

1 to 2 in [2.5 to 5 cm] piece charcoal

1 Tbsp ghee

Place the metal bowl or onion in the center of the dal. Using a pair of tongs, burn the charcoal over a flame until it turns red hot. Carefully place the live charcoal in the center of the bowl and drop the ghee on the hot charcoal. It will start to smoke.

Cover the saucepan with a lid to trap the smoke and let it sit for 5 minutes. Remove the lid, the wire rack (if using), and the bowl or onion and safely discard the charcoal. Proceed with the fried ginger in the recipe.

Parathas + Masala Parathas

Parathas were the flatbreads that I ate at home in India. With breakfast, I'd lightly butter the bread and scoop in a bit of marmalade; for dinner, it served as the vehicle to scoop up the various savory dishes served with it. Parathas are soft, flaky, unleavened flatbreads. In principle, they're similar to the idea behind puff pastry, with the dough folded into layers and a fat like ghee keeping those layers separate. As the dough cooks, the moisture is converted to steam, further supporting the flaky layers.

Parathas are shaped by several different methods. The method here is the one used for the *lachha* (pronounced "lutch-ha") paratha, in which the dough is rolled out, drawn into a rope, coiled, and then rolled out again to form a disc. This method introduces many layers into the bread, giving it a flaky texture. Because ghee solidifies at room temperature, the parathas will become stiff when cold. Simply rewarm them on a hot skillet or wrap 4 or 5 parathas in a layer of parchment paper, then in foil, and warm them in an oven at 300°F [149°C] for 6 to 8 minutes.

MAKES 8 PARATHAS

2 cups [320 g] atta *or* 1½ cups [210 g] all-purpose flour plus ½ cup [70 g] whole-wheat flour

1 tsp fine sea salt

½ cup [100 g] plus 2 Tbsp melted ghee

1 cup [240 ml] water, warmed to 160°F [71°C]

THE FLAVOR APPROACH

In India, unleavened whole-wheat breads, such as parathas and rotis, are made with a stone-ground flour called *atta*. American whole-wheat flours do not yield the same texture as atta for several reasons. There are two types of wheat: hard and soft. These labels are used in reference to the amount of force needed to break the grain (in hard wheat, the protein and starch are tightly bound).

When wheat is ground, the grains pass through a mill, where they are fractured and then broken down to a fine flour using smooth rollers. During this process, the starch granules inside the grain fracture and "damage." Greater *starch damage* leads to more water absorption, a more pliable dough, and increased starch gelatinization.

Because American whole-wheat flour is less finely ground, its starch damage values are much lower than atta's. Atta, made from hard wheat, has a starch damage value between 13% and 18%. American soft wheat is between 1% and 4%, and hard wheat is between 6% and 12%. Atta also contains a higher protein content.

American whole-wheat flours contain larger bits of bran than atta does. These bits of bran act like blades and cut the gluten strands that form in the dough.

cont'd

To achieve the same texture as atta in my Indian breads, I use a mixture of American whole-wheat and all-purpose flours and reduce the kneading time.

I prefer ghee for its richer flavor, but canola or grapeseed oil can be used.

Sift the atta and salt over the bowl of a stand mixer with a fine-mesh sieve. Using your fingers, massage 2 Tbsp of the ghee into the atta. Attach the paddle attachment to the stand mixer and set the speed to low. While mixing, slowly drizzle in the warm water, 2 Tbsp at a time. Stop adding water when the dough just comes together; you may not need all the water. Stop the stand mixer and scrape any dough off the paddle. Switch in the dough blade and knead the dough for 10 minutes on low speed. For the combination of all-purpose and whole-wheat flours, knead for 5 minutes. If the dough sticks to the bottom of the bowl, stop and scrape it with a bowl scraper, bring the dough together, and continue to knead. The dough will be soft and pliable when done. Transfer the dough to a clean, dry, lightly floured surface. Knead it for 1 minute and shape it into a ball. Cover the dough with bowl or a wet kitchen towel and let it rest for at least 30 minutes. At this stage you can wrap the dough and refrigerate it in an airtight container for up to 1 week. Be sure to leave it out on the kitchen counter to warm up for at least 30 to 45 minutes and then roll out the parathas.

To prepare the parathas, divide the rested dough into 8 equal parts by weight and shape them into individual balls. Flatten one ball of dough on a dry, flat, lightly floured surface. Roll out the dough into a 6 in [15 cm] disk. Spread a minimal amount of ghee, about 1 tsp, over the surface.

Starting from one edge of the circle, pleat the dough over itself in strips, back and forth, until you reach the other edge, to resemble the pleats of an accordion. Press down the pleats so the stack forms a thick strip. Take one end of the strip and coil it into a solid spiral. Press gently so the spiral becomes a flattened disk. Sprinkle a little flour over the dough and roll it out to again form a 6 in [15 cm] disk. Prepare the remaining balls of dough in this way.

To cook, heat a large skillet over medium-low heat. Once the skillet is hot, set the paratha on the skillet, spread a little ghee on the surface, and cook until the bread starts to turn golden brown and develops blisters, 2 to 3 minutes per side.

Masala Parathas

1 shallot (2 oz [60 g]), finely minced

1 tsp garam masala, homemade (page 312) or store-bought

1 green or red chilli, thinly sliced

2 Tbsp chopped cilantro

2 tsp dried mint

1 tsp amchur

Make sure these ingredients are chopped extremely fine. This helps prevent the dough from tearing while you gently roll out the parathas.

Combine all of the ingredients. Follow the preceding paratha recipe, and after the ghee is massaged into the atta, add this mixture. Then continue with the remainder of the recipe.

Caldine (Goan Yellow Fish Curry)

In terms of heat, this is a mild fish curry from Goa that's very popular with kids; as a bonus, it's a quick and easy recipe. You can use a milder fresh green chilli or skip it, as you prefer. Serve this with bread or rice and a fresh salad or pickle (see Cauliflower Aachar, page 320). Any type of white fish and even shrimp work great here but avoid salmon; it doesn't work as well in curries.

SERVES 4

4 garlic cloves, peeled

1 in [2.5 cm] piece fresh ginger, peeled and chopped

1 green chilli

½ tsp ground black pepper

½ tsp cumin seeds

½ tsp coriander seeds

2 Tbsp coconut oil, ghee, or extra-virgin olive oil

1 medium white onion (9¼ oz [260 g]), diced

½ tsp ground turmeric

One 13½ fl oz [400 ml] can full-fat unsweetened coconut milk

1 lb [455 g] fish such as cod, cut into 1 in [2.5 cm] cubes

1 Tbsp tamarind paste, homemade (see page 67) or store-bought

Fine sea salt

2 Tbsp whole cilantro leaves, for garnish

THE FLAVOR APPROACH

Coconut milk, rich in fat, gives this curry its creamy feel.

Coconut milk is an emulsion made up of water, fat, and proteins; the addition of an acid such as that present in the tamarind can destabilize the emulsion in the presence of heat and stirring, so the coconut proteins separate and form aggregates. To avoid this, stir gently, and add the tamarind at the end when the fish is cooked.

Grind the garlic, ginger, green chilli, black pepper, cumin seeds, and coriander seeds to a smooth paste in a blender. Add a few tablespoons of water if needed to loosen things up in the blender.

Heat the coconut oil in a medium saucepan over medium-high heat. When the oil is hot, sauté the onions until they turn translucent, 4 to 5 minutes. Add the ground garlic mixture and turmeric and cook, stirring occasionally, until most of the liquid is cooked off and the fat starts to separate from the mixture, 4 to 8 minutes.

Turn the heat to low and stir in the coconut milk. Bring the mixture to simmer. Add the fish and cook until the fish turns opaque and flakes easily, 3 to 4 minutes. Stir in the tamarind and let it simmer for 1 minute. Taste and season with salt and remove from the heat. Garnish with the cilantro and serve warm.

Chicken Coconut Curry

Whenever my grandfather picked up extra coconuts on his trips to the market, my grand-mother would separate the flesh from the mature coconuts and dry them in the sun to increase their shelf life. The dried coconut pieces were then ground as needed, and they often made an appearance in curries like this one. Serve this chicken curry over a bowl of warm rice or with large chunks of sourdough bread to sop up the flavorful liquid.

SERVES 4

1 cup [115 g] packed unsweetened fresh, thawed, or desiccated coconut

4 cloves

1 tsp black peppercorns

1 tsp ground coriander

½ tsp ground cumin

6 garlic cloves, peeled

1 in [2.5 cm] piece fresh ginger, peeled and chopped

1 green chilli

2 Tbsp coconut oil, ghee, or a neutral oil

1 large white onion (14 oz [400 g]), halved and thinly sliced

1 tsp ground turmeric

½ tsp Kashmiri red chilli powder

3 lb [1.4 kg] bone-in chicken thighs and drumsticks

2 Tbsp cider vinegar

Fine sea salt

2 Tbsp chopped cilantro, for garnish

THE FLAVOR APPROACH

As in the Caldine (page 301) and the Black Pepper Chicken (page 260), coconut provides the luxurious texture of fat as the foundation of this dish.

Toasting shredded coconut amplifies the aroma and creates a deeper and richer flavor in this curry. I prefer either frozen or fresh coconut, but you can also use desiccated; just make sure your blender pulverizes the shreds completely.

Vinegar is added at the end to reduce the risk of the coconut milk emulsion falling apart.

Heat a large saucepan over medium-low heat. Add the coconut and toast, stirring occasionally, until it turns golden brown, 5 to 6 minutes. Add the cloves, peppercorns, coriander, and cumin and cook until the spices get fragrant, 30 to 45 seconds. Remove from the heat and transfer the contents of the saucepan to a blender. Add the garlic, ginger, and chilli. Boil 1 cup [240 ml] of water in a kettle and pour it over the coconut spice mixture in the blender. Pulse until it forms a smooth paste.

In the same saucepan, heat the coconut oil over medium-high heat. Sauté the onion slices until they turn golden brown, 8 to 15 minutes. Add the turmeric and cook for 30 seconds. Transfer the coconut spice paste from the blender to the saucepan, add the chilli powder, and cook for 2 minutes. Add the chicken pieces and brown for 4 to 5 minutes. Stir in 1 cup [240 ml] of water, bring to a boil, and lower the heat to low. Simmer until the chicken is completely cooked, 30 to 45 minutes. Stir in the vinegar. Taste and season with salt and cook for 1 more minute. Remove from the heat, garnish with the chopped cilantro, and serve hot or warm.

Chickpea, Spinach + Potato "Samosa Pie"

Samosas are individual hand pie–size creations that encase tasty fillings in an equally tasty crust. The choices for fillings are endless, including the popular spiced potatoes, spiced chickpeas, paneer, and ground lamb. I make this larger version that I've nicknamed the "samosa pie" whenever I want the flavor and texture of a samosa for dinner but I'm low on time. I've replaced the samosa pastry with store-bought phyllo sheets; they give the crust a delicate, paper-thin texture that crumbles with a crunch in every bite.

SERVES 4

For the filling:

Fine sea salt

2 medium russet potatoes (total weight 15½ oz [440 g]), peeled and diced

2 Tbsp extra-virgin olive oil

1 medium white or yellow onion (9¼ oz [260 g]), diced

1 in [2.5 cm] piece fresh ginger, cut into matchsticks

1 tsp garam masala, homemade (page 312) or store-bought

1 tsp ground black pepper

½ tsp ground turmeric

½ tsp red chilli powder

5 oz [140 g] fresh baby spinach leaves, chopped

Two 15½ oz [445 g] cans chickpeas, rinsed and drained

1 tsp amchur

2 Tbsp chopped cilantro

1 fresh chilli, minced

For the phyllo crust:

¼ cup [55 g] unsalted butter, melted

¼ cup [60 ml] extra-virgin olive oil

10 sheets phyllo, thawed

1 tsp cumin seeds

1 tsp nigella seeds

THE FLAVOR APPROACH

A mixture of butter and olive oil moisturizes the phyllo sheets and helps turn them crisp as they cook in the oven.

Black pepper and chilli with ginger and the spices in the garam masala add heat and flavor as well as aroma.

Nigella and cumin seeds add flavor and crunchiness to the pastry.

Set a rack on the lower one-third level of the oven and preheat to 350°F [177°C].

Set a large pot of salted water to boil over medium-high heat. Add the diced potatoes and cook until they are just tender but retain their structure, 4 to 5 minutes. Drain the potatoes.

Heat the olive oil in a medium saucepan over medium-high heat. Add the onions and sauté until they turn pale and translucent, 4 to 5 minutes. Lower the heat to medium-low and add the ginger, garam masala, black pepper, turmeric, and chilli powder. Sauté until the spices are fragrant, 30 to 45 seconds. Add the potatoes and cook for 2 minutes, until they are completely tender in the center. Add the spinach and cook until the leaves have wilted and released most of their liquid, 2 to 3 minutes. Fold in the chickpeas and amchur, season with salt, and cook for about 1 minute. Remove from the heat. Add the cilantro and chilli. Taste and season with salt if needed.

To prepare the phyllo crust, combine the butter and olive oil in a small bowl. Brush a 9 by 12 by 2 in [23 by 30.5 by 5 cm] rectangular baking pan with the butter–olive oil mixture. Line the base of the pan with 5 sheets of phyllo, brushing each sheet with a little bit of the butter–olive oil mixture. Make sure any overhanging phyllo sheets are also brushed with the mixture. Add the

chickpea mixture and level it with a large spoon or spatula.

Add the remaining phyllo sheets on top, brushing each with the butter–olive oil mixture. As you place each one, pleat slightly to create a ruffled surface. Sprinkle the cumin and nigella seeds on top. Fold in any overhanging phyllo and neatly tuck

them in around the sides. Bake the pie in the preheated oven until the crust is golden brown on top and on the sides, 30 to 45 minutes, rotating halfway through baking. Let cool in the pan for 5 minutes before serving.

The pie is best eaten the day it is prepared.

Coconut Milk Cake

This coconut cake was born out of two very different cakes. As coconuts are a staple in Goan kitchens, we make a coconut cake with semolina, called *baath*, that's highly fragrant. The second cake that gave inspiration for this dessert was the Mexican tres leches, a marvelous cake made soft and rich by the addition of milk, which I find extremely soothing at all times of the year. Let the cake soak in the infused coconut milk, and serve some extra milk on the side in a pitcher for your guests.

MAKES ONE 9 IN [23 CM] SQUARE CAKE

For the cake:

1 cup [115 g] packed unsweetened shredded fresh or desiccated coconut

½ cup [110 g] unsalted butter, cubed, at room temperature, plus a little extra for greasing

2 cups [320 g] fine-grade semolina flour

½ tsp baking powder

¼ tsp fine sea salt

One 13½ fl oz [400 ml] can full-fat unsweetened coconut milk

One 5.4 fl oz [160 ml] can unsweetened coconut cream

2 cups [280 g] sugar

4 large eggs, at room temperature

1½ tsp rose water

For the coconut-cardamom milk:

Two 13½ fl oz [400 ml] cans full-fat unsweetened coconut milk

½ cup [50 g] sugar

½ tsp ground green cardamom

THE FLAVOR APPROACH

Coconut comes into play at several stages in this cake. Toasting shredded coconut intensifies the nutty, tropical aroma.

Adding coconut milk and coconut cream adds the next layer of flavor and also provides the fat that, along with the butter and eggs, gives this cake its structure.

Rose water and cardamom help intensify the perception of sweetness in the cake.

Preheat the oven to 300°F [149°C].

Line a baking sheet with parchment paper and spread the coconut out in an even layer. Toast the coconut in the oven until it starts to turn a light golden brown, 5 to 8 minutes. Remove from the oven and let cool completely before using. Increase the oven temperature to 350°F [180°C]. Grease a 9 by 9 by 2 in [23 by 23 by 5 cm] square baking pan with a little butter.

In a large bowl, whisk together the semolina, baking powder, and salt. In a small bowl, whisk together the coconut milk and coconut cream.

In the bowl of a stand mixer fitted with a paddle attachment, cream the butter with the sugar on medium-high speed until light and fluffy, 4 to 5 minutes. Stop and scrape the sides and bottom of the bowl. Add the eggs, one at a time, beating after each addition. Lower the mixer speed to medium-low and add half the dry ingredients, beating until combined, 1 to 1½ minutes. Beat in the coconut milk–cream mixture and rose water and then the remaining dry ingredients, and beat until well combined. Transfer the batter to the prepared pan.

Bake for 60 to 75 minutes, rotating the pan halfway through baking, until the surface is golden brown, the center is firm yet spongy, and a skewer inserted into the center comes out clean.

Meanwhile, to prepare the coconut-cardamom-milk, mix the coconut milk with the sugar and cardamom and stir until the sugar is dissolved. Store, refrigerated, until ready to use.

Set the pan on a wire rack to cool for 10 minutes. Run a knife around the edges of the pan to loosen the cake. Using a skewer, poke several holes in the cake. Pour 2 cups [480 ml] of the milk over the cake. Wrap with plastic wrap and refrigerate until chilled, at least 4 hours and up to 2 days.

Warm the cake and leftover coconut-cardamom-milk before serving.

PANTRY ESSENTIALS

Plain Rice

For the most part, I cook with basmati rice at home. Basmati rice is renowned not only for its spectacular long grains but also for its aroma. Being a creature of habit, I purchase my basmati rice from my Indian food market. When purchasing basmati, always ask for rice that's from India and has been aged for at least 1 year; the aroma will be richer.

When I cook basmati for plain rice, pulaos, or biryani, I follow these three rules:

1. Once water is added to the rice on the stove, avoid stirring or mixing it.

2. For plain rice, I do not add any salt or oil because they reduce the natural fragrance of basmati rice.

3. To add a bit of color, add a pinch of ground saffron, a few drops of beet juice, or turmeric powder.

SERVES 2 (ABOUT 1¼ LB [570 G] COOKED RICE)

1 cup [200 g] basmati rice

4 cups [960 ml] water

Pick through the rice and remove any stones or debris. Place the rice in a fine-mesh sieve and rinse under cool running water until the water is no longer cloudy. Transfer the rice to a medium bowl, cover with 2 cups [480 ml] of the water or enough water to cover the grains by at least 1 in [2.5 cm], and soak for 30 minutes. Drain the water. Place the rice in a medium saucepan or a small Dutch oven with a lid and add the remaining 2 cups [480 ml] of water or enough water to cover the grains by at least 1 in [2.5 cm]. Bring to a rolling boil over medium-high heat. Turn the heat to low, cover, and cook until most of the water has evaporated, 10 to 12 minutes. Remove from heat and let sit, covered, for another 5 minutes. Just before serving, fluff the rice with a fork.

Rice Crumbs

While breadcrumbs and semolina have long been staples in my kitchen for adding a crunchy coating when I bake or deep-fry food and as a binding agent in meatballs and meatloaf, recently I've been trying to re-create those same textures with rice. These rice crumbs are a fantastic way to achieve this, and a great way to use up leftover cooked

rice. You'll probably want to double this recipe and make some extra.

MAKES APPROXIMATELY 3½ OZ [90 G]

2 cups (12 oz [340 g]) leftover plain boiled basmati rice

Preheat the oven to 250°F [120°C].

Line a baking sheet with parchment paper. Spread the rice out in a single layer on the prepared baking sheet, breaking any clumps of rice with your hand. Place the rice in the oven until the grains dry out completely, at least 45 to 60 minutes. The rice crumbs should not turn golden brown; if you notice that happening, this means your oven is too hot and you need to lower the temperature. Your drying time will vary depending on your oven; it can take an additional 30 minutes or more than the suggested time.

Remove the baking sheet from the oven and let the rice cool completely to room temperature. Grind the cooled toasted rice grains in a spice grinder or coffee mill to a tiny but coarse consistency. The degree of grinding will depend on your preference. Transfer the rice crumbs to an airtight container and store in a cool, dark place for up to 1 month.

SPICE BLENDS

Spice blends and masalas (the Hindi word for any spice blend) are a fantastic resource to keep on hand in your kitchen. To make them last longer and get their maximum flavor, make them in small batches and store them in dark containers in a cool spot away from sunlight.

THE FLAVOR APPROACH

+ Toasting spices provides heat, helping drive out the moisture that accumulates in the dried spices during storage.

+ Heat also helps draw out the flavor molecules in the seeds, and some of these molecules undergo changes in their chemical structure, which changes their flavor and makes them tastier.

+ Grinding whole spices breaks them down into tiny particles, which increases their surface area. Extraction of the flavor molecules is more efficient when the particles are smaller. When added to a dish in a ground powder form, their flavor and pigments are released at a higher rate than if they were kept whole.

Garam Masala

I'm including two different versions of garam masala that I cook with at home. You can use either version in the recipes here. Let the spices cool before you grind them or they will release moisture, which can cause a bit of clumping when the spices are ground.

My Shahi Garam Masala

A bit different from the classic garam masala, this *shahi* ("royal" in Urdu) version is highly aromatic and is used on special occasions to flavor rice, lentils, meats, and vegetables. But you don't need to wait for a special celebration to use it; I certainly don't!

You can prepare an intensely floral and aromatic version of shahi garam masala by adding 1 Tbsp of edible dried rose petals to the toasted spice mix when grinding the mixture. I find this version goes well with meat dishes.

MAKES JUST UNDER ½ CUP [40 G]

2 Tbsp cumin seeds

2 Tbsp coriander seeds

2 Tbsp fennel seeds

1 Tbsp whole black peppercorns

2 dried bay leaves

One 2 in [5 cm] cinnamon stick

12 whole cloves

8 whole green cardamom pods

1 whole black cardamom pod

1 whole star anise

1 tsp freshly grated nutmeg

Heat a small, dry stainless-steel or cast-iron skillet over medium-high heat. Turn the heat to medium-low and add the cumin seeds, coriander seeds, fennel seeds, black peppercorns, bay leaves, cinnamon, cloves, green and black cardamom pods, and star anise. Toast gently by rotating the pan to circulate the spices until the spices become fragrant, 30 to 45 seconds. Be careful not to burn them; if they do burn, discard them and start fresh.

Transfer the toasted spices to a small plate and let cool completely. Transfer the cooled spices to a mortar or spice

cont'd

grinder. Add the nutmeg and grind to a fine powder. Store the spice mix in an airtight container in a cool, dark place for up to 6 months.

My Garam Masala

This is my regular garam masala; note the absence of a few aromatic spices such as fennel and a smaller amount of green cardamom in this version.

MAKES ABOUT ¼ CUP [25 G]

2 Tbsp cumin seeds

2 Tbsp coriander seeds

1 Tbsp black peppercorns

2 dried bay leaves

One 2 in [5 cm] cinnamon stick

12 whole cloves

1 whole black cardamom pod

3 or 4 green cardamom pods

1 tsp freshly grated nutmeg

Follow the method for the Shahi Garam Masala (page 311).

My "Gunpowder" Nut Masala

The classic fiery gunpowder masala of Southern India is made with a mixture of lentils and served as a seasoning alongside a variety of foods. This nut-based version of gunpowder masala arose out of necessity, because I don't regularly stock my pantry with the specific lentils used, but this turns out to be a great way to use up extra bits of nuts and seeds stored in the back of your freezer.

To use, generously sprinkle the masala over savory dishes like dals, vegetables, and salads.

MAKES 2 CUPS [210 G]

3½ oz [100 g] raw cashews

½ cup [35 g] raw pepitas (pumpkin seeds)

1 oz [30 g] dried red chillies

20 to 25 fresh curry leaves

2 Tbsp white or black sesame seeds

½ tsp asafetida

Heat a small, dry skillet over medium heat. When the pan is hot, add the cashews, pumpkin seeds, chillies, curry leaves, and sesame seeds and toast for 4 to 5 minutes until the seeds start to turn brown and the leaves begin to slightly curl. Transfer to a medium bowl and let cool to room temperature. Once cooled, grind the mixture with the asafetida to a coarse or fine powder, depending on your preference, in a food processor or a blender. Transfer to an airtight container and store for up to 2 weeks in the refrigerator.

Salt-Cured Egg Yolks

Salt-cured egg yolks are used for their savory appeal; when shaved, they taste like finely grated Parmesan. Use them over pasta or as a garnish in dishes to give an extra bit of saltiness and umami. They must be prepared a few days ahead of when you want to use them.

MAKES 2 CURED YOLKS

1½ cups [450 g] fine sea salt

½ cup [50 g] sugar

2 large eggs

Oil spray, such as canola

THE FLAVOR APPROACH

+ Salt and sugar draw out the water from the yolk through osmosis. The reduced availability of water helps preserve the yolk.

+ The glutamic acid in the yolk concentrates it and gives a richer umami taste.

+ The kala namak variation provides a stronger sulfurous aroma in addition to the rich umami notes.

In a small flat container or dish, spread out half of the salt. Make two small depressions in the center.

Working with one egg at a time, carefully separate the yolk from the white and place the yolk in a depression in the salt. Reserve the whites for another purpose. Cover the yolks with the remaining sea salt. Cover the container loosely with a lid and leave in the refrigerator for 1 week.

After a week, position a rack in the middle of the oven and preheat the oven to 200°F [93°C]. Remove the lid and carefully remove the yolks. The yolks will be firm but slightly sticky to the touch; be careful when handling them. Using a pastry brush, lightly dust off the excess salt. Quickly rinse the yolks under running tap water and dab dry with a clean paper towel. Set a wire rack on a baking sheet and spray the rack with the oil. Set the cured yolks on the rack and place it in the oven to dry completely, at least 45 minutes to 1 hour. Once the yolks are dried, remove them from the oven and allow to cool completely before storing in an airtight container in the refrigerator for up to 2 weeks or in the freezer for up to 1 month.

To use, shave the yolk with a zester or grater and use it as a topping or garnish for salads, soups, and so on, as you would a hard cheese.

VARIATION: *For a stronger sulfurous flavor, use kala namak mixed in with the salt and sugar.*

1 cup [300 g] fine sea salt + ¼ cup [50 g] kala namak + ½ cup [100 g] sugar

Trim and discard the ends of the shallots and peel them. Cut them in half lengthwise and brush them generously with the grapeseed oil.

Heat a small skillet over high heat. When the pan is hot, char the shallots on each side for 3 to 4 minutes; the surface should be slightly burnt. Remove from the heat and transfer the shallots to a bowl to cool. When the shallots are cool enough to handle, mince them and add to a mixing bowl along with the yogurt, lemon juice and zest, and pepper. Season with salt. Fold to combine. Taste and adjust the seasoning.

In the same skillet, heat the olive oil over medium-high heat. When the oil is hot, add the nigella seeds and cook until fragrant, 30 to 45 seconds. Pour the hot oil with the nigella over the dip in the bowl. Garnish with the chives and serve.

Sundried Tomatoes + Red Bell Pepper Spread

Bright red, with sweet, rich flavors, this spread can be used as a dip with a platter of crudité or in sandwiches (it's especially great in grilled cheese sandwiches and even as a dip on the side). For an extra kick of garlic, use 3 garlic cloves.

MAKES APPROXIMATELY 2½ CUPS [590 G]

1 medium red bell pepper (7 oz [200 g])

8½ oz [240 g] sun-dried tomatoes, packed in olive oil

6 scallions

2 garlic cloves, peeled

2 Tbsp fresh lemon juice

1 tsp coriander seeds

1 tsp nigella seeds

1 tsp red chilli flakes

1 tsp fine sea salt

Trim the stalks off the bell pepper and discard the seeds. Cut the bell pepper into chunks and place them in a blender. Add the tomatoes and ¼ cup [60 ml] of their oil; reserve the remaining oil for another purpose. Add the scallions, garlic, lemon juice, coriander and nigella seeds, red chilli flakes, and salt and pulse on high speed until it forms a smooth paste. You might need to add 1 to 2 Tbsp

DIPS + SPREADS

Dips and spreads are a great resource for entertaining. Serve either of these dips with toasted bread or a bright, colorful platter of crisp vegetables as a crudité.

Burnt Shallot Dip

MAKES APPROXIMATELY 1½ CUPS [350 G]

2 shallots (total weight 4¼ oz [120 g])

1 Tbsp grapeseed oil or other neutral oil

1 cup [240 g] plain unsweetened Greek yogurt

1 Tbsp fresh lemon juice

1 tsp fresh lemon zest

½ tsp coarsely ground black pepper

Fine sea salt

1 Tbsp extra-virgin olive oil

1 tsp nigella seeds

1 Tbsp chopped chives, for garnish

of water to get the ingredients to move in the blender. Taste and adjust the seasoning.

DIPPING OILS

One of my earliest experiences with Italian food involved the simplest yet the most splendid appetizer—warm focaccia served with dipping oil and balsamic vinegar on a large plate. The formula for this is very straightforward:

[Spices + Herbs + Good Oil] + Good Vinegar + Flaky Salt + Warm Bread = Happiness

Here are some playful takes on this concept. Serve the oil with 1 to 2 Tbsp of a good fruity or sweet vinegar, like balsamic, fig, plum, or sherry vinegar.

FLAVOR MAP FOR DIPPING OILS

Basic Recipe (feel free to tweak the amounts here):

½ cup [120 ml] oil + ½ tsp spices and/or chillies + 1 tsp fresh herbs or ½ tsp dried herbs + 2 to 3 Tbsp acid (vinegar) + salt and pepper

EMULSIONS

Here are two types of emulsions that use different emulsifiers to stabilize the emulsion created by the oil and water. Toum uses the pectin in garlic, while mayonnaise relies on the lecithin in egg yolks and mustard to hold that luscious texture together.

Toum

You don't need to restrict yourself to using toum as a dipping sauce. Because it lasts for a long time, you can use it as a quick garlic flavor booster in various ways: Fold a spoonful or two into soft goat cheese to serve with crostini, the Oven "Fries" (page 144), or the Lamb Chops with Scallion Mint Salsa (page 163); or combine it with the Goat Cheese Dip (page 144) and use it as a condiment on sandwiches or as a dip.

MAKES ABOUT 1 QT [960 ML]

1 large head garlic (4¼ oz [120 g])

¼ cup [60 ml] fresh lemon juice

½ cup [120 ml] ice-cold water

3 cups [720 ml] grapeseed oil or debittered extra-virgin olive oil (see case study, page 104)

Fine sea salt

Peel the garlic cloves and trim the bottom ends. Remove and discard any green parts.

Place the garlic with the lemon juice and water in the bowl of a food processor and pulse until combined. Continue to pulse as you slowly drizzle in the grapeseed oil, one drop at a time, until the mixture is completely emulsified and smooth. Taste and season with salt.

Store the toum in an airtight container in the refrigerator for up to 1 month.

Curry Leaf + Mustard Oil Mayonnaise

The wasabi-like heat of golden-yellow mustard oil matched with the perfume of curry leaves gives this mayonnaise its bold flavorful character. Use it as you would regular mayonnaise, over your fries, and on your summer tomato sandwiches as I do, with a few crispy fried curry leaves.

MAKES JUST OVER 1 CUP [150 G]

½ cup [120 ml] debittered mustard oil or debittered extra-virgin olive oil (see case study, page 104)

12 to 15 fresh curry leaves

1 large egg yolk, at room temperature

2 Tbsp fresh lime juice or rice vinegar

1 Tbsp prepared yellow mustard

2 tsp honey

½ tsp red chilli powder

½ tsp freshly ground black pepper

Fine sea salt

THE FLAVOR APPROACH

+ Here the fiery-tasting substances in mustard oil come into play when making an emulsion.

+ The yellow mustard is optional; it acts as a second emulsifier along with the lecithin (in the egg yolk) and honey.

Heat the oil in a small, dry stainless-steel saucepan over medium-high heat. While the oil is heating, rinse the curry leaves under cold tap water and dab them dry with a clean kitchen towel. When the oil is hot, add the curry leaves, cover the saucepan with a lid, and remove from the heat. Once the oil has cooled to room temperature, transfer it to small container. Transfer the fried leaves to a small plate lined with a paper towel to get rid of any excess oil, and reserve to use as a garnish.

Place the egg yolk, lime juice, yellow mustard, honey, chilli powder, and black pepper in a medium mixing bowl. Whisk the mixture until smooth and combined. Slowly drizzle the cooled infused mustard oil into the center of the egg yolk mixture and whisk. The mixture will start to thicken. Once the oil is incorporated, taste and season with salt. Store the mayonnaise in an airtight container in the refrigerator for 3 to 4 days.

VARIATION: *For an extra kick of heat, use cayenne instead of red chilli powder. To give the mayonnaise a deeper yellow color, mix in ¼ tsp of ground turmeric with the egg yolk.*

My Quick Marinara

When I don't have a marinara sauce on hand for pizza, this is my go-to. It's a bit unconventional but works beautifully. Use a good-quality tomato paste; I like to buy it in tubes.

Depending on your preference, you can use the olive oil that the anchovies were packed in or just regular extra-virgin olive oil.

MAKES 1 CUP [ABOUT 200 G]

2 Tbsp unsalted butter or extra-virgin olive oil

1 tsp nigella seeds

1 garlic clove, peeled and finely grated

½ tsp dried oregano

½ tsp ground black pepper

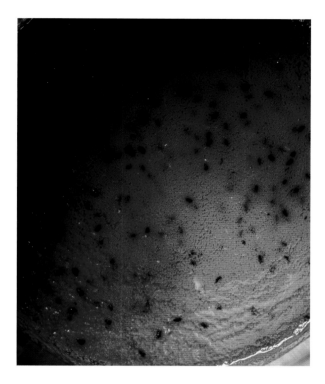

4½ oz [130 g] tomato paste

2 anchovies, packed in olive oil, drained

Sea salt

Sugar

THE FLAVOR APPROACH

+ Anchovies and tomatoes add umami character. The anchovies fall apart and melt away as they cook.

+ Nigella seeds are often erroneously referred to as onion seeds or black cumin, even though they are completely unrelated. Nigella produce an onion-like aroma when cooked; this becomes evident here when they're added to the hot oil.

Heat the olive oil in a small saucepan over medium-low heat. When the oil is hot, add the nigella seeds and garlic and cook for 15 seconds, until fragrant, taking care to prevent the garlic from burning. Add the oregano and cook for an additional 10 seconds. Stir in the black pepper, tomato paste, anchovies, and ½ cup [120 ml] of water and whisk to combine. Increase the heat to medium-high and bring to a boil, then turn the heat to low and simmer for

5 minutes. Taste and season with salt and sugar. Store in an airtight container in the refrigerator and use within 1 week.

INDO-CHINESE CONDIMENTS

Heat plays a significant role in many Indo-Chinese dishes. Whenever we ate at the Chinese restaurants in India, these two sauces were always provided on the side. And if we ordered takeout, you can bet I asked for a couple extra servings of these.

THE FLAVOR APPROACH

+ Vinegar in both sauces provides sourness.

+ In the Indo-Sichuan Sauce (page 318), the vinegar also acts as preservative along with the chillies and garlic.

Chilli-Soy Vinegar Sauce

This sauce is usually prepared without the addition of soy sauce; however, I find mixing the two together with the chillies gives a more robust flavor. A quick and easy sauce to prepare, it's got acidity, umami, and heat all rolled into one. Sprinkle a few drops of the liquid into your Manchow Soup (page 255) or over your noodles to kick things up.

MAKES ½ CUP [120 ML]

¼ cup [60 ml] rice vinegar

¼ cup [60 ml] soy sauce

1 green chilli, such as serrano or bird's eye, thinly sliced

Fine sea salt

Place the vinegar, soy sauce, and chilli in a small serving bowl. Season with salt and let sit for 1 hour before serving. Store in a covered container in the refrigerator for up to 2 days.

Indo-Sichuan Sauce

The name of this sauce is a bit misleading; it does not use Sichuan peppercorns but instead refers to the Hakka.

While this sauce is served with Chinese food in India, I use it as a dipping sauce for everything; it even goes on top of my fried eggs. The oil extracts the bright red pigment of the red chillies, and you end up with a brilliant shade of rouge. While Kashmiri chillies are mild in their level of heat, you can further reduce the level of fieriness in the dish by simply removing and discarding the seeds from half the chillies, then proceeding with the recipe.

MAKES 1¼ LB [570 G], 3 TO 3½ CUPS

1½ oz [40 g] dried whole Kashmiri chillies, stalks removed and discarded

1 cup [240 ml] boiling water

½ cup [120 ml] grapeseed oil or other neutral oil

2 Tbsp minced shallot or red onion

3¼ oz [90 g] garlic, peeled and minced

2¼ oz [65 g] fresh ginger, peeled and minced

¼ cup [55 g] tomato paste

½ cup [120 ml] cider vinegar

2 Tbsp soy sauce

½ tsp sugar

Fine sea salt

Place the chillies in a medium bowl or cup and cover with the boiling water. Push down the chillies to submerge them and let stand for 30 minutes to soften and rehydrate.

Remove the chillies and transfer them to a blender with half of the soaking water. Reserve the remaining water. Pulse for a few short seconds until a coarse paste forms.

Heat the oil in a medium saucepan over medium heat. When the oil is hot, add the chilli paste and cook, stirring constantly, for 1 minute. Add the shallot and cook for 1 minute. Add the garlic, ginger, and tomato paste and cook for 2 minutes. Lower the heat to a simmer and add the vinegar, soy sauce, sugar, and the reserved water. Cover the saucepan with a lid and cook, stirring occasionally, until the ginger is completely tender and cooked, almost all the water has cooked off, and the oil separates, 25 to 30 minutes.

Taste and season with salt. Transfer the sauce to an airtight container and refrigerate for up to 1 month.

PRESERVED LEMONS, TWO WAYS (CLASSIC + QUICK)

You can certainly purchase preserved lemons in most stores now, but for those of you who want to give it a try, here are two methods. Meyer lemons remain my top choice for this preserve because of their thin skins, but any type of lemon will work in this recipe. Before serving, rinse the preserved lemons under running tap water, then scrape and discard the flesh. Dice the peel and use as needed. You can blend it into mayonnaise, fold it into sauces, or add it to salad dressings.

THE FLAVOR APPROACH

+ Salt works by masking the bitterness in the lemon.

+ Using a combination of salt and acid (citric acid) helps soften cell structure and preserve lemons.

Classic Method

I first learned to make preserved lemons via the legendary writer Claudia Roden, from her book *Arabesque: A Taste of Morocco, Turkey, and Lebanon*. Here, the combined actions of the salt and the acid (citric acid) of the lemon soften the fruit. The salt also plays a second role: It helps alleviate the perception of bitterness from the white pith. If a white mold develops on the exposed skin of the peel, simply rinse it off. Classically, the lemons are not cut all the way but in a crisscross pattern that holds the entire lemon together. I've tried this in a few different ways and haven't noticed any difference in taste.

MAKES 1½ CUPS, OR APPROXIMATELY 15¾ OZ [450 G]

4 lemons (total weight about 10 oz [280 g])

¼ cup [50 g] fine sea salt

½ cup [120 ml] fresh lemon juice from 4 additional lemons

Wash and scrub the lemons under warm tap water. Cut the lemons in quarters and remove and discard the seeds. Rub the lemons with the salt and transfer them to a sterilized preserving jar. Press the lemons down with a ladle

to crush them and cover the lemons with the remaining juice. Seal the jar and keep in a dark cool spot for at least 1 month before using. Store indefinitely, refrigerated.

Quick Method

The quick method is a shortcut that I use when I've run out of my jars of preserved lemons. First, heat is applied by dropping the lemons into a bath of boiling water to soften them. They are then chopped up to increase the surface area so the salt and acid can rapidly penetrate the lemons' flesh.

MAKES 1½ CUPS, OR APPROXIMATELY 15¾ OZ [450 G]

4 lemons (total weight about 10 oz [280 g])

¼ cup [50 g] fine sea salt

½ cup [120 ml] fresh lemon juice from 4 additional lemons

Wash and scrub the lemons under warm tap water. Cut the lemons in quarters, then cut each in half. Remove and discard the seeds. Rub the lemons with half the salt and place them in a small bowl for 2 hours. Rinse the lemons under cold running tap water and discard the liquid left behind in the bowl. Place the lemons in a small saucepan with the remaining salt, the lemon juice, and ½ cup [120 ml] of water. Bring to a boil over medium-high heat, then lower the heat to a simmer and cook until the liquid volume is reduced by half and it is thick and syrupy, 25 to 30 minutes. Remove from the heat, transfer to a sterilized, nonreactive (glass or plastic), airtight container, and refrigerate overnight. The preserves will be ready to use the next day.

Quick Pickled Nectarines with Mint + Serrano

This is a fresh pickle made with sweet, ripe nectarines; you can use peaches in a pinch.

Because capsaicin is soluble in fat and alcohol and only weakly soluble in water, most of the heat stays concentrated in the chilli to give a pop of heat when you bite into the chilli slices. I find this pickle delicious with soft cheeses such as fresh creamy burrata or with salads or grilled meats and seafood.

cont'd

Heat a small, dry skillet over medium-high heat. Once the pan is hot, toast the coriander seeds until they just start to release their aroma, about 30 seconds. Transfer the seeds to a mortar and pestle and crush into a coarse powder, then transfer to a small mixing bowl.

Cut the nectarines into halves and remove and discard the stones. Cut the nectarine halves into thin slices and place them in a large bowl with a lid. Tear the mint leaves and add them with the chilli to the nectarines in the bowl.

Add the lime juice, date syrup, and black pepper to the crushed coriander seeds and mix with a spoon until evenly combined. Pour this liquid over the nectarines in the bowl. Season with salt. Fold carefully, cover the bowl with the lid, and let sit at room temperature for 30 minutes. Serve at room temperature or chilled. This pickle will keep for up to 1 day.

Cauliflower Aachar (Pickle)

There are two types of people in my life—those who love this cauliflower pickle slightly sweet and those who prefer it spicy—so I leave the decision whether to add jaggery (or sugar) entirely to you.

Mustard oil is the classic choice for this aachar or Indian-style pickle, and it imparts its special note of pungency, but you can replace it with extra-virgin olive oil, sesame oil, or a neutral oil such as grapeseed. To make the pickle more visually exciting, I sometimes use equal parts black and yellow mustard seeds. In this recipe, asafetida acts as an allium flavor substitute. The pickle does not need to be canned.

Serve a little bit of this aachar on the side with meals, and add a generous spoonful to your sandwiches (make a sandwich with the Lamb Koftas, page 264) for an extra bump of texture and flavor. Use up the leftover oil and vinegar mixture as a dip served with bread.

SERVES 4

1 tsp coriander seeds

2 ripe but firm yellow nectarines
(total weight 15½ oz [440 g])

¼ cup [5 g] fresh mint leaves

1 green chilli such as serrano, thinly sliced

¼ cup [60 ml] fresh lime juice

2 to 3 Tbsp date syrup, homemade (page 324)
or store-bought

½ tsp coarsely ground black pepper

Fine sea salt

THE FLAVOR APPROACH

+ Capsaicin does not dissolve well in water; as a result, you'll notice different grades of heat in this dish; it's more concentrated when you bite into the chilli rather than in the pickle's liquid.

+ As time progresses and the acids break the cells down, the capsaicin will start to spread and the heat will become more uniform.

MAKES ABOUT 2 LB [910 G]

2 lb [910 g] cauliflower, broken into bite-size florets—after trimming you should have 1.7 lb [760 g]

1 cup [240 ml] mustard oil, extra-virgin olive oil, sesame oil, or grapeseed oil

¼ cup [36 g] black or yellow mustard seeds (or both)

2 Tbsp cumin seeds

1 Tbsp red chilli powder

2 tsp ground turmeric

1 tsp asafetida

2 Tbsp fine sea salt

2 Tbsp jaggery or dark brown sugar (optional)

¾ cup [180 ml] cider or malt vinegar

Clean, wash, and sterilize a 3 qt [2.8 L] canning jar. Keep the jar dry.

Rinse the cauliflower florets and arrange them on a clean kitchen towel to drain off any excess water. A salad spinner will also do a fantastic job of removing any excess water.

Warm the oil in a large saucepan over medium heat. Lightly crush the mustard and cumin seeds with a mortar and pestle and add them to the hot oil. Cook for 30 seconds, until the spices just start to get fragrant. Remove from the heat and add the red chilli powder, turmeric, and asafetida. Fold in the cauliflower to coat well. Transfer the cauliflower with the oil-spice mixture to the prepared jar.

In a medium bowl, dissolve the salt and jaggery in the vinegar. Pour this mixture over the cauliflower in the jar, seal with a lid, and shake to coat well. Leave the jar at room temperature overnight, after which the aachar will be ready to eat. This aachar can be stored in the refrigerator for up to 1 month.

CHUTNEYS

I could happily devote an entire chapter to the luscious, gorgeous nature of savory and sweet chutneys. Chutneys are condiments that provide a complex assortment of flavors, and a little bit goes along way. Serve them alongside snacks or as a condiment with a large meal.

Green Apple Chutney

This recipe is based on one that I found in my late maternal grandmother's recipe notebook for apple chutney. Every year, she'd make a few jars and I'd eat it on a plate filled with rice, her cabbage foogath (page 291), and Caldine (page 301). This chutney pairs well with grilled pork chops. Cooking the apples in a large, wide skillet increases the available surface area for evaporation. Adjust the amount of red chilli flakes based on your preference.

cont'd

2 lb [910 g] Granny Smith or other firm, tart green apples, peeled and cored

½ cup [70 g] packed raisins or sweetened cranberries

2 in [5 cm] piece fresh ginger, peeled and cut into 1 in [2.5 cm] matchsticks

2 tsp to 1 Tbsp red chilli flakes, such as Aleppo

1 cup [200 g] packed brown sugar

1 cup [240 ml] cider or malt vinegar

1 tsp fine sea salt

Prepare four clean, sterile 8 oz [250 ml] canning jars.

Shred the apples using the coarse blades of a grater or a food processor.

Combine the shredded apples, raisins, ginger, and chilli flakes with ¼ cup [60 ml] of water in a deep nonreactive stainless-steel skillet and heat over medium-high heat. Bring to a boil, then lower the heat to a simmer and cover with a lid. Cook until the apples get soft, stirring occasionally with a silicone spatula, 10 to 12 minutes. Stir in the sugar, vinegar, and salt and continue to cook, uncovered, stirring occasionally, until the apple mixture gets thick and most of the liquid evaporates, 30 to 40 minutes. Remove from the heat and pack into a clean, sterile jar. This pickle is good for 1 month.

Tamarind-Date Chutney

This chutney is sweet from the date syrup and gets its acidity from the tamarind. Dried ginger gives it heat, while kala namak adds a special note of saltiness. This chutney is served with fried snacks such as samosas and is a part of the family of street foods called *chaat* in India. Drizzle the chutney over fresh or grilled ripe fruit; serve it with a little sweetened crème fraîche as a dessert.

MAKES 1 CUP [280 G]

½ tsp ground cumin

½ cup [120 ml] date syrup, homemade (page 324) or store-bought

2 Tbsp tamarind paste, homemade (page 67) or store-bought

2 Tbsp ground jaggery or dark brown sugar

1 tsp amchur

1 tsp dried ground ginger

½ tsp red chilli flakes, such as Aleppo or Maras

½ tsp kala namak, plus more as needed

Toast the cumin in a small saucepan over medium heat until fragrant, 30 to 45 seconds. Whisk in the date syrup, ½ cup [120 ml] of water, the tamarind, jaggery, amchur, ginger, and chilli flakes. Bring to a boil over high heat. Lower the heat to a simmer and cook until the liquid reduces to 1 cup [240 ml], scraping the sides of the saucepan as it cooks, 5 to 8 minutes. Remove from the heat and add the kala namak. Taste and add more kala namak if needed. Serve at room temperature or chilled. Store in an airtight container for up to 2 weeks in the refrigerator.

Mint Chutney

This classic chutney is served with fried Indian snacks such as samosas and pakoras; it reduces some of the heaviness associated with these foods. The cooling effects of the menthol in mint along with the heat of fresh green chillies come through in this chutney. The acids from lime juice and vinegar provide a sour note but also stop the polyphenol oxidases in the leaves from turning the green

chlorophyll pigment dark black. This chutney works great on wraps and especially well with roasted vegetables.

MAKES 1 CUP [240 G]

1 bunch [75 g] cilantro

1 bunch [55 g] mint

2 green chillies such as serrano

1 in [2.5 cm] piece fresh ginger, peeled and chopped

¼ cup [60 ml] fresh lime juice

3 Tbsp rice vinegar

Fine sea salt

Place the cilantro, mint, chillies, ginger, lime juice, and vinegar in a blender or a food processor. Pulse for a few seconds at intervals until the ingredients are completely pulverized to a paste. You might need to use a spatula to move things around in the blender. Taste and add salt as needed. Transfer to an airtight container and store in the refrigerator for up to 3 to 4 days.

Pumpkin Seed Chutney

This chutney arose out of necessity. Several years ago, I learned to make dosas and idlis, and while I could find other ingredients, it was trickier to find a source for fresh or frozen coconut. Pumpkin seeds and olive oil helped me re-create that texture with a similar flavor profile. As with the Mint Chutney (left), the addition of lime juice provides a sour note and inactivates the polyphenol oxidase, which reduces the chances of the green chlorophyll pigment turning brown. A second level of protection comes from the olive oil; chlorophyll is soluble in oil, which helps reduce access to the oxygen necessary for the oxidase enzyme. Grinding the herbs in the olive oil first helps with this. This chutney is a much brighter green than the Mint Chutney.

MAKES 2 CUPS [380 G]

1 cup [130 g] pepitas (pumpkin seeds)

1 bunch [75 g] cilantro

½ cup [6 g] packed fresh mint

¼ cup [60 ml] fresh lime juice

¼ cup [60 ml] extra-virgin olive oil

12 black peppercorns

2 garlic cloves, peeled

2 green chillies such as serrano

1 in [2.5 cm] piece fresh ginger, peeled

½ tsp cumin

Fine sea salt

Place the pumpkin seeds, cilantro, mint, and lime juice in a blender or food processor. Pulse for a few seconds at intervals until you get a coarse paste. Add the olive oil, peppercorns, garlic, chillies, ginger, and cumin. Pulse for a few seconds at intervals until the ingredients are pulverized to a paste. Taste and season with salt. Store this chutney in an airtight container with a piece of plastic wrap pressed against the surface to block off any air; it will keep for up to 1 week in the refrigerator.

Cardamom Toffee Sauce

This is my all-purpose toffee sauce. I drizzle it over cakes and tart crunchy slices of apples—pretty much anywhere I can squeeze it in, this sauce will make an appearance. Toffee gets its rich flavor notes from the molasses present in brown sugar.

THE FLAVOR APPROACH

+ Brown sugar undergoes caramelization as it starts to heat up.

+ Cream of tartar prevents recrystallization of the sugar by "inverting" sucrose, and it splits to produce glucose and fructose, which interferes with crystal formation.

+ Cardamom is added toward the end, once the sauce is warm, to prevent the spice from burning.

MAKES 1½ CUPS [360 ML] SAUCE

1 cup [200 g] packed dark brown sugar

¼ tsp fine sea salt

⅛ tsp cream of tartar

½ cup [120 ml] heavy cream

2 Tbsp unsalted butter, cubed

½ tsp ground green cardamom

cont'd

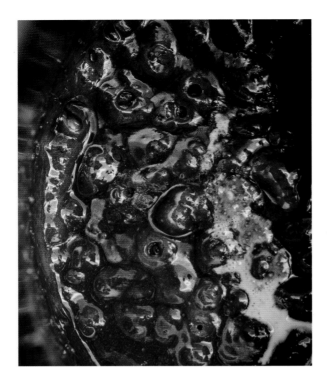

Place the sugar, ¼ cup [60 ml] of water, the salt, and cream of tartar in a medium heavy-bottomed saucepan and heat over medium-high heat, stirring continuously. Cook until the sugar dissolves completely and starts to caramelize and develop a deep amber color. Remove from the heat and carefully stir in the heavy cream. Add the butter and stir until the liquid is completely smooth. Transfer the caramel sauce to a heatproof glass jar and let it cool until it is warm to the touch. Stir in the cardamom, cover with a lid, and let cool completely. Refrigerate for up to 1 month.

Homemade Date Syrup

For those who want to try making your own date syrup at home, this recipe is for you.

Homemade date syrup can take some time to prepare, and often dried dates, despite being soft, can be resistant to creating the right texture needed in a syrup. Dates contain about 0.5% to 3.9% pectin by weight, which contributes to this resistance. You can solve this problem by adding a bit of baking soda combined with heating and blending in a high-speed blender. It is fascinating to see how the color and the texture of the date purée evolves during the processing; it will transform from a viscous

toffee-colored substance to a smooth reddish-brown syrup.

Do not concentrate the molasses too much; it will continue to thicken and can even harden as it cools. If it becomes too stiff on cooling, add a few tablespoons boiling water to thin it out, or warm the jar in a pot of simmering water for a few minutes until it loosens.

MAKES JUST UNDER 1 CUP [240 ML]

1 lb [455 g] Medjool dates

½ tsp baking soda

4 cups [960 ml] warm filtered water at 100°F [35°C]

1 tsp lemon juice or rice wine vinegar

Fine sea salt (optional)

THE FLAVOR APPROACH

+ Baking soda helps dissolve the pectin in the dried dates.

+ Heat and the mechanical action of the blades will aid in pulverizing the dates and increasing the surface area of the dates for the baking soda to act on.

+ Dried dates typically contain very low amounts of pH-sensitive anthocyanin pigments (compared to fresh dates). Despite this, the color of dried dates changes along with the pH during various stages of cooking. This is likely due to the activity of residual anthocyanin or other pigments. Baking soda will increase the pH, turning the dates a light toffee brown. As the puréed dates are heated, the baking soda breaks down at 176°F [80°C], producing sodium carbonate, which is more alkaline than baking soda. Heating the date mixture at an alkaline pH promotes caramelization and the Maillard reaction, turning the dates a dark brown color and then dark violet. Add acid (lemon juice or vinegar) and the pH decreases, turning the liquid a dark wine red. Using filtered water is recommended, as it includes less dissolved substances than tap water, which could interfere with the baking soda. Notice how the date syrup gives off a toasty sweet perfume.

Cut the dates to extract the pits from the centers; discard the pits. Chop the dates and transfer them to a medium bowl. Sprinkle the baking soda over the dates and, using a

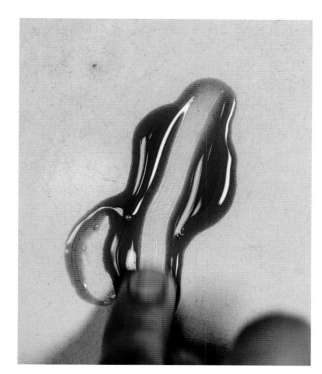

fork, toss to coat well. Add the warm water and mash the dates with the fork. Let the dates sit covered for 30 minutes; stir them occasionally with the fork.

After 30 minutes, the date pulp will resemble a thick, gloopy, soup-like mass. Using a spatula, transfer the mixture to a blender or the bowl of a food processor fitted with a blade. Pulse for a few seconds until you get a smooth toffee-brown purée. Transfer the date purée to a deep, medium saucepan, cover partially with a lid, and bring to a boil over medium-high heat. Lower the heat to low and cook, stirring occasionally, for 30 minutes, until you get a thick purée and the color switches to a dark reddish brown. Scrape the bottom of the saucepan to avoid burning. Stir in the lemon juice and remove from the heat.

Set a fine-mesh sieve lined with a few layers of cheesecloth over a funnel set over a bottle or medium bowl. Filter the date syrup through it in batches. Squeeze out any liquid and discard the date pulp left behind in the cloth. You should get about 2½ cups [600 ml] of liquid.

Transfer the liquid to a wide medium saucepan and bring to a boil over medium-high heat. Lower the heat to medium and cook until the liquid reduces to about 1 cup

[240 ml]; it should be the consistency of a thick syrup and coat the back of a metal spoon or a plate; when you draw a line through the syrup, you should be able to leave a clean trail on the back of the spoon or the plate. This takes 25 to 30 minutes. If the syrup starts to stiffen on cooling, add a few tablespoons of boiling water to loosen it up. Transfer to a clean, sterile jar, seal with a lid, and store in the refrigerator for up to 3 to 4 weeks.

Flavor Reactions

In the kitchen, various types of food reactions contribute to the creation of flavor molecules. Some of these flavor reactions require enzymes. Others do not.

An enzyme is a protein molecule that acts as a catalyst, making things happen in cells. They usually have an "-ase" suffix, like protease (an enzyme that breaks downs proteins). For example, proteases are present in raw fruits such as papayas, pineapples, kiwi, passion fruit, and mangoes; they are also produced by yeast and are used to tenderize meat and reduce the bitterness in cheese. Proteases tenderize meat and produce peptides that give meat an appetizing flavor.

All of the sensations covered in this book are affected by enzyme reactions. Some enzymes make fruits taste sweeter during ripening by converting the acids to sugars. Lipases are enzymes that break down fat molecules and can affect the texture of the crumb in a cake or a loaf of bread. Sourness is enhanced by enzymes in lactobacilli and yeast; think buttermilk, kefir, cultured butter, yogurt, kimchi, vinegar, and sourdough bread.

Enzymes are also responsible for browning. When a peach is sliced or a mint leaf is bruised, the cells in the tissue break open and release enzymes called polyphenol oxidases that use the oxygen in the surrounding air to create a brown pigmentation. There are a couple of ways to reduce or avoid the undesirable browning of food: either blocking oxygen or killing the enzyme.

- Citric acid and ascorbic acid present in citrus fruits can temporarily inhibit browning. You can also take advantage of the low pH in acidic ingredients present in vinegar and pineapple juice.

- Block the oxygen from air by coating the fruit with a sugar syrup or immersing it in cold water. But freezing and refrigeration are temporary fixes; as soon as the ingredient warms up, browning will resume.

- Heat will destroy enzymes; blanching at 212°F [100°C] kills the enzyme's activity.

In contrast, this browning reaction is highly desirable in the production of black tea, coffee, and cocoa; for example, tea leaves are crushed to release the enzyme to allow the browning of the leaves to proceed.

Let's take a closer look at some of the most common flavor-producing reactions, taking place in our kitchens.

Oxidation of Fats: When fats are exposed to the oxygen in air, they undergo a few chemical changes that might be desirable or undesirable. For instance, sometimes this produces delicious flavor molecules in poultry and meat. When red meat is allowed to age at low temperatures over a period of several months, the fats react with oxygen and develop desirable flavors. The marbled fats and phospholipids in the muscle tissue of beef create "meaty" aromas, while the proteins, sugars, and vitamins contribute to the development of sweet, salty, sour, and bitter tastes.

Cooking by heat can also help with oxidation. When pork is roasted at temperatures below 212°F [100°C], the number of lipid-derived molecules increases, which give it that characteristic aroma loved by meat eaters. In deep-frying, fat undergoes several changes in its texture and flavor, and oxidation is one of the key participants in these reactions.

Temperature: When food is heated, the molecules gain energy, start to vibrate faster, and move more quickly; aroma molecules evaporate and travel through air much faster, while other activated molecules collide with other molecules and cause changes that can affect the appearance and flavor of food. Warm temperatures applied during cooking can contribute to the oxidation of lipids and create aroma and taste molecules; for example, when meats like beef are heated, vitamin B1 (thiamine) creates a variety of flavor molecules that create meaty flavors.

Heat is of course responsible for caramelization and the Maillard reaction, both of which create both a complex array of flavor molecules and browning in food, without the use of enzymes.

Caramelization: When sugar is heated, the crystals lose their structure and turn into a liquid that, on continued heating, starts to decompose and turn brown. This is caramelization, and depending on how long you heat it, you can produce different degrees of the brown caramel color and its characteristic bittersweet taste. When table sugar or sucrose is heated, it first splits into its two constituents, glucose and fructose (Hot Honeycomb Candy, page 199), which go on to form three brown molecules—caramelins, caramelens, and caramelans—and a complex array of flavor molecules that contribute to various tastes: butterscotch (diacetyl), nutty (furan), fruity (ethyl acetate), and toasty (maltol). Caramel is also acidic, because acetic acid, the key ingredient in vinegar, is one of the acids created by the chemical reactions taking place (formic acid is another acid produced).

The darker the caramel, the greater the amount of sugar has decomposed; consequently, there is a decrease in sweetness and an increase in bitterness. Sugar can caramelize at a wide range of temperatures and the crystals don't need to liquefy to caramelize. When table sugar (sucrose) is heated, the solid crystals start to change to a liquid state but simultaneously, some of the sugar molecules in the crystal begin to break down and turn to caramel. Caramelization can occur way before the sugar crystals break down, but the lower the temperature, the longer it takes for the color pigments and caramel flavor molecules to develop. Adding an ingredient like baking soda to sugar will push the reaction forward quickly because it increases the pH. Acids do not promote caramelization.

The Maillard Reaction: The complex bundle of flavors that arises when carrots are roasted in an oven, when buns are brushed with a whisked egg to form a shiny brown coat on baking, and when a cake bakes in an oven and acquires its delicious golden-brown top, all stem from the Maillard reaction, a process discovered by Louis-Camille Maillard. While similar to caramelization, which involves sugars and heat, the Maillard reaction is distinctly different. Here a new player jumps in: the amino acids present in proteins. In the Maillard reaction, special types of sugars called reducing sugars like glucose, fructose, maltose, and lactose react with amino acids, such as lysine, present in proteins and undergo a series of changes that produce a complex set of flavor substances.

When a cake is baked in an oven at 350°F [180°C], the ingredient molecules start to move and meet each other. Once the batter reaches 285°F [140°C], the amino acids react with the reducing sugars and kick off a series of reactions that produce a variety of aroma and taste molecules as well as brown pigments, called melanoidins, that give the cake its flavor and golden-brown color.

Both caramelization and the Maillard reaction can occur simultaneously during cooking in the same food, but they are not one and the same. When sugar is heated by itself or with a bit of water, there are no proteins or amino acids present; this is caramelization. But if you pour in some heavy cream and stir it into the browned sugar to make caramel sauce, it will also involve the Maillard reaction, as the milk proteins provide the necessary amino acids. The Maillard reaction helps develop the color and flavor of chocolate, coffee, maple syrup, and tea, a function almost universally capitalized on in food manufacturing and processing.

I apply baking soda on the surface of the skin to make my baked pomegranate and poppy seed chicken wings (page 95); the baking soda provides an alkaline pH (9.0), helping brown the chicken skin by promoting the Maillard reaction. The same logic applies to bagels and pretzels, which are often sprayed or dipped into a boiling solution of lye (sodium hydroxide) or baking soda—both alkalis—and water right before they're baked, which facilitates the development of a deep brown color. Acids do not promote the Maillard reaction. The Maillard reaction does not require very high temperatures; it can also occur at low temperatures, below the boiling point of water and even at room temperature, as long as plenty of sugars and amino acids are available. However, the effects on flavor and color are much more noticeable at 250°F [120°C].

Water must be present for the Maillard reaction, but in smaller amounts. Water can help prevent the formation of unpleasant flavors during the Maillard reaction that can be formed during the making of ghee (see page 278). It's a balancing act: Both temperature and time play a role in how much of the Maillard pigments and flavors form during cooking, in addition to the other factors mentioned. If you bake a cake at a low temperature, the cake will eventually turn golden brown on the surface as it would if you baked it at a higher temperature, but the browning will take a longer time.

Appendix

A Basic Primer on Flavor Science

At its very essence, cooking is a thoughtful scientific approach—discovery through trial and error—married to our emotions and improved through repetition. I've always viewed cooking as an experiment that is driven by the hopeful outcome of pleasure and nourishment.

Be it the water in your drinking glass, the butter you slather on your morning toast, the lime juice you squeeze over your salad, or the saffron you grind to add fragrance and color to your rice, every ingredient we use is made up, at the microscopic level, of molecules that influence the way we approach our food—the way we think, see, choose, cook, smell, and taste. A splash of malt vinegar over a bag of hot, freshly fried fish and chips adds sourness because of the acid molecules it carries; a sweet potato that's roasted tastes sweeter than it did when uncooked because the starch is converted to sweet-tasting sugar molecules; the jolt of heat that you feel when you bite into a fresh serrano chilli comes from a molecule that triggers your nerves; even that creamy velvety texture of yogurt is the result of a complex mixture of fat, proteins, sugars, acids, and water (among other molecules) that give yogurt its flavor and shape.

As we interact with our food and environment, we're actually interacting with the molecules that make up their colors, shapes, aromas, and tastes, as well as the sounds that accompany them. Our brains translate these interactions and make us respond, and our actions are accompanied by our emotions and thoughts. The simplest action in the kitchen can involve a multitude of sensations.

When rolling out dough to make the pastry for a pie, you pick up the scent molecules emanating from the flour and butter; you watch the fat and water turn the flour into a crumb-like texture, and then shape that into a soft dough and use it to line a pie dish. The pie is baked, and you pick up new scents of toasted warm grain, fat, and sugar, and taste a crust that's flaky, crisp, and mildly sweet with a hint of saltiness. If you learned to make pie with a family member, you might feel nostalgic. In my case, I made my first pie crust alone while living in a dorm, and the memories of what a disaster that experience was immediately come to mind and make me chuckle.

Each molecule, in turn, is made up of tinier particles called atoms. The diverse combinations in which these atoms bond to each other create the limitless repertoire of molecules in nature. Though we aren't always conscious of it, we're working with them as we cook and manipulating them to our advantage.

Knowing what's actually inside our ingredients gives us insight into their charisma; for example, why a fat or oil acts like a solid or liquid at room temperature, or why a Granny Smith apple is simultaneously tart and sweet. Understanding how the molecules in our food behave helps open up new ways to manipulate flavor and improve the ones with which we are already familiar.

Let's take a close look at some of the most common ingredients in the kitchen, starting with water.

Water

Water is essential for survival and life on earth: It covers more than 70% of the world's surface and makes up about 60% of our body mass. When two atoms of hydrogen and one molecule of oxygen unite, the result is a molecule of water. Water takes on a few avatars: when room temperature at sea level, fresh water exists as a liquid; at freezing temperatures, it's a solid; at high temperatures, it transforms into a gas. These states all depend on the arrangement of molecules, how loosely or tightly packed they are. Water is called a universal solvent because more ingredients can dissolve in it than in any other liquid, by far. As a result, it is nearly impossible to find pure water in nature. You can see this for yourself. Take a few drops of tap water and let them dry on a glass surface; depending on the quality of the water, you'll see a faint to thick residue of a grayish white powder. This powder is made up of the various minerals and salts the water encountered and dissolved along its journey to your faucet.

When we used to visit my paternal grandparents' home in Mathura in northern India, soap would not lather as it did back in Bombay; the water came from the ground and was referred to as "hard water." Hard water contains a large number of salts and minerals that dissolve in the water in the rocks and mineral deposits in soil and deep underground. Calcium and magnesium ions in hard water prevent soap from lathering and produce a scum; hard water also leaves a salt crust at the bottom of tea kettles, pots, and pans, which builds up over time (acids such as vinegar help get rid of this). Using hard water to cook can affect the taste and texture of food, notably the quality of cheese; it can also affect the ability of yeast to work properly in fermented and baked foods.

Depending on where you live, your city or town might use a water purification facility that filters out and eliminates most of these minerals and salts (and other harmful substances, such as lead) to produce soft water. This is the water most of us cook with. Absolutely pure water contains water and nothing else.

In the labs I've worked in, we always used distilled water, a highly purified form of water, because even a tiny amount of chemicals or salts could show up in our measurements and affect our results. Distilled water is prepared by boiling filtered water in a big chamber; the steam vapors rise to the top and are collected by cooling in a separate chamber (most labs do this procedure twice to keep it extremely pure, calling the water double distilled). For the most part, I don't recommend using distilled water or double distilled water at home. It's not necessary to achieve that high degree of purity in ordinary cooking; you'd have to also wash all your cooking utensils with distilled water, as they do in labs, to ensure that they're completely free from any waterborne substances.

Filtered soft water is great for yeast and other ingredients. The salts of calcium and magnesium present in hard water can affect how some vegetables, such as dried beans, cook. Beans contain a fiber called pectin, which contains calcium and magnesium, that makes them resistant to cooking. Using filtered water that is free from salts helps reduce cooking time (see Dal Makhani, page 292, and Oven "Fries," page 144).

Water's ability to dissolve substances comes from its uncanny capacity to insert itself between other molecules. A molecule of water contains two atoms of hydrogen, each attached to one atom of oxygen by polar covalent bonds. Hydrogen and oxygen have different affinities for the shared electrons, which creates a bit of an imbalance; there is a partial negative charge near the oxygen atom and a partial positive charge near the hydrogen atoms. In addition, in liquid water, the partially negatively charged hydrogen atoms that form one molecule of water are attracted to the slightly positively charged oxygen atom of another molecule of water, and they form a weak hydrogen bond.

When salt is mixed with water, the weaker ionic bonds that hold the sodium and chlorine atoms together split because the covalent bonds of water are much stronger and pull the two atoms in different directions. The positive sodium is surrounded by the negatively charged oxygen atom of water, while the negatively charged chlorine atom is surrounded by hydrogen atoms of the water. As a result, water inserts itself between the sodium and chloride ions, and salt dissolves in water. Water's ability to pull apart the bonds of other molecules is so strong that many substances, such as sugar and vinegar (acetic acid), will dissolve when added to water. That is how most of the taste molecules dissolve in the water in our saliva and reach our taste receptors.

Ingredients that dissolve in water, such as sugar and the proteins in egg whites, are called *hydrophilic* (water-loving), and water is called a *polar solvent*. Ingredients that do not dissolve in water, such as olive oil and butter, are considered *hydrophobic* (water-hating); these dissolve in nonpolar solvents, such as the turpentine employed by artists who use oil paint. Nonpolar solvents will not mix with water, staying in distinct separate layers. When vinegar and oil are mixed together in a vinaigrette, they eventually separate into two layers; the oil floats to the surface while the vinegar (the water phase) settles at the bottom.

Water is used as a standard in many culinary matters. For example, to get a rough check on the accuracy of my cooking scale at home, I use two tricks that I learned from my days working in the lab. First make sure the scale is sitting on a flat, level surface (use a carpenter's spirit level if you have one). Second, purchase a small 3.52 oz [100 g] standard metal weight and check to see if your scale reads the weight correctly. Alternatively, measure 3.4 fl oz [100 ml] of pure filtered or distilled water and weigh it. If the scale is accurate, you should get a rough reading of 3.52 oz [100 g]. (Give your scale some room for error; most home kitchen scales, though very good, might not be as precise as one used in a lab.)

Many cooking techniques rely on the constant boiling point of water (212°F [100°C]); we use it to tenderize vegetables through steaming and to hard-boil eggs. You can use the following to test the accuracy of your food thermometer: When water starts to boil vigorously (a rolling boil), your thermometer should read 212°F [100°C] at sea level. The first tiny bubbles that form contain vaporized water but still don't have enough energy to reach the surface and escape. As the water continues to heat up, more energy is supplied, and the bubbles escape from the surface at a constant vigorous rate. If you brown onions

Boiling point	212°F [100°C] at sea level
Freezing point	32°F [0°C] at sea level
Weight	0.034 fl oz [1 ml] weighs 0.04 oz [1 g]
pH of pure water	7.0 at 77°F [25°C]

in an oven (see the case study on page 64), you'll start to notice some spots turning brown faster than others; these spots are dryer than the others because they lost their water early on. The thinner tips of the onion slices and those exposed to the hottest parts of the oven will heat faster and lose water first.

Water is a bit unusual when compared to other substances; an extremely large amount of energy is needed to change its temperature by a single degree. The specific heat of water is one of the highest in nature; it takes 1 calorie of heat to raise the temperature of 0.035 oz [1 g] of water by 33.8°F [1°C]. This is why water can absorb a lot of energy in the form of heat during cooking. As long as water is present in excess, it will do its best to suck up all the heat energy and keep all ingredients at their boiling point (as seen in a stock or soup); as soon as the water starts to evaporate and reduce, the temperature in the rest of the ingredients will start to rise.

Where you live can affect the boiling point of water. At altitudes above 3,000 ft [914.4 m], the air pressure starts to decrease and the temperature at which water boils decreases. For every 500 ft [152.4 m] rise in altitude from sea level, the boiling temperature of water drops by 1°F [-17.2°C]. Think of it like this: If you press a soft piece of foam with maximum strength and pressure, it compresses; as you start to pull away and reduce the pressure, the foam will expand.

A similar principle applies here: The air pressure at high altitudes is lower because there is less air, so the pressure applied to the surface of the water is much lower than it would be at sea level; as a result, the water boils at a lower temperature. It's important to note that this temperature is not sufficient to kill harmful microbes or cook food to the desired texture. Thus, when canning and cooking food at high altitudes, you'll need to cook it longer. There's also less moisture at high altitudes, so you'll notice food drying out

quickly. Devices such as pressure cookers help alleviate this problem by providing a constant source of high pressure in a sealed chamber.

Salts and sugars can affect the temperatures at which water boils (the more salt or sugar in your water, the higher the boiling point) or freezes (the more salt or sugar in your water, the lower the freezing point); we see this in ice creams and sorbets. Older ice-cream makers feature a tub where the ice-cream custard is inserted snugly into a larger tub containing a mixture of ice and salt. Salt lowers the freezing point of water and allows the ice cream mixture to get cool enough to freeze and firm up. This is necessary because ice creams (and sorbets) contain salts, sugars, and other ingredients that lower the freezing point and freeze only once the temperature in the ice bucket gets low enough. When making sugar for candies or caramel, we start by adding a large quantity of sugar to a small volume of water; you'll notice that the liquid's temperature rises beyond the boiling point of water as it continues to heat.

When my grandmother made her stock, she slowly simmered meat and bones with garlic, onions, herbs, and spices in a large pot of water. As the water bubbled, it drew out different molecules, like proteins, sugars, and salts, from the ingredients that gave the stock its delicious flavor. As we saw earlier, a wide variety of molecules dissolve in water with ease, more so than with any other liquid in nature, giving it the appropriate moniker of "the universal solvent." A large component of taste relies on the ability of molecules in food to dissolve in the water present in our saliva. The result is an unveiling of information that reveals the sweetness of a blueberry or the saltiness of capers on a sliver of gravlax.

Carbon

If you heat a bit of sugar in a spoon over an open flame, it will transition from a white crystalline solid to a dark-brown liquid and eventually incinerate to produce a hard black material: carbon. Every living thing on earth, from us humans to all the other animals to all the plant life, is composed of carbon-based molecules. Carbon is similar to the extremely popular person you went to school with, the one who could make friends with almost anyone and with whom everyone wanted to be friends. Carbon's unique ability to form "friendships" or bonds with other elements, and even itself, results in the creation of chains and rings of varying lengths, a property called *concatenation*.

A single atom of carbon must form four bonds to be stable; it does this by linking to itself or other elements, such as oxygen, hydrogen, nitrogen, and sulfur. This creates the various molecules that make up the building blocks of living organisms; consequently, almost all the food we eat is carbon based, except for water and some minerals like calcium and magnesium. Organic chemistry and biochemistry are scientific branches that study carbon-based molecules; you'll hear the word *organic* used to describe certain ingredients; for example, cooking acids—vinegar and lemon juice—are called *organic acids*.

Our food contains many different types of carbon-based molecules: the carbohydrates in our grains, fruits, and starchy vegetables; the fats and oils (collectively known as *lipids*) present in avocados, nuts, seeds, dairy, and meat; the proteins in our beans, eggs, dairy, meat, and seafood. We eat *macronutrients*—carbohydrates, fats and oils, and proteins—in large quantities to support our body's functions. Other substances, called *micronutrients*—such as minerals like sulfur, iron, calcium, and sodium and vitamins like the B vitamin group and vitamin C (ascorbic acid)—also come through our food, but we need these in much smaller quantities.

Beyond giving us energy and supporting our day-to-day functions and needs, almost all these groups of nutrients contribute in some way to the flavor equation. Some vitamins and minerals, such as magnesium (part of the green chlorophyll pigment in plants), are responsible for the color of our food; carbohydrates include the sugars, such as honey and maple syrup, that provide the sweet taste in our food; and starches provide the texture of foods like mashed potatoes and the fiber in fruit and vegetables.

Proteins contribute to a variety of tastes, and glutamate gives us a savory taste. Fats and oils help us fry food and give foods like yogurt a luxurious velvety texture. The ways in which we perceive the touch, shape, and colors of a salad, or the aroma and the taste of a cake, involve communication from specialized, sensor-like cells called *receptors*, which line the outer surface of our nose, mouth, eyes, ears, and skin and communicate with our brain through chemicals. I've mentioned organic acids; there are also nucleic acids. Both play an important role in two tastes—sourness and savoriness. Alcohol is another special group of organic molecules, of which we consume only ethanol.

Carbohydrates and Sugars

Because I have a terrible sweet tooth, I have a special relationship with carbohydrates, be they fresh, seasonal fruit, or my favorite food group, ice cream. Carbohydrates, or *saccharides*, are made up of molecules called, helpfully, sugars. Sugars in turn are made up of carbon (C), hydrogen (H), and oxygen (O) atoms. Carbohydrates include simple sugars and more complex sugars like starch. Any action performed by your body requires energy, similar to your car requiring gas (or electricity), and sugar is our primary source of fuel.

Sugars can be categorized as either *monosaccharides*, with one molecule of sugar, like the fructose in honey; disaccharides, which have two monosaccharides joined together, like the lactose in milk; or polysaccharides, like starch, which have several sugar molecules attached. The bond that holds two or more molecules of sugar together is called a glyosidic bond.

Sugars, as we know, taste sweet, but some carbohydrates, such as starch, do not and must be broken down by enzymes called *amylases* in our saliva before we can appreciate their taste. *Polysaccharides*, like starch in plants and glycogen in animals, act as energy stores; whenever the body is low on fuel, it calls in these reserves. Some polysaccharides provide structural integrity, like the cellulose in plants (a source of dietary fiber in the vegetables and fruits we eat) and some animals; for example, crustaceans use a molecule called *chitin*, which forms the outer shell of crabs.

Besides the sweetness they add to desserts, sugars also help create flavor compounds and pigments in the caramelization and Maillard reactions and aid in the development of textures, such as the crust on the surface of cakes and the soft texture of ice creams. The fermentation of sugars by bacteria and yeast produces alcohol and vinegar. Agar, a seaweed polysaccharide composed mostly of molecules of galactose, is used as a thickener and a solidifying agent in food. Fruits like apples and oranges contain the polysaccharide pectin, which is used to help

FLAVOR WHEEL OF AMINO ACIDS

Of the twenty-two amino acids we use, only twenty are encoded by the genes in our DNA. Here is a summary of their taste profiles.

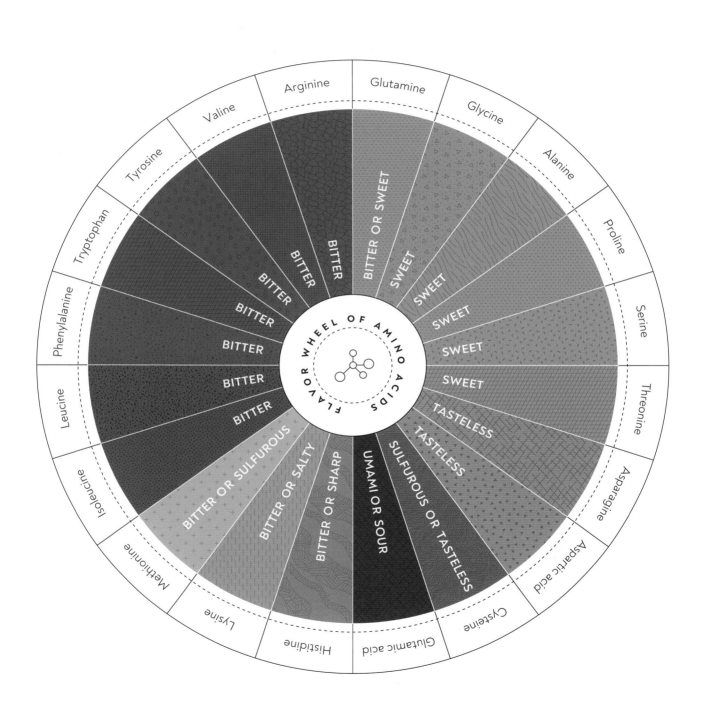

thicken marmalades, jams, jellies, and pie fillings and as an emulsifying agent (see Toum, page 315).

Amino Acids, Peptides, and Proteins

When winter arrives, all I crave is a bowl of hot ramen from the restaurant near our home in Oakland. Every spoonful is a marvelous combination of savory and salty notes, with a tiny hint of sweetness and a variety of textures from the slices of *chashu* (braised pork belly) and ramen. This soup owes much of its savory flavor to the presence of amino acids.

AMINO ACIDS

Amino acids are the building blocks that make up protein molecules. Each amino acid is made of nitrogen in the form of an amino ($-NH_2$) group and a carboxylic acid group ($-COOH$) (see Carbon, page 331). Amino acids can exist in one of two forms—an L-form or a D-form—depending on how the amino and carboxylic acid groups are arranged around the central atom of carbon. In nature, the L-form predominates, though a few bacteria can synthesize some amino acids in the D-form. Humans can synthesize and use only the L-form of amino acids.

There are more than five hundred types of amino acids in nature, but we utilize only twenty-two of them. The amino acids we can synthesize in our bodies are called *nonessential*; the ten amino acids we cannot synthesize but must obtain through our food are called *essential amino acids*. Amino acids are also classified by what is present in the "R" group—any chemical group that is attached via a carbon or hydrogen atom to the rest of the molecule (e.g., in the case of the amino acid alanine, hydrogen is attached to the general structure of the amino acid molecule).

Depending on what's in this R group, amino acids can be: nonpolar; polar; basic (those with a positive charge on their R group); or acidic (those with negative charges on their R group, due to having an extra carboxylic acid group). The type of R group affects how a protein folds and behaves. Nonpolar amino acids do not like water (they are hydrophobic); polar amino acids like water (they are hydrophilic). The behavior of acidic and basic amino acids changes depending on the pH of their environment.

Our taste receptors are made up of long proteins that look like a snake. Some parts of this snake contain a higher proportion of hydrophobic amino acids on their surfaces; these portions are embedded in the lipid (see Lipids, page 335), part of our cell's membrane, while the surfaces that are richer in hydrophilic amino acids will be exposed to the sides of the membrane that come into contact with water. Only two amino acids contain sulfur (S): cysteine and methionine. Cysteine is the starting material for the flavor and odor compounds of garlic, onions, and other members of the *Allium* plant family; methionine is the first amino acid produced when our cells create peptides or proteins.

Free amino acids contribute taste, especially in protein-rich foods like meats and cheeses. The amino acid glutamate is responsible for the savory or umami taste (see How Savoriness Works, page 205). Glycine and alanine can come across as sweet, while tryptophan and tyrosine are bitter. Lysine is one of the key players in the Maillard reaction that occurs when food is cooked using heat; in foods containing a mixture of sugars and proteins, lysine reacts with reducing sugars, such as glucose and fructose, to produce a complex set of flavors and even some brown-colored molecules, called pigments, that make the surface of a baked cake, for example, appear golden brown or cause the formation of the brown surface that develops when steak is seared on a hot pan.

Note: Essential amino acids are the ones our bodies cannot synthesize, so we must get them through our diets. Nonessential amino acids are the ones our bodies produce. In some instances, when we're sick, our bodies will be unable to synthesize some nonessential amino acids; these are called *conditional* nonessential amino acids.

PEPTIDES

Amino acids attach to each other by forming a chemical bond, called a *peptide bond*, between the amino and carboxylic acid groups to form chains of varying lengths called peptides. Peptides can be short—*oligopeptides* contain two to twenty amino acids—or long—*polypeptides* contain more than twenty amino acids. *Glutathione*, a short oligopeptide made up of three amino acids (cysteine, glycine, and glutamate) might play a role in enhancing the combined taste of savory and salty as well as the *kokumi* taste (see page 50).

Proteins

Proteins are large molecules, much longer than peptides, made up of long polypeptides or several polypeptides attached to each other by chemical bonds, such as disulfide bonds, between the sulfur-containing amino acids. Proteins in the form of enzymes act as catalysts to enable biological reactions: *amylase* in our saliva breaks down starch, and *alcohol dehydrogenase* in yeast produces alcohol from glucose. Some proteins provide structural integrity to cells and tissues, such as the *actin* and *myosin* proteins that give

CASE STUDY:
PROTEIN DENATURATION AND CHEESE MAKING

Paneer, the classic, unsalted Indian cottage cheese, is prepared by the application of heat and acid (see page 61) to milk. The proteins in milk undergo a drastic change in their shape; they denature and separate into a white crumbly mass and a pale greenish liquid, the whey. For the most part, homemade paneer is great for crumbling into salads and shaping into blocks to be cut, but even these tender blocks fall apart when sliced with a knife. Although it's the simplest cheese to make, and I make good paneer at home, it never resembles the firm stuff I get from the store that easily slices for kebabs.

After much research, I realized the answer lay in the type of milk used and the chemical differences between them. Cow's milk contains less calcium than buffalo's milk, which affects the quality of paneer. To produce paneer with a firm texture, I would need to increase the calcium content of the mixture I used. To do this, I used food-grade calcium chloride, an acidic salt of calcium that imparts a low pH (in the form of hydrogen ions), which also helps with protein denaturation. (Calcium chloride is available online as well as at specialty cheese and fermentation stores.)

Buffalo's milk, which is commonly used in India, has a total calcium content of 0.19%, and the recommended temperature to which it is heated in commercial production of paneer is 203°F to 244.4°F [95°C to 118°C]. Cow's milk has a total calcium content of 0.12% and the recommended temperature to which it is heated in commercial production of paneer is 176°F to 185°F [80°C to 85°C].

Paneer

Firm Paneer: Add ½ tsp [2 g] calcium chloride to ½ gal [1.9 L] whole milk and heat over medium heat to 185°F [85°C]. Remove from the heat and stir in 2 Tbsp fresh lemon juice. Strain the curdled milk proteins through a fine-mesh sieve lined with cheese cloth. Rinse under running tap water several times. Squeeze the cloth tight to drain excess water, and hang the cloth with the paneer over a bowl at room temperature for 1 hour. Remove and then set a heavy weight like a Dutch oven over the cheesecloth for 1 hour. Remove the drained paneer from the cloth and cut as needed. Paneer can be stored in an airtight container in the refrigerator for up to 3 days or in the freezer for up to 3 weeks. Makes 10 oz [280 g].

Soft paneer: Mix ½ gal [1.9 L] milk with ½ cup [120 ml] fresh lemon juice instead of calcium chloride and proceed as above. Makes 8¾ oz [250 g].

the muscle tissues in meat their firm texture. Others form the receptors in our bodies that help us sense light, sound, aroma, taste, and pain through extremely complex communication pathways.

When we drink a glass of chilled lemonade, receptors in specific cells on the tongue's surface bind the acids and sugars in the drink to tell us how sour and sweet it tastes; a different set of receptors recognizes and senses the chilly temperature of the drink. Protein fact: During starvation, when the body is depleted of its energy reserves of carbohydrates and fats, it utilizes proteins (our own muscle tissue) as a final resort.

Proteins are finicky, so a tiny change in their molecular shape can cause a dramatic change in their behavior and function. Alterations in temperatures, the low pH of acids like vinegar, excess salt, ultraviolet light, and even mechanical disturbances can morph the shape of a protein. This alteration, called *denaturation*, is akin to a coil or spring that gets stretched out when pulled. We take full advantage of this when we cook. When we make a meringue, egg whites are whisked with sugar fast enough that the proteins get stretched by mechanical forces and form a light and airy structure (see Peppermint Marshmallows, page 196). Another case of denaturation occurs when we stir lightly whisked eggs into a pot of boiling broth (see Manchow Soup, page 255); the proteins in the egg quickly denature and change shape to form the "threads" that give this soup its unique textural character.

You may come across recipes that call for the use of certain types of fresh fruit to tenderize meat, such as figs, pineapples, papaya, or mangoes (even dried mango powder, amchur, will do; see Grilled Spiced Chicken Salad with Amchur, page 159). Each of these fruits contains enzymes called *proteases* that cut the peptide bond in the proteins present in meat tissues to improve the meat's palatability and taste. Note: Only raw fruits will work, as these enzymes are destroyed when heated, so skip the canned pineapple.

Lipids

I like to dip my crispy french fries in mayonnaise, as the creamy texture of the mayonnaise gives the entire experience an exciting contrast of textures and flavors. The fries and mayonnaise both owe their textures to the presence of fats, which belong to a special group of macronutrients, the *lipids*. The lipid family includes fats and oils; fat-soluble vitamins, such as vitamin E; some pigments, such as beta-carotene; cholesterol; and even waxes. Here, we will focus on fats and oils.

I need to delve a little bit into the structure of fats, because it affects their behavior and, ultimately, our cooking; for example, the molecular structure of a fat determines why butter is solid and sesame oil is liquid at room temperature.

A fat or oil, called a *triglyceride*, is made up of two types of molecules: three fatty acids, each of which is a long chain of C and H atoms attached to a carboxylic acid group (-COOH), the same chemical group that defines the organic acids; and a water-soluble alcohol, glycerol. Because long-chain fatty acids do not dissolve in water, this fatty acid is called hydrophobic or lipophilic (fat loving).

Let's take a look at fatty acids. Fatty acids come in a variety of forms and sizes, which affects the behavior and properties of fats and oils. If all the carbon atoms in a fatty acid chain are completely filled with hydrogen atoms, they form a *saturated* fat. If one or more carbon atoms in the fatty acid chain are not completely filled up by hydrogen atoms, they form "double bonds" between the adjacent carbon atoms, creating an *unsaturated* fat. Saturated fats are stable; they don't readily react with air, water, or even sunlight.

In comparison, unsaturated fats are a little more reactive and less stable; the double bond they contain can make them turn rancid easily. This is why oils rich in unsaturated fatty acids must be stored away from sunlight and tightly sealed to reduce exposure to air. Grain flours, nuts, and seeds are all rich in oils, so to increase their shelf life and prevent them from going bad, they should be stored in the freezer. Fats behave like solids at room temperature because they are rich in saturated fatty acids and contain little to no unsaturated fatty acids; oils behave like liquids at room temperature because they usually contain a large number of unsaturated fatty acids.

If there is only one unsaturated bond in the fatty acid chain, they're called *monounsaturated fatty acids* (MUFAs); if there is more than one unsaturated bond, they're called *polyunsaturated fatty acids* (PUFAs). These unsaturated double bonds cause a kink in the otherwise linear chain of the fatty acid molecule, so the molecule can bend at this spot; this makes the fat behave like a liquid at room temperature, as we see with olive and sesame oils. When the carbon chains on both sides of the double bond point toward the same side, they're called *cis-unsaturated fatty acids*; when the two chains point in opposite directions, they're called *trans-unsaturated fatty acids*. Our bodies contain predominantly cis-unsaturated fatty acids; the retinoic acid present in our eyes is the only trans-unsaturated fatty acid in the human body.

Notice that some of the unsaturated fatty acids have extremely low melting points compared to the saturated fatty acids in the table (facing page); they're lower than the average room temperature of 73.4°F [23°C]. Most fats and oils, including those we cook with, contain varying combinations of saturated fatty acids with monounsaturated and polyunsaturated fatty acids. Consequently, many plant-based fats, like olive, canola, and walnut oils, are liquids at room temperature because they have a higher proportion of unsaturated fatty acids. Most animal fats, like butter and lard, and some plant-based fats, like coconut oil, are considerably richer in saturated fatty acids, so they are solids at room temperature. A fat like olive or walnut oil that remains liquid at room temperature or lower is an excellent choice for a salad dressing like a vinaigrette because it will not coagulate and create an unpleasant clumpy texture when it meets cool ingredients—unlike butter or ghee—and it gives a smooth, silky mouthfeel on the tongue.

Chemists, observing that saturated fats last longer and don't go bad as quickly as unsaturated fats, developed a method called *hydrogenation* to protect unsaturated fats from going bad. The premise was pretty simple: Hydrogen was added to fill up those double bonds in the fatty acid molecule and saturate them. However, during this process, some of the cis-unsaturated fatty acids do not saturate; instead, they change to a trans-form. When you see "partially hydrogenated fats" on a food label, this refers to the presence of both cis- and trans-unsaturated fatty acids. Because of their structure around the double bond, cis-unsaturated fatty acids don't pack easily when compressed, which creates fluidity. Trans-fats, in contrast, have a rigid structure. One reason why trans-saturated fatty acids (better known as *trans fats*) are considered unhealthy is that our cell membranes contain cis-unsaturated fatty acids; if trans-fatty acids replace them, the cell membranes lose fluidity and break down.

As with amino acids (see page 333), which are sorted into essential and nonessential categories depending on whether we synthesize them ourselves or get them through our food, we can synthesize saturated fatty acids and some MUFAs. However, we lack certain enzymes (see Proteins, page 333) for creating the cis-double bond needed in linoleic and alpha-linolenic (ALA) fatty acids. As a result, we must obtain them through our food.

Some fats and oils carry unique tastes, so choosing the appropriate oil when frying or dressing a dish can make a big difference in flavor. Olive and mustard oils will leave a noticeable taste in food, whereas others, such as grapeseed oil, are considered neutral tasting because they are flavorless. Most unsaturated fatty acids taste bitter when emulsified in water; some might even taste pungent. When frying, it's essential to know not only the fat's melting point temperature but also the temperature at which the fat starts to break down and burn, called the *smoke point* (see table, facing page). Using a fat beyond its smoke point is not just dangerous (because it is a fire hazard) but also imparts an undesirable flavor to food as it disintegrates into a bunch of chemicals.

Fats are an important source of energy and contain more than twice the amount stored in carbohydrates. In fact, once the body is depleted of its ready sources of sugar, it starts to utilize fat for its energy needs. Both fats and oils are responsible for luxurious, silky-smooth textures and carry various kinds of flavors, like the pungent mustard oil used in Indian cooking and the fruity olive oils of the Mediterranean and Middle East regions. Fats and oils are also less dense than water, which is why olive oil forms a layer on top of vinegar (water based) in a bottle of a vinaigrette. (At room temperature, 77°F [25°C], the density of water is 62.24 lb/ft^3 [1.0 g/cm^3]; olive oil is lighter, around 58.81 lb/ft^3 [0.91 g/cm^3].)

Lipids not only provide some of the most satisfying mouthfeel experiences, like velvety and crunchy textures, but also help dissolve several types of taste and aroma molecules. Lipids present in meat contribute to the formation of various flavor molecules seen in chicken broth and pork when they are cooked. They also provide a variety of color pigments produced by plants, such as the carotenoids present in carrots and egg yolks (animals, including chickens, get carotene from their plant-based diets, which makes their yolks appear yellow).

Lipids also contain another prominent food molecule, *phospholipids*. These building blocks of cell membranes resemble a clothespin with two hydrophobic fatty acid molecules, called "the tails," attached to a phosphate group called "the head," which is hydrophilic. Lecithin, present in egg yolks and soybeans, is perhaps the best-known example of a phospholipid. Because lecithin contains two water-hating (fat-loving) tails and one water-loving head, it is able to act as a go-between by stably holding fat and water molecules together, forming an emulsion. This is the basis of the technique behind mayonnaise.

Nucleic Acids

Deep inside our cells lie long chains called *nucleic acids*. These chains are extremely important because they carry and transmit genetic information and participate in the production of proteins. (In a little bit, we will see how nucleic acids contribute to flavor.) At its core, a nucleic acid is a polymer of many single units called *nucleotides*. Each

COOKING FATS AND OILS

A summary of the smoke points and physical and chemical changes of common cooking fats and oils.

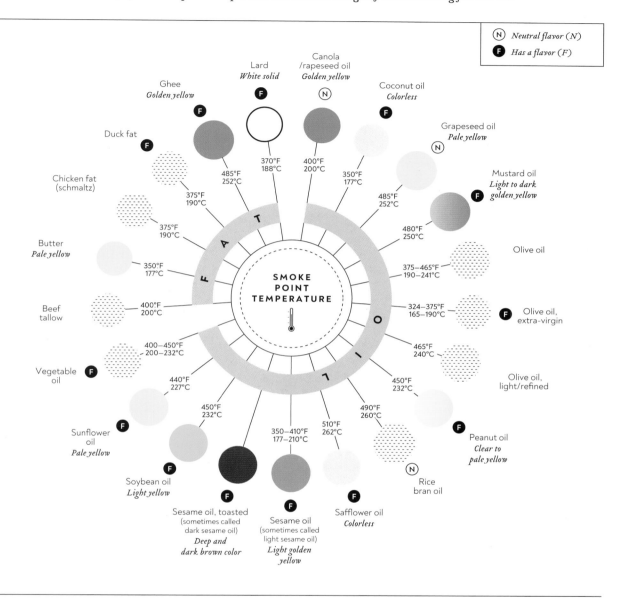

N Neutral flavor (N)
F Has a flavor (F)

Lard
White solid

Canola /rapeseed oil
Golden yellow

Ghee
Golden yellow

Coconut oil
Colorless

Duck fat

Grapeseed oil
Pale yellow

Chicken fat
(schmaltz)

Mustard oil
Light to dark golden yellow

Butter
Pale yellow

Olive oil

Beef tallow

SMOKE POINT TEMPERATURE

Olive oil, extra-virgin

Vegetable oil

Olive oil, light/refined

Sunflower oil
Pale yellow

Peanut oil
Clear to pale yellow

Soybean oil
Light yellow

Rice bran oil

Sesame oil, toasted
(sometimes called dark sesame oil)
Deep and dark brown color

Sesame oil
(sometimes called light sesame oil)
Light golden yellow

Safflower oil
Colorless

485°F 252°C
370°F 188°C
400°F 200°C
350°F 177°C
375°F 190°C
485°F 252°C
375°F 190°C
480°F 250°C
350°F 177°C
375–465°F 190–241°C
400°F 200°C
324–375°F 165–190°C
400–450°F 200–232°C
465°F 240°C
440°F 227°C
450°F 232°C
450°F 232°C
350–410°F 177–210°C
510°F 262°C
490°F 260°C

FATS AND OILS UNDERGO DIFFERENT PHYSICAL AND CHEMICAL CHANGES DURING DEEP FRYING AS TIME PROGRESSES

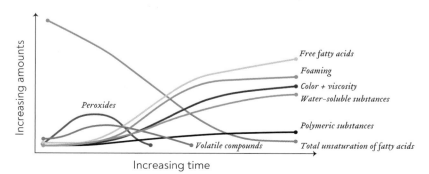

Increasing amounts

Peroxides

Free fatty acids
Foaming
Color + viscosity
Water-soluble substances
Polymeric substances
Volatile compounds
Total unsaturation of fatty acids

Increasing time

nucleotide is attached to a sugar (with five carbon atoms, called a *pentose*), a phosphate group, and a nitrogen base.

There are two types of slightly different nucleic acids in our cells: deoxyribonucleic acid (DNA) and ribonucleic acid (RNA). The sugar in DNA, called *deoxyribose*, differs from the one in RNA, *ribose*, in that it lacks a hydroxyl group (-OH). To distinguish between the two types of nucleic acids, "d" is included in the name to signify the presence of deoxyribose in DNA while the absence of "d" refers to the presence of ribose in RNA. There are five nitrogen bases—adenine (A), cytosine (C), thymine (T), guanine (G), and uracil (U); DNA contains A, C, T, and G; RNA contains A, C, U, and G. Individual nucleotides are sometimes called *adenylate* (AMP) or *adenosine 5'-monophosphate* in RNA or *deoxyadenylate (dAMP)* or *deoxyribose adenosine 5'-monophosphate* in DNA.

Nitrogen bases are extremely important because their arrangement on our DNA defines our genes. RNA, along with a complex set of protein machinery, runs across our DNA strands to read and transcribe information and eventually produce proteins. These proteins are then transported to cells in our bodies and make up our receptors, such as the light-sensing receptors in our eyes, the aroma receptors in our nose, the taste receptors on our tongue, and the sensory receptors that recognize pressure and the texture of food. Other proteins, such as enzymes, help us digest our food. In addition to their role in producing various flavor molecules, such as amino acids, proteins, and the enzyme machinery that play a role in flavor, nucleic acids also directly contribute to taste; as taste molecules, they play an important role in savoriness or umami.

To understand how nucleic acids act as taste molecules, let's take a brief look at savoriness using the example of the shiitake mushroom. Savoriness is produced by free glutamate and also by three different nucleotides present in RNA—adenylate (AMP), guanylate (GMP), and inosinate (IMP). Even though IMP is not present in nucleic acids, it gives rise to the AMP and GMP needed for RNA. In the meat industry, IMP is used as a flavor enhancer to increase the perception of savoriness and give a meaty profile to food.

In fresh shiitake mushrooms, the levels of both glutamate and GMP are very low, but when dried, the amount of both ingredients rises dramatically (see table, page 341). When a mushroom is left to dry, the cells start to dehydrate and the mushroom shrivels up. Certain enzymes, called *ribonucleases*, break down the RNA and release GMP, causing a massive rise in the umami-tasting molecules and making the savory taste of a dried shiitake much greater than that of a fresh one. This is why it is better to use dried shiitake when you want to boost the umami profile of a dish.

AMP, GMP, and IMP are also seen in other ingredients, such as katsuobushi, anchovies, scallops, and squid. Glutamate and these three nucleotides create a synergism when together in a dish, increasing the overall perception of savoriness (see Blistered Shishito/Padrón Peppers with Bonito Flakes, page 213). When you want a deeper note of umami in a dish, include ingredients that are rich in glutamate and one or more of the nucleotides. The total amount of glutamate appears to increase because the weight of the mushrooms per unit increases.

A Short Introduction to the Biology Behind Flavor

Open any cookbook, and you'll find that the recipes provide instructions asking you to consider and make a note of the changes that happen and sensations that arise as you proceed through the steps. Watch a cooking show, and your mind steps into a world of excitement and wonderment. Eat at a restaurant, and your mind is instantly intrigued by the ambience, the meal, and, perhaps, the people you're seated with. Biology plays an integral role in cooking and eating, and for any discussion on flavor, knowing why and how things work is important.

Our ability to detect the different sensory aspects of the food we eat in relation to our environment is one of the most remarkable attributes of our body, one that I forget to appreciate often enough. Arrive at a farmers' market, and you'll encounter a bustling and noisy mix of wondrous sensations—the color and smell of all sorts of varieties of oranges sitting in their crates, the stacks of freshly baked loaves of bread studded with sesame and poppy seeds, the little dim sum food stall, where a sizzling wok gives off an aroma of sautéed scallions and ginger. Your senses kick into action, all working simultaneously and quickly, converting signals from the external environment and sending them to your brain, which in turn figures out what they mean and tells you how to respond. The different parts and components of this complex machinery form a part of the somatic nervous system.

Our bodies contain special sensory organs covered with tiny receptors that can detect physical and chemical changes in our environment that we call *stimuli*, such as sound, light, and texture, as well as the aroma and taste molecules in our food. Despite their small size, these receptor cells are extremely powerful, instantly converting physical and chemical stimuli from our environment and food into electrochemical signals. The receptors are attached to nerves that run throughout the body and directly to the brain, similar to the way in which wires from a keyboard run through a laptop and send information to the microchip. The brain processes the electrochemical signals sent by the nerves, describes the stimulus to us, and triggers our emotions, so we instantly know whether we should love it or not. A lot of this information is also stored in the brain in the form of memories; if we reencounter a food, it might evoke a memory, but it can also train us to avoid harmful stimuli and appreciate beneficial ones.

SOME COMMON COOKING STARCHES (ARRANGED BY TYPE) AND THEIR PROPERTIES

Find your cooking starch and add it to the liquid you're using when it's at the "start" thickening temperature.

Common Cooking Starches	Type	Thickening Temperature (Start Temperature to End Temperature)	Amylose (%)	Some Applications
Cornstarch	Grain	143.6°F to 158°F [62°C to 70°C]	28	Thickener, dredging fried food
Rice	Short-grain (waxy rice)	131°F to 149°F [55°C to 65°C]	1	Rice starch can be used as a thickener
	Long-grain (starchy rice), e.g., basmati, jasmine rice	140°F to 176°F [60°C to 80°C]	73.24	
	Sticky rice (Thai glutinous rice)		Nearly 0%	
Oats	Grain	132.8°F to 143.6°F [56°C to 62°C]	27	Thickener
Wheat	Grain	127.4°F to 149°F [53°C to 65°C]	26 to 31	Flours are used as thickeners
Arrowroot	Root	147.1°F [63.94°C]	25.6 to 21.9	Thickener
Sweet potato (Ipomoea batatas)	Root	140°F to 167°F [60°C to 75°C]	18	Japchae (Korean noodle dish)
Tapioca* (Cassava)	Root	125.6°F to 147.2°F [52°C to 64°C]	17	Thickener, bubble tea (boba), puddings
Potato starch	Tuber	136.4°F to 150.8°F [58°C to 66°C]	23	Thickener
Yams (Dioscorea spp.)	Tuber	165.2°F to 170.6°F [74°C to 77°C]	22	Flours are used as thickeners
Chickpea flour	Legume	149°F to 158.4°F [65°C to 70°C]	30	Thickener
Mung bean starch	Legume	159.8°F to 165.2°F [71°C to 74°C]	40	Glass noodles
Peas	Legume	158.4°F [70°C]	30	Thickener

Note: Some of these values will vary depending on the method used to determine the ratio of amylose and amylopectin as well as the source and specific variety of the root or grain.

*Sago is sometimes used to refer to tapioca but can also refer to starch extracted from palms.

DIFFERENCES BETWEEN GRAIN AND ROOT OR WAXY STARCHES

	Grain Starches	Root and Waxy Starches
Examples	Wheat flour, cornstarch, rice starch	Arrowroot, potato, tapioca
Contains	High amylose content	High amylopectin content
Appearance	An opaque finish when cool	A transparent, glossy finish when cool
Thickening temperature	Starts to thicken near the boiling point of water and is stable at (212°F [100°C]). Will become even thicker as it cools and can be cut into pieces.	Starts to thicken at a low temperature (167°F [75°C]) and overheating might thin it. It thins slightly once it cools.

TROUBLESHOOTING STARCHES

	Things to Watch Out For	Solutions
Stirring after thickening	Will thin down	Add flavoring agents before the sauce is thickened so you can minimize stirring.
Reheating	Does not thin	Use a mix of grain and root/waxy starch when thickening.
After freezing and thawing	Weeps water	Use a mix of grain and root/waxy starch when thickening.
Exposure to air	Might form a skin on cooling	Press a piece of parchment or plastic wrap against the surface of the sauce to avoid skin formation.

Because cooking usually involves the use of different types of ingredients, these can in turn affect the thickening capacity of a starch (see table, Ingredients Affecting Sauces Thickened by Starches, following).

*Adapted from Cookwise *by Shirley O. Corriher (William Morrow and Company, 1997).*

INGREDIENTS AFFECTING SAUCES THICKENED BY STARCHES

Problem	Source	What It Does	Solution
Salts	Table salt (sodium chloride), baking soda, baking powder, bones (in bone broth), naturally present salts in fruits and vegetables	Sodium chloride decreases the thickening temperature slightly, depending on how much is present.	Since almost every ingredient contains some type of salt, including tap water, it is harder to control. Add salt at the end if possible, once the sauce has thickened to the desired consistency.
Sugars	Natural sweeteners like table sugar (sucrose) and sugars present in foods, like milk sugar (lactose)	They lock water molecules, making them unavailable for starch granules. Increases the thickening temperature.	Start by adding less sugar while thickening. Once thickened, dissolve the remaining sugar in a small quantity of water and fold it in.
Acids	Acids naturally present in fruits or those, like vinegar, added during cooking	Acids break starch granules and reduce their ability to thicken.	Preferably add them toward the end, after the liquid has thickened to the desired consistency.
Amylases (a special type of protein molecule called enzyme)	Raw fruits, vegetables, grains, yeast, fermented food products like beer, eggs, and animal tissues	Amylases tear starch molecules apart and prevent the sauce from thickening.	Heating the liquid close to the boiling point of water for about a minute helps to avoid this by destroying the enzyme's function. Some recipes might call for the addition of cornstarch to egg-based custards to ensure thickening. Pay extra attention and heat the liquid to 185°F [85°C] for 1 minute to get the "nappe" or coat. By the time the liquid reaches this temperature, the egg proteins change their shape just enough to thicken the base, and the amylase's activity is also destroyed.

ND = not detected
Blank space = not measured

Ingredients		Glutamate	IMP	GMP	AMP	Theanine
Meat + Poultry	Beef	0.01	0.07	0.004	0.008	
	Pork	0.009	0.2	0.002	0.009	
	Aged Cured Ham	0.34				
	Chicken	0.022	0.201	0.005	0.013	
	Egg Yolk	0.05				
Seafood	Tuna		0.286	ND	0.006	
	Snow Crab		0.005	0.004	0.032	
	Scallop		ND	ND	0.172	
	Blue Crab	0.043				
	Alaska King Crab	0.072				
	Shrimp	0.02				
	Anchovies	0.63 to 1.44				
	Dried Bonito		0.47 to 0.80			
	Dried Sardine					
Seaweed	Dried laver	1.383				
	Kelp	1.608				
	Wakame	0.009				
Vegetables + Fruit	Carrot	0.04 to 0.08				
	Cabbage	0.05				
	Tomato	0.246	ND	ND	0.021	
	Garlic	0.11				
	Green Peas	0.106	ND		0.002	
	Onion	0.02 to 0.05				
	Shiitake Fresh	0.071	ND	0.016 to 0.045		
	Shiitake Dried	1.06	ND	0.15		
	Avocado	0.018	ND			
Fish Sauce	China	0.828				
	Japan	1.383				
	Vietnam	1.37				
Soy Sauce	China	0.926				
	Japan	0.782				
	Korea	1.262				
Cheese	Emmenthaler	0.308				
	Parmigiano-Reggiano	1.68				
	Cheddar	0.182				
Milk	Cow	0.001				
Fermented Beans	Locust Beans	1.7				
	Soy Beans (Douchi)	0.476				
Tea	Green Tea	0.22 to 0.67				1.78
	Darjeeling Black					1.45
	Assam					1.05

Adapted from Yamaguchi S., Ninomiya K. "Umami and food palatability." *Journal of Nutrition* 130, 4S (2000).

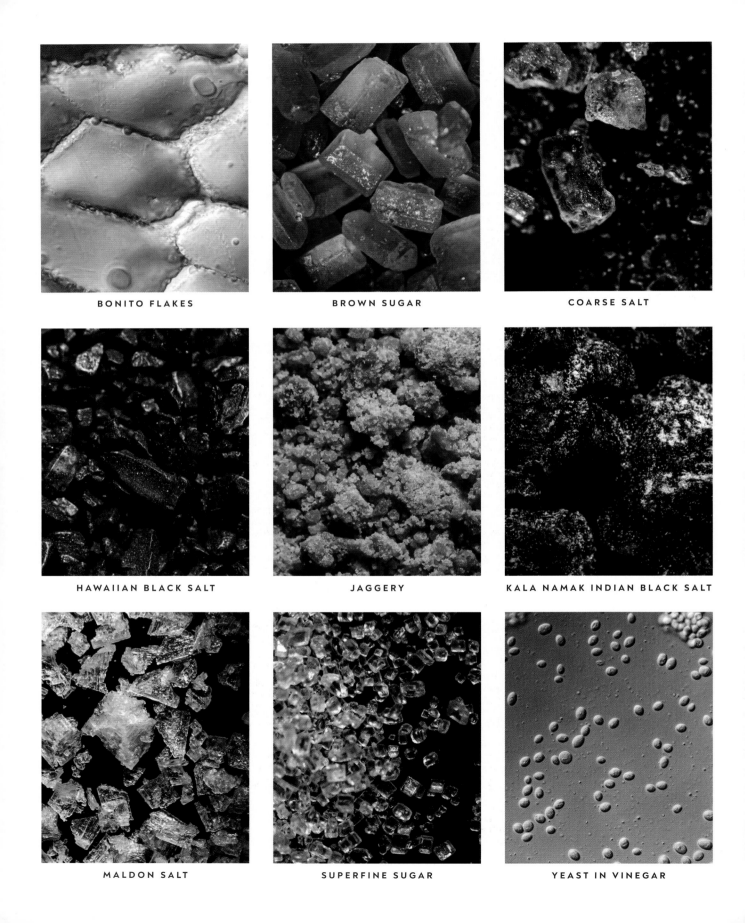

BONITO FLAKES

BROWN SUGAR

COARSE SALT

HAWAIIAN BLACK SALT

JAGGERY

KALA NAMAK INDIAN BLACK SALT

MALDON SALT

SUPERFINE SUGAR

YEAST IN VINEGAR

Sources Consulted

Books

Achaya, K. T. *A Historical Dictionary of Indian Food.* Oxford: Oxford University Press, 2002.

Barham, Peter. *The Science of Cooking.* Berlin: Springer, 1950.

Belitz, H. D., W. Grosch, and P. Schieberle. *Food Chemistry, 3rd ed.* Translated by M. M. Burghagen. Berlin: Springer, 2004

Corriher, Shirley O. *Bakewise.* New York: Scribner, 2008.

The Culinary Institute of America. *Baking and Pastry, 3rd ed.* New York: John Wiley & Sons, 2016.

Davidson, Alan. *The Oxford Companion to Food, 3rd ed.* Edited by Tom Jaine. Oxford: Oxford University Press, 2014.

Editors at America's Test Kitchen. *Cooks Illustrated: Cook's Science.* Brookline, MA: America's Test Kitchen, 2016.

Friberg, Bo. *The Professional Pastry Chef, 3rd ed.* New York: John Wiley & Sons, 1995.

Grigson, Jane. *Jane Grigson's Fruit Book.* Lincoln, Nebraska: University of Nebraska Press, 2007.

Kapoor, Sybil. *Sight, Sound, Touch, Taste, Sound: A New Way to Cook.* London: Pavilion, 2018.

Kho, Kian Lam. *Phoenix Claws and Jade Trees.* New York: Clarkson Potter, 2015

Lawson, Nigella. *How to Eat.* New York: John Wiley & Sons, 2000.

Lett, Travis. *Gjelina: Cooking From Venice, California.* San Francisco: Chronicle Books, 2015.

Lopez-Alt, J. Kenji. *The Food Lab.* New York: W. W. Norton & Company, 2015.

McGee, Harold. *On Food and Cooking, Rev. ed.* New York: Scribner, 2004.

Migoya, Francis and The Culinary Institute of America. *The Elements of Dessert.* New York: John Wiley & Sons, 2012.

Nostrat, Samin. *Salt, Fat, Acid, Heat.* New York: Simon & Schuster, 2017.

Parks, Stella. *Bravetart.* New York: W. W. Norton & Company, 2017.

Roden, Claudia. *Arabesque—A Taste of Morocco, Turkey, and Lebanon.* New York: Alfred A. Knopf, 2006.

Roden, Claudia. *A Book of Middle Eastern Food.* New York: Alfred A. Knopf, 1972.

Spence, Charles. *Gastrophysics: The Science of Eating.* New York: Viking, 2017.

This, Hervé. *Molecular Gastronomy: Exploring the Science of Flavor.* Translated by Malcolm DeBevoise. New York: Columbia University Press, 2008.

Introduction

Ahn, Yong-Yeol, Sebastian E. Ahnert, James P. Bagrow and Albert-László Barabási. "Flavor network and the principles of food pairing." *Scientific Reports* 1, (January 2011). https://doi.org/10.1038/srep00196.

Emotion

Eskine, Kendall J., Natalie A. Kacinik, and Jesse J. Prinz. "A Bad Taste in the Mouth: Gustatory Disgust Influences Moral Judgment." *Psychological Science* 22, no. 3 (March 2011): 295–99. https://doi.org/10.1177/0956797611398497.

Katz, DB and BF Sadacca. "Taste." *Neurobiology of Sensation and Reward,* edited by JA Gottfried, Chapter 6. Boca Raton (FL): CRC Press/Taylor & Francis, 2011. https://www.ncbi.nlm.nih.gov/books/NBK92789/.

Noel, Corinna and Robin Dando. "The effect of emotional state on taste perception." *Appetite* 95 (December 2015): 89–95. https://doi.org/10.1016/j.appet.2015.06.003.

Wang, Qian Janice, Sheila Wang, and Charles Spence. "'Turn Up the Taste': Assessing the Role of Taste Intensity and Emotion in Mediating Crossmodal Correspondences between Basic Tastes and Pitch." *Chemical Senses* 14, No. 4 (May 2016): 345-356. https://doi.org/10.1093/chemse/bjw007.

Yamamoto, Takashi. "Central mechanisms of taste: Cognition, emotion and taste-elicited behaviors." *Japanese Dental Science Review* 44, No. 2 (October 2008): 91-99. https://doi.org/10.1016/j.jdsr.2008.07.003.

Sight

Gambino, Megan. "Do Our Brains Find Certain Shapes More Attractive Than Others?" *Smithsonian Magazine,* November 14, 2013. https://www.smithsonianmag.com/science-nature/do-our-brains-find-certain-shapes-more-attractive-than-others-180947692/.

Spence, Charles and Mary Kim Ngo. "Assessing the shape symbolism of the taste, flavour, and texture of foods and beverages." *Flavour* 1 (July 2012). https://doi.org/10.1186/2044-7248-1-12.

Spence, Charles. "On the psychological impact of food colour." *Flavour* 4 (April 2015). https://doi.org/10.1186/s13411-015-0031-3.

Spence, Charles, Qian Jance Wang, and Jozef Youssef. "Pairing flavours and the temporal order of tasting." *Flavour* 6 (March 2017). https://doi.org/10.1186/s13411-017-0053-0.

Sound

BBC News. "Music to enhance taste of the sea." BBC News, April 17, 2007. http://news.bbc.co.uk/2/hi/uk_news/england/berkshire/6562519.stm.

Spence, Charles, Charles Michel, and Barry Smith. "Airplane noise and the taste of umami" *Flavour* 3, (February 2014). https://doi.org/10.1186/2044-7248-3-2.

Mouthfeel

American Egg Board. "Coagulation/Thickening" *Egg Functionality.* Accessed January 6, 2020. https://www.aeb.org/food-manufacturers/egg-functionality/coagulation-thickening.

Ho, Thao and Athapol Noomhorm. "Physiochemical Properties of Sweet Potato and Mung Bean Starch and Their Blends for Noodle Production." *Journal of Food Processing & Technology* (2011).

Jeltema, Melissa, Jacqueline Beckley, and Jennifer Vahalik. "Model for understanding consumer textural food choice." *Food Science & Nutrition* 3, No. 3 (May 2015): 202-212. https://doi.org/10.1002/fsn3.205.

Nadia, Lula, M. Aman Wirakartakusumah, Nuri Andarwulan, Eko Hari Purnomo, Hiroshi Koaze, and Takahiro Noda. "Characterization of Physicochemical and Functional Properties of Starch from Five Yam (Dioscorea Alata) Cultivars in Indonesia." *International Journal of Chemical Engineering and Applications* 5, No. 6 (December 2014): 489–96. https://pdfs.semanticscholar.org/f5f5/c144eee8dbff570da8dce6018fe07d1323aa.pdf.

Aroma

Aprotosoaie, Ana Clara, Simon Vlad Luca, and Anca Miron. "Flavor Chemistry of Cocoa and Cocoa Products—An Overview." *Comprehensive Reviews in Food Science and Food Safety* 15 (November 2015): 73-91. https://doi.org/10.1111/1541-4337.12180.

Baritaux, O., H. Richard, J. Touche, and M. Derbesy. "Effects of drying and storage of herbs and spices on the essential oil. Part I. Basil, ocimum basilicum L." *Flavour and Fragrance Journal* 7, No. 5 (October 1992): 267-271. https://doi.org/10.1002/ffj.2730070507.

Hammer, Michaela and Peter Schieberle. "Model Studies on the Key Aroma Compounds Formed by an Oxidative Degradation of Ð-3 Fatty Acids Initiated by either Copper(II) Ions or Lipoxygenase." *Journal of Agricultural and Food Chemistry* 61, No. 46 (November 2013): 10891-10900. https://doi.org/10.1021/jf403827p

Tocmo, Restituto, Dong Liang, Yi Lin and Dejian Huang. "Chemical and biochemical mechanisms underlying the cardioprotective roles of dietary organopolysulfides" *Frontiers in Nutrition* 2, (February 2015). https://doi.org/10.3389/fnut.2015.00001.

Taste

Achatz, Grant. "Grant Achatz: The Chef Who Lost His Sense of Taste." Interviewed by Terry Gross. *Fresh Air,* NPR, March 3, 2011. Audio. https://www.npr.org/2011/03/03/134195812/grant-achatz-the-chef-who-lost-his-sense-of-taste.

Bachmanov, Alexander A., Natalia P. Bosak, Cailu Lin, Ichiro Matsumoto, Makoto Ohmoto, Danielle R. Reed, and Theodore M. Nelson. "Genetics of Taste Receptors." *Current Pharmaceutical Design* 20, No 16 (2014): 2669 – 2683. https://doi.org/10.2174/13816128113199990566.

Beauchamp, GK and JA Mennella. "Flavor perception in human infants: development and functional significance." *Digestion 83, Suppl* (March 2011): 1-6. https://doi.org/10.1159/000323397.

Breslin, Paul A.S. "An evolutionary perspective on food and human taste." *Current Biology* 23, No. 9 (May 2013): 409-418. https://doi.org/10.1016/j.cub.2013.04.010.

Chamoun, Elie, David M. Mutch, Emma Allen-Vercoe, Andrea C. Buchholz, Alison M. Duncan, Lawrence L. Spriet, Jess Haines and David W. L. Ma on behalf of the Guelph Family Health Study. "A review of the associations between single nucleotide polymorphisms in taste receptors, eating behaviors, and health." *Critical Reviews in Food Science and Nutrition* 58, No. 2 (2018): 194–207. https://doi.org/10.1080/10408398.2016.1152229.

Keast, Russell S.J and Paul A.S Breslin. "An overview of binary taste–taste interactions." *Food Quality and Preference* 14, No. 2 (March 2003): 111-124. https://doi.org/10.1016/S0950-3293(02)00110-6.

Mojet, Jos, Johannes Heidema, and Elly Christ-Hazelhof,. "Effect of Concentration on Taste-Taste Interactions in Foods for Elderly and Young Subjects." *Chemical Senses* 29, No. 8 (October 2004): 671-81. https://doi.org/10.1093/chemse/bjh070

Flavor Reactions

Food Enzymes

Raveendran, Sindhu, Binod Parameswaran, Sabeela Beevi Ummalyma, Amith Abraham, Anil Kuruvilla Mathew, Aravind Madhavan, Sharrel Rebello and Ashok Pandey. "Applications of Microbial Enzymes in Food Industry." *Food Technology and Biotechnology* 56, No. 1 (March 2018): 16–30. https://doi.org/10.17113/ftb.56.01.18.5491.

Oxidation of Fats

Stephen, N.M., R. Jeya Shakila, G. Jeyasekaran, and D. Sukumar. "Effect of different types of heat processing on chemical changes in tuna." *Journal of Food Science and Technology* 47, No. 2 (March 2010): 174–81. https://doi.org/10.1007/s13197-010-0024-2.

Sucan, Mathias K. and Deepthi K. Weerasinghe. "Process and Reaction Flavors: An Overview" *ACS Symposium Series* 905, (July 2005): 1–23. https://doi.org/10.1021/bk-2005-0905.ch001.

Caramelization and the Maillard Reaction

Ajandouz, E., Tchiakpe, L., Ore, F.D., Benajiba, A., and Puigserver, A. "Effects of pH on Caramelization and Maillard Reaction Kinetics in Fructose-Lysine Model Systems." *Journal of Food Science* 66 (2001): 926–31. https://doi.org/10.1111/j.1365-2621.2001.tb08213.x.

Jackson, Scott F., C.O. Chichester, and M.A. Joslyn. "The Browning of Ascorbic Acid." *Journal of Food Science* 25, No.4 (July 1960): 484–90. https://doi.org/10.1111/j.1365-2621.1960.tb00358.x.

Van Boekel, MA. "Formation of flavour compounds in the Maillard Reaction." *Biotechnology Advances* 24, No. 2 (Mar-Apr 2006): 230–33. https://doi.org/10.1016/j.biotechadv.2005.11.004.

Temperature and Taste

Lipscomb, Keri, James Rieck, and Paul Dawson. "Effect of temperature on the intensity of basic tastes: Sweet, Salty, and Sour." *Journal of Food Research* 5, No. 4 (2016). http://dx.doi.org/10.5539/jfr.v5n4p1.

Brightness

Berger, Dan. "Acid, pH, wine and food." *Napa Valley Register*, January 30, 2015. https://napavalleyregister.com/wine/columnists/dan-berger/acid-ph-wine-and-food/article_f0637ece-f631-52b5-adb7-05cd3270f8d0.html.

Brandt, Laura M., Melissa A. Jeltema, Mary E. Zabik, and Brian D. Jeltema. "Effects of Cooking in Solutions of Varying pH on the Dietary Fiber Components of Vegetables." *Journal of Food Science* 49, No. 3 (May 1984): 900-904. https://doi.org/10.1111/j.1365-2621.1984.tb13237.x.

Krueger, D. A. "Composition of pomegranate juice." *Journal of AOAC International* 95, No. 1 (Jan–Feb 2001): 163–68. https://doi.org/10.5740/jaoacint.11-178.

Mazaheri Tehrani M, MA Hesarinejad, MA Razavi Seyed, R Mohammadian, and S Poorkian. "Comparing physicochemical properties and antioxidant potential of sumac from Iran and Turkey." *MOJ Food Processing & Technology* 5, No. 2 (2017): 288–94. https://pdfs.semanticscholar.org/209d/1e69140050fa9641a5de5cf0719f75bfc408.pdf.

McGee, Harold. "For Old-Fashioned Flavor, Bake the Baking Soda." *New York Times*, September 14, 2010. https://www.nytimes.com/2010/09/15/dining/15curious.html.

Bitterness

Cutraro, Jennifer. "Coffee's Bitter Mystery." *Science Magazine*, August 21, 2007. https://www.sciencemag.org/news/2007/08/coffees-bitter-mystery.

Drewnowski, Adam and Carmen Gomez-Carneros. "Bitter taste, phytonutrients, and the consumer: a review." *American Journal of Clinical Nutrition* 72, No. 6 (December 2000): 1424–1435. https://ucanr.edu/datastoreFiles/608-47.pdf.

John Martin's Brewery. "Where does the bitterness in beer come from?" Accessed on January 7, 2020. https://anthonymartin.be/en/news/where-does-the-bitterness-of-beer-come-from/#.

Keast, Russell, Thomas M. Canty, and Paul A.S. Breslin. "The Influence of Sodium Salts on Binary Mixtures of Bitter-tasting Compounds." *Chemical Senses* 29, No. 5 (2004): 431–9. https://doi.org/10.1093/chemse/bjh045.

Saltiness

Algers, Ann. "Low salt pig-meat products and novel formulations: Effect of salt content on chemical and physical properties and implications for organoleptic properties.", Accessed January 7, 2020. http://qpc.adm.slu.se/Low_salt_pig-meat_products/page_23.htm.

Sweetness

Ajandouz, E.H., L.S. Tchiakpe, F. Dalle Ore, A. Benajiba, and A. Puigserver. "Effects of pH on Caramelization and Maillard Reaction Kinetics in Fructose-Lysine Model Systems." *Journal of Food Science* 66, No. 7 (September 2001): 926–31. https://doi.org/10.1111/j.1365-2621.2001.tb08213.x.

Beck, Tove K., Sidsel Jensen, Gitte K. Bjoern, and Ulla Kidmose. "The Masking Effect of Sucrose on Perception of Bitter Compounds in Brassica Vegetables." *Journal of Sensory Studies* 29, No. 3 (June 2014): 190-200. https://doi.org/10.1111/joss.12094.

DuBois, Grant E., D. Eric Walters, Susan S. Schiffman, Zoe S. Warwick, Barbara J. Booth, Suzanne D. Pecore, Kernon Gibes, B. Thomas Carr, and Linda M. Brands. "Concentration—Response Relationships of Sweeteners." *ACS Symposium Series* 450 (December 1991): 261–76. https://doi.org/10.1021/bk-1991-0450.ch020.

Shimizua, Seishi. "Caffeine dimerization: effects of sugar, salts, and water structure." *Food & Function* 5 (2015): 3228–3235. https://doi.org/10.1039/C5FO00610D.

Savoriness

Kurihara, Kenzo. " Umami the Fifth Basic Taste: History of Studies on Receptor Mechanisms and Role as a Food Flavor." *BioMed Research International* (June 9, 2015). http://dx.doi.org/10.1155/2015/189402

Fieriness

Block, Eric. "The Chemistry of Garlic and Onions." *Scientific American* 252, No. 3 (March 1985): 114–9. https://doi.org/10.1038/scientificamerican0385-114.

Bosland, Paul W. and Stephanie J. Walker. "Measuring Chile Pepper Heat." New Mexico State University, Distributed February 2010. https://aces.nmsu.edu/pubs/_h/H237/welcome.html.

Cicerale, Sara, Xavier A. Conlan, Neil W. Barnett, Andrew J. Sinclair, and Russell S. J. Keast. "Influence of Heat on Biological Activity and Concentration of Oleocanthal—a Natural Anti-inflammatory Agent in Virgin Olive Oil." *Journal of Agricultural and Food Chemistry* 57, No. 4 (January 2009): 1326-1330. https://doi.org/10.1021/jf803154w.

Green, Barry G. "Heat as a Factor in the Perception of Taste, Smell, and Oral Sensation." Institute of Medicine (US) Committee on Military Nutrition Research, edited by BM Marriott. National Academies Press 9, (1993). https://www.ncbi.nlm.nih.gov/books/NBK236241/.

Lim, T. K. *Edible Medicinal and Non-Medicinal Plants: Volume 4, Fruits*. Berlin: Springer, 2012. https://www.springer.com/gp/book/9789400740525.

Richness

Keast, R.S. and A. Costanzo. "Is fat the sixth taste primary? Evidence and implications." *Flavour* 4, (2015). https://doi.org/10.1186/2044-7248-4-5.

Wiktorowska-Owczarek, Anna, Małgorzata BereziĐska, and Jerzy Z. Nowak. "PUFAs: Structures, Metabolism and Functions." *Advances in Clinical and Experimental Medicine* 24, No. 6 (2015): 931-941. https://doi.org/10.17219/acem/31243.

Toschi, Tullia Gallina, Giovanni Lercker, and Lorenzo Cerretani. "The scientific truth on cooking with extra virgin olive oil." *Teatro Naturale International* (April 2010). http://www.teatronaturale.com/technical-area/olive-and-oil/1769-the-scientific-truth-on-cooking-with-extra-virgin-olive-oil.htm.

Tangsuphoom, N., and J.N. Coupland. "Effect of pH and Ionic Strength on the Physicochemical Properties of Coconut Milk Emulsions." *Journal of Food Science* 73, No. 6 (August 2008): E274-E280. https://doi.org/10.1111/j.1750-3841.2008.00819.x.

A Basic Primer on Flavor Science

Bernard, Rudy A. and Bruce P. Halpern. "Taste Changes in Vitamin A Deficiency." *Journal of General Physiology* 52, No. 3 (September 1968): 444-464. https://doi.org/10.1085/jgp.52.3.444.

Henkin, R.I and J.D Hoetker. "Deficient dietary intake of vitamin E in patients with taste and smell dysfunctions: is vitamin E a cofactor in taste bud and olfactory epithelium apoptosis and in stem cell maturation and development?" *Nutrition* 19, No. 11–12 (November–December 2003): 1013-1021. https://doi.org/10.1016/j.nut.2003.08.006.

Tamura, Takayuki, Kiyoshi Taniguchi, Yumiko Suzuki, Toshiyuki Okubo, Ryoji Takata, and Tomonori Konno. "Iron Is an Essential Cause of Fishy Aftertaste Formation in Wine and Seafood Pairing." *Journal of Agricultural and Food Chemistry* 57, No. 18 (August 2009): 8550-8556. https://doi.org/10.1021/jf901656k.

With Gratitude

This book exists because of the support and encouragement of people who've been with me on my journey. From my time spent working in numerous labs and cooking in kitchens, this book is influenced by the people who, in different ways over the years, pushed me to be inquisitive cook.

I owe thanks to many people who generously shared their knowledge and helped point me in the right direction to find the answers to my many questions while I researched this book. Alice Medrich, Amy Guittard, Andrew Janjigian, Arielle Johnson, Bee Wilson, Cenk Sönmezsoy, David Lebovitz, Edd Kimber, Elizabeth Vecchiarelli, Grant Achatz, Helen Goh, Helen Rosner, Jeff Yankellow, Kayoko Akabori, Kenji López-Alt, Kian Lam Kho, Lisa Vega, Melissa Clark, Nigella Lawson, Samin Nosrat, Stella Parks, and Tucker Shaw—thank you.

To Diana Henry and John Birdsall; who remind me that all things are possible and to believe in myself.

Will Butler for sharing his experience and helping me understand how the loss of vision affects our senses and reshapes the way we cook.

I am grateful to my friends who each played a very special part in the different components of this book during its creation; Tina Antolini, Bryant Terry, Emma Bajaj, Charlotte Druckman, Perry Lucina, Ben Mims, Farideh Sadeghin, Khushbu Shah, Mayukh Sen, Michaele Manigrasso, Qin Xu, and Phi Tran—thank you for your energy and love.

Julie Sahni, Harold McGee, Shirley O. Corriher, and the folks at *Cook's Illustrated*, whose illuminative work let me view food through the wonderful geeky lens of science.

A special shout out and thank you to the brilliant Anna Jones, whose flavor maps inspired the ones I created for this book.

To the many editors over the years who've shaped the way I write, taken a chance on me, and given me new opportunities to share my work; Allan Jenkins, Anna Hezel, Brian Hart Hoffman, Brooke Bell, Christopher Kimball, Daniel Gritzer, Eric Kim, Emma Laperruque, Janine Ratcliffe, Josh Miller, Adam Bush, Joe Yonan, Kat Kinsman, Karen Barnes, Matt Rodbard, Kristen Miglore, Molly Tait-Hyland, Paolo Lucchesi, Sho Spaeth, Emily Weinstein, and Tara Duggan—thank you.

My community of recipe testers that carefully worked their way through my recipes; Abby Parsons, Abby Pressel, Abraham Scott, Akshay Mehta, Andrea David, Angie Lee, Anikah Shaokat, Anuradha Srinivasan, Ariadne Yulo, Becky Crowder, Ben Kantor, Calla-Marie Norman, Catherine Tierney, Chandra Ram, Cheryl M. Gomes, Christina C. Hanson, Clare Christoph, Constantinos Megalemos, Danielle Wayada, Deirdre de Wijze, Diella Lee, Donecia Collins, Eric Ritskes, Gene-Lyn Ngian, Ginny Bonifacino, Giverny Tattersfield, Gwen Krosnick, Harriet Arnold McEwen, Jacquelyn Scott, Jaime Woo, James Ekstrom, James Jones, Jasmine Lukuku, Jennifer Bigio, Jenny Louisa Esquivel, Jessica Jones, John Wilburn, Jordan Wellin, Judson Kniffen, Kara Weinstein, Katie Brigham, Maren Ellingboe, Margaret Eby, Matt Golowczynski, Matt Sartwell, Meleyna Nomura, Melissa de Castro, Monique Llamas, Myles Tucker, Neelesh Varde, Neyat Daniel, Nick Stanzione, Nicole Washington, Nina Fogel, Noé Suruy, Pippa Robe, Rachael Krishna, Ranchel Garg, Renée Alvi, Robin Pridgen, Rukhsana Uddin, Safira Adam, Sally Dexter, Sarah Corrigan, Shailini Vijayan, Shantini Gamage, Sharon Hern, Sheela Lal, Sreeparna Banerjee, Stacey Ballis, Steven Pungdumri, Suchi Modi, Sukesh Miryala, Susan Pinette, Susan R. Jensen, Tacia Coleman, Tiffany Chiu, Tiffany Langston, Tina Ujlaki, Todd Emerson, Tom Beamont, Tom Natan, and Vallery Lomas—you're the best, thank you.

Since this is a book that focuses on the science of flavor, I would be remiss if I didn't thank my professors and the folk whose labs I trained and worked in, both in India and America, who made this an exciting world to explore and encouraged me to think and question everything. To my professors and colleagues at the University of Cincinnati College of Medicine, Ohio, and Georgetown University, Washington DC, where I learned to design experiments, form ideas, and test their validity, as I sought answers. At the time, I never realized how valuable this approach would eventually become to my cooking.

My one dream for this book was to include a few photographs that gave an appreciation for food at the microscopic level. A huge thank you to Dr. Steven Ruzin and the Biological Imaging Facility at the University of California, Berkeley, for generously providing access to their microscopes and making this a reality.

I owe deep gratitude to the lovely people at California Olive Ranch, Dandelion Chocolate, King Arthur Flour, the Guittard Chocolate Company, Miyabi USA, Oaktown Spice Shop, Staub USA, Yandilla, and Market Hall Foods for their help with my research, sourcing ingredients, and providing some of the kitchen tools that you see in this book.

While the concept for this book lay stashed away in my mind for years, I owe immense gratitude to my literary agent, champion, advisor, and dear friend, Maria Ribas, who helped me transform an abstract idea into this book that you now hold in your hands. The entire team at Stonesong and Alison Fargis for being there whenever I needed help, thank you.

This book has a lot of different pieces that needed to cohesively unite and make sense. Thank you to everyone at Chronicle Books for being my dream team and listening to my ideas, which I'm quite aware, often sound a bit crazy. My editor, Sarah Billingsley, for your grace under pressure and dedication to bring all the different components of this book together. My designer, Lizzie Vaughan, thank you for your patience and artful attention to detail; I'm in awe of how beautiful you made this book by seamlessly weaving it all together. Christina Loff, Cynthia Shannon, and Joyce Lin, for your enthusiasm, counsel, and friendship, you are absolutely stellar, thank you. The international marketing and publicity teams especially; Cora Siedlecka, Sally Oliphant, and Jennie Brockie, thank you for all the love you poured into spreading the word about my books. To Matteo Riva, whose spectacular illustrations playfully translate the science in this book rather spectacularly, your art completes this book.

To my family, especially my mom, my aunts, Anu Sharma, Zane Futardo, and Joy Futardo, for all their help and support with this book.

Finally, to my husband, Michael, for whom I love to cook and share our adventures in life. And yes, you can have the first copy!

—Nik

Index

A

Achatz, Grant, 29, 50
acids, 61–62, 65, 70–71, 339
actin, 334
agar, 331
alanine, 333
alcohol dehydrogenase, 334
alkalinity, 61, 62
almonds
  Lamb Koftas in Almond Gravy, 264–65
  Raspberry + Stone Fruit Crisp, 188
  Saffron Swirl Buns with Dried Fruit, 193–95
amchur, 66
amino acids, 332, 333
AMP (adenosine monophosphate), 338
amylase, 331, 334, 339
anchovies
  about, 206
  My Quick Marinara, 316–17
anthocyanins, 22, 23, 24
anthoxanthins, 23
apples
  Green Apple Chutney, 321–22
  Green Olives + Chouriço Stuffing, 149–51
apricots
  Polenta Kheer, 185
  Saffron Swirl Buns with Dried Fruit, 193–95
aroma, 41–45
ASCOs, 237
Asparagus, Charred, with "Gunpowder" Nut Masala, 115

B

beans. *See also* chickpeas
  Chicken Hakka Noodles (Indo-Chinese), 216
  Dal Makhani, 292–95
  Green Beans with Preserved Lemons + Crème Fraîche, 76–77
  Manchow Soup, 255

pH and, 70
  Warm Kale, White Bean + Mushroom Salad with Chilli Tahini, 111
beef
  Beef Chilli Fry with Pancetta, 160
  Coffee-Spiced Steak with Burnt Kachumber Salad, 229–30
beer
  bitterness in, 103, 105
  Sweet Potato Honey Beer Pie, 129–31
beets
  about, 24
  Paneer + Beet Salad with Mango-Lime Dressing, 147–48
  preventing staining from, 279
betacyanin, 24
betalains, 23, 279
biology, role of, 338–40
bitterness
  about, 102–4
  boosters, 105–7
  delayed, 106
  measuring, 103
  quick tips for boosting flavor with, 107
  using, in the kitchen, 107
blueberries
  Blueberry + Omani Lime Ice Cream, 98
  color of, 22
  Roasted Fruit with Coffee Miso Tahini, 125
  Saffron Swirl Buns with Dried Fruit, 193–95
Blumenthal, Heston, 28
Bolinhas (Semolina Coconut Cookies), 191–92
bonito flakes, 206, 208
bread. *See also* buns
  Chocolate Miso Bread Pudding, 133
  croutons, 32
  Green Olives + Chouriço Stuffing, 149–51
  Masala Cheddar Cornbread, 183
  Parathas + Masala Parathas, 297–98
  "Pizza" Toast, 143
brightness
  about, 60–62
  boosters, 65–67

tips for boosting flavor with, 70–71
brining, 34
Broccolini + Chickpea Pancakes, Roasted, 214
broths, bone-based, 71
Brussels Sprouts Salad, Shaved, 112
buns
  Chouriço Pao (Buns), 91–93
  Saffron Swirl Buns with Dried Fruit, 193–95
Burrata with Chilli Oil + Thai Basil, 283
butter, 276
buttermilk, 65, 66

C

cabbage
  Braised Cabbage with Coconut, 291
  Chicken Hakka Noodles (Indo-Chinese), 216
  Manchow Soup, 255
  Stir-Fried Cabbage, 219
cacao, 105
cakes
  Coconut Milk Cake, 306–7
  Gingerbread Cake with Date Syrup Bourbon Sauce, 268–69
Caldine (Goan Yellow Fish Curry), 301
Candy, Hot Honeycomb, 199
carbohydrates, 331
carbon, 331
carbonated beverages, 67
cardamom
  Cardamom Toffee Sauce, 323–24
  Green Cardamom Extract, 47
carotenoids, 23
carrots
  Couscous with Sesame-Roasted Carrots + Feta, 154–55
  Crispy Carrots with Garlic + Mint Tahini, 178
cashews
  Cherry + Pepper Granola Bars, 186
  My "Gunpowder" Nut Masala, 312
  Polenta Kheer, 185

I

ice cream
   Blueberry + Omani Lime Ice Cream, 98
   No-Churn Falooda Ice Cream, 200
Ikeda, Kikunae, 204
IMP (inosine monophosphate), 338
Indo-Sichuan Sauce, 318

J

Jones, Jessica, 154

K

kala namak, 20, 139, 312–13
kale
   Garlic + Ginger Dal with Greens, 256
   Vegetable Pakoras, 116
   Warm Kale, White Bean + Mushroom
     Salad with Chilli Tahini, 111
Kanji, Chicken, 222–23
Kebabs, Honey + Turmeric Chicken, with
   Pineapple, 180–81
kefir
   about, 65–66
   Blueberry + Omani Lime Ice Cream, 98
   Roasted Cauliflower in Turmeric Kefir,
     54–55, 83
Kheer, Polenta, 185
Kho, Kian Lam, 283
Kimber, Edd, 193
Koftas, Lamb, in Almond Gravy, 264–65
kokumi, 50
kosher salt, 139
Kulfi, Spiced Coffee, 123

L

lamb
   Lamb Chops with Scallion Mint Salsa,
     163
   Lamb Koftas in Almond Gravy, 264–65
   Shepherd's Pie with Kheema +
     Chouriço, 226–27
lard, 277
lecithin, 38, 337

lemons
   about, 66
   Lemon + Lime Mintade, 97
   Preserved Lemons, Two Ways (Classic +
     Quick), 318–19
lentils
   Collard Greens, Chickpea + Lentil
     Soup, 118
   Garlic + Ginger Dal with Greens, 256
lettuce
   Grilled Hearts of Romaine with Chilli
     Pumpkin Seeds, 73
   Grilled Spiced Chicken Salad with
     Amchur, 159
limes
   about, 66
   Blueberry + Omani Lime Ice Cream, 98
   Lemon + Lime Mintade, 97
limonin, 106
lipids, 331, 335–36. *See also* fats; oils
long pepper, 236
lysine, 333

M

macronutrients, 331
Maillard reaction, 104, 105, 107, 171, 333
Maldon salt flakes, 139
malt syrup, 173
Manchow Soup, 255
mangoes
   Mango-Lime Dressing, 147–48
   unripe, 66
maple syrup, 170, 173
marinades, 70
Marinara, My Quick, 316–17
Marshmallows, Peppermint, 196–97
masalas. *See* spice blends
mayonnaise
   Curry Leaf + Mustard Oil Mayonnaise,
     316
   making, 36, 38
McGee, Harold, 34, 236
meal ideas, 326–27
micronutrients, 331
minerals, 331
mint
   Lemon + Lime Mintade, 97
   Mint Chutney, 322–23
   Peppermint Marshmallows, 196–97
   Scallion Mint Salsa, 163

miraculin, 170
miso
   about, 208, 211
   Chocolate Miso Bread Pudding, 133
   Coffee Miso Tahini, 125
monosaccharides, 331
monounsaturated fatty acids (MUFAs),
   274, 335
mouthfeel, 30–39
MSG (monosodium glutamate), 206
mucilage, 38
mushrooms
   Manchow Soup, 255
   Roast Chicken Thighs + Vegetables, 225
   savoriness and, 208, 338, 339
   Warm Kale, White Bean + Mushroom
     Salad with Chilli Tahini, 111
mustard
   about, 237
   bitterness in, 107
   powder, 237
mustard oil
   about, 106, 237, 277
   Mustard Oil Herb Salsa, 250
   using, 241
myoglobin, 23
myosin, 140, 334

N

nectarines
   Quick Pickled Nectarines with Mint +
     Serrano, 319–20
   Raspberry + Stone Fruit Crisp, 188
   Spiced Fruit Salad, 164
Noodles, Chicken Hakka (Indo-Chinese),
   216
nucleic acids, 336–38
nucleotides, 205, 337–38
nuts, 277. *See also individual nuts*

O

oats
   Cherry + Pepper Granola Bars, 186
   Raspberry + Stone Fruit Crisp, 188
oils. *See also individual oils*
   choosing, 279, 337
   cooking with, 106, 275–76

NIK SHARMA is the writer, photographer, and recipe developer behind *A Brown Table*, an award-winning blog that has garnered best-ofs from *Saveur*, *Parade*, *Better Homes & Gardens*, and the International Association of Culinary Professionals. Nik lives in Los Angeles, California.

Chronicle Books publishes distinctive books and gifts. From award-winning children's titles, bestselling cookbooks, and eclectic pop culture to acclaimed works of art and design, stationery, and journals, we craft publishing that's instantly recognizable for its spirit and creativity. Enjoy our publishing and become part of our community at www.chroniclebooks.com.

Also available: *Season*
Season was named one of the best cookbooks of the year by the *New York Times*, NPR, the *Guardian*, and *Bon Appétit*, was selected as an Amazon Book of the Month, and was a finalist for the 2018 James Beard Award.

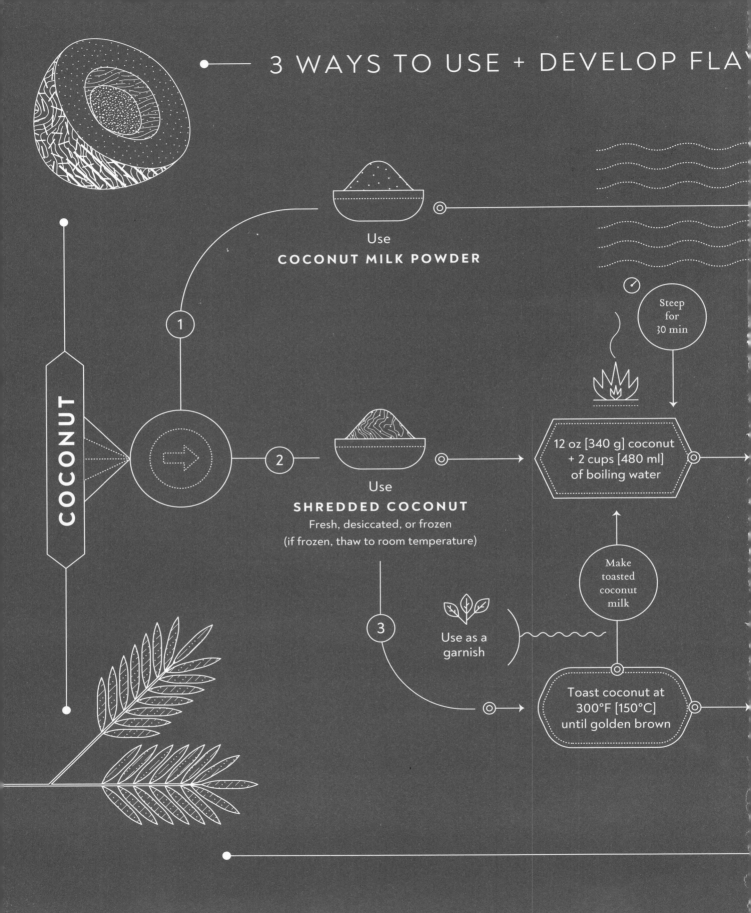

COCONUT

Use
COCONUT MILK POWDER

1

2

Use
SHREDDED COCONUT
Fresh, desiccated, or frozen
(if frozen, thaw to room temperature)

3

Use as a
garnish

Steep
for
30 min

12 oz [340 g] coconut
+ 2 cups [480 ml]
of boiling water

Make
toasted
coconut
milk

Toast coconut at
300°F [150°C]
until golden brown